Impertinences

Impertinences

Selected Writings of Elia Peattie,
a Journalist in the Gilded Age

Edited and with a biography by
Susanne George Bloomfield

University of Nebraska Press
Lincoln and London

Publication of this book was supported by the University of Nebraska at Kearney. Manufactured in the United States of America.

Set in Adobe Minion by Kim Essman. Designed by R. Eckersley. Printed by Edwards Brothers, Inc.

∞

Library of Congress Cataloging-in-Publication Data
Peattie, Elia Wilkinson, 1862–
Impertinences : selected writings of Elia Peattie, a journalist in the Gilded Age / edited and with a biography by Susanne George Bloomfield.
p. cm.
Includes bibliographical references and index.
ISBN 0-8032-3748-0 (hardcover : alkaline paper) –
ISBN 0-8032-8786-0 (paperback : alkaline paper)
1. Omaha (Nebraska) – Social life and customs. 2. Nebraska – Social life and customs. 3. Peattie, Elia Wilkinson, 1862– 4. Authors, American – 19th century – Biography. 5. Journalists – United States – Biography. I. George Bloomfield, Susanne, 1947– II. Title.
PS3531.E255A6 2005 814'.52–dc22 2004025703

To Terry,
finally

Pardon all this impertinence. I am no crank, though you may suspect it. I am nobody at all except a woman who loves to see her country grow, and the literature of her country grow.

Elia Wilkinson Peattie to Hamlin Garland, 30 September 1891

CONTENTS

xiii List of Illustrations

xv Preface

xix Elia Wilkinson Peattie Chronology

1 Introduction: A Writer's Beginnings, 1862–1896

CHAPTER 1. EARLY OMAHA

21 "A Word with the Women" – Defending Omaha

23 "Seen with One's Eyes Open: What Is to Be Seen from an Open Motor Car in Omaha"

29 "How They Live at Sheely: Pen Picture of a Strange Settlement and Its Queer Set of Inhabitants"

33 "A Sociological Soliloquy: Some Thoughts Suggested by the Proposed Exodus from the Bottoms"

39 "Mrs. Peattie in Rebuttal: Just a Word or Two in Passing Concerning the Society Question"

42 "Work of the Day Nursery: The Creche and What It Does for Women Who Must Work"

46 "The Working Girls' Home: A Description of the Place on Seventeenth Street, between Douglas and Dodge"

53 "With Works of Charity: St. Joseph's Hospital and the Good Sisters Who Do Its Work"

58 "Omaha's Black Population: The Negroes of This City – Who They Are and Where They Live"

65 "Killing, Yet No Murder: A Day at the Stock Yards in South Omaha"

CHAPTER 2. FACT AND FICTION

75 "No Need of Prostitution: Mrs. Peattie Refuses to Accept the Claim That the Wanton Is a Necessity"

83 "Leda"

88 "Lovely Woman and Indians"

92 "The Triumph of Starved Crow"

97 "A Word with the Women" – Francis Schlatter, Faith Healer

99 "A Word with the Women" – For the Sake of Love
103 "The Law and the Lynchers"

CHAPTER 3. COMMUNITY CONCERNS

115 "Stand Up, Ye Social Lions: Mrs. Peattie Arraigns the Sickly Forms That Sin from Nature's Rule"
119 "What Women Are Doing" – The Art of Shopping
123 "All Fuss and Feathers: Wedding Ceremonies Which Are Almost Grotesque Because of Their Flummery"
128 "The Mockery of Mourning: Thoughts upon Outward Signs of Inward Grief Prescribed by Convention"
134 "Want to See a Knock-Out: Americans Seem to Feel That Way in Spite of Their Civilization"
141 "The Work of the Worker: Qualities in Evangelist Mills That Give Him Success in Soul Winning"
148 "A Salvation Army Funeral"
152 "Brains in the School Room: Some Pertinent Remarks Regarding the Needs of the Public Schools"

CHAPTER 4. A WORD WITH THE WOMEN

164 "Ties Which Do Not Bind: The Matrimonial Knot and the Ease with Which It Is Broken"
169 "How Not to Treat Babies"
176 "Where Are the Children? A Lay Sermon Suggested by Chief Seavey to Colonel Hogeland"
182 "The Women on the Farms: A Chapter of Advice for Them Which City Women Need Not Read"
188 "Barriers against Women: They Are Mostly Erected by the Women Themselves through Blind Superstition"
192 "What Women Are Doing" – Protection for Working Women
195 "The Woman's Club: It Will Be Distinctively Feminine and Run to Please Women"
198 "A Word with the Women" – Stromsburg's Woman's Club
201 "No Distinction as to Color: Chicago Woman's Club Abolishes the Prohibitory Rule at Its Last Meeting"

CHAPTER 5. PEOPLE AND PLACES

208 "A Bohemian in Nebraska: A Peep at a Home Which Is a Slice Out of Bohemia"

214 "A Word with the Women" – Willa Cather

217 "Some Pigs and a Woman: Mrs. A. M. Edwards and Her Herd of Poland China Porkers"

223 "The Lady of the Cloister"

229 "A Woman Doctor"

234 "A Singular Institution: The Christian Home of Council Bluffs and Its Founder"

241 "Grand Island and Its Beets: The County Seat of Hall and What Beet Cultivation Has Done"

249 "The State Fish Hatchery: Where the Rivers of Nebraska Get Their Stock of Gamey Fish"

254 "A Word with the Women" – The Hunting Mania

257 Conclusion: A Writing Life, 1896–1935

269 Notes

287 Works Cited

295 A Bibliography of the Works of Elia Wilkinson Peattie

331 Index

ILLUSTRATIONS

INTRODUCTION

2 Composing room, *Omaha World-Herald*
3 Robert Burns Peattie
6 Elia Wilkinson Peattie
7 Omaha Daily Herald Building
9 Cover of *A Journey through Wonderland*
11 Page from "Jim Lancy's Waterloo"
13 Frances M. Ford

CHAPTER 1. EARLY OMAHA

20 Farnham Street
22 Omahans at Krug Park
25 Omaha streetcar
31 Jim Dahlman and Nick Dargaczewski
35 Immigrant A. J. Smith
41 Thirteenth Street saloon
44 Children and merry-go-round
48 Omaha telephone operator
54 St. Joseph's Hospital
59 Dr. Matthew Oliver Ricketts
66 Omaha stockyards

CHAPTER 2. FACT AND FICTION

74 Peattie as Omaha Woman's Club president
76 Prostitute Maud Raymond
77 Prostitute "Red Nora" Courier
84 Unidentified girl
89 Soldiers at Wounded Knee
93 Starving Indian woman
98 Francis Schlatter
100 Francis Schlatter and crippled woman
104 Crowd awaiting execution of Ed Neal

CHAPTER 3. COMMUNITY CONCERNS

114 Omaha residence of Christian Hartman
116 Emma Schaper

120 Unidentified woman shopper
124 "The Wedding March"
129 Woman in mourning
133 Girl in full mourning
136 John L. Sullivan and Jim Corbett
143 Benjamin Fay Mills poster
149 Unknown Salvation Army sister
153 Miss Mary Reid's seventh-grade class

CHAPTER 4. A WORD WITH THE WOMEN
162 Elia Peattie, 1904
165 An unknown family
170 Rural mother and child
177 Three mischievous boys
183 Charles Smith farmhouse
189 Elia Peattie and daughter
193 Women workers at cigar factory
196 Club women at Lininger gallery
199 Women's group in historical costumes
203 Helen Muhammitt

CHAPTER 5. PEOPLE AND PLACES
208 Agricultural exhibit at Sugar Palace
209 Kate and Michael Cleary and E. A. Downey
215 Willa Cather
218 August Swanson's livestock
224 Academy of the Visitation
230 Omaha Medical College
235 Rev. Joseph Lemen's Christian Home
242 Boys thinning sugar beets
250 Gretna fish hatchery
255 Hunters with Canada geese

CONCLUSION
258 Elia Peattie at home in Chicago
259 Elia Peattie with her son Donald
262 Elia Peattie, 1918
264 Robert Burns Peattie, ca. 1920
266 Elia Peattie shortly before her death

PREFACE

Impertinences is a collection of editorials, columns, and stories written by Elia Wilkinson Peattie for the *Omaha World-Herald* during her sojourn in Omaha, Nebraska, from 1888 to 1896. It attempts to enlarge our ever-growing understanding of women's writings at the end of the nineteenth century and to help clarify a major turning point in American history, especially in the booming West.

Peattie grew up during the Gilded Age, roughly the two decades after the Civil War, when industry expanded, the transcontinental railroad united the country physically, and waves of immigration increased America's population. It was the age of the Victorian True Woman, when piety, purity, submissiveness, and domesticity defined the role of women and centered them firmly in the home. Toward the end of the century, new scientific thought ushered in the Progressive Era, and the New Woman, a product of the Woman's Movement initiated in the late 1840s, began to challenge the status quo.[1] Women started demanding the right to equal educational and career opportunities as well as stronger political rights and responsibilities.

Entering adulthood as the Progressive Era merged into the Gilded Age suited Peattie perfectly; she was an intellectual woman who wanted a career, but she was also a devoted wife and mother. Described as "tall, dignified, and kindly, and possessing a wicked sense of humor" (Raftery 53), Peattie exemplified an increasing number of late-nineteenth-century women who balanced their desire for independence and universal rights with their maternal, womanly instincts and needs. For the first time, American women had a choice: they could remain contentedly in the home, follow a professional career, or, as in Peattie's case, attempt to harmonize the private and public spheres. Peattie's struggle to grow as an individual, to gain respect as a professional, and to balance family and career is one that women still face today.

Peattie spent most of her life in the Midwest, but the nine years she spent in Omaha were important to her as a writer and as a woman at the close of the nineteenth century. While raising four children, tending a husband with recurring health problems, and helping with the family finances, Peattie authored a prodigious number of editorials, columns, short stories, poems, articles, novels, histories, plays, literary criticism, popular domestic fiction, and children's novels and stories. One book cannot do justice to the expanse and variety of writings produced by Elia W. Peattie during her lifetime.

Although much of Peattie's work was published to help support her family, some of her best works – her writings appearing regularly in the *Omaha World-Herald* and her short stories collected in *The Mountain Woman* – were written while she was living in Omaha. During her years on the *World-Herald*, Peattie influenced the women of Nebraska as well as people across the United States, not only in the dignity with which she led her life, the compassion she felt for others, and the fierceness with which she defended her beliefs, but also with her professionalism. Her writing served political, cultural, and social functions as it expanded her own horizons as a writer and as a woman.

I am beginning and ending *Impertinences* with an overview of Peattie's life, but my primary focus is the journalistic writings Peattie penned while she resided in Omaha. Choosing which writings to include among the literally hundreds she published in the *World-Herald* and how to group them proved to be a monumental task, and a somewhat disappointing one, since I had to exclude many of my favorites because of lack of space. As I firmly believe in the importance of context as well as text, I have provided short, general backgrounds for the chapters as well as details about each of the writings. Some of Peattie's subjects, such as faith healer Francis Schlatter, though well known at the time, have faded into obscurity. Others, such as the Omaha stockyards or mourning rituals, concern people, events, or customs that have changed greatly over the last century. Most of Peattie's topics, however, show us just how little has changed in the last one-hundred-plus years.

This volume includes the most definitive Peattie bibliography that presently exists. It has been compiled entry by entry over the last ten years as I read newspapers and periodicals published during her lifetime. However, it is far from complete, since she published prolifically in diverse venues. The only archive of Peattie works is housed at the University of California–Santa Barbara; it contains mainly books that Peattie has published as well as papers relating to her children. Peattie's letters are scattered throughout the United States in the archives of her correspondents. More disappointing, two house fires, one in 1899 in South Haven, Illinois, and another in 1903 at Bond Avenue in Windsor Park, Illinois, destroyed most of the Peatties' manuscripts, letters, photographs, and memorabilia. The biographical introduction is meant to give a background of her life, focusing primarily on her Nebraska years and her writings in the *World-Herald*, and it should not be considered a definitive biography of her multifaceted life.

Fortunately for me, Peattie had not been completely forgotten when I began this project. Sidney Bremer has done an excellent job in recovering Peattie's Chicago years as well as interpreting and republishing *The Precipice*, Peattie's feminist social work novel of Chicago. Joan Falcone is editing Peattie's memoir, "Star Wagon," and has researched Peattie's later years in Chicago and North Carolina. I am deeply indebted to both of these supportive scholars, especially Joan, who has shared her manuscript of "Star Wagon" with me. I also have another manuscript in progress, "Proving Up: Turn-of-the-Century Stories of Western Women by Elia Peattie," a collection of Peattie's short stories about the West with a critical foreword that will discuss her place within western American literature. However, Peattie's eighteen years of literary criticism for the *Chicago Tribune*, her other periodical and popular fiction, her children's stories and novels, her poetry, her histories and historical stories, and her plays still need to be explored. In addition, two of Peattie's sons, Donald and Roderick, and one of her daughters-in-law, Barbara Culross Peattie, were themselves significant writers who carried on the family writing tradition.

I have chosen to print Peattie's *Omaha World-Herald* columns and editorials in their entirety, for the most part, except for long lists, extended quotations from other publications, occasional rambling asides, and statistical insertions. I have also silently edited typographical errors and omissions found in the originals, for Peattie was a perfectionist and probably cringed at every misspelling the typesetters made and the proofreaders missed.[2] In addition, many of the issues were in poor condition when microfilmed, and portions of some texts are unreadable; occasionally, entire issues are missing.

Fifteen years ago, I began researching turn-of-the-century family periodicals to find stories about the West written by people with firsthand experience in the settlement process. This is the second book to result from this discovery process, and two more manuscripts are nearing completion. The Nebraska Humanities Council funded me in my initial research and set me on a route I could never have imagined. I am deeply grateful to them for the assistance they provided. Two other women, Nancy Johnson and Jean Keezer-Clayton, have aided and encouraged me from the beginning and throughout the accumulating years.

I am indebted to many people, also, for their aid in my work on Elia Peattie. Grandchildren Mark and Noel Peattie, scholars and writers themselves, along with Mark's wife, Alice, searched among family letters and photographs, granted me permission to use the autobiographies of their father, uncle, and grandparents, and offered assistance with biographical questions. Peattie biographer Joan Falcone as well as scholar Judy Boss, who collaborated on the Peattie website, graciously shared essential research with me. Research assistant Eric Reed, the fastest typist in the West, provided indispensable help, while N'deye Atatouba helped with the complexities of the index. Alta Kramer and Sheryl Heidenreich, University of Nebraska at Kearney's Inter-Library Loan marvels, unearthed obscure books and documents and efficiently dispatched hundreds of requests for microfilm, articles, books, and periodicals. Without their assistance, I truly could not have completed this book.

Financial support, too, was essential, for I needed to search the *Chicago Tribune*, *Chicago Daily News*, *Omaha Bee*, and *Omaha World-Herald*, available only on microfilm, make copies of hundreds of pages of Peattie's published works, and explore the archives of the Douglas County Historical Society in Omaha, the Nebraska State Historical Society in Lincoln, and Stuhr Museum in Grand Island. I received summer fellowships from the University of Nebraska at Kearney (UNK) and the Center for Great Plains Studies in Lincoln as well as several grants from UNK's Research Services Council. Chancellor Douglas Kristensen, Dr. Kenneth Nikels, and Dr. James Roark played a key role in this institutional encouragement. Dr. Barbara Emrys, English Department chair, provided invaluable moral support and reams of copy paper.

Several museums and organizations supplied materials in my historical and literary quest. I am indebted to so many for their interest and indispensable assistance: the Chicago Historical Society; Barbara Lage, Don Snoddy, Helene Quigley, and especially Joann Meyer, Douglas County Historical Society; Terri Raburn, Nebraska State Historical Society; Karen Keehr, Stuhr Museum of the Prairie Pioneer; Catherine Renschler, Adams County Historical Society; Dorothy Langdon-Conry, Omaha Woman's Club; Ann Walding-Phillips, *Omaha World-Herald*; David Wetzel and Barbara Dey, Colorado Historical Society; Carol Wood and Cathy Peterson, Children's Square USA; Vern Lenzen, Durham Western Heritage Museum; Sarah J. Johnson, Nebraska Game and Parks Commission; Eric Gillespie, Catigny First Division Foundation; John B. Ahouse and the University of Southern California Doheny Memorial Library; Patty Manhart, May Museum in Fremont; Elaine Westering, Geraldine Rystrom, and Mary Ulffers of Stromsburg; and Jim Calloway, Great Plains Black Museum. Susan Mahr, Robert Chrisman, and Debra Bunting of Omaha helped too in trying to locate essential photographs.

Very special friends Ladette Randolph, Margie Rine, Mary Clearman Blew, Steve Shively, and Nancy Johnson not only responded with helpful suggestions on my manuscript but also offered unwavering moral support. Charles Peek, Kate and Mike Benzel, John Damon, Marguerite Tassi, Ruth Behlmann, Marguerite (Cleary) Remien, Jeanette Marcy, and Linda Oberle tracked my progress and encouraged me, while my family, with our ever-multiplying grandchildren, kept me rooted in the twenty-first century. My husband, Terry, understood the seemingly unending hours needed for researching, writing, and revising and knew when to help, when to leave me alone, and when to have the horses ready to go riding. I truly appreciate them all!

ELIA WILKINSON PEATTIE CHRONOLOGY

1857	Robert Burns Peattie born in Waushara County, Wisconsin
1862	15 January. Elia Wilkinson born in Kalamazoo, Michigan, to Frederick and Amanda Wilkinson
1871	Wilkinsons move to Chicago
1883	5 May. Elia marries Robert Peattie
1884	6 February. Son Edward Cahill born in Chicago
1884	Elia joins *Tribune* as first "girl reporter"
1885	5 May. Daughter Barbara is born
1888	Moves to Omaha
1889	Publishes *The Story of America*; takes a trip to Alaska
1890	Robert goes to Colorado Springs to recuperate; Elia publishes *A Journey Through Wonderland*; publishes *The Judge*; meets William Jennings Bryan in Omaha
1891	Son Roderick Peattie born 1 August; publishes *With Scrip and Staf*
1892	Publishes *The American Peasant*; meets Hamlin Garland at People's Convention in Omaha
1893	Reads three papers at World's Fair; helps found Omaha Woman's Club
1894	Attends General Federation of Women's Clubs in Philadelphia, shares stage with Susan B. Anthony
1895	Publishes *The Pictorial Story of America* and *Our Lady of Liberty*
1896	Peatties move back to Chicago; publishes *A Mountain Woman* and *Our Chosen Land*
1897	Publishes *History of United States, Indiana and Gibson County*, and *Pippins and Cheese*
1898	21 June. Son Donald Culross born
1898–99	Elia joins Chicago Women's Club, Little Room, Fortnightly Club; lectures extensively; publishes *America in War and Peace*, *The Shape of Fear*, *The Love of a Caliban*; writes 100 stories in 100

	days for the *Chicago Tribune*; moves to old Wilkinson "House-Home" on Bond Avenue where they will live for twenty years
1901	Publishes *The Beleaguered Forest* and *How Jacques Came into the Forest of Arden: An Impertinence*
1901–17	Elia is literary critic for *Chicago Tribune*
1903	Publishes *The Edge of Things*
1908	Helps to found the Cordon Club for women authors when they are ousted from the all-male Cliff Dwellers Club
1914	Publishes *The Precipice*
1915	Barbara Peattie Erskine dies
1918	Publishes *Painted Windows*
1920	Robert retires from *Tribune* after twenty years; Peatties retire at "Dunwandrin" in Tryon, North Carolina
1930	Robert dies at age sixty-three in Tryon
1935	12 July. Elia dies at age seventy-three in Wellingford, Vermont

Impertinences

INTRODUCTION

A Writer's Beginnings

1862–1896

"That any day seems dull is a confession of personal limitation."

Entering the pressroom of the *Omaha World-Herald*, Elia Wilkinson Peattie, her long, brown hair lifted softly into a bun, gathered her black twill skirt in her left hand to keep it from trailing on the tobacco-stained floor and clutched the typescript of her latest editorial in her right. She scanned the smoke-filled room as she swept toward the editor's desk, smiling and joking with her fellow journalists. The clatter of typewriters and the swoosh-clank of the presses never skipped a beat as they once did when she first took up her position at the newspaper. As a matter of fact, few of the reporters even gave her more than a glance anymore. The men had finally become used to having a woman around the newspaper office.

Acceptance, however, hadn't come easily. Perhaps tolerance would be a better word.[1] Peattie was one of the first women on a major Omaha newspaper and one of the first plains women to write editorial columns in a major newspaper that addressed public issues, and her outspoken and sometimes irreverent remarks often made her as many detractors as friends. However, her intellectual background, her use of irony and humor, her ability to employ various genres and literary approaches, and her undaunted "impertinence" produced a strong voice in America at the turn of the century.

Born in Kalamazoo, Michigan, on 15 January 1862, Peattie was prepared in her early years for the economic struggles she would later encounter. During her childhood in Michigan she enjoyed few social or cultural diversions, for her father's tight control of the family budget allowed only the necessities – especially the necessities that he considered important. In 1871 Peattie's father decided to move the family to Chicago, believing many opportunities would arise for enterprising men after the great fire, and the family, which now included three daughters, lived frugally. Elia's father built the family a small, boxlike duplex on the corner of Polk and Robey Streets, which was at that time on the outskirts of the city, and rented out the other half for income. In her memoirs, Peattie recalled having no books or magazines in the house.[2]

By the time Peattie was thirteen and had reached the seventh grade, she had

Intertype machines in the composing room of the *Omaha World-Herald* in 1894. (Omaha World-Herald)

to drop out of school to assist her father in setting type at his job-printing office. Although Peattie never returned to school, she seized every opportunity to learn. She became devoted to the dictionary, learning definitions and phrases and studying punctuation. One of her uncles, Edward Cahill, often invited her to Lansing, where he practiced law. There she luxuriated in their gracious hospitality, their abundance of books and magazines, and the company of another uncle, Frank, who instilled in her a passion for Shakespeare.

In 1877, when Peattie was fifteen, Bertha, the fourth daughter, was born, so Elia had to quit working at the print shop and stay home to help her mother with the children and the housework. That same year, Peattie met her future husband, Robert Burns Peattie, twenty, at a dance on Chicago's West Side. Their love and commitment sparked instantaneously. Of Scottish ancestry, Robert, born in 1857 to John and Elizabeth Culross Peattie, grew up on a farm in Wisconsin and later in the Gas House region of Chicago, where his father owned a machine shop. Robert began a career in journalism while in high school, distributing the evening newspaper over a five-mile route to earn money for books, and then moved up to clerk in the business office of the *Chicago Times*. Later this persistence would reward him with the chance to become a full-time reporter. Robert won Elia's heart, in part, by

Robert Burns Peattie as a reporter for the *Chicago Times* in the 1880s. (Chicago Historical Society)

his gift offerings of books and flowers, although her puritanical father, who was victim to "periods of excessive piety," was not impressed by a slender and delicate young fellow who would waste so much money and bring the unorthodox theories of Spencer and Darwin into his home.

By 1880, Peattie's father grew restless in Chicago and decided to move the family to Windsor Park and into a small house in the woods, far from any neighbors. Peattie's father had to walk three miles each day to take the train to work in Chicago. Robert, likewise, had to spend hours traveling to visit her. Their relationship became complicated that year because Wilbur F. Storey of the *Chicago Times* hired Robert as a reporter, a tremendous career move for the young journalist. At that time, the newspaper comprised four pages and employed only six reporters with no telegraph franchise. Storey's philosophy that it was "a newspaper's duty to print the news and raise hell" would have appealed to the young "radical" ("Detroit Free Press"). Robert often worked nights, so months would pass before the lovers would be able to see each other. Conditions improved slightly for the couple after the entire staff of the *Chicago Times* walked out and went to work for Melville E. Stone, editor of the *Morning News* or *Daily News*. At the *News*, Robert worked at various times as reporter, editorial paragrapher, exchange editor, and dramatic critic on both the morning and evening editions. Elia's father, dismayed, asked why Robert could not hold a "regular" job where he could be earning up to ten dollars a week. When he learned that Robert was making twenty-five dollars a week as a reporter, he viewed him with more respect (Robert Peattie 20).

In 1882, when Peattie was twenty and still living at home, Hazel, her youngest sister, was born, the last of seven children. Both of her mother's sons had died in infancy (Bremer and Falcone 678). Her mother had trouble recovering her strength, so Peattie worked feverishly to maintain the household and care for her four younger sisters. After three of her father's sisters died within a short period, her father, overtaken with sorrow, fell into a dark depression. The burden of her mother's invalidism, her sisters' rebelliousness, and her father's despondency became more than Peattie could bear. Suddenly one day, when Peattie was mending, she suffered what the family physician termed "nervous prostration." The doctor recommended that she stay with a friend, Lizzie Chase, in Chicago. Elia took his advice and never returned to the log cabin at Windsor Park. She published her first poem that year, "Ode to Neptune," in the *Chicago Times* (Raftery 51).

Marriage and a New Career

The next year, on 5 May 1883, after a six-year engagement, Robert and Elia married, with poet Eugene Field, who wrote a column called "Sharps and Flats" for the *Chicago Daily News*, serving as best man (Raftery 51).[3] In a characteristic moment of exuberance, Robert paid the minister fifteen dollars for performing the ceremony and hailed a cab to take them to their little cottage on the North Side. They arrived home with five cents left over but formed a partnership in life as well as business that never faltered (Roderick Peattie 32). Elia always considered her marriage with Robert as fortunate. Although they fell in love at first sight, she grew to realize that his support of her immutable ambition to write, as well as his valuable assistance in editing and proofreading, was what made her life happy and complete ("Mrs. Elia Wilkinson Peattie" 562). They moved in with Robert's widowed mother in her house on Pearson Street. Exactly nine months later, on 6 February 1884, their first son, Edward Cahill, was born. Fifteen months after that, on the couple's second anniversary, daughter Barbara arrived.

The Peatties continued living and working in Chicago, with both Elia and Robert writing for Stone's *Daily News*. Stone considered the couple "locally distinguished" journalists and allowed them to choose their own subjects. His practice of making the news lively and reliable and his policy of guiding the opinion of the public served as a useful training ground for Elia's future writing (Duffey 11). In addition, Robert and Elia spent their evenings writing stories together to supplement their newspaper income. Elia's Christmas story, published by the *Chicago Tribune* on 26 December 1885 and celebrated by the editors as "worthy to rank with the tales of the best-known authors of the day," fueled her creative efforts ("Mrs. Elia Wilkinson Peattie" 562).[4]

Soon both Elia and Robert joined the staff of the *Chicago Tribune*. After Elia had won several short-story contests for the newspaper, the editor, Robert Wilson Patterson, realized that it would be more economical to add her to his staff than to continue paying her the weekly prizes she continued to win, so Elia officially joined the *Tribune* in 1886. It is unknown when Robert began. Patterson asked Elia to take on the responsibilities of their Art and Society page, and she accepted quickly, even though she knew little about either. Her writing needed improvement too. City editor Fred Hall often caused Peattie to shed tears. Once he returned an article to her with all of the writing crossed out. He turned it over and upside down, telling her, "There's some blank paper. Please try again" (Robert Peattie 30). Although Peattie acknowledged that she might not have been the best society editor in Chicago's history, she did gain an enduring love and knowledge of art and made lasting friendships with Chicago artists.

Peattie's modest columns led to larger fields, and she became the first female reporter for the *Tribune* and the second "girl" reporter in Chicago.[5] Although married and the mother of two children, she worked day and night beside some of Chicago's best male journalists, interviewing public figures such as American anarchist Emma Goldberg, Union general Benjamin Franklin Butler, and journalist Kate Field as well as exposing fraudulent spiritualists (Roderick Peattie 33; Raftery 51; Bremer and Falcone 678). In addition, Peattie traveled around the Midwest as the *Tribune*'s correspondent and wrote special articles for the Sunday edition.

Elia Wilkinson Peattie from *A Woman of the Century*, published by Frances E. Willard and Mary A. Livermore in 1892.

Four years later, the couple could afford their own home on Woodlawn Street. Peattie had her first magazine fiction, "Grizel Cochrane's Ride," published in February 1887 in the prestigious family magazine *St. Nicholas*. Robert, meanwhile, had moved back to the *Chicago Times* and was also editing the evening edition, *The Mail*. Although the Peatties lived on a modest income and kept incredibly busy, they were warm, well fed, and very happy.

The Omaha Daily Herald Building ca. 1880s. (Nebraska State Historical Society Photograph Collections)

Nebraska and the *Omaha World-Herald*

The Peatties moved from Chicago to Omaha in 1888 when Robert accepted the position of managing editor of the *Omaha Daily Herald*, established by George L. Miller, Omaha's first physician. Elia had urged Robert to accept the position because Miller had also offered her the chance to publish bylined writings, putting both of them on the payroll. They left the children with Robert's mother for several months while they established themselves in Omaha, cramped into the back bedroom of a shabby boardinghouse.

Peattie's first contribution to the *Herald* was a short story titled "A Diminuendo," published on 16 December 1888, her introduction to Omaha readers. The *Herald* announced that Peattie would begin as a "regular staff correspondent" the following week. However, "The Women of the World," Peattie's "Column of Original Chat about Well-Known Women and Current Fashion," did not begin until 6 January 1889 and ran for only four weeks. She also published a gossipy article, "The Wabash Corner," and two short stories, "Dr. de Launy of Omaha," in January, and "Lisette," in April. She may have contributed other writings, but these are the only ones that carried her byline or initials.

Meanwhile, both the *Omaha Daily World*, founded by Gilbert Hitchcock in 1885, and the *Omaha Daily Herald* were floundering financially. By 1889 the *World*'s deficits totaled one thousand dollars a month, while the *Herald* was losing nearly five thousand dollars a month. Hitchcock decided to buy the *Herald* and merge the two newspapers into the *Omaha World-Herald*. Robert would continue as managing editor of both editions. Hitchcock's chief rival, Edward Rosewater of the *Omaha Bee*, commented sarcastically, "If Mr. Hitchcock couldn't make *The World* pay, how can he expect to make still another newspaper, also a financial failure, pay by consolidation?" Rosewater's words were, unfortunately, prophetic (Limprecht 4–5).[6] The Peatties did not receive the financial security they had envisioned. Instead, they were plunged into economic and transitional uncertainty, once more living on credit and hope. They rented a house on the western edge of Omaha at 1213 South Thirty-third Street. Both Robert's mother and Elia's sister Bertha soon joined them and lived with the family throughout the Omaha years.

Shortly after the Peatties arrived in Omaha, Mr. Hyde, one of their next-door neighbors, gave Elia a letter of introduction to the Northwestern Railroad's passenger superintendent. Hyde, perhaps a Northwestern employee, had heard that the railroad company wanted a travel book written to acquaint people with its route from Minneapolis to Seattle and Tacoma as well as its steamship line to Alaska. After Peattie met with the superintendent in Minneapolis, the railroad commissioned her to write a guidebook about every town of importance along the line. Offering free vacations as incentives, railroad investors across the United States had begun hiring writers and photographers to travel on their lines and promote historic monuments, scenic wonders, and local color along their routes to interest the public in "discovering" America for themselves – by rail, of course. To accommodate American sightseeing, railroads began investing in feeder lines and in luxury hotels at select locations, offering package deals on vacations.[7] Peattie's travel narrative, *A Journey Through Wonderland: Or, The Pacific Northwest and Alaska, With a Description of the Country Traversed by the Northern Pacific Railroad*, published by Rand McNally in 1890, described her pleasurable but anxious journey, one she termed "a very liberating experience." Unwilling to conform to the typical travel narrative, Peattie decided to incorporate a romantic, fictional subplot. For her account she created the persona of Scott Key, a young New York businessman who has never traveled farther than five hundred miles from home. Spicing the recitation of obligatory city statistics, famous landmarks, and alluring railway accommodations with her trademark wit and ironic insight, Peattie elevated advertisement to art.

Cover of Peattie's 1890 travel narrative, *A Journey Through Wonderland: Or, the Pacific Northwest and Alaska, with a Description of the Country Traversed by the Northern Pacific Railroad.*

At first, Elia was a sporadic feature and fiction writer for the newspaper, contributing bylined articles such as "Tragedy of Ward 3" and "Christmas at Goldberg." Most of her time was consumed by her family and the young people's history book that she was commissioned to write: *The Story of America: Containing the Romantic Incidents of History, from the Discovery of America to the Present Time.* Remarkably, she produced the volume of over seven hundred pages in four months, dictating the entire history to two stenographers ("Mrs. Elia Wilkinson Peattie" 563).

In 1890, Peattie increased her output of editorials and initiated her own bylined column, "What Women Are Doing," featured in the Sunday edition and reprinted on Wednesdays, contributing twenty-eight pieces total. She also completed *The Judge*, a murder mystery set in Chicago about a young girl torn between her fiancé, accused of murder, and her father, the judge who presides over the trial. A Chicago reporter cracks the case, contributing an intriguing subnarrative about journalistic integrity and the interference of the press in crime investigation and in the courts of law.

After *The Judge* won a nine-hundred-dollar prize from the *Detroit Free Press*, Rand McNally published it in 1890. The family could now afford to move into a home of their own at 3224 Poppleton Avenue, approximately two miles from their jobs at the *Omaha World-Herald* building located at 1412 Farnham Street. The Peatties put down a thousand dollars for a house with "a nice living room, a dining room and excellent kitchen, a good basement, four bedrooms, an attic with a servant's room, a fine porch and a yard with trees." The house, then on the outskirts of Omaha, looked out on the "wild lands" that later became Hanscom Park. The *Omaha City Directory* for 1889 listed Robert B. as "Managing Editor of the *World-Herald*." Now, Elia's name was listed under Robert's as "Editorial Writer."

During the winter of 1890, Peattie's literary career was complicated when her husband became critically ill with double pneumonia. She took him on a recuperative trip to Colorado Springs. While at the hotel, his congestion became so acute that when the doctor informed Peattie her husband would never recover, she sat by his bedside and fashioned a black cashmere mourning dress. However, she added silver braid and rosettes so as not to alarm Robert. Later, when they were able to dine together, Robert complimented her on her new dress, but she never told him the use for which it had been designed. Reluctantly, Peattie had to leave Robert in Colorado Springs and return to care for her children and continue working to support the family. Throughout the next several years, Robert attempted cures again in Colorado and then Texas, but he never fully recovered, nor was he ever physically strong again.

Peattie's publications increased in 1891 as the need to help support the family grew more imperative. As prestigious periodicals such as *Atlantic Monthly*, *Harper's Bazaar*, *Harper's Weekly*, *Cosmopolitan*, *Lippincott's*, *Saint Nicholas*, *Wide Awake*, *Youth's Companion*, and *Judge's Young People* began publishing her fiction, she gained professional respect and a national reputation. She also published *With Scrip and Staf*, a tale of the Children's Crusade. She wrote only two daily columns for the *Omaha World-Herald* in 1891, perhaps because she gave birth to their third child, Roderick, on 1 August. However, she wrote a half dozen stories and more than twenty editorials, usually published in the Sunday edition.

Peattie and the Populists

Peattie became more regular in her contributions to the *World-Herald* in 1892, penning fifty-two "editorials." Usually printed in the second section of the *Sunday World-Herald*, the subjects were eclectic and covered in depth. A high point of that year was the People's Party Convention in Omaha. Peattie helped Thomas Henry Tibbles write a pamphlet on "Free Silver" titled "The American Peasant: A Timely Allegory" for *The Independent*, the national Populist magazine, which he founded in Lincoln, Nebraska. The article, a utopian morality tale dealing with the problems of farmers as well as the debate over the gold and silver standard, was written by T. H. Tibbles and "Another." Peattie explained that she was "Another."[8] Active in the Populist Party, she campaigned diligently for William Jennings Bryan through her speaking and her writing. "The West was hard-pressed at that time," wrote Peattie in "Star Wagon." "Railroads and Eastern investors were milking the hard-working and inexperienced West and causing hardship."

Influenced by Tibbles's description of the desolation of Nebraska's prairie farm families, Peattie also wrote "Jim Lancy's Waterloo." This grim tale narrated the failed attempt of a farmer to make a living on the Nebraska prairie. After it was published with an illustration in *Cosmopolitan* magazine, the

Page from Peattie's short story "Jim Lancy's Waterloo," published in *Cosmopolitan* in 1894 and illustrated by Alice Barber Stephens.

Populists printed a million copies of this naturalistic short story and distributed it as propaganda. Later Peattie included it in her short-story collection *A Mountain Woman*, published in 1898 by Way and Williams.

In appreciation of her support for him and the Populist Party, Bryan presented Peattie with a full set of the poetry of William Cullen Bryant. His inscription read: "To my friend Elia Peattie the first Bryan man, with the warm regards of William Jennings Bryan." Later, Peattie described him as "one of the most magnetic orators this country has ever produced, though it has been rich in orators," but she added, "We did not then dream how, in time, vanity would mar his idealism, or how inadequate were the ideas we held as the solution of the distress about us."

Traveling dominated 1893 for Peattie. She visited several Nebraska cities for material for articles on their communities, and she attended, along with many other Nebraskans, the Chicago World's Fair. In addition to enjoying the sights, visiting family, and renewing acquaintances, she read three papers at the exposition with James Whitcomb Riley and Eugene Field.[9] Meanwhile, Peattie continued her outpouring of editorials, writing forty-six in 1893 on such diverse subjects as the Keeley Gold Cure for alcoholism, the annexation of Cuba, mortgages, children's books, the character of furniture, and funerals.

The Woman's Club

Most important this year, however, was Peattie's work in establishing the Omaha Woman's Club. As her Omaha contacts and reputation as a journalist grew, she began creating networks with the women around her to ease her feelings of isolation from her friends and family back in Chicago as well as from its diverse cultural and intellectual opportunities, to form new friendships with other women who shared her interests, and to find a forum for her views on women's roles in society. Frances Ford, a Woman's Club member from New Jersey now living in Nebraska, visited her and persuaded her to help found the organization in Omaha.[10] Peattie wrote an article in the *Omaha World-Herald* suggesting such a club and received an overwhelming response.

Although the first Woman's Club, Sorosis, founded by newspaper columnist Jane Croly, began in 1868 in New York City, the movement expanded quickly throughout the 1880s and exploded in the 1890s. Often begun as literary societies that studied music, art, and drama as well as literature, the clubs soon enlarged their focus on self-education to include social and civic concerns. Usually composed of middle- and upper-class white women, they sometimes were viewed by outsiders as rather exclusive (Thomas 41–42).

Frances M. Ford of Omaha, who helped found the Omaha Woman's Club and served as its president from 1894 to 1895. (Omaha Woman's Club)

Women's clubs helped unite women by offering a close-knit, supportive community where they could establish friendships, further their self-education, and engage in social reform without neglecting their homes and families, all the while maintaining their middle-class respectability (Thomas 36; Goldberg 42; Ammons 6).[11] Clubwomen, for the most part, saw themselves as wives and mothers first but wanted to be considered as homemakers who had enlarged their duties to include the community and the state as their larger home (Lerner xvii, 32; Blair 32–34).

The concept appealed to Omaha women. The next year, 1894, with a Woman's Club membership of more than four hundred, Peattie represented Omaha at the national conference of the General Federation of Woman's

Clubs in Philadelphia, sharing the stage with Susan B. Anthony. That fall, Peattie helped form the Nebraska State Federation of Women's Clubs. She served first as vice-president and then president of the state organization, and persuaded the state clubs to join the General Federation of Women's Clubs. As a result, Nebraska became the seventh state to join the national organization.

Committed to the group's ideals of promoting culture and philanthropy and working for social and educational reform, Peattie traveled across the state to organize local groups. "I made many friends on these excursions and loved the making of them," she wrote. Their greatest value, she believed, was in "reaching out toward knowledge and beauty and social pleasure in the midst of toil and hardship; uniting women who needed unity; putting the social factor in lives that would have been sordid and heartbreakingly dull but for this deep impulse toward education and friendship and service." Peattie was most proud of the Omaha Woman's Club's creation of a traveling state library that made it possible for everyone in Nebraska, no matter how remote the location, to have the opportunity to borrow a book.

Peattie continued her weekly Sunday features and editorials and renewed her column, renamed "A Word with the Women." Appearing on page eight, the last page of the newspaper, it often served as a vehicle for promoting the Omaha Woman's Club and as a newsletter for its members. Her name and occupation as "Editorial Writer, World Herald" were now in boldface type in the 1894 *Omaha City Directory*.

In 1895, Peattie's contributions to the *World-Herald* peaked at 321 editorials and columns, including two serialized novels, "The Fountain of Youth" and "Jan Paulsen: The Bookman," and a three-part story, "Witch's Gold." As she was also gathering stories for *A Mountain Woman*, to be published the next year with Way and Williams, her columns often became a patchwork of short commentaries, news about women from Omaha and around the world, and Woman's Club notes. Her aim, it appears, was to elevate the status of women by holding up models of success, admonishing foolish and selfish behavior, and promoting her own exemplar of the "New Woman."

Leaving Omaha

Peattie's last year in Omaha, 1896, witnessed an increased emphasis on women's issues and a decrease in sustained feature articles and editorials, perhaps owing to Robert's precarious health and her need to find additional income by writing magazine stories to "keep the pot boiling." Because he had been forced to travel for his health frequently, Robert had finally lost his position at the *Omaha World-Herald*. After an unsatisfying stint on a Council Bluffs, Iowa, newspaper, he decided to leave Omaha and try his luck in New York City.

That fall, *A Mountain Woman* came out to positive reviews. The short stories, many previously published in periodicals, presented western themes and settings that echoed the naturalistic tones of Hamlin Garland. Peattie also revised and reissued her American history, *Our Chosen Land: A Romantic Story of America from the Present Time of Its Discovery and Conquest to the Present Day*, with Wabash in Chicago, adding material about the Chicago World's Fair (Bremer and Falcone 679). In addition, she compiled another history, *The Pictorial Story of America: Part 3, Fulton County, Indiana.*

Peattie remained in Omaha with the family until October but struggled financially and emotionally, continuing her work at the *World-Herald* and sending out fiction for publication to many magazines to "pay the grocer, the coal man and buy the clothes." With her husband no longer managing editor, her tenuous relationship with the men on the staff became strained, and Peattie speculated that they were jealous of her celebrity. Unable to keep up the mortgage on their home and worried about supporting her mother-in-law, Bertha, and the three children, all of whom were residing with her, Peattie decided to move back to Chicago where her husband would join her in his new position as correspondent for the *New York Tribune*.

In a farewell "A Word with the Women" column to her Omaha readers on 11 October 1896, Peattie revealed her emotional ties to the newspaper and Nebraska:

> I have just written that familiar headline for the last time. . . . When I first came to Omaha newspaper women were not common here. People suspected that women would not make practical newspaper workers. Dear Dean Gardner asked me, I remember, if I was going to carry some notes I had taken about the cathedral chimes to a reporter to have him write it up! But since that time women have become well known on the newspapers in Omaha, and there are several efficient women writers engaged on the various papers of the city. I have had the privilege of watching this young city pass from its pioneer stage, with all the materialism that implies, into the state of intellectual aspiration. It cares for power more now than for land; it likes music and books, painting and ideas, better than houses and horses. Its evolution goes on, and those who remain will have the privilege of assisting it. . . .
>
> This column has never essayed to be brilliant or remarkable. It has quietly followed the mood of the day and the town – for towns and days have moods. It has commented casually upon what happened to be happening.

It has been merely a mirror, idly held up, that the public might see in it its own face. Whatever of good or bad there has been in it, the public is almost as responsible for it as I.

I am tempted to hope that some people, seeing this familiar column in the paper no more, will miss it for a week or two – it would be folly to expect to be remembered longer than that. And I, having lost my occupation, will also miss my audience – for a longer time than two weeks.

And so, bon soir, la compagnie!

The next evening, the Woman's Club and the Sundown Club hosted a farewell reception for Peattie. By nine o'clock nearly five hundred people filled the rooms of the Commercial Club, lavishly decorated with palms and ferns by the House and Home Committee. Mr. W. H. Alexander, in his farewell remarks, stated: "Gifted beyond most women, with conspicuous intellectual graces, you have awakened the interest and challenged the approval of the brightest minds in the country. You have done more than this; forgetful of personal convenience, you have ever been ready for service. In the church, in the school, in the clubroom, where ever your voice and your pen could be useful to others, they have both been employed."

On behalf of the group, Alexander presented Peattie with a gold-mounted oak chest containing silver tableware. Wearing a simple white gown with a red rose in her hair, Peattie replied, "You cannot expect me, Mr. Alexander and ladies of the club and members of the Sundown club, to speak. I cannot tell in words how your presence here tonight has affected me more than this beautiful gift – and it is beautiful. It is the prettiest thing that I have. I shall feel, when I leave Omaha, like a barnacle rubbed off a ship" ("Farewell to Mrs. Peattie").

The accolades continued, perhaps none so heartfelt as an anonymous column written in tribute to her "By the Women who miss Mrs. Peattie – By one of their number": "And now she is gone! What a lonely corner there will be in the paper – how we will miss her cheery words! Who will ever be to us at once critic, teacher, preacher, and playmate? Who will guide us to good literature, show us good pictures and tell us where good music may be heard? Who will introduce to us new authors and address to us eulogies on buried ones?" ("A Word from the Women").

Years later, when Peattie was invited back to Omaha by the Omaha Woman's Press Club, another audience of more than five hundred came to hear her speak. She reflected that during her eight years working on the *World-Herald* she had written nearly every kind of story that her editor could assign and had traveled all across Nebraska. She believed herself to have been Omaha's first woman reporter ("Large Audience"). This could well be true, for in 1880, out of a total of 12,308 journalists in the United States, only 288 were women (Beasley and Gibbons 10). Expected to marry, raise children, and stay within the safe confines of the home, women needed a "good excuse" to choose a career in journalism – "a dead husband or starving children." If they tried to combine a vocation in journalism with marriage, they either "kept it to themselves" or "flirted with disaster" (Saltzman 1).

Most women writing for Nebraska newspapers held low-paying jobs, such as preparing copy for the women's or social pages (Riedesel 37). By the fall of 1893, not only did Peattie's writings have bylines, but her name often adorned the headline of her article or editorial, as in the following examples: "That Vital Thing, Debt: Mrs. Peattie Discourses on It in Connection with Mortgage Statistics" and "Salvation Lasses at Home: Mrs. Peattie Writes of the Blue Frocked Sisterhood of the Lord."

When Peattie began publishing in Nebraska in 1889, few bylined news stories, articles, editorials, or even fiction written by women appeared regularly in the two major daily Omaha newspapers, the *World-Herald* and the *Bee*. A few Omaha women edited or wrote in women's weeklies, like Mary Fairbrother, job printer and editor of the *Woman's Weekly*, the official publication of the Nebraska Woman's Club. Some women, like Mora Balcombe and Viola Pratt, contributed freelance articles that appeared occasionally in Omaha newspapers; others, like Willa Cather in the weekly *Lincoln Courier*, wrote literary or dramatic reviews. Still others were weekly newspaper editors who published, edited, typeset, and wrote local news for small-town newspapers sprinkled across the state, like Maggie Mobley of the *Grand Island Independent*, Minnie Williams of the *Hastings Nebraskan*, and Mrs. Datus Brooks of the *Omaha Republican*.[12] Nebraska did boast of a nationally known female editor, Clara Bewick Colby, a leading activist in the West who established the *Woman's Tribune* in Beatrice in 1883. This suffragist newspaper, which had one of the largest and longest-running circulations of such reform publications, was published in Nebraska until 1889 and remained in print until 1909 (Lomicky 102). In addition to advancing the vote for women by printing appeals by Elizabeth Cady Stanton and Susan B. Anthony and writing editorials on political issues in Nebraska, Colby published information of general interest to women, such as literary reviews, household hints, and child-rearing tips; promoted women's accomplishments; reported on women's clubs and organizations; and supported the Nebraska Home for the Friendless, a state institution dedicated to helping destitute women and children (Lomicky 106). However, as the *Hebron Journal* proclaimed in an 1895 article titled "Women in Journalism," Peattie was "the leader of them all," her name "so well known that she needs no introduction to the public that has so long admired her work."

By 1900 the newspaper field had grown, and of the 30,098 journalists, now 2,193 were women (Beasley and Gibbons 10). As the twentieth century approached, women were gaining more and more recognition in the field of journalism all across the United States. A few daring women, like Jane Cunningham Croly, Ida Wells, Nellie Bly, and Frances Willard, worked side by side with newspapermen and won international reputations as journalists.[13] The major cause for this increase was the urbanization of America in the late nineteenth century, which supported the expansion of the daily newspaper.[14]

Meanwhile, Peattie enjoyed her own celebrity in Omaha. "There was something about [Omaha] that appealed to me," she said in a 1923 interview. "There was a chance to do many formative things. I tried in my own untrained way, and with more disinterestedness than less impulsive people could understand, to do some of that work. I knew afterward that I made as many enemies as friends and I suppose that I must have been a perfect nuisance. But anyway it was the breath of life" ("Writer").

Being a nuisance, or "unseemly," was an attitude that Peattie cultivated. In reply to a letter to the *Omaha World-Herald* signed A. M. M., Peattie wrote an editorial titled "In Defense of Her Own Sex." She declared, "You think, do you madam, that a wrangle over 'rights' is unseemly? Why, then, so was the American Revolution unseemly; so was the wrangle which secured the manumission of slaves, so has been every struggle for liberty! Unseemly! All vital things are unseemly." She continued, "To be perfectly respectable one must needs have done nothing at all. A sawdust doll, dear madam, is always seemly."

Peattie had vitality, intellect, and dedication. During her Omaha years she gained strength from her various roles as writer and woman in her struggle for self-definition and economic survival. A passion for writing burned within her throughout her life, but the works that she published during these years would attain the greatest depth and breadth and vitality that she would ever achieve. Her energy and commitment to personal, intellectual, cultural, and social improvement not only serve effectively in presenting a balanced portrait of America as the Gilded Age merged into the Progressive Era, but they also depict a region and a people having interminable possibilities. Despite her impertinence, or, perhaps, because of it, she emerged as a spirited voice in the late nineteenth and early twentieth centuries.

CHAPTER 1

Early Omaha

"To know the hour and to be the man – that is magnificent."

The Peatties moved from Chicago to Omaha in 1888, and their son Roderick, born in Omaha in 1891, claimed that he was raised on the border of the frontier. He remembered the drovers' trail from the open range that he could observe from his nursery window, where herds of tired cattle and sweaty horses stirred up the dusty roads. He said of his parents, "With pioneer courage bred in them, no obstacle seemed too great for Robert Burns and Elia Wilkinson Peattie. They made light of hardship and took every advantage of chance" (Roderick Peattie 5).

In reality, Omaha had been growing as a city for more than thirty years when the Peatties arrived. It was established in 1854, shortly after Nebraska was organized as a territory and President Pierce ratified a treaty with the Omaha Indians. The Council Bluffs and Nebraska Ferry Company completed their official survey on July 4 and began promoting the town of "Omaha," translated, according to Indian legend, as "above all others upon a stream" ("A History of Omaha" 1). The political leaders, who owned most of the land, were of British, German, and Irish ancestry, men like Byron Reed (real estate), Augustus Kountz (banking), and Edward Creighton (lumber and telegraph).

When Grenville Dodge, a surveyor, convinced Abraham Lincoln to build the railroad along the Platte River valley, securing the location of the Union Pacific through Omaha, the city's future was assured. Union Pacific spokesmen declared that "Omaha was the starting point of the grandest undertaking God ever witnessed in the history of the world" (Larsen 27). In 1865 Omaha doubled in size with the arrival of thousands of workers in their teens and early twenties, many of them Irish, Civil War veterans, or former slaves. With wages ranging from $2.50 to $4.00 a day, they flocked to Omaha to lay the rails for the Union Pacific across the Great Plains (Ambrose 167, 177–78). The rail line encouraged the growth of industry, especially the stockyards and packinghouses, which, in turn, lured more European immigrants. The population and regional dominance of Omaha grew steadily.

Omaha served as the first territorial capital until Nebraska was admitted to the Union in 1867, when the legislature voted to move it to a site to be called

A busy day on Farnham Street, 1889. (Nebraska State Historical Society Photograph Collections)

Lincoln, but that did not slow the town's progress. Soon four more railroads reached Omaha and, in partnership with Council Bluffs, constructed the Union Pacific bridge across the Missouri River. In the 1870s Omaha offered young men a chance to make a fortune in several types of enterprises: working for the railroads, providing agricultural products and services, and developing commerce.

Omaha had grown steadily from a frontier town of 16,083 in 1870 to an urban crossroads with a population of 30,518 by 1880. With its large number of German immigrants and its abundance of grains nearby, the city soon challenged Milwaukee and Cincinnati in beer production, producing 31,755 barrels annually. The Iler distillery was reportedly the fourth largest in the world. By 1885, three years before the Peatties arrived, Omaha's population had reached about 60,000, and real estate transfers peaked at $31 million (Limprecht 4; Chudacoff 14). Omaha had thirteen public schools, four parochial schools, two colleges, and thirty-nine churches.

At thirty-one years of age, however, the city also displayed its exuberant youthfulness. Prostitutes, gamblers, and saloons competed for the business of thousands of young people seeking their fortunes in the West. Brothels were raided monthly, with advance notice given to the house, and police collected five dollars for each madam and one dollar for each prostitute daily – the price of doing business (Limprecht 4). Although vice flourished and cattle may have passed near the Peattie home on the way to the stockyards, Omaha was hardly the frontier outpost of Roderick's memory.

Peattie's editorials, peopled by all layers of society, have become important historical records of a rapidly changing era. Even the controversy they once generated informs today's readers of a region's past at its best and its worst. Strongly against censorship, Peattie argued that "Omaha is like the rest of the world – made up of good and bad, the detestable and the admirable. It cannot whip history into even respectability by expunging leaves from its books. It is just as bound to preserve historical accuracy – if there is such a thing – as any other town, city, state or country. . . . History can never be respectable. It must be full of storms."[1] *Peattie fearlessly recorded the history of Omaha in the making, holding its people accountable for their actions, no matter their social status, and providing today's readers with an intimate look into the people and places of historic Omaha.*

"A Word with the Women" – Defending Omaha

24 July 1896

Many of Peattie's columns expressed her delight in the scenery around Omaha. Having been raised in the forests of Michigan and moved to the woods of Windsor Park north of Chicago, she had grown to appreciate the beauty of nature. After residing in Omaha for over six years, she came to love the city and poetically described her scenic surroundings. In her daily column "A Word with the Women," Peattie, a staunch booster of Omaha, defended the city from detractors, even finding positive attributes in the sweltering Nebraska summer along the Missouri River.

❧ There is a funny trick out in the state of depreciating Omaha. The people in the country do it to a small extent, and the people in the towns do it to a great extent. Even the visitors at present in town attending the Law League convention maintain that Omaha is a great deal hotter than the country. Now the plains are hot in summer. Nebraska is hot from the Iowa to the Colorado line. The nights are cool, thank heaven, and so strength is found to endure the heat. But the sun comes up in a cloudless sky, and the wind that blows is a land wind, and so does not much cool the air. Sometimes at midday on the treeless plains the thermometer gets up where it astonishes people. It has been known to be at 135 before now – though of course many Nebraskans will deny it. But I saw it, so I know. It was a good thermometer, too. But all

Omahans enjoying a summer day at Krug Park, ca. 1900. (Douglas County Historical Society Collections, Omaha, Nebraska)

that doesn't matter. The heat is good for us. It's better yet for corn. We like it hot. But we wish to insist that Omaha is no hotter than the other places in the state. This may seem to be a foolish insistence upon a small point. But we Omaha people never go out in the state without hearing that Omaha is commercial, which we grant, or without being told that it is not so pleasant to live in as Lincoln, or Fremont, or Beatrice, or Crete, which may or may not be true, or without being informed that it is very wicked, which we do not seem to see so many evidences of as the country people when they come to town. But we will not admit that Omaha is hotter than other places. Wicked, commercial, unpleasant we may be, but we are not any hotter than any other place. It seems such a small point to stick for that our critical neighbors might grant it to us.

"Seen with One's Eyes Open: What Is to Be Seen from an Open Motor Car in Omaha"

19 July 1891

In the late 1880s and 1890s, streetcars played a significant role in Omaha's development. The horse-drawn railway, and the later cable and trolley lines, began extending their service to the suburbs, avoiding the crowding typical of most cities. Some suburbs, such as Benson Place and Dundee Place, built their own lines that connected with the city's trolley system. By 1890 Omaha boasted of ninety miles of street railway (Chudacoff 15). Elia and Robert rode the Omaha streetcars from their home on Poppleton Avenue to their jobs at the World-Herald Building downtown – and sometimes just for pleasure.

In this editorial, Peattie began her journey in Hanscom Park, seventy-three unimproved acres donated in 1872 to the city by civic leaders Andrew J. Hanscom and James G. Megeath. That the proposed park lay at the end of the horse car line and near the real estate holdings owned by these two businessmen elicited many raised eyebrows, but it soon became a showpiece for the city and established a tradition of park development. Peattie's 1891 pleasure ride entered the suburbs; passed by the Missouri River, where the Omaha and Grant Smelting and Refining Works, which employed more than six hundred workers and processed over sixty-five thousand tons of ore in 1890, spewed out smoke (Larsen and Cottrel 79); traveled through the downtown area; and crossed into the ethnic neighborhoods inhabited by the Swedes, Czechs, and Germans.

❧ We have some friends who ride in carriages – they are nice folks, too, and we don't lay their carriages up against them.

Personally, we ride in motors. And the second reason is that we like motors.

By walking a little way we can get on the Hanscom Park motor at its southern extremity, right when you can look down into the dell of the park and see the fountain spouting up like a sort of domesticated geyser in the midst of the pond. We do not walk down to the end of the line with a desire to get any more than our money's worth out of the motor company, and we would be grieved if any suspected us of such motives. The truth is, there is a kind of proletarian pleasure in getting on at the very end of the line and riding to the terminus. You feel like one of the people. You almost think for a time that you are an honest workingman. And then you get a view of that fine hill which lies at the southeastern extremity of the city, which has a grove on it and two white houses. This hill is banked up at sunset with purple mist. The grassy slopes become a luminous green. The groves have a sort of translucence. No doubt they are very commonplace hills indeed, but under this transfiguration they look like the hills of the blessed. Some time we are going over to see what kind of people live in those white houses. Probably we shall find that they are nothing out of the usual and that they do not live up to their purple mists and their illuminated grass slopes.

This is the beginning of the motor ride.

For a few blocks one rides along the western suburbs of the city. The lawns are close-clipped. The clematis turns the porches into royal pavilions; the curtains fluttering back from the windows reveal cool and dainty interiors. The neighborhood is the dwelling place of those who neither make millions nor carry dinner baskets; but industrious, self-respecting and social, spend their days in a wholesome round of work and simple pleasures. Some of the men work a little too hard and get a strained look on their faces; some of them are too young to have such gray hair. The women are a little too much addicted to playing high five. But still they are sensible folk who try to do their duty in the world, who raise their children with love and judgment and who are the very back bone of the municipality.

The motor swings 'round onto a more commonplace street, but one which gives you glimpses down many fine avenues. There is an old pioneer judge watering his lawn with his own hands, while his servant stands watching him. The "hired man" cannot imagine why a man should want to do a piece of work like that when he has a servant to do it for him. He does not know the love of the soil that lives in the breast of these old pioneers. He cannot guess at the rest to brain and nerve that comes up from that fresh, keen-scented grass to the old man, who, for a time, forgets his responsibilities, his many conflicts, his growing feebleness, and in short sleeves, with hose in hand, seems to have gone back to simpler days, when his children played about him as he worked. . . .

The saloons begin to increase in number as the motor spins on. Here and there a little child plods up the stairs to a hot flat with a jug of beer in her hands. Out on the narrow balconies in the rear of these flats sit the men with their shoes off, feet on railing, heads swimming a little from the heat and toil, minds rather numb from the same reason. They wonder dimly why the baby will cry so much, and if it couldn't be taken better care of than it is. The mother within looks a trifle frowzy. Her face is flushed. Once when she lays the baby down after a long period of patient hushing, and the little one cries out angrily, the mother raises a nervous hand and slaps its soft cheek.

Omaha streetcar and conductors, ca. 1890s. (Nebraska State Historical Society Photograph Collections)

Then she kisses the place she has slapped, and the baby sobs, really grieved this time, and falls asleep, and the mother comes out and sits on the pile of inverted washtubs, on the rear balcony, beside her husband.

How uninviting the little ice cream houses look! There seem to be more flies in them than there are anywhere else, and the cases full of cakes are nauseating. You know there is a smell of oilcloth in the rooms; and can see just how the sweating proprietor will wipe three dead flies, two dried currants and a splash of pale pink cream off the table when you sit down to it, and you can taste the metal-poisoned jelly in the cake just as well as if you had been within and paid your money for all these luxuries.

A dead, heavy smell comes up from the river, where the black towers of the smelter are etched against the sky: You give a thought to the men working there, half-naked, short of breath, unconscious of the wind stealing so sweetly down from those southern heights. There are the fires that never die; the fumes that never perish; the work that never ceases – there in the smelter. The description would fit what the children refer to in awed and ambiguous tones as the "Other Place." Only there is this difference. The smelter accomplishes something. It sends out precious metal for the uses of man. But the "Other Place" – well, no one, not even the Presbyterians, have found out what good it is going to do.

There's an odd place up that embankment! From below, seeing ragged, yellow clay rising forty feet it looks uninviting enough. But once up there you have an orchard, garden plates filled with sweet, old-fashioned flowers; melancholy cedars sending their balsamic scents in through the lattices of the long verandahs. The noise of the city steals into the shaded rooms so softly that it might be the murmur of the sea. The dust never rises to powder the dew in the hearts of the roses. Here, sometimes, at twilight, the passerby, glancing up suddenly, sees a languid woman moving, dressed in white. On her face is a calm, deep and fixed. Her movements are gentle; the very foldings of her white garments suggest refinement. A man on the cars says to a friend:

"She has not been down those stairs for fifteen years. She will never go down again till she is carried out in her coffin."

"How do you explain it?"

"You can't explain it. If a man did that you would call him a philosopher. But this is a woman."

"To be sure," said the other in a tone that dismissed the subject, "there is then no explanation."

Opposite is where the young electrician lives – just a lad, you know, but given to experimenting, not unsuccessfully, with the liquid of life and light and heat. He has a little shop where he works, in the rear of his father's house, and he has done some work there which marks him as no common experimenter. Already his labors have brought him recognition in pecuniary as well as more gratifying ways, and it is said by those who are qualified to speak that his prospects are good for making a name.

There is the mysterious "Students' Home"; an ominous building suggestive of midnight crimes. You wonder who the students are, and what they study; and looking at the door that opens into space midway between the street and the rotting balcony, you feel that the "Straggler's Retreat" or the "Assassin's Rest" would be a more appropriate appellation for such a lugubrious edifice. Next come the great office buildings, and the Commercial national bank, which from the standpoint of the artist is the finest building in Omaha. The business streets look strange and deserted at this hour of the day. There are tired little crowds in the drug stores; the streets are strewn with paper. The pavement smells hot. The windows of the dry goods shops present alluring bargains in white lawns. It is wonderful how the fine stores are spreading out now. One finds thriving patches of them a mile from what used to be considered the business district. Banks with great, gleaming windows, spic-and-span grocery stores, dashing "gentlemen's furnishing houses," are now where a time ago there was only an array of old junk shops and hay markets. Omaha is getting to have her little race quarters now. You can tell when you are coming to a neighborhood where the Swedes are raising up their broods of white headed babies. There are places where the milliner who invites you to come in and get a green and pink bonnet, and the saddler who depends his name on the creaking sign from below his windows are evidently catering to Bohemian trade. Sometimes you know by the quality of laughter that floats out from behind the shutters that a company of darkies are within. The funny little summer houses that clutter up the yards in this block and the thriving condition of the flower gardens tell you that they are Germans in this block.

A German must have his flower patch. He can make a country anywhere if you will give him a few flower seeds and a frau who understands soups. Then he lives; he grows. Work is no hardship. He delights in his meals, he loves the comforts of his bed, he smokes his pipe and reads his paper. He loves his little children from the bottom of his heart, and if he is sometimes unnecessarily stern with them, it is more to indulge himself to the exercise of authority than to afflict them. And as for taking a day's pleasure without them, that is not to be thought of. So he builds him a horrid little summer house and paints it in astonishing colors; and all round about are flowers which grow as American tended flowers cannot be persuaded to; and so with his frau and his kinder and his pipe he is not only a contented man, but an excellent citizen, and the kindest and heartiest of neighbors.

There is no life more uneven than that of the fireman. Ninety-nine hundredths of the time he is forced to lead the life of a vegetable. The other hundredth he is a hero. He is tied to his post day and night. At most stations he is permitted to sleep at home with his family. The rest of the time he lies on a cot with his boots beside him, his trousers on and his coat at his right hand. He never has a mild diversion. Any break in the monotony of his life is sure to be a violent one. He sits for six days, for example, playing cards. But he has to do something. Now and then he pauses before dealing out the next hand, to gently abuse the department. And once he gets up enough energy to say that he thinks no man can show a card that compares with Hill's for the next presidency. Then suddenly there is a metallic ringing; a tickling, a whirring of the electric indicator; the doors of the stalls fall automatically; the horses trot for their places by the shaft; there is the crack of the lighted match and the smell of the burning kindling; a little hoarse shouting, unintelligible as a military command; over the incline dash the animals, harnessed in three movements; on go coat and helmets as the men cling to the swaying engine; the horn sounds its alarm; the travel in the street stops to let the lumbering, plunging thing pass. And then the men who were so like sponges clinging to a rock become the very impersonation of terrible activity. They obey commands without question; they fight death and disaster with the odds against them.

And sometimes when the dull game of cards is taken up the next day, the players are a hand short. Because one of them is in the little back room at the undertaker's, and his place has not yet been supplied at the engine house. And outside festoons of black and white bunting drip over the red brick facade.

Why is it some streets look shabby in spite of anything that can be done to them? Look up the hill there toward the west. The houses look well enough, there are trees and lawns, yet nothing has that fine order that you see in spruce neighborhoods. You feel someway that the people in them prefer baseball to lectures and would rather see Sullivan than hear Patti.

Deep in tree-shade sit some rambling old houses, conservative and tempting. The grass lies lush under the dying orchard. The currants fall from overripeness and lie rotting. A catbird cries out from this miniature wilderness and mingles his clamor with the shrill noise of the motor. Omaha is full of such surprises. It is one of her greatest charms.

Now the spaces between the houses widen out. You get a glimpse of another suburb, well paved, with urns dripping vines in the trim lawns, houses fantastic but sprightly of architecture – a general atmosphere of aspiring and mortgaged prosperity over all. Then the roll westward of the interminable plains; the slope to the east of the yellow river sands; the sluggish, huge stream like a half-chilled snake, crawling southward, and you are at a little box of a place where the conductor goes to get a plug of tobacco to entertain him on his home journey, or, if he is of a mind, buys a nickel's worth of cakes and washes them over with ginger ale.

And meanwhile your fellow passengers have been absorbingly interesting as – well, as only men, women and children can be. There was the young man with the compelling perfume, who carried a roll of music, and whose barber had put oil on his hair. He was going to the lawn party of a certain boarding-house keeper's daughter and was expected to sing "Last Night, the Nightingale," while the daughter played the accompaniment with her foot on the loud pedal and her eye on the singer. There was the kindergarten teacher with her sweet face and her Jenness-Miller gown; and the man with the look of a London missionary who gave a tract and punched nickel to the conductor. And the lady who looked like a Parisian, and who gave little gasps as if she was exploding with unexpended conversation; and there was the old Bohemian woman who took a wallet out of a bag, and a purse out of the wallet and a nickel out of the purse with which to pay her fare.

And there was a man in blue jeans who sat with a little child in his arms, his head hanging heavily, his eyes dull. And every now and then he drew the little one closer to him, half baring his arm as he did so. And though it was not very hot there were great drops of sweat on that arm, showing through the dirt and tan. And there were other drops on the man's brow. But the child did not notice them and fell asleep in his arms, holding one brawny thumb in its little fist. And then a drop fell on its face right where the lash swept over the cheek. But the drop did not come from the brow of the man nor yet from the arm.

"How They Live at Sheely: Pen Picture of a Strange Settlement and Its Queer Set of Inhabitants"

31 March 1895

Sheelytown, a Polish neighborhood clinging to Omaha's southwest outskirts and named for the Sheely Brothers Packing Company, was settled by the Irish, who founded Union Stock Yards and several packinghouses. Its boundaries extended roughly to Hanscom Park on the north, Thirty-first Street on the west, Frederick Street on the south, and Twenty-fourth Street on the east (Otis 247). The first Poles came to Omaha in the 1870s to work in the meatpacking plants, stockyards, smelting works, and railroads, with more arriving in the 1880s and 1890s (Larsen and Cottrell 161). Although the majority of the Polish immigrants were hard workers with close-knit families and strong ties to the Catholic faith, 95 percent of them did not speak English, nor did they have an education or job skills (Casper 183).

Around 1890 an estimated two hundred Polish families lived in Omaha. They constructed a frame church, St. Paul's, at the corner of Twenty-ninth and Elm so that they could conduct services in Polish. In 1891, Father T. Jakimowicz was transferred from Elba to take charge of the Omaha congregation, but he left after a couple of years, "reportedly because of misunderstandings of an undisclosed nature." In the meantime, dissidents from the congregation brought in Stephen Kaminski, a Polish nationalist who posed as a priest. The faction who stood behind Kaminski obtained title to the church property, and when the parish took legal action to correct the scandal, Kaminski barricaded himself in the sanctuary and used firearms to retain control, wounding Xavier Dargaczewski and Frank Kraycki. The case was taken to the district court, which decided that the church should remain under the control of the Roman Catholic bishop. On 27 March 1895, after hearing the verdict, Kaminski and his supporters set fire to the church, completely destroying it (Casper 185–87).[2]

❧ "The priest, he say: 'I never leave this town till I see the bare bones of this church!' And he is seein' 'em!"

The gaunt, wooden structure of St. Paul's Catholic church was blazing, and around on the clay hills was gathered a silent people. Not a cry went into the air. Hardly a word was spoken. A group of weeping and shivering little ones, in their night clothes, huddled together trembling on a mattress on the ground. Their home was flaming before their eyes, and the wild, fire-lit sky, the ominous, unnaturally silent gathering of people, the subdued tones in which all spoke, seemed to fill the night with a terrible menace. It was no wonder the little ones trembled and wept.

The girl who told what the priest had said was silenced by a young man who pulled at her sleeve. He said something to her in Polish. The girl flushed and disappeared in the crowd. No one, it seemed, could talk English. It might be that as you approached a group, the persons would be talking in what seemed to you to be the familiar tongue. But if one ventured to ask a question one was told in German or Polish, or Swede, that English was a tongue unknown to the speaker. The night took on an air of conspiracy. Women hurried to the fire with their faces so muffled that they could not be recognized. Men watched the weeping flames from the near hills, content to stand up there among the treacherous water gullies, rather than to approach nearer. A solitary policeman walked among the crowd, with apprehension in his eye. A subtle, deadly, repressed excitement made itself felt. One knew that in the hearts of the silent people round about was a smoldering and hot hatred. One suspected that in the pockets of those sullen looking men were weapons of destruction, and could easily imagine that those taciturn, yet emotional women would have enjoyed the flurry of a sudden riot, and that their strong brown hands could have hurled stones with energy and effect.

St. Paul's church, which has been the scene of a battle, and which was burned at last, the priest being forced to flee for his life, leaving behind him the vestments and vessels of the sacred edifice, stood well upon a western hill, midway between Omaha and South Omaha. Below the treeless hill on which the "bare bones" of the church rest there lies a rugged and dusty valley in which clutters what is known as Sheely station. It is a foreign country – Sheely station, and is a little village by itself, sustained by the not far distant packing houses. It is hemmed in by the railroad and brick yards on the eastern side, by the city at the north, and by the nothingness of the plains on the west and south. It has an aspect of peculiar poverty, yet it is not squalid. It looks distinctly un-American, but at first one has difficulty in classifying its foreign aspect, and at last concludes that it is heterogeneous. There are, in fact, Germans, English, Irish, Italians and Poles living there. Numerically

Omaha mayor Jim Dahlman and Sheelytown "mayor" Nick Dargaczewski, ca. 1906. (Douglas County Historical Society Collections, Omaha, Nebraska)

considered the Poles may not be more than half of the community, but they exercise, without doubt, a greater influence than any of the transplanted foreigners, and form the most restless and positive force in the neighborhood.

Up the irregular and ungraded streets small cottages are perched precariously on the edges of bluffs, or on the slope of a hill. Unwholesome scents distress the nostrils. In some of the yards there lies the debris that indicates slovenly living. Yet, in among the untidy huts are many clean, attractive cottages, with pleasant windows, and an aspect of cleanliness and frugality. Such places are especially to be found on the edge of the community toward the south, and appear to be homes erected by their owners, and representing that home-getting, self-respecting quality which is one of the best elements of this country.

There are a number of grocery stores at Sheely, at which the necessaries of life may be purchased, and several saloons, at which may be obtained the luxuries of existence – as luxuries are regarded by a large part of the community at Sheely station. In the midst of these are the dance halls, where, late into the morning, the sound of gay music can be heard almost every Sunday night, and where, it is hinted, the extravagances of conduct are such as to require the most aggressive work of the Parkvale Congregational mission to counteract them.

Among the many conservative church people the action of the Hanscom Park Methodist church in holding stereopticon entertainments in its edifice Sunday evenings has been not a little criticized. But the truth is, those entertainments were held largely to attract the young men and women of Sheely station, and were meant as a rival to the dance houses, at which it is believed much mischief is worked. A good deal of missionary work has been done at Parkvale – much more is evidently needed. St. Paul's might have exercised the strongest influence of all had it not been rent with factions, permeated with politics, and cursed with the spirit of hatred and malice. Such members of it as might have enjoyed their worship were never permitted to remain in a quiet frame of mind, and though they no doubt grieved deeply the other evening as they saw the church burn, they must have felt that on the whole it was better to have the strife end so, and to erect a new house for purposes of prayer, and not of battle.

One of the features of Sheely station is the "Beehive," a rotten and miserable structure, built for a tenement house, but come to be a mere haunt of the impecunious, from whom it would be absurdity to expect the payment of rent. The great desolate brown building got its name of the Beehive because it swarmed with human beings, who were so closely cluttered as to make the decencies of life an impossibility. During the rigors of the winter the place has been partly deserted, for so dilapidated has it become that even the most hardy would not select it for a winter's residence, except from lack of choice. In the summer it runs with humans, as one has sometimes seen a freshly lifted board run with ants. Its odors are an alarm to the nostrils. Its visible dirt is excessive – its hidden dirt not to be imagined. The sun beats on it, the dust whirls about it, the half naked children pour from it upon the verandas, and rags of all colors hang from the railings of the balconies. The place is a riot of shiftless misery.

There are so many good, industrious and desirable citizens living at or near Sheely station that one hesitates to describe the worst features of the place, lest it should involve these, who are innocent, in the contumely which attaches to those who have made the place a by-word. But, admitting the existence of these respectable men and women, who are fighting poverty honestly, and raising their children safely in pleasant little homes, there is a tribe of swarthy, angry, skulking men who spend their money in the saloons, who work all day and whose leisure is spent in almost any way except an innocent one. Among this tribe are certain leaders who are nothing more nor less than bandits. Only the other day a physician was in that part of the town on a professional visit. One of the most formidable of these banditti, who terrorizes the whole community, saw the physician, evidently did not like the cut of his coat or the curve of his nose, and, sallying out, assaulted him with serious results. It would not be fair to say that such occurrences have been frequent. But certainly they have been known before. Sheely station has several crimes to its record.

It is, probably, only a transient community. The city is reaching out toward this cluttering of cots. Some day it will disappear in the mysterious way that such communities do, or form elsewhere. Now it is undeniably one of the most foreign and peculiar neighborhoods in Omaha.

Its deserted and dismantled buildings, of which there are several, its great bleak places between the clay cuts, its odd crooked streets, its unexpected flights of stairs leading up banks over which the path runs, its little ravines and curious nooks make it a veritable paradise for the adventurous boy. And since conspiracies and plots are in the air, it is not strange that the adventurous boy has his share of the same thing.

Yet there are good and honest little boys there, and sweet and modest girls, as any one can see by looking over the faces at the Dupont school, or as they look out of the windows of their own little homes. There are rooms which are cosy and inviting, and very dear to the occupants in those cottages, and many a loving mother in them, and a father who deprecates the necessity which forces him to live in a neighborhood where there is a turbulent and treacherous element.

"A Sociological Soliloquy: Some Thoughts Suggested by the Proposed Exodus from the Bottoms"

14 May 1893

Peattie attempted to put into clearer perspective the forced exodus of "squatters" from their tar-paper shacks in the "Bottoms," the poor section of Omaha. The impetus for this particular incident was the arrival in New York the previous September of immigrants carrying the dreaded disease of cholera.[3] *Residents of Omaha, fearing an outbreak with the return of warm weather, looked with apprehension at the dirt and disease so prevalent in the poverty-ridden immigrants' homes and demanded that they be cleaned up.*

Peattie was an avid reader and active in the Populist Party, and her response exemplifies her knowledge of contemporary economic philosophies and political trends that reinforced her own campaign to right social wrongs. She looked with skepticism at contemporary theorists such as Edward Bellamy, American socialist and author of Looking Backward *(1888), who believed in the equitable distribution of wealth, complete social equality, and the nationalization of public services, and Henry George, American economist and social reformer best known for his work* Progress and Poverty *(1879), who was also horrified by the contrast between the wealthy classes and the poor and who pleaded for an economically just society. Although Peattie supported the principle of social equality, she also believed in free will and self-determination and had little patience with those who would not help themselves.*

❧ Over this town, with its abrupt yellow clay banks, its sudden sodden declivities where the willow saplings grow around little stagnant pools, its low, long-reaching, picturesque river bottoms, there are a number of colonies of cluttering huts. They are occupied by persons who do not own land, and who, for the most part, do not expect to do so. And they are living on land on which some man is paying taxes, and for which he may have paid money – or may not. Just why the very poor are so frequently the very dirtiest is a little hard to determine. It is all a part of the general relaxation of pride, frugality, industry and courage that makes or accompanies abject poverty. Perhaps it would not be amiss to say that in this country where hope flies out of the window, dirt flies in at the door. In the Latin countries of Europe, among the peasantry of other nations, dirt is familiar, natural and to be expected. But in America dirt is a sign of wreck and ruin. It is not natural to the clime. And where ever it is seen, it is safe to infer that very much more misery than that which dirt can cause is to be found within the lowly doors of the "tar paper huts."

With the cholera sending its black shadow over the world, the health authorities of Omaha have decided that these colonies of "squatters," which are, decidedly, the dirtiest places in Omaha, must be broken up. And the squatters all over the city have been requested to move. From a sanitary point of view this is the only wise thing to do. The ground on which these people live has become a putrifaction [*sic*], the wells from which they drink are poisoned, all about is a litter of rags, rotting stuff, dirt, and the small horrible chaos that dirty men alone can produce. There's an idea abroad among some persons – perhaps chiefly among the squatters – that the whole movement is only a subterfuge on the parts of the land owners to get these poor wretches off their property. There may be something in this, but probably not much. The land owners are, of course, perfectly willing to have these bands of unsanitary folks – to speak of them as scientifically as possible – move from their premises – but it is no more than right to assume that the property owners chiefly wish to co-operate with the board of health in cleaning up this much neglected city.

An Immigrant, A. J. Smith of Custer County, Nebraska, documents his arrival in Nebraska, 1886. (Nebraska State Historical Society Photograph Collections)

Meanwhile, the question arises, where are the squatters to go? They are persons who have not the ability or the desire to accumulate property. Some are old, some are sick, some are shiftless, some are carrion who prey on civilization and live off its garbage heaps, some are foreigners, confused by the strange country, ignorant of its language, unequipped with a means of making a trade. All are miserable. All are dangerous because very poor. A man or woman who is near starvation is always dangerous.

There is nothing sentimental in this view of the case. I am not sentimental about people who prefer dirt, laziness, lying, begging and even stealing to honesty, temperance, frugality, cleanliness and self respect. But society has to deal with all sorts. And I am still concerned about these unconscious disciples of Mr. George, who have assumed with childlike simplicity that earth, like air or water, is free to all men. (Did I say water was free? It was a slip of the pen.) That it ought to be, all the good men must believe. That men who have not ground must pay tribute all their lives to men who have is, without question, a fine form of robbery and has been at the bottom of much of life's misery. But we are dealing, after all, not with possible conditions, but with present conditions.

The land owner in these particular cases, may or may not be grasping, but they own the land, and the law gives them a right to it, and will protect them in the maintenance of those rights. And the law will stand opposed to the man and woman who interferes with those rights. And who settles down upon those lands without paying the tribute in the way of rental, which the law requires, have no right to expect anything but that they will be ousted whenever the owners or the city sees fit. They must go. But where will they go?

What the character of these people on the bottoms is, there are three women in this city who know better, perhaps, than any man. One of them is Mrs. Jardine, who for many years, has been an angel of mercy to the poor, an intelligent, sensible worker in the cause of judicious charity and a woman whom this whole city respects. Mrs. Hopkins, Sr., a woman of great judgment and energy, has acted the part of friendly visitor all during the last winter among these miserable ones, and knows the inside of those houses and the insides of the people's hearts. Miss Anna Millard, a young lady for whom "society" was too small, has been, day after day, a nurse among such of these people as were sick, leaving her beautiful home to work there among the huts, armed with scientific knowledge, much experience and a womanly heart that made her stop at the performance of no kindly deed. These women, who know the struggles that some of these people on the bottoms have had, who know how fate has made playthings of them, how ill health has followed them, how friends have deserted them, who have seen the women bearing their children in terrible poverty, deserted, horrified at the prospect of the future, who have brought comforts to the children in the dead of winter, who have seen the sullen despair of the discouraged men, know one side of the question.

We, who see the filthy yard, read of the quarrels, dread the outbreak of cholera, know of the beggings, the pilferings, the horrible low-lived existence see another side.

A girl who said she lived on the bottoms called at my house the other day. She was about 16 years old, with a dull, sensual, rather handsome face. She had a paper on which was written in excellent chirography the fact that her father had been hurt by the cable cars two years ago and was a confirmed invalid, that her mother, who had supported the family by washing, had been dead two months, that she had three little sisters, who were at home, and who needed – everything. We found a bundle of clothing for the girl and then tried to fit a pair of shoes on her. After trying on five or six pairs of half worn shoes, we found a pair that exactly fitted. But the buttons had been cut off. I said: "You can sew the buttons on. Sit here, and I'll give you a needle and thread."

"I don't think the shoes fit," the girl said sullenly.

"They fit perfectly," I replied. "Here are the buttons, and a thimble and some linen thread."

She looked at the shoes on her feet, which literally had no soles, and then at the shoes in her hand, and the little pile of buttons.

"I don't believe I'll have time," she objected. "I ought to be getting home to the children."

"You will go home to the children," I said, "when you have sewed those buttons on, and not before. Your time cannot be very precious, if you spend it wandering the streets. And if you come here begging for shoes – and if I were in your place I would go barefooted before I would do it – you must take the shoes that are given you, and you must make them fit to wear."

She sewed on sullenly, while I wrenched from her the fact that she had never been to school but two days, that she didn't like it, and could neither read nor write. None of her sisters had ever been at school. They were not going. She knew they wouldn't like it. She didn't know where they lived. It was somewhere on the bottoms. Yes, she was American. Pure American. Her last name was Duncan. She didn't know what her first name was. Never heard of such a thing as a "first name." There were two buttons lacking, and I went in an adjoining room to get them. When I returned she was flying down the stairs as if pursued by the furies.

"Aren't you going to take the things?" I called after her. She shook her head angrily and sped on. I saw her throwing sullen glances back at the house as she walked away – the hated house where she had actually been made to do ten minutes' work.

That's one example of the sort of people who will not earn. And they are just as vicious, though not quite so dangerous, as the millionaire who has not earned his money, but who makes money by imposing tributes on those who do earn. But there is another sort of person also living down on the bottoms. It is the widow, with four small children, who washes every day of the week, and receives $1.50 per day, and who cannot pay rent out of such small earnings. At least, I cannot imagine how she can, although really it must be possible to do it, since so many do.

If only Mr. Bellamy's plan or Mr. George's plan, or the plan of the populists, or even the socialists would right these things, who would not be eager to adopt any or all of them? But are you, who get up early and work late, going to stand for any scheme that will make you the enforced equal of the girl who fled as if pursued by the furies because she was asked to do a little work? Truly, you may. I will not. Neither will I be put on an equal with the millionaire, who makes his money out of others, just as the vulture gets his flesh by preying upon bodies. Neither the deliberate millionaire nor the deliberate pauper move in my set. I want to be put on an equal only with those who earn what they have. The law that will keep the millionaire from acquiring only so much and that will force the pauper to earn would be the law that would remedy our worst social evils. But there can never be any such law. You can not make men good by legislation. For legislation is the result of social conditions, not the cause of them. The law must always lag a little way behind the mental condition of the people. They must loathe slavery before they abolish it; they must outgrow superstition before they cease to kill their witches; they must learn to hold life sacred before they cease to hang. Law shows the condition of popular opinion merely, and is a device of society for making itself durable.

The thing that will better us, and the only thing, is a sense of high philosophy, and this present century is far too material to hope to see it. We must learn as much socialism as will make us perceive that a harm done to another is a harm to us. We must learn that the ignorance of one hurts and degrades all; that we cannot be dishonest without lowering the whole body politic; that bad politics reflects upon each of us as well as upon the "others." But when will we learn this? Not today nor tomorrow. The successful man is too often the smart man – that is, the man who knows how to seize his advantage to the disadvantage of others. In Omaha, on one hand, we are trying to push the weaker to the wall, and with the other we are lifting the fallen out of the mire. We call the first business principles, we call the second charity. What's the result? The standard of business honor is low. And the very poor are numerous.

Omaha is full of charity. It has half a dozen hospitals; it has its Creche, its orphanage, its Boys and Girls' home, its W.C.T.U. institutions, its Y.W.C.A. institutions, its refuge home, its City mission, its Open Door, and its Associated Charities. Too frequently all of these institutions are but used as a cover for laziness of the most criminal sort. Thieves warm themselves by the fires, while good women and men shiver alone in their misery and will ask no help. It is necessary to watch the men at the wood yard to see that they do not fling their chunks back on the pile instead of splitting them. The liquor given to dying women is drunk by their drunken husbands. The comforts provided for children are pawned for drink. An old woman dies alone with no one to give her bite or sup, within calling distance of a hundred Christian homes. It is all confusion. All perplexity. And if any form of "scientific charity" or any arrangement of politics, or any changing of the social order will do away with it, I would like very much to have some one tell me what it is.

There are so many things that are wrong. Social conditions, religious attempts at curing all this, municipal management, laws, customs, prejudices – all are partly wrong. But the people are more wrong than any of these things – far more wrong! How to make them better is a part of the great mystery of evolution. If everyone would begin with learning the control of self and the subjugation of one lawless person, we would soon have the world subdued. But that does not seem to be likely.

And meanwhile, as one talks and idly philosophizes, the poor are being driven from the shanties in the name of science and the march of civilization goes on. But still, at odd moments, I wonder where they are going – those people who are being driven from the tar paper houses, those people who would as lief [*sic*] as not drink from pestiferous wells, those people who do not care for schools and who are very sullen and miserable and estranged from all the rest of us?

There is no sequence or logic in all the foregoing. It is not written to influence anybody to form any sort of an opinion. It is a soliloquy.

"Mrs. Peattie in Rebuttal: Just a Word or Two in Passing Concerning the Society Question"

21 January 1894

Peattie was often taken to task for voicing her forthright views regarding Omaha's social problems. Several months after her editorial on the Bottoms, she commented on the myriad abstract philosophies that sought to solve the problem of poverty. Although she condemned the materialism of the upper classes and abhorred the living conditions of the poorer classes, she supported the legions of philanthropic women who were, at least, offering concrete aid, whatever their motives.

❧ The few remarks I made about a part of Omaha society the other day have aroused much comment. This may have been because these remarks were just or because they were unjust. It does not much matter. I could have retorted with personalities, but that would have been disagreeable. And life is so short it is surely not worthwhile to be disagreeable unless there is something to accomplish by being so. I know what the facts were that prompted me to make the criticism that I did. . . .

I am told a great many remedies for the social disturbance. One man says land is at the bottom of all our trouble. He tells me that Henry George is the philosopher of basic truth. My friend who tells me this is a cobbler, with a beautiful smile, and a perfect trust is the ultimate happiness of mankind. He thinks we would all be free if we all owned land, and if we paid but one tax and that on land. Another friend says money is the trouble, and that if we had money enough to pay for the earnings of man, no one would be hungry, and men could not then speculate in money and acquire wealth at the expense of others. Some tell me that whisky enslaves us, and that intemperance in this and other directions is what is at the bottom of our woes. There are those who think that the practical disappearance of handwork and the introduction of machinery is to blame for much of the speculation in the labor of men's hands, and the consequent inequality in the distribution of profits, and I even met a man the other day who said he thought the stress and distress of these days was due to the invention of electric lights. Of course everyone says we need socialism. And it is that fact that I suppose the Western Laborer thinks I am afraid to face. And I am. God knows we all are. For the woes that would come of it are as terrible, surely, as any we have now.

"Now understand me well – it is provided in the essence of things that from any fruition of success, no matter what, shall come forth something to make a greater struggle necessary."

That's what Walt Whitman said, and what he thinks. But Hamlin Garland thinks and says constantly that the day will come when all men will be free – when none will be at the bidding of the other.

There are certainly enough opinions about what we ought to do to be saved. We are all conscious one way and another of the insidious means which some men employ to rob other men of the results of their labor. But we make strange prescriptions for the cure, and we diagnose the social disease in eccentric ways. Perhaps this confusion comes partly from the fact that none of us are willing to be veritists. We exaggerate conditions. We make them worse than they are, or else we idealize them. We decide that all well-bred people are kind people, when as a matter of fact the best bred and most delightful gentlemen we know may be grinding the face of the poor. And while he compliments us in elegant phrase, he may be driving some other woman to shame from the miserable wages he pays her for her service in his store or factory. Or we decide that the poor are all deserving, that they are languishing for work, and that they are crushed by society. Whereas, it may be that the one we most pitied would run from work as from the plague, and, so far from being a victim of society, is, and always will be, a prey upon it. It is the constant taking into cognizance of these things that has made charity come at last to its scientific basis, and gives it the statistical aspect which is so offensive to our sensibilities yet which we all admit is a necessity of our present conditions.

A man well known in this city in "labor circles," as the newspapers say,

Men and women enjoying a beer at a saloon on Thirteen Street between Harney and Farnham, 1886. (Nebraska State Historical Society Photograph Collections)

wrote me the other day, and, in the course of his letter, spoke with much impatience of the fad for charitable work which the fashionable were now amusing themselves with. I think he underestimated the purity of motive which prompts most of these women in their work. We have all been telling them they ought to divide their surplus with the needy, and they are trying to do it the best way they know how. They have given of their surplus, and even of that which was not surplus; they have also given of their time, and of themselves. I don't say that it may not have filled some of them with virtuous self-gratification. Or that it may not have served to lull into temporary peace a heart much troubled with private griefs, or that it may not have a diversion for some who have not enough to fill their lives, or that it may not have been a mere part of that somewhat perfunctory giving of goodness in which some women indulge themselves. But what of it? Women have a right to their consolations. If they want to use an opiate for a broken heart, or fill idle hours, or deliberately add to their good acts, they surely have the right. No one can escape from selfishness. For, finally, everything is selfish. But to be selfish in that sense is no sin – it is quite the opposite. We are born to make the most of self – to do that is selfishness, or, at least, it is selfism.

This much good has come of the dread year of 1893 – we are all trying to look more closely at the fabric of society which each one of us assists in weaving. We are noticing, for the first time, how gigantic and impressive is the pattern. We are astonished to find how gray and dun the whole thing looks, and how startling those splashes of red in it are. Whether we lie on the floor of Rescue hall, rolled in an old blanket, or under eiderdown in a perfumed chamber, we are troubled with inquiries which will not let us rest, but which din at us with imperative voices, and ask us for how much of this suffering we have been personally responsible.

"The times," said a well-known lady of Omaha the other day, in a meeting of women assembled to consider the need for systematic relief measures, "are revolutionary or evolutionary, and I defy anyone to tell me which." No one ventured a reply.

"Work of the Day Nursery: The Creche and What It Does for Women Who Must Work"

7 February 1892

One organization that Peattie wholeheartedly endorsed was the Omaha Creche, established in 1877. Led by Mrs. T. L. Kimball and supported by wives of other prominent Omaha businessmen, the group, funded by public contributions, erected a brick building on Nineteenth and Harney Streets on a lot rented from the city. As a day nursery for children of single parents, it had been situated well out of the business district; however, the city grew up around it, and its purpose changed. At first the Creche charged ten cents a day per child, with parents dropping the children off on the way to work and picking them up afterward, but the organizers discovered that many young mothers or widowers could only find low-paying jobs such as waitressing, clerking, or working in factories. Many of these jobs demanded unusual hours, and parents were unable to keep their babies at night, especially in the unheated, cramped apartments that they could afford. In response, the Creche began taking children as week boarders at $1.25 each ("Caring for the Children").

Many organizations sponsored entertainments to aid the Creche during the year; several businesses donated clothing, bedding, and yard goods to the cause, and a group of women formed a sewing circle to make clothing for the children.[4] *Because Peattie understood that politics played a key role in generating social reforms, her role in alleviating the suffering of Omaha's disadvantaged groups was to publicize their problems and marshal philanthropic forces to prompt change.*[5]

❧ There are thirty-two children there now – at the Creche – and not one of them is equipped with the complement of parents. There is either a father or a mother lacking for all of them, and some of them are absolutely without any such possessions. It's about three years ago since the Creche started. It was the idea of some good women who had practical ideas. It seemed to them that there was no better way of helping hard working women and men who had been unfortunate than by taking care of their children for them. But these ladies knew better than to rob any of the people they intend to help of an atom of their self-respect. So they made a business basis for the thing. The men and women who confide their little ones to the care of the Creche pay for them. If one child is put in, $1.50 is paid for what "little orphan Annie" called its "board and keep." If two children are placed there by the same person, $2.50 is charged for both of them. If three are sent $3 is charged.

Of course, if the money thus received was relied upon to run this beneficent little establishment, it would be a failure in a week. It is supported chiefly by charity. But the charity is so contrived that it does not make beggars out of its beneficiaries.

The great play room is clean and warm, and the windows open to the south. On the walls is a blackboard, and above the board are pictures of babies not prettier than those who play beneath. Thirty-two is a comfortable family for the Creche, for it has room only for thirty-six. It is doing at present about its full amount of usefulness. The matron, Mrs. Smith, has been in her place during the greater part of the existence of the institution, and she has got the matter down to a science. She knows just how much it will take to feed those hungry mouths: she has an idea of what to do for every sort of ailment. She can oversee the cooking in the way to make it at once most frugal and most tempting. There is a cook and two nurses, and these comprise the entire working force. And it certainly takes that many women to comfortably look after such a family.

The mere labor of combing thirty-two heads every morning is nothing to laugh at. There are a few day boarders, that is to say, little children whose parents call for them at night and take them home, but those are few compared with those who live week in and week out at the Creche. A number of the little ones have now arisen to the dignity of attending public school. But the majority play around all day. There was once a kindergarten run in the play room. And an excellent scheme it was. It gave method to the play of the children. It educated their eyes, ears, perceptions; it taught them gentleness and love – two lessons that these children in common with others have some need to learn. Not that the little things at the Creche are naughty. Not a bit

Omaha children of diverse backgrounds enjoying a merry-go-round ride, ca. 1900. (Nebraska State Historical Society Photograph Collections)

of it. We would not be willing to look them in the face again if anything so slanderous were said. On the contrary, they are very nice babies, and their nurses say that they have no trouble whatever in taking care of them and managing them. A punishment is rarely needed.

Their days are all much the same. By 7:30 they are tucked in their little blue iron beds up in the dormitories – such an innocent, piteous company of little sleepers! In the morning they are up early, and are dressed from top to toe, and washed clean as whistles before they [sit] down to breakfast. There are two tables, made low to accommodate such little chaps. And it takes the two nurses and the matron to satisfy the demands. Then there is school for those who go, and a long day of fascinating idleness for those who stay.

The fathers and mothers generally clothe their own, but the Creche furnishes some things for the needy and puts blue gingham aprons on all of them. There is a veranda where an airing can be had when the weather is fine, but there is no playground, for the reason that the good ladies who built the place could not raise sufficient funds for such a purpose, and were not willing to run into debt. . . .

The ladies have always been hoping for an endowment, however modest. Not that they are expecting it. But we all have a shadowy idea that some day our rich uncle – of whom we have never heard – may come home from East India or Australia and give us a fortune, don't we? Well, that is the way the ladies who manage the Creche look forward to an endowment. The chief reason why they continue to hope for such an undeniable blessing is that every little while some children are brought here whose parents cannot or will not pay for their keeping. The sums given to the Creche are so meager that it is simply impossible to keep children under such circumstances. Only the other day two little children had to be sent from the Creche for this very reason. They had been there until a bill of over $50 stood against their guardian, who, in this case happened to be their grandfather. The ladies would not have let them go if the grandfather would have promised to pay in the future, but this he would not do. Yet he earns a comfortable living. He evidently was willing to have them taken care of. But the time came when the disagreeable question could not be set aside even by the tender-hearted ladies any longer. They were establishing a precedent which they could not afford to establish. It was decided to send the children to their "home" in Council Bluffs. They had been in the Creche a long time, and were happy there, happy as only children can be. A lady good-naturedly offered to take them to Council Bluffs in her carriage. She did not dream of the task she had taken upon herself.

Once out on the road the children grew suspicious. The baby, who is a little boy, set up a lamb-like bleat for "Mamma," by whom he meant Mrs. Smith, who was the matron at the Creche. That was the only mamma he knew. But the little girl, who was 3, and who had already begun to know something of the world, said nothing. She would not even answer when she was spoken to. She sat perched on the carriage seat with her little lips tightly pressed. She darted a suspicious glance at the lady. Now she looked at her poor baby brother, with the fierce solicitude of one who knows the maternal apprehension of danger to its young.

The lady made inquiries. She found the wretched little home. The grandfather was not in it. He was away at his work. The young aunt, 15 years of age, was off on the streets. The neighbors said she was a hoyden and was seldom at home. A neighbor offered to keep the children till the aunt returned. So these modern babes in the woods were dropped like blind kittens into the sea of uncertainty. Once in the house the girl, seeing that her worst apprehensions had been realized, broke her stubborn silence with a burst of bitter tears as it ever falls to the lot of childhood to shed, and the baby set up his old plaint for his fictitious "Mamma."

The lady who brought them fled with an aching heart. She did not sleep that night. She has not been herself since. And she has a conspiracy on foot to rescue them, in some way, from this neglected life. But her plans are vague. She only knows that she cannot, in justice to herself, permit herself to be associated, in her own mind, with the very wicked uncle who took the babes into the woods and left them to the mercies of the robins.

An endowment would do away with the necessity for such a thing! That is what the ladies are saying. The question is, will a rich Australian uncle turn up for this beautiful little home? Very likely not. Things do not fall in so nicely with the requirements of the unfortunate in this world.

A number of well-known people are going to give a bright dramatic performance on the evening of the 17th at Germania hall. And it will be a good thing for those who want to help make these little youngsters comfortable, to drop in. The price of a day's cigars set apart by a number of young men who have good young hearts thumping away in the right sort of manner under their coats, will be acceptable.

"The Working Girls' Home: A Description of the Place on Seventeenth Street, between Douglas and Dodge"

5 June 1892

Affordable housing for single women became another crucial issue in Omaha, and Peattie championed any organization that alleviated their problems. The Young Women's Christian Association (YWCA) in Omaha led the way in 1892 by providing room and board for a modest fee on Seventeenth Street between Douglas and Dodge.[6]

As with all charitable societies, the Omaha YWCA in the 1890s was in a state of "perplexity," wrote Peattie, because there was "a constant deficit in the accounts." Neither society women nor working women nor even the benevolent ladies of the governing board escaped Peattie's reproach. Women, she demanded, must all join together and work toward a common good.

The YWCA also operated the Noonday Rest, next door to the boardinghouse, where working women received a luncheon at a minimal cost. In 1895 about 250 women took advantage of the food, friendship, and assistance in finding employment. In the evenings the Noonday Rest provided members with free study courses in subjects such as English, physical culture, and current topics as well as Bible classes.

❧ Omaha has a working girls' home – though so few seem to know of it.

Now a working girls' home is not in any sense a charitable institution, although it is certainly a benevolent one. In New York, Boston, Philadelphia, Chicago, and doubtless many other cities, there are hundreds of young women living in working women's homes, who, if these institutions were charitable, could never be induced to enter them.

It was to avoid any confusion of this point that the young women now at the Omaha institution suggested that it be called the working woman's boarding house.

But at the same time, any concern of this sort needs the constant superintendence of women of benevolence and executive ability, as so far as known there is not a working women's home in this country which has not been started by women of practical benevolence, and which is not practically guarded and controlled by a "board."

The Women's Christian association mothers the home in Omaha, and at present it is in a state of perplexity.

The cause of this perplexity is that there is a constant deficit in the accounts, and this has to be made up by members of the Christian association.

To tell why both ends refuse to meet would be to tell the history of every "home" in this city. They do not meet because the price charged for rent is out of all proportion with the value received. This is not saying that the landlord is a Shylock, but it is saying that money is unnecessarily scarce and interest criminally high. I do not know who owns the very comfortable four-story brick structure on Seventeenth between Douglas and Dodge, in which the home has its existence at present, and nothing personal is intended in the foregoing remarks. Another reason that both ends will not meet is because coal is outrageously dear – and it will get dearer and dearer, be sure! Those unscathed conspirators in the east who, with assured complacency, have made it impossible even to lay in the supply of coal in the summer by raising their prices to winter rates in the month of June, are largely responsible for the difficulty. Light is dear, water is dear! It is a marvel that there is not a tax on air, or that a meter is not attached to our blood in order to discover the quality in circulation and make a charge.

These are the reasons that every one in Omaha finds it difficult to make their expenditures come within their income.

I went up to the home the other evening. The matron, Miss Evans, who has recently come to her present, useful position, was kind enough to say that I might stay to dinner. So I went down stairs when the bell sounded at 6 and found myself seated with fifteen other working girls, all of them looking a little tired about the eyes, and having appetites quite equal to my

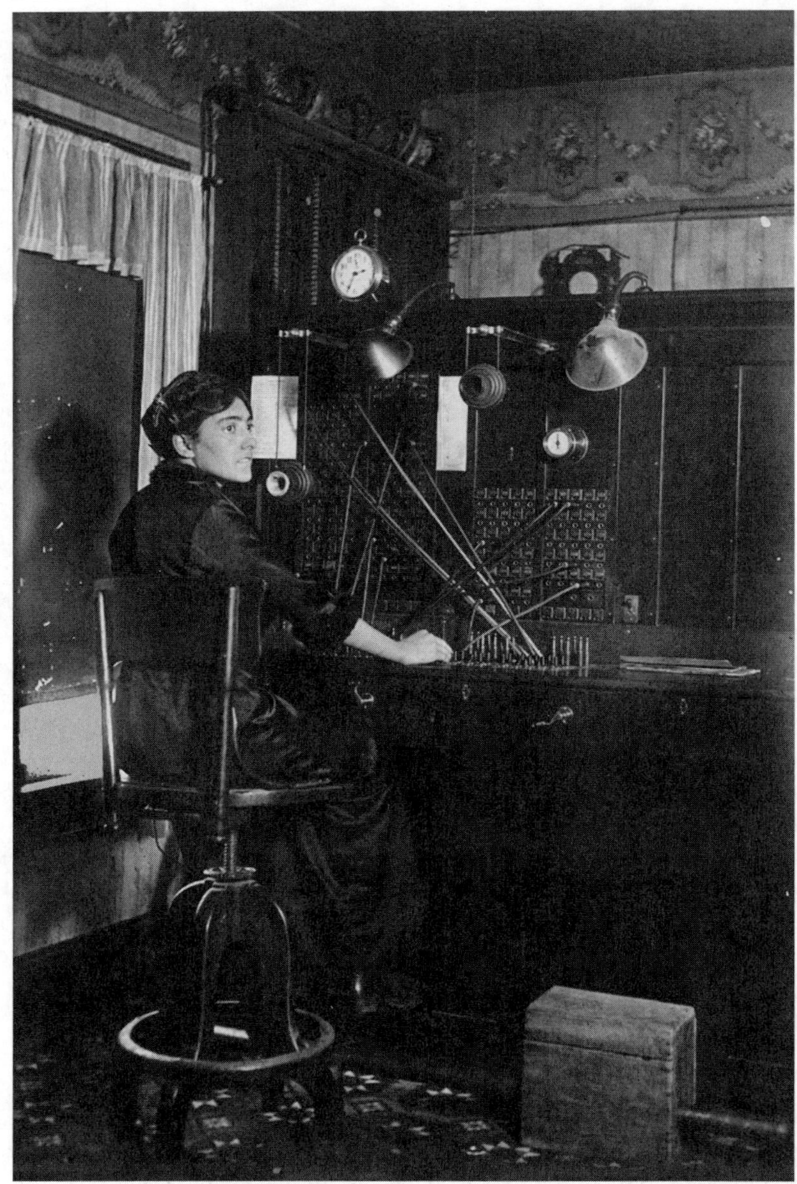

Omaha telephone operator, ca. 1900.
(Nebraska State Historical Society Photograph Collections)

own. Miss Evans got them to chatting. There is nothing about Miss Evans that freezes your young blood. She has very brown eyes, which are amiable in their expression, and white hair – prematurely white – and a way of dressing that somehow suggests New England, tho' why it would be difficult to say.

The girls were in good spirits – why should they not be, when work was over for the day, and a plentiful dinner was before them, and their dining room was illumined with the cordial glow of a young June sun.

Besides, they were talking about Nora McCafferty, who had more relatives than any other girl.

"I once went to a party," said one, "and the room was full. And I was introduced. Nora did the introducing. And well she might. For there wasn't a blessed soul there who wasn't a cousin or a sister or a brother of Nora's." They were full of such talk. There was one foreman, so a clerk in one of the dry goods stores said, who was so cross-eyed that the tears ran down his back.

A number of the girls were clerks in stores. Some of them were stenographers, some were dressmakers – and "Central" was there. Now I have often wanted to see "Central." She has always seemed to me a very capricious young lady. Also she has seemed very political – that is to say, a great manipulator of wires. But – when I saw her she looked like any other nice young woman. It seemed queer to me that this young autocrat, who holds the wills of all of us in the hollow of her hand, so to speak, and can, if she has a mind, prevent us from carrying our designs into effect at the most critical moments, should be liable to hunger and sleepiness and fatigue quite after the manner of an ordinary person. To see "Central" eating in an ordinary manner instead of saying "number" or "hello" affected me very much as if I had seen Kaiser William dusting the dining room chairs.

We had a good dinner.

"You can't work all day and thrive on weak food," said Miss Evans, and the girls all said, as if they had been a chorus in a comic opera, that you couldn't.

We had roast pork and potatoes, with very fine gravy, and radishes red as her lips – I don't know whose lips, but everybody can select lips to suit himself – and beans which were cooked so well that even Oliver Wendell Holmes would have approved of them, and lettuce, crisp and crinkley, and tea, and good bread, and "cottage" pudding.

Good enough for anyone not occupied in cutting off coupons, eh?

After dinner some of the girls went walking and others went to their rooms to sew – for when your income is a certain sum it happens that you have to make your own dresses after you have done your other work. Some of them went with generously disposed young men to see Amy Leslie coquet in rags and French silk stockings through "La Mascotte."

There are no rules at the home which oppress any one. Girls are expected, as they would be at their own homes, to be in at a reasonable hour, and do not stand on the front porch and talk to a young man! The rule seems almost like a reflection on my sex, and I am tempted to resent it.

Now, the girls say that if the home is broken up they do not know what they will do. Of course they will go somewhere and continue to live right along, but they will not, for a reasonable sum a week, have a parlor furnished with a piano and an organ and books and pictures which they can call their own, and where they are at perfect liberty to invite their friends.

The working girls' boarding house is a much more valuable concern than folk generally appear to realize. It is valuable not so much because of what it has done as because of what it is capable of doing.

Now, I want to know if the girls in this city who are working independently and earnestly for their living mean to let this invitation go to pieces.

It may be that you have a good home yourself, and so have no need of a home with a capital H. But I beg you to reflect on the girls who do need such a place, and who, if they do not have it, will be able to pay only for the most wretched lodging, who will have no friends, no social life, no feeling that any one cares for her! When a woman gets that frame of mind she is not very far from destruction.

You see, it is the atmosphere of the home, the little socialities, the amenities, the feeling of organization, very much more than the cheap board which makes the place grateful to the young girls.

Now if the home had more borders it would thrive. Instead of having fifteen girls in it, it ought to have a hundred. If the present house will not accommodate those who apply, then the ladies should get a larger house. They ought never to turn away an applicant. If there isn't a bed vacant, a cot can be procured. In this spirit only can the place be made to succeed. You young women who sleep in hall bedrooms and eat bad dishes in the company of strangers, get out of the whole desolate environment and go over to the home and be sociable. The girls over there are nice – there is no mistake about that – and you can have no end of fun together. You can have musicales, and tableaux, and literary evenings, and games, and fine times generally. I think myself that now and then some of the people in this town who have both talent and leisure might go over there now and then and brighten things up a bit. Miss Bradley might go and give the girls a physical culture evening, though to be sure Miss Bradley has more talent than leisure. Mr. Bert Butler or Miss Luella Allen might take violins and good fellowship with them and make a delightful evening. Mr. Cahn might play on the home piano. Mr. Estabrook might give a little address; he would have an appreciative and comely audience. Mr. J. Laurie Wallace might give a sketch talk. There are really no end of people who might do delightful things, and who I know would be glad to do them if they only realized that by doing so they would confer real pleasure.

And, by the way, I know that almost every house in this town is littered with magazines. But the home has no such happy litter. Can you not put your magazines in your carriage and send them to the home? The girls would not only get pleasure, but benefit out of them.

By the way, speaking of carriages, did you ever meet one of those elaborate clerks who say:

"Madam, permit me to carry this bundle to your carriage?"

It is almost harder on the clerk than it is on yourself when you are obliged to reply:

"But I could not keep you from your duties so long, you see, I have to wait for a car."

I don't know why it makes some clerks so happy to labor under the pleasing fiction that they encounter only persons of wealth and consideration.

To return to the subject in hand, I think it would be a great loss to the women of this city if that home is permitted to go by the board. Because if it is, it will be difficult to start another home. And the older this city grows, the more such a place will be needed. How much it is needed when a woman earns five or six dollars only as a result of a week's arduous and monotonous labor, only God, who reads each hot temptation of the heart, can ever know. To be lonely, shabby, weary, to go without joy, without anticipation – do you know what it means? Why it means that even sin is acceptable, if it comes in happy guise. That is why a working girls' home is needed. It is a safeguard that is inestimable.

We could afford to lose a church or two. We cannot afford to lose the Working Girls boarding house.

Women out of town often wish they had some place to go that would be less expensive and public than a hotel. Besides, a woman always runs the chance of being refused admission to a hotel unless she is accompanied by a man – which is surely a curious condition of things and rather paradoxical. But so it is. Such visitors to Omaha may be glad to know that they can have a good room and home-like surroundings at the home, at rates which are moderate. If country women would get in the habit of staying at the home, they would find it a great convenience. For the place has, in fact, the advantage of a club, and could be made much of if the women would enter into the scheme in the right spirit. I think the board makes a mistake not to advertise the place. Working women are not clairvoyants and cannot know of the existence of such a place unless they are apprised of it. Why are not cards put in the dry goods shops, the factories, the dressmaking establishments, the telephone and telegraph headquarters, in the office buildings and restaurants?

A few very clammy men might refuse to allow the putting up of the cards, but clams are always in the minority, and it is a comfort to know that the world continues to move without their cooperation. Then there should be a sign or placard letting the passer-by know the nature of the home. At present it is not distinguished from any other house.

"The Working Woman's Boarding House" should make itself known.

Considered from both a benevolent and a business point of view, I think that whenever one of the inmates leaves a line in the paper should announce the vacancy, in order that some one else may take advantage of the fact.

Then there should always be rooms kept for transients, and a few painted signs announcing the ability to entertain them should be put at the outskirts of the city along the railways.

I think myself that the good women of this city make a great mistake to diffuse their energies in the way that they do. It is said that the Episcopalian ladies are working to start some sort of a home. Why are they not invited to join in sustaining the one which already exists?

The ladies of the Women's Christian Temperance Union are struggling to start rooms where friendless and penniless girls who are looking for work may find a safe abiding place. Why do they not unite with the Women's Christian association and have a few rooms set apart for such a purpose, thus saving cost of two establishments and appealing more directly to the public by one successful institution than by several which are not successful?

This city has a large number of benevolent institutions and none of them are succeeding. The reason is lack of co-operation and indifference.

It has sometimes seemed to me that the reason is a lack of beneficiaries.

You can not, of course, help the friendless until you have found someone who is friendless.

However, the Working Girls' Home is needed. And it is not charitable. The working women ought to sustain it from motives of self-interest. I am sorry to use language that is not perfectly elegant, but I am constrained to suggest that they "get a move on them."

"With Works of Charity: St. Joseph's Hospital and the Good Sisters Who Do Its Work"

1 November 1891

During Omaha's boom years, the need for hospitals to care for the poor also grew. John A. Creighton came to Omaha in the 1850s with his younger brother Edward. When Edward died in 1874, he left $100,000 to found a university. John established his own legacy as well: the John A. Creighton Medical College and the Creighton Memorial St. Joseph Hospital, which replaced a five-year-old wooden structure and became the medical school's primary resource for clinical instruction.

When the hospital opened in June 1892, Peattie publicly lauded philanthropists like John Creighton, who selflessly gave of himself and his fortune to help the destitute people of Omaha. In 1895 Pope Leo XIII bestowed upon Creighton the title "Count of the Holy Roman Empire" for his philanthropy. The Omaha World-Herald *announced, "Nobility has perched on Omaha's brow," and it went on to boast that Creighton's honor is "one degree higher than that of Marquis George M. Pullman" ("Count John R. Creighton").*

❧ There are 150,000 persons in Omaha, and it is safe to assume that a few of them do not know who John A. Creighton is.

He is one of that fast diminishing group of Omaha pioneers who invented, created, utilized, constructed and organized, and by their united efforts made a city. He is also one of that downtrodden class known as capitalists.

That is why he has been able to give $100,000 in addition to the sum of $50,000 left by his wife, for a new structure in which to place St. Joseph's hospital.

Was it in '69 that St. Joseph's hospital was first started in this city? No one seems definitely to know. The Sisters of Mercy opened its hospitable doors and continued their kindly ministrations till Bishop O'Corman found an opportunity of putting them in the work of which they make a specialty – that of teaching. Then the hospital was placed in the charge of the sisterhood of St. Francis – women who are educated to care for the sick. The school in which they study is the hospital. They learn nothing theoretically. Their work is all practical. Some suffering unfortunate illustrates every new fact acquired. Surgery, therapeutics, anatomy, physiology, obstetrics, are all learned in the school of experience. If you would like to know how it is done, you can go any

St. Joseph's Hospital, Creighton Memorial, in Omaha, 1913. (Douglas County Historical Society Collections, Omaha, Nebraska)

day to St. Joseph's hospital up on the ragged clay bluff beyond the Eleventh street viaduct, and see for yourself. Look in the dark little laboratory at the west side of the building. There you will see a pale postulant, her face framed in white gossamer, standing immovable as a sentinel, while the compounder of drugs delivers her daily lecture – a woman past middle age, in the black draping of the perpetual vows, who understands pharmacy and is capable of preparing all of the drugs used in the hospital. In another room there is one of those long, clean tables which, taken in connection with the smell of carbolic acid, always strikes a chill to the heart. Here, in the operating room, there are other Sisters, who assist in the work of the physicians. Some of them are indeed fitted for bold surgery, and there is one Sister now at the hospital who can take up an artery as well as a physician. Their nursing is skillful – they know what to do in every emergency. They understand the treatment of the most lingering and of the most violent of diseases. They can care for a man in the crisis of pneumonia, or take one through the run of typhoid fever and its dangerous convalesce; they do not need assistance in midwifery, and they know every device for mitigating suffering. Day and night they toil up there in that dun brown building on the hill. Their steps are noiseless, their voices are low, their bodies capable of great endurance. In the wards at night they can stand from 8 to 8, caring for the dying, if necessity requires. They have no servants, but themselves perform all of the work. They prepare the meals, wash the floors, do the washing and the ironing – it is the toil of the household multiplied a hundred times. At present there are about twenty-five of them at the hospital, and such a number enables them to do the work without too great exertion. It has not infrequently happened that the force has been insufficient and that the Sisters have been overworked.

The Sister Superior is Sister Xavier, a woman of much experience, notable for the courageous work she did in this city at the time of the smallpox epidemic. She is not only a woman of executive ability and one who understands the work of the Sisterhood, but she is a capable business woman, and Mr. Creighton entrusts her with the payment of the contractors and much other business concerned with the building of the new hospital. Sister Hedwig, who has been Sister Superior at the hospital for five years, and who has won innumerable friends here, has gone elsewhere, and it is but a few weeks since Sister Xavier entered upon the performance of her duties.

The building, old as it is, and therefore difficult to keep clean, is kept in that perfect condition of order which is perhaps only found in hospitals. The rooms are plain. But the linen room is well stocked, the pleasant private dining room has its semblance to home, and the individuality of the women has made itself apparent in the tiny chapel. Here the altar is always trimmed, a few lights always burning, and here, in the pauses of their work, the Sisters come each day to kneel for prayers – prayers all the more acceptable because many duties make them brief.

The hospital is maintained by desultory charity – and it is hinted that whenever there is a deficit that Mr. John A. Creighton attends to it. However, it would not be easy to get Mr. Creighton himself to admit to this. It is really a wonder that he does not deny any knowledge of that fine building, which by next March will be opened to the public on the corner of Castellar and Tenth streets, and which will refute the charge that Omaha has no good hospital buildings.

This enormous building is built in the shape of a hollow square, with one side missing, that is to say, it is built around three sides of an open court. Its facade is noble and simple, presenting four gables and a square tower. The doorway is of dark red stone, with pillars supporting a triangle, in which is graven the name of the hospital. At the rear there are nine covered porticoes, each long and commodious, and commanding a view of bluffs, white river bottoms, green fringes of willows, rolling, tree-covered plain and here and there a glimpse of vineyards and gardens. No scene could better suggest comfort and prosperity – it is one in which even the perturbed and the diseased mind must find peaceful contemplation. The site of the hospital is well up out of the smoke of the city on those pleasant heights at the southeast.

There is always an atmosphere of rest there – the work and the murk have not reached up to it. Next to the hospital ground, for instance, is a quaint, quiet home with a number of "Ls" [*sic*] leaning against it nonchalantly, and a poplar, yellow with the premonition of winter, stands guard before the door; cherry and apple trees ornament the lawn, and rose bushes hug the walk. No doubt in a few years the city will go noisily clambering up the hill, but at present the place is quiet and beautiful.

In the firm walls of this new building there are provisions for 300 patients, and they will lie in rooms as well ventilated and heated as ingenuity has yet made possible. Mr. Voss is the architect and the undertaking has been one of such magnitude that he has done his best on it – and it is said to be a good best. Certainly the utmost care has been used in carrying out each particular of the plan. Mr. Creighton has his nephew of the same name overseeing the construction, and he says with pride that the building is as stanch as it can be made and that not a brick or beam has been laid carelessly.

It is Mr. Creighton's hope that when it comes to furnishing the building all of the money contributed will be put in a common fund, and that the rooms will not differ greatly one from another in the expansiveness of their fittings. He has had enough experience to know that there are drawbacks to having rooms furnished by individuals. In the nature of things a hospital cannot be hampered in the use of its rooms, and there is always the possibility that persons who have furnished rooms may assume some right over them. It is imperative that the Sisters should not feel under the necessity of considering any such trivial matters. They are doing a great work now and they will do a greater one when they get in this fine new building, and it is not well that they should be limited or hindered. I wish I knew the dimensions of the building because there are some folk who are interested in dimensions. Personally, I detest dimensions. I once visited a red wood forest in company with a friend of mine who had a passion for facts. Now a red wood forest is a cathedral built by God. The air is so clear and fine, so filled with balsamic odors, so free from all defilement, that the soul is unconsciously lifted up. The music of the needles is mournfully iterant. The sky above is as blue as the heart of an arctic berg; the strong straight shooting of the majestic trunks toward heaven makes even the irreligious pray. My friend – well, he took out a tape measure and told me the circumference of the trees, as if I cared how many miserable inches it took to produce that majesty! I told him if he ever got to the pearly gates he would refuse to go in till he got the measurements.

That's the way I felt about the hospital. It does not matter in the least how many feet its foundation stands on, and if anyone wants to know he is at liberty to find out. But it does matter a great deal that those fine walls are going to shelter 300 persons at one time – 300 persons who but for the protection afforded them there might by dying in loneliness and misery.

Omaha herself does not seem likely to have a hospital. The county of Douglas has a hospital building, but no appropriation. The city pays for a few patients when necessity demands at one and another of the hospitals. For months past when any man fell sick on the street, the city and county have wrangled over his dead body; not to secure possession of it, but to get rid of it. At times men who were dying from some casualty have actually been permitted to die before provision was made for them. Physicians have, in very humanity, kept unknown persons in their offices, not knowing whither to send them. As the matter stands at present any non-resident or any person not coming within the category of a pauper will be cared for by the county, but in emergency cases, the city will take care of the sufferer, particularly when he or she is a pauper. It must be admitted that there seems to the lay mind to be some difficulty in obtaining from a man with a fractured head or an epileptic fit any information concerning the state of his finances, but doubtless the council can tell how it may be managed. The adjustment would never have been as good as it is even if it had not been for the constant agitation by Dr. Gapen. He has done what he could. A man less aggressive and uninterested would have despaired long ago.

Within the walls of St. Joseph's hospital, without regard to color, sex or religious belief, all will be welcome. It is a shame that the people of Omaha should be willing to depend upon an institution to whose maintenance they do not contribute to care for their indigent sick. And the best thing they can do is to remove a part of that stigma by sending to St. Joseph's the money they would be forced to pay out in taxes for the support of a city hospital if one existed. I was over at St. Joseph's hospital the other day, at the old building, I mean – where the patients now are. The big gate yielded slowly. By the side of it I noticed a box on which it was announced in white letters that any papers or magazines would be gratefully received. The Sister who opened the door for me wore the black swathings that showed her to be under perpetual vows. She led me from room to room; here I saw a Sister holding the head of a woman hideous with the last emaciation of consumption, her breath coming in rattling reluctance, her lips burned with fever, her eyes starting, yet seeing nothing. Back and forth over that distrait head, went the slow hand of the patient Sister. With a never failing smile the water was lifted and put between those lips, paralyzed with pain. In another room I saw a little boy in the first shock that followed the amputation of his limbs, and beside him sat a Sister with her hand on his pulse, her whole being alive to his necessity, her skill required to its utmost. On the porches, in the quiet wards, holding throbbing stumps or enduring the dreadful languor that follows fever, were men and women of all ages, and among them moved the Sisters, speaking gentle words and doing gentle deeds.

Heavens! How far away it seemed from the fret and the fume and the littleness of the rest of us women! To say that I felt secular is putting it mildly. I felt actually profane, and was relieved when I got out among people just as frivolous, as selfish and heedless as I was myself.

"Omaha's Black Population: The Negroes of This City – Who They Are and Where They Live"

25 September 1892

Some African Americans who came to Nebraska tried life as homesteaders, but out of twelve black settlements, most failed by the end of the 1880s. The majority of African Americans who settled in Nebraska were lured there by the railways. The Union Pacific and Union Stock Yards, especially, used them as "scabs," or strikebreakers, to force mostly immigrant laborers to accept low wages and grueling working conditions. By 1880, 2,385 African Americans had settled in Nebraska, out of a population of 452,402, and by 1890 the total had risen to 8,913 out of a state population of 1,062,656 (Walakafra-Wills 2–3).

Peattie acknowledged several prominent members of the African American community in Omaha. Dr. Matthew Oliver Ricketts, the first African American to graduate from a Nebraska university or college, was the controversial political leader of Omaha's black community. A modest man yet a compelling speaker, he was elected to a seat in the Nebraska legislature in 1892 and 1894, the first black Nebraskan to hold that position.[7]

❧"You want to know something about the men of my race?" repeated Letter Carrier Overall. "I am an American."

And so he is. But he is also a Negro.

There is certainly no race which has a better right to call itself American than that which, before this country became a republic, was brought here by the hundreds, and which has grown to millions by the process of nature. None of the other peoples which make up this heterogeneous body politic has had such slight accessions in the way of immigration.

The Afro-American is a nation within a nation.

In Omaha there are 6,000 of them. That does not seem to be a large number, and yet it is a fact that to the stranger the percentage of Afro-Americans upon the streets of this city appears to be large.

Dr. Matthew Oliver Ricketts, physician and first black Nebraska legislator, ca. 1890s. (Nebraska State Historical Society Photograph Collections)

But it is my opinion that the reason this seems to be the case is because so large a part of them are persons of independence, activity and a greater or less degree of importance, such as one naturally would not expect from a race which has labored under tremendous disadvantages.

That these disadvantages did not disappear with the enfranchisement of the Negro anyone will admit. A senseless race prejudice, the direct and undeniable result of the institution of slavery, has held the Afro-American back as relentlessly as did the mandates of his former master. Prejudice hunts him out and tracks him down with an instinct as keen as that of the bloodhound which used to track him through the midnight forest.

It would have made anarchists of another race.

But a man who laughs more naturally than he weeps, who sings more naturally than he curses, is not the stuff of which anarchists are made. For the sunshine that made the skin of the Negro dark, went deeper and shone into his heart, and made him merry – so merry that the hate, the contempt and the misrepresentation of two centuries has not been able to make him sad.

Besides, the racial enmity of the Anglo-American for the Afro-American has fallen harmless. If it was the intention of the white man to break the spirit of the black man, then he may as well suffer the mortification of knowing that he has failed.

The black man is having a good time. He has learned to govern himself, which is a difficult thing for any man to do, but particularly difficult for a man who has been allowed the exercise of no moral responsibility, but has been ruled with arrogance and tyranny.

After the systematic effort of this country for over 200 years to destroy the self-respect of the Afro-American, is it not a good deal to expect that in a quarter of a century that self-respect will reach par?

The honest and accurate knowledge of what the colored Americans are in this city is enough in itself to remove the last remnant of prejudice from the mind of any fair man or woman.

There are, then, as stated before, about 6,000. The children are in the public schools. The women are almost all in their homes, comparatively few of them being at any sort of work which takes them away from home. The employments of the men are many. But they would have been yet more varied if it had not been that the doors of opportunity have so often been closed to the man with colored blood in his veins. Certain occupations have thus far been closed to such. It is doubtful, for example, if a colored merchant would succeed. There are none in Omaha.

The Rev. John A. Williams, pastor of St. Phillip's Protestant Episcopal church, is a young man who has but recently taken up his ministerial duties. He is a man of strong opinions, and he stands very staunchly for the rights of his race. He has sent many communications to the *World-Herald* upon this subject, particularly those in protest against the frequent lynchings of Negroes in the south. Among the other ordained ministers who have now or have recently held pastorates in this city are the Rev. Thomas H. Ewing, the Rev. W. D. Benable, the Rev. G. W. Woodbey, and the Rev. John R. Richardson.

The attorneys are Silas Robbins, Daniel Lapsley and Mr. Kelly. The practice of these attorneys is almost exclusively among men of their own race.

For many years Dr. W. H. C. Stephenson has alleviated the physical ills of his compatriots; and for a less length of time Dr. M. O. Ricketts has been here, and has won the reputation of being a very careful physician as well as an exceedingly likeable young man.

The *Progress* is the journalistic organ of the Afro-Americans. It is a weekly paper, and it stands in every way for the progress of the Negro. F. L. Barnett is the editor, and his labors since 1889, when the paper was started, have been unceasing, and in the face of no inconsiderable difficulties. The circulation of the paper is 5,000.

It is, as a general thing, earnest in its tone, and does not materially differ from any other weekly paper with an avowed object, except in one department, which is edited by some incognito, who signs himself "The Owl," presumably because he sees in the dark. The self-assumed duties of this individual are unique in journalism. He reminds Sister J. that she cannot expect to keep one foot on the church choir and the other on the ball room floor. He tells Brother R. that it is very well for him to shout at the prayer meeting on Wednesday nights, but asks him where he was last Friday at 11:30 in the evening. The position of public censor appears to be far from quiet, judging from the retorts "The Owl" makes, but he apparently never halts in the execution of what he considers his duty.

The *Progress* is the only paper in the world, so far as I have seen, with a clean composing room. The floor of the average composing room is generally coated with mud and tobacco juice. It is never washed, though it is sometimes scraped. The wall reminds one of Lew Wallace's descriptions of the walls of an Aztec house of worship. Cockroaches sport gaily over everything and mice play about the feet of the proof readers as they sit jabbering off their interminable columns.

But the composing room of the *Progress* is clean as most people's sitting rooms, and on high stools sit two very agreeable and comely young women setting type. These are Miss Virgie Johnson and Miss Laura Barnett, and with the assistance of Mr. J. M. Darsey, who is one of the handsomest men, black or white, among the printers in this city, they set up the type for their paper. There are a number of colored men employed in the municipal offices. James S. Bryan is stenographer and secretary in the comptroller's office; A. W. Parker is an inspector of seals, weights and measures; A. Brown is a clerk in the office of the register of deeds; Millard F. Singleton is in the employ of the government as an inspector at Willow Springs distillery.

There are three colored men "on the police force now." They are B. Walker,

J. Russell and A. Salters. At the post-office E. S. Clenians is a clerk, having been appointed to that position by ex-Postmaster Gallagher. And E. R. Overall, R. A. Freeman, A. Noonan and C. Parker are mail carriers.

Mr. Overall is also president of the Missouri and Nebraska Coal Mining company, and is known in politics and in the assemblies of the Knights of Labor as an advanced radical. Twice he has been sent as a delegate to the national labor assembly.

Mr. Overall has written some and talked a great deal in public upon labor questions. Generally speaking, the colored men are not given to labor unions. They do not take very kindly to organization, at least in relation to work. The reason for this may be that they are very adaptable and are willing to take a hand at anything likely to earn them a livelihood. Mr. Overall said that recently there had been some dispositions shown to join the Knights of Labor, and that there were five colored members of his assembly – No. 140, which is a mixed assembly and not a trades union. There is but one saloon kept by a colored man, and the owner of that is Wright Newman. . . .

If one were to reply to the question, "In what part of the city do the colored people live?" he would probably reply, "The Third ward." And perhaps more do live there than anywhere else. At the recent primary for the nomination of candidates for the city council, the officers of the primary were colored men, though the majority of the voters are white. But the truth is that the homes of the colored men are scattered all over the city. And many of these homes are of comfort and of beauty. One of the finest – probably the most expensive – is that of Mr. Singleton, at Twenty-second and Charles streets. It is said to have beauty of architecture, to be finished in hard woods, and to have the latest modern improvements. If any one man were to be named as foremost in the republican element among the colored men, it would probably be Mr. Singleton.

It is roughly estimated that the property owned by Afro-Americans in this city would aggregate $700,000.

John Lewis is one of the richest, and is said to be worth $50,000 in cash, not to mention much property. Thomas Campbell is thought to have $40,000 over and above his property. Mrs. Lizzie King has $60,000; A. O. Adams, $40,000. A large number own their homes, and though, as is inevitable, some of these homes have mortgages upon them, yet far the greater number are unencumbered.

The patriarch of the community is Father Washington, who has watched the flight of 108 years and who has reminiscences about many illustrious persons who have been gathered to their fathers, and had monuments erected to their memory. Two men have gone from Omaha to Washington in the employment of the government. One is H. W. Crasley, who has some position of trust in connection with the senate; and the other is P. J. Williams, who is in the binding department.

There is a fair proportion of society movement among the colored race in this city. The Ancient Free and Accepted Masons has five lodges. The Independent Order of Odd Fellows has one lodge for men and one for women. The Knights of Tabor are strong: there are certain clubs ostensibly of a political nature, but in reality of a sporting character, and it is unnecessary to say that the women do not belong to them. The young colored men have a passion for gaming, which is greatly deplored by their elders, and against which the clergymen and all judicious persons lend their influence.

It is easy to understand why this thirst for gaming exists among them. If this age is distinguished by any distinct trait in commerce, it is the desire to get something for nothing. Since the young colored man cannot do this in wheat deals, in commercial speculation, or in the judicious management of bogus stock, both because of his inexperience in bold financial ventures and because of his ostracism from business circles, what more natural that he should try to win his pile at "policy?" But the tendency is none the less to be deplored for all that.

The anti-Broatch club and the North Side Colored Citizens' Protective Association are flourishing clubs and lend a hand to each other financially, politically and socially.

It is the fashion of some people to say that, aside from the fact that the federal authority of our government was asserted in the civil war, that the whole strife and agony was a waste. In short, they assert that the abolition of slavery was not worth the price paid for it.

Setting aside the abstract moral question of the degrading effects of slavery upon the race of enslavers, and the absence of liberty, which is the life of life, to the enslaved, there still remains the fact that a body of humans, now numbering about 11,000,000, have become factors in a free government. Whether they are factors for good or for evil is a question about which there is some disagreement.

The other day I drove out over the hills that lie just west of the city. The sunflower was in bloom there, and raised its royal head all along the roadside and in the midst of the fields. The plume of the golden rod waved in the sunlight, and the meadows were thick with that other golden flower, which apes the golden rod, but the name of which I do not know. The sky was bluer than anything else in the world except the crevasse of a glacier; and the wind that came rioting in from the plains was such a wind as blows only here in the west, where neither mountain nor lake disturbs the mellow warmth of its gay progress. I came across a little house set down in the midst of the sunflowers. A young wind-break of willows and cotton wood trembled, and shook, and glittered in sunlight and breeze. About on the grass clucked a group of barnyard fowls; they chattered importantly to each other in the shade of the barn or scratched up the dust of the road. The house was painted tastily, and at the windows the muslin curtains sucked in and out, and threatened to knock the pots of pink geraniums off the window sill. Someone was singing, and the voice was that of a Negro. No other voice has that unctuous swell, that trick of modulation, that capricious ebb and swell of sound.

A man came out with a little girl in his arms. She tried to pull his hat off. She showed her adorable teeth. Her little curly head bobbed up and down. The young man got her under his arm and held her there while she laughed and struggled. Then her mother came, looking out to see what the noise was, and she made the baby she had in her arms wave its tiny dark hand at them. I was so near I could see in the house. The pine floor was like snow. The chairs suggested comfort; the dishes were blue and white; two high chairs stood side by side and on the corner of the sewing machine was a copy of the *Century*. The children wore blue gingham, trimmed with bits of embroidery; the mother was dainty in her dress, and her face was round and sweet and full of content.

And someway over me there came a vision of the slave cabin; and the motherhood which meant but shame, and the toil that stood for servitude. Lies and theft took the place of this truth and industry. Stealth displaced this candor. Fear usurped this self-respect. The whip of the slave driver was the spur to activity instead of the love of success. And the babies, with their merry faces, changed into the sad victims of the slave market – they became a part of the traffic in human flesh, in human hearts!

And I wondered how in the name of all that freedom means anyone could be so dull, so selfish, so criminal as to say this liberty counts for nothing!

Why, if it counted for nothing more than the sacredness of home, the inviolate love of one man for one woman, and the hope and honesty and paternity and citizenship that comes as the sequence of that love, it would have been worth while!

Out of ignorance, superstition, fear, servility, enforced deception, the Afro-American is making his way. He is not to be judged by his blunders, but by his successes. His crimes are far easier to account for than his virtues. We have made but part of the reprisal we owe him. The chains with which we once held him are broken, the bonds of our prejudice, which hold us slaves, will not let us assert ourselves free men – free to find our friends wherever soul responds to soul, regardless of the color of the skin.

In colleges and schools, in churches, in shops, fields, kitchens, and offices, this great people is working out its emancipation from ignorance. They present no problem to this republic except that which was first made and is not sustained by the white race.

I wish them whatever of knowledge that may fit them to work better, read deeper, vote truer. But I do not wish them so much knowledge as will take the song from their lips, nor the jest and the lightness from their hearts.

"Killing, Yet No Murder: A Day at the Stock Yards in South Omaha"

7 February 1892

Next to the railroads, the livestock industry dominated the Omaha economy. On 1 December 1883, Alexander Swan, a Wyoming cattle baron, and Omaha tycoon William Paxton, who operated a cattle ranch near Ogallala, Nebraska, along with Irishmen John A. Creighton, John A. McShane, Frank Murphy, and John H. Donnelly, organized the Union Stock Yards Company on land south of the city purchased from the Union Pacific Railroad (Otis 45; Chudacoff 13–16). Although livestock-slaughtering operations had existed in Omaha on a small scale since 1871, McShane, with generous subsidies of stock, land, and cash, lured the Fowler brothers, Philip D. Armour, Michael Cudahy, Gustavus Swift, and Nelson Morris to build meat-packing plants near the Union Stock Yards (Leighton 173–74). The town of South Omaha, which had grown up around the stockyards, soon came to be called the "Magic City." By 1890 it had more than ten thousand inhabitants and claimed to have 327 businesses, including 3 banks and 37 cattle companies (Larsen and Cottrell 74–77).

In 1887, Michael Cudahy and his younger brother, Edward, with the help of Philip Armour, started a meat-packing business in Omaha, the Armour-Cudahy Company.[8] *Within the next two years, the Omaha plant grew to fifteen hundred employees with a payroll of $700,000 and boasted sales of over $13 million (Kennedy 57–60).*

❧ Nebraska has two industries, corn and stock – but without the corn there would, of course, be little stock. The corn is the backbone, and the stock is the sinews of Nebraska prosperity. And out at South Omaha a business is done in the shipping, the buying, selling, killing, and packing of stock which makes any other one business in this community sink in significance.

Unloading pens at the Omaha stockyards, ca. 1900.
(Nebraska State Historical Society Photograph Collection)

South Omaha is indeed a rim around the stock yards. Every one in that town, with a very few exceptions, is dependent directly or indirectly upon the packing houses. It is a remarkably hard working town. It gets up early and it goes to bed early, and though it enjoys the content which comes from hard labor, it does not have a very gay time. It has not, indeed, much inclination for amusements. It is too tired at night. The unceasing push, push, push in the great packing houses will tire out anyone. And to eat and sleep is what the body cries for.

There is an idea abroad that men who work always among the cattle are very rough – even turbulent. Some folk have an idea that they spend most of their time when they are out of work hours fighting or drinking. The truth of the matter is that nine-tenths of the men in the packing houses at South Omaha are men with families, and that they go home to those families when they are through with work, and that, while they may not be distinguished for any superfluous graces, they are in reality very industrious and quiet-going fellows, who like to have their wives and their children think well of them. There is a fight occasionally – it is little wonder with such muscles and such animalism as those men have. Some of them are like gladiators. They can handle the carcass of a steer much as a woman handles her baby. Such men fight for two reasons: first, because they are in places where there is a good deal of irritation, and because their resentment lies near the surface, and second, because they are conscious of their strength, and fight for amusement. As all their life is a mere outputting of strength, and as they earn their living by the mere exercise of muscular energy, it is not strange that their idea of amusement is an exhibition of strength. It would be surprising if they did not enjoy the prize fight above all other things. They understand it. It is in their line.

But men who care nothing about exhibitions of physical strength, and who do not like prize fights must not be too hard on them. A prize fight is not nearly so vicious as some novels, and books of alleged philosophy, and it is moral compared with certain dramatic entertainments. The little homes at South Omaha are rather surprisingly comfortable. And there are a great many children in them. And all day the mothers are working for the children, and the fathers are toiling in the ill-smelling dimness of the packing houses for the children. And the children themselves are running about in the midst of the great clay draws, where the grader has made those astonishing clean cuts; or going to the pretty school house on the hill. And that is all there is to it. They have money enough to live comfortably on – even money enough to pay for a home, with the exercise of a little self-denial – or perhaps a good deal of self-denial. If some of them are intemperate, why so are men in every other walk of life, and most of them have far less excuse than these out at South Omaha. But there is one comfort. They feel pretty sure that the work will not shut down. For man must eat – and as long as he does so, the packing houses must run. There is no danger of overstocking the market for any great length of time.[9] . . .

This company is incorporated as a common carrier. From the moment that animals are put in its care until they leave it, the company feeds them and is responsible for them, precisely as if it owned them. It has in South Omaha twenty-three miles of tracks and six fine engines. It can accommodate, at once, 20,000 hogs, 10,000 cattle, 5,000 sheep and 500 horses.

It is not seven years since this organization started. Yet it is one of the most successful in the country. This is not due entirely to the efforts of the officers. It happened to be the right thing in the right place. It supplied a need. John A. McShane is the president, William A. Paxton the vice president, J. C. Sharp the secretary and treasurer and W. N. Babcock the general manager. The board of directors consists of W. A. Paxton, John A. McShane, John A. Creighton, A. C. Foster, Milton Rogers, E. A. Cudahy, Isaac Waixel, B. F. Smith and M. C. Keith.

The enormous establishments of Cudahy, the Omaha, Swift and Hammond are in convenient juxtaposition, and the stock can be driven easily from the yards to the pens of any of these houses. But the quantity of business done by these yards cannot be estimated by the connection with these local packing houses, for there are buyers from a dozen cities, from Buffalo to Denver, always on the ground.[10] . . .

The establishment of Cudahy is larger than any other packing house in South Omaha, although it turns out no better material. It, however, has introduced various departments which arise out of the primary industry, which the other establishments have not adopted.

For example, Cudahy makes all of his own boxes for packing his preserved meats in. He makes the tin pails for lard and the tin cans for his prepared meat, and recently a chemical department has been started, in which is made pepsin, prepared beef, both liquid and solid, for beef tea, pepsin tablets, and a sort of lacto-peptine used particularly for infants.

Nearly 2,000 men and women are engaged in Cudahy's packing house. And the stranger who visits there could easily believe there were more, for the place, vast as it is, seems swarming with men, boys and girls who, over and over, with a swiftness almost incredible, do the same thing every day of the year, till they learn to do it with accuracy and decision not to be excelled. The wonderful system is amazing. It comes through what may be termed a subletting of authority. There are a number of heads of departments – men of experience and reliability. . . .

The work is unrelenting from the time the whistle blows in the morning, till night. The young Bohemian who stands with his legs well apart, and his fine arms half bared out at the end of a chute where the cattle run from the brown hillside, never alters from the steady down-falling of his big hammer. And each fall of that hammer knocks into insensibility a "beef." From the moment it descends with its unerring aim, the cow or steer ceases to be anything but a "beef," although for several seconds it lives. As a precautionary measure against suffering, its throat is also cut and then a moment later it is swung up, its hide pulled off as neatly and quite as quietly as a lady pulls a glove from her hand, and down the carcass, cutting cleanly and opening up the animal, goes the keen knife. A moment later the entrails are out, and the axe divides the huge body in two; the animal is slid along into the cooling room, weighed, examined in death, as it had before been examined in life by the government inspectors, and left there to cool, forming one figure in the long avenues of carcasses, down which one might walk for the better part of an hour without coming to the end. An ammonia machine keeps the temperature of the rooms at the desired degree of coolness.

Each beef or hog is marked in such a manner that it can be traced to the very ranch or range from which it came. In a way the identity of the animal is never lost until it is cut up into steaks for the table at some retail meat market, or thrown into the great soup cauldrons for the prepared beef at the packing houses. The waste from these animals, in the way of cuttings of wholesome meat, makes this broth, and the process of distillation and of condensation is a tedious one. How savory are the results, everyone knows, and it may be comforting to the thousands who enjoy a cap of prepared bouillon to assure them that greater cleanliness could not be observed even in a private kitchen. Indeed, everywhere the cleanliness is remarkable. Even in the room where the cattle are cut up and the blood literally streams down upon the floor, there is cleanliness, for men with brooms and water sweep the floor continually and longitudinal drains carry away the blood. And even this is not wasted. It is dried and bagged and used for fertilizing purposes.

Some one said some time that nothing was wasted of the hog excepting the squeal. That is literally true, not only of the hog, but of the cow. The bones of the cow make fine buttons and knife handles, and various other articles, and are shipped away in enormous quantities. The bristles of the pig are used for brushes. The entrails serve for the covering of sausage and similar things, the lining of the stomach goes for pepsin, and every part of the animal which cannot be sold as it stands is preserved in one way and another.

Cudahy not only puts up beef extract, but corned beef, and roast beef and potted beef and ham. Each of these commodities is prepared in a different room, and each must be weighed and placed in the cans prepared, then soldered, painted, labeled and packed. To see the way in which the meat, without halting, goes from one department to another, until the animal which stood bellowing on the hoof in the yard finally appears before your eyes in a little glass bottle as the double distilled extract of beef, is, indeed, amazing. Or perhaps he arrays himself as yellow butterine – a product of which the Cudahy is now turning out 10,000 pounds a day. It ships a deal of this to the south, for, as is well know, butterine never becomes rancid, and is therefore especially valued in the south. The machinery which makes this butterine is simple, and the process anything but offensive. In the clean whitewashed room, where it is finally beaten up into shape, the workers stand with their bared arms and white aprons, and the operations of separation from the water, and the mixing and putting into pails are agreeable to the eye and the nostril. Up in the room above, where the boiling is done, and the introduction of the oleo and neutral oils is made, perhaps it is not quite so pleasant, though equally clean. It is really amazing that people will continue to pay an outrageous price for bad butter when butterine could be bought for a sum so comparatively small, and always be good. There are, by the way, a good many pleasant rooms in the establishment. That where a dozen girls stand about among the clean pine tables, bottling the pepsin and prepared beef, is very agreeable, with its white curtained shelves. The tin rooms, with their incessant whirl of machinery, and the bright tin cuttings sprinkling the floor, and the piles of pails and cans is far from unpleasant. The machinery is amusingly clever. It has elbows and wrists, and adroit fingers, and knows how to use them. In one year the average amount of tin used was 35,000 boxes. The room where the boxes are made is very pleasant. This is one of the first places where a man is put when he comes into the establishment if he has no knowledge of any particular part of the work. It's a good place for him to learn English if he is unacquainted with the tongue, and to get used to work. They call it Castle Garden because of its polyglot characteristics. Beyond this room stretch out the lumber rooms, filled with pine cuttings all ready for putting together into boxes from the south and west. The room where the smoked beef is prepared for shipment is a pleasant room. In a way the vast cold cellars are pleasant, with the orderly array of meat by the millions of pounds.

But there are rooms in the place that seem like hell. Such a room is that where the hogs are cut up. It is much more offensive than the corresponding room in the beef house. A hog under all circumstances is obnoxious, until as chop or roast, well seasoned, he comes onto your table. And even then a little of him will go a long way.

A well directed thrust of the knife enters the heart of the hog, as, squealing with the anticipation of another meal, this prince of gluttons trots along the chute that brings him to the killing room. The next second he is deluged with hot water and rolled over in a machine which at one revolution takes every bristle off him. Then he is slit up, his entrails cut out, and while some men continue the process of cutting him up others clean these entrails. The steam from the boiling water fills the place with obscurity, and in this sickly dimness hideous odors arise. The men, with their hands in filth and their garments thick with blood, are all working fiercely. Their faces have blood on them; they stand in blood; they breathe the perfume of scalded flesh. This detestable animal does occasionally look well when he is converted into a smoked ham, well jacketed in his yellow coat and labeled, but until he reaches that state of disguise he is hideous from first to last. He is hideous as he wallows and grunts out in the pens. He is hideous and comical at once when he dies. He is loathsome as he hangs on his hook in the cooling room. The raw fat of the pork, salted and otherwise prepared for shipment, is enough to disgust a Greenlander – although the meat is white as purest lard, and is carefully prepared. In much of this hog meat that is shipped to the south there is not a vein of lean. They like this over in Holland also, and large quantities are sent there.

In contrast to this is the pork intended for the Omaha market, which is lean and "sightly." Cudahy's keeps meat for every sort of market, and can satisfy folks of all kinds of tastes. With lard it is the same. There are brands of lard sent exclusively to the south, brands intended alone for sale in San Francisco and on the Pacific coast, and brands sold here in the central west. The manufacturing of lard is one of the largest departments, it is quite needless to say, in the institution.

Outside of the buildings, for there are two – and running the full length of them is a covered walk – it is as wide as a boulevard and as busy as a market place. By the side of it run the railroad tracks, and here from morning till night the roustabouts wheel and drag and assort and carry the endless variety of stuff that finds its way in and out of this enormous plant. Now it is twenty cars of tin to be unloaded. Swift furnishes the ice for all the packing houses at South Omaha, except the Hammond Packing company, and last year he sent 200,000 tons of it there. Of this Cudahy uses his share. The magnitude of Cudahy's establishment is never more thoroughly impressed upon the mind than in going the length of this long walk on this crowded thoroughfare among the oil, the boxed beef, the lard, the ice, the butterine, the tin, the lumber and the hurrying men.[11] . . .

It may be interesting to know that 75 percent of all the hogs brought to the Union stocks yards are killed in South Omaha and 33 1/3 per cent of all the cattle. There are at present thirty-nine commission firms doing business there.

One of the peculiar features of the Cudahy establishment is the fire department. Ten men sleep in a pleasant room over the general offices, and by their beds lie firemen's outfits, just as one sees them in the room of the regular firemen in the city. A pole runs from the convenient balcony to the ground, and the hose are conveniently at hand. There is always pressure enough to throw a good column of water. In three minutes these well-drilled fellows can be in working order at any part of the plant. The men belonging to the fire department work in the day in the packing house.

Another convenience which must be highly appreciated is the grill room over the offices. Here for a modest sum it is possible to obtain an excellent dinner, and the men from the offices, the heads of departments and the firemen previously mentioned dine every day. Perhaps 100 men sit down here each day to an agreeable meal of three courses.

There is a fine retail market in connection with Cudahy's designed especially for the convenience of the men working at the establishment, but it is so fine, such excellent cuts are to be obtained there, and the appearance of the great market is so inviting that it is visited not only by a large part of South Omaha, but by many persons from Omaha also. Enough can be saved on the meat to make it well worth the while of any one with a conveyance to drive over there from this city and get a supply, now that the weather is of the sort to permit the meat to keep.

To describe fully this enormous concern – Cudahy's – would require far more space than could be afforded in this paper. From the engine room where the great Corliss engine works with noiseless alertness, and the dynamos, pumps and churns, and the water pumps lie in idleness to be ready in case of need, and the great furnaces stand, to the remote apartment where the silent girls with their busy hands paint and paste the bright little boxes for the canned meat there is perfect system and order and economy. There are little boys just able to keep their heads in the midst of the hurly burly, and there are gigantic fellows strong enough to lay low with a blow of the fist the fiercest of the cattle that camp out in the yards, but all are parts of this enormous machine and must never falter in their work. They are all paid by the hour since the eight-hour law went into effect, and their wages are not of a sort that cause that cause them to grumble.

Not the least interesting feature of Cudahy's is Mr. Cudahy himself. He is a young man and a nonchalant one. He controls this whole business. And to do this he has to keep apprised of the market all over the world. Speculation is necessary. The dealing in futures is not to be avoided – not that there is any desire to avoid it. And in the midst of all this excitement, with a telegram handed to him almost every minute of the day, with a force of seventy clerks directly under him, and a telegraph instrument ticking by his side, this young man is as quiet and as comfortable as if his life were given up to the most leisurely pursuits. He is down as early as anyone in the office in the morning, and he is home last, but in spite of incessant work and continual contriving he looks anything but nervous or worn. No one could be in more robust health, apparently, and his occupation appears to be his chief delight. He is a perfect type of the successful business man of the latter part of the nineteenth century – a time when the successful men make their stake while they are young. And it may be remarked that most of the men who are in important positions at Cudahy's are young. Thirty-four years appears to be quite aged among this crowd of young fellows. The corps confesses to a little vanity on the subject. They are young and glad of it.

CHAPTER 2

Fact and Fiction

"Fiction is but the modification of fact for use."

At heart a writer of fiction and poetry, Elia Peattie declared, "I enjoyed my writing on the paper, and was given a free hand, putting the fictional touch on most of the things I did and being permitted to sign my articles" ("Star Wagon").[1] She prided herself on the controversial nature of her editorials, which were often a cross between a feature story, a personal essay, and political or social commentary, and her voice became stronger and stronger as she grew in experience and maturity.

Peattie's style and personality harmonized well with the "new journalism," introduced by Joseph Pulitzer in 1883 when he transformed the New York World *into a newspaper targeting the working-class men and women of America by offering "lively coverage of the day's news, aggressive crusading for civic improvements, and entertaining reading about the drama and pathos of city life" (Marzolf 7).[2] To make the* Omaha World-Herald *competitive, Gilbert Hitchcock, along with other publishers across the United States, began to follow the examples of Pulitzer and William Randolph Hearst, publishing a newspaper to entertain as well as to inform.*

Sensational and dramatic headlines were what sold newspapers in the 1890s. Peattie was an avid newspaper reader – not just of local papers but also of news from around the world – and her most engaging writings dealt with stories and issues that made front-page news. Aware of her audience's diverse intellectual and emotional background, Peattie would often take different approaches to a headline story. Sometimes she wrote purely factual editorials, reasoning with her readers. Occasionally she would insert short narratives, usually fictionalized, as examples to support her viewpoints. At other times Peattie wrote fictionalized sketches based on a real person or event in order to personalize the news and increase empathy with her readers. For subjects that impassioned her the most, such as prostitution and unwed mothers, the unjust treatment of Native Americans, and unconventional religions, Peattie worked the issues from various angles, with one article engaging logic and facts, another appealing to the more personal and human side of the issue, and a third, more fictionalized approach inviting emotional responses.

Portrait of Elia Peattie as Omaha Woman's Club president, 1896. (Omaha Woman's Club)

Peattie's reactions to the headline news of the day combined intellectual research, human interest, spunky personality, and fiction. The fact that some of Peattie's local color may have been invented did not seem to bother her sense of journalistic integrity. After all, she was writing during the time of the realists, who believed that people and events were representative of all mankind. Leda may not have been an actual Omaha shop girl, but many like her worked in the stores on Farnham Street and were seduced by the same sorts of men. Perhaps, by giving her characters symbolic names like Leda or Starved Crow, she assumed her readers would accept them more as parables of life than as verifiable reports of real people. She understood that facts and examples went far to prove an argument, but she also recognized the idiosyncrasies of human nature and the impact of a good story well told.

Peattie loved best the challenges that controversial issues and events provoked, and in most cases she confronted them unswervingly. She admitted, "At that time Nebraska had no writers of celebrity and it did not take long to make a gay little reputation. There were great fights on, too, and it was the fun of the world breaking lances against established trends and misbehaving folk" ("Star Wagon").[3]

"No Need of Prostitution: Mrs. Peattie Refuses to Accept the Claim That the Wanton Is a Necessity"

4 March 1894

Peattie sincerely empathized with the plight of "fallen women." She supported the Open Door, a charitable institution where unmarried women could obtain medical assistance during pregnancy and childbirth; campaigned for affordable room and board for single women; and tried to change public attitudes toward prostitutes, many of whom she believed had made a mistake in their lives or had been condemned by society's double standard.

Prostitution ran rampant in early Nebraska, especially in the Burnt District in Omaha during the years of the 1890s depression.[4] *Saloons, brothels catering to all classes of men, and cribs proliferated in Omaha's vice district.*[5] *The issue embroiled all of the state in 1894 when Lincoln's mayor, Austen H. Weir, ordered that all brothels in the city be closed on 1 March. Weir proclaimed that the women could either "secure respectable employment or permanent homes in respectable families," or go to the girls' home in Milford where special provision had been made for their care.*[6] *According to the account, two hundred prostitutes made their living in Lincoln at that time, and there were fifteen "houses of sin."*

❧ This is a law-abiding state. Of course. Do we not hasten to arrest the freezing man who steals coal, or the shivering woman who steals clothes? We must do this or the foundations of the law will crumble.

But we are nevertheless convulsed with amazement when the mayor of Lincoln suggests that a certain law on the statute books be enforced.

Police mug shot of Omaha prostitute Maud Raymond, arrested for horse stealing, 1896. (Nebraska State Historical Society Photograph Collections)

Nor are we alone in our amazement. The rest of the world looks with equal surprise and not a little amusement at this extraordinary man, who proposes to see to the enforcement of the statutes of his state and the ordinances of his city providing against professional prostitution.

That anarchy is not necessarily so unpopular among men as it is commonly held up to be whenever a redistribution of property is suggested is evidenced

Police mug shot of Omaha prostitute "Red Nora" Courier, arrested for shoplifting, 1896. (Nebraska State Historical Society Photograph Collections)

by the fact that we have been living in anarchy all along and never noticed it. For if it is not anarchy to disregard a law, then what is it? And the form of anarchy in which we have been so openly indulging appears not alone to have been encouraged by common citizens, but to have been encouraged and supported to the utmost by the makers of the law themselves, the legislators at Lincoln.

Ray Cameron, who has the reputation of being one of the most charming and witty cyrians [hedonists] in Nebraska, says, "I predict that the girls will continue their work secretly until the legislature opens. Then they will come back to their quarters as usual. There is too much money in circulation during the legislative sessions for them not to take some risks."

It is incidentally understood that the business interests of Lincoln are likely to suffer greatly from this order of Mayor Weir's and that the business men feel that the order should not be enforced at a time so financially stringent. I have lived in the West too long to underestimate the necessity of systematic "booming" and am tremendously impressed with the last argument: feeling that the continuance in crime of 200 sister women is merest trifle compared with the dividends which Lincoln merchants will receive as the outcome of flush pocketbooks in the demi-monde. But setting aside for the moment the embarrassment in trade, which must naturally result from the failure of 200 women to offer their bodies daily for sale (immortal souls thrown in, as a cap to the bargain) I am obliged to confess that I see no reason why Mayor Weir's direction to the chief of police to enforce a law should awaken any discussion. Once before and quite recently has a similar effort been made. That was in Pittsburg, but the authority of the mayor went for nothing; the majesty of the law was scoffed at as if it were no more than the majesty of a king of carnival. Trade reasserted itself, and men continued to break the laws which they themselves had enacted.

It passes my comprehension to understand why the legislatures of every state should go to the trouble to enact laws which they do not respect themselves nor anticipate others will respect. Can it be that they merely put these statutes on their books to impress posterity? Or is it a fact that society unites in holding up before its composite eye a colossal image of fictitious virtues?

However that may be the 200 prostitutes of Lincoln are told to move on, and move on they will to Omaha, Kearney, Beatrice, and Hastings. They will stay away for a brief time, until the vigilance of the police is relaxed, and then they will return. Everyone seems to recognize the fact that they must be back in time for the legislative session. Real politics appear to have difficulty in proceeding without the aid of prostitution.

Men and women who do not believe in innocence are apt to denominate themselves men and women of the world, and they appear to think that by this open confession of their sophistication they have made sufficient apology to society for any vicious views that they may hold, and any overt actions they may commit.

Men and women of the world have often assured me that prostitution is a necessity. I know the Queen of England thinks it is. And I am acquainted with a great many wives who assure me that they believe so, and that if professional prostitution were not permitted, it would not be safe for any pure woman to walk the streets alone. I always wonder what sort of a personal experience these women must have had to give them such an idea of the brutishness of man. I have noticed, too, that women who tell me this are invariably the women who tell me that they think such institutions as the Florence Crittenton homes, or the Open Door, immoral. And when they assure me that they consider it injudicious to restrict men in their vices, and immoral to rescue the women these men have ruined, then, indeed do I look with pity, knowing that a black leaf of shame lies in their life's book. Only the last great heart sacrifice that a woman can make will cause her to become so indecent in her mode of thinking. When a pure woman thus condones sin it is because her husband or her son is a sinner, and she had to do one of two things – disapprove of the sinner or approve of the sin.

There are hundreds of thousands of women who think they are Christians, who have done the latter.

I do not know whether or not these women are as bad as the prostitutes. I suppose God knows. But there are some things that I do know.

I know a young wife who says she is glad John has sowed his wild oats, and that she could never have married a ninny. I saw her baby the other day on the street. Its eyes were as blue and innocent as heaven. And on its cheek was a dull, angry sore. I wondered what that sore meant.

I know a young man dying of softening of the brain, and his sweet wife and little children weep for him, loving him still. And the heaven of a home he might have had is guarded from him by angels with flaming swords.

He, too, was a man who had sowed his wild oats.

I know a woman who for years has lived with a polluted man and been forced to acknowledge him as her husband. And she shrinks from him in loathing; she cringes before his tyranny; and she lives with him in bitterness and hate. Why? Because she preferred to live with him as a legalized concubine and enjoy the approval of society rather than leave him for poverty and the loss of social position. How is she better than the prostitute? Did I say I knew one such woman? I know twenty. And some are young and beautiful, and some are old and plain, but from the eyes of all looks a sorrow ancient as sin, and a bitterness that comes alone with loss of self-respect.

For such things is professional prostitution responsible.

As to who is responsible for professional prostitution, that is another matter.

Anyone who chooses to read Chariton Edholm's "Traffic in Girls" will perhaps learn something of the subject. This book is published by the Woman's Temperance Publishing association of Chicago, and contains reports concerning the Florence Crittenton missions, with incidental descriptions of the way in which young girls are entrapped into lives of shame. It also contains the famous reports which Mr. William T. Stead made in his *Pall Mall Gazette* of the slavery of the brothel.

After reading this book, with its terrible revelations, I have no doubt that many would contend that it held little of general interest, and that such things do not happen in Nebraska. I have no means of knowing how bad Nebraska may be. But I do know of a girl 14 years of age who this week found the shelter of the Open Door. The man who ruined her was over twice her age. The girl has been placed in the Milford home, where she has been cared for physically and morally, and taught a trade, so that when she leaves she will not have to join the ranks of the unhappy sisterhood. Two other girls, barely past 16, also found shelter in the Open Door this last week, and will be sent to the state home in Milford. They will leave there, let us hope, armed with the courage to be true to their better selves. Had it not been for the provision that these institutions make they would have had no choice but to accept the hospitality of wholesale midwifery from which one emerges only to enter the doors of a house of debauchery.

That the recruits to the sad sisterhood are young maidens, deliberately ruined by men much older than themselves, I am convinced. What else is there for the ordinary women to do when she finds herself betrayed but to join these miserable ones? The frantic fear, the shame, the suffering, the cruelty of society, leave little choice.

I have often heard it said that women are much more cruel than men to their fallen sisters. My experience has not corroborated this. On the contrary, the cruelest acts of uncharity of which I have ever known, have been perpetuated by men. The most unjust situations which are today poisoning the ear of Omaha society, were concocted in the offices or the clubs, and are being circulated with an assiduity worthy of a better cause. As for the women, they have not encouraged these reports, which they believe to be unjust, and to have no substantiation in fact.

If a good woman desires to take a fallen sister into her home for the purpose of helping her to a better life, the good woman's husband is almost sure to overbear her impulses with objections. And I distinctly remember reading a sermon preached in this city by a young and dogmatic clergyman, in which society was cautioned against forgiving the fallen woman. He seemed to think the Lord had a monopoly on forgiveness. I think he afterwards apologized for his attitude by saying that the standard of womanhood ought not to be lowered by her presence in society. But I could not see how the standard of womanly purity could be lowered by the reform of a bad woman. And as for the possible contamination, that counts for nothing. There used to be a saw which said: "Evil communications corrupt good manners." Like most saws, it is only partly true. Mr. George W. Cable puts it very much better when he says that it is not the company we seek, but the reason we have for seeking it, that makes the difference.

I do not want to be unfair or one-sided. But I feel convinced that in nine cases out of ten it is the brutality of man which is directly responsible for the downfall of woman, and not any innate viciousness in the woman herself. There are stories today being enacted as sad and as tragic as that of Virginia. I will admit that anyone who sees a company of these fallen women together in "the cage" at the city jail, swearing, jeering and laughing with a gaiety more dreadful than any grief, will find it difficult to believe that they were ever pure. But the very violence and excess of their obscenity shows to the thoughtful mind how far they have fallen and what a killing shock their sensibilities received when, in some black moment, life was suddenly transformed for them into death – a death without the peace of the grave.

I know that they seem happy. I know they resent pity. I know all their coarseness, their hardness and their folly. Yet my heart aches for them, and I could weep for the curse that curses women, and which never seems to rest on man.

Some time ago a widow, with a child, tried in some Christian city of New York to find a place as housekeeper for a widower. She knew of no other way in which she could earn a living without parting from her child. One morning she blew out the brains of her baby and then herself. Her act was that of a Lucrece.

At the Mission of Our Merciful Savior in Omaha there is today a young widow with a child who tried in Omaha to get a position similar to that desired by the young woman in New York. The experiences she met with caused her to fly to the Mission for refuge.

Apropos of all this, I cannot help recalling a little "etching" once shown me by Miss Higgins, a young writer in this town, who has much originality of theme and method. Miss Higgins' little sketch was abrupt, tragic and not to be forgotten. Divested of all the phraseology which gave it charm, the story was briefly this:

A young gentleman had an episode – all men must have episodes, of course, if they would cut their eye-teeth. The girl he ruined crept away into a wretched life, cheated of all her birthright of happiness and innocence. The man outgrew his infatuation, forgot his wrong doing, married a lovely woman and was happy. Moreover, he was good. He thought no evil. If he ever remembered his escapade it was to think of himself merely as having been selfish. In time he and his sweet wife had a little daughter. One day she was stolen from her cradle. No human ingenuity availed to find her. But eighteen years later the woman the young man had been selfish with stood before him, hardened by years of sin into a dreadful thing, with the soul dead in her, and by her side stood the daughter he had lost in her babyhood. And in her face, triumphing over the fair lineament her mother had bestowed upon her, was the same look as of a demon that blasted the face of her companion. It was Nemesis, of course. It was fair play – turn and turn about. Yet the writer knew that everyone would sympathize with the man and condemn the woman.

Such things go on constantly under our eyes. These tragedies are never to be escaped from.

"It cost me a thousand dollars," said a well-known young man in this town, speaking of a girl who had left the city, driven away by the hue and cry made against her when her shame was found out. "It cost me $1,000. But it was worth it."

It certainly was, to the woman. A thousand dollars is dirt cheap for the price of damnation.

If one were to ask me the cause of the present financial misery, and the hunger of so many men, I would say that it was the aggregated result of millions of small, greedy and unjust acts.

If one were to ask me the cause of the prevalence of prostitution, I would say that it is the aggregated result of innumerable acts of brutality and deception.

How quick men are to protest against any folly or trivial selfishness in which women indulge! Yet this satanic crime of selfishness, this black sacrilege, this compounded hellishness of action by which they create and sustain prostitution, they say is "necessary." They object to its discontinuance because it will "hurt trade."

Mammon! Is trade more than the souls of women, the purity of home, or the health of young men?

Do not talk of "necessity," for science stands ready with a voice cold and clear as that of justice itself to give you the lie! There is no necessity for the debasement of the human body – else God were a fiend and it would be best to curse him and die.

Mayor Weir of Lincoln, the prostitutes may defy and the profligates jeer at you, and men blind with their own egotism find epithets for you; but women – who sometimes see clearer than men, and who find out sophistries sooner – hold out to you pure hands, and thank you. For they have had the sweetness of their lips sullied by kisses that bore the taint of wantons' lips; they have known the fear of nursing their children with plagues worse than Egypt ever knew, because the crimes of the father are visited upon the children, and their hearts have been torn because of those other women, once wholesome as themselves, whose pitiful feet have taken hold on hell.

Never mind the censure, Mayor Weir. There's an exalted pleasure to be found in persecution which most of the world will never know.

"Leda"

1 February 1891

In 1891, three years before the Lincoln prostitution scandal had made headlines, Peattie had written a sentimental sketch titled "Leda" that personalized her empathy for the "fallen woman." Alluding to the classical myth of Leda, a queen of Sparta raped by Zeus when he had taken the form of a swan, Peattie described the all-too-common example of a young, naive girl victimized by a man who also falsely represented himself. In the Greek myth, the beautiful Helen of Troy was born of the union of Zeus and Leda; however, Peattie's Leda was herself reborn with the help of the charitable women at the Open Door. Given a second chance at honor and respect, both Leda and her child were saved. This parable, Peattie hoped, would appeal to readers not swayed by facts and logic.

Josie Washburn, an Omaha prostitute who worked for madam Anna Wilson, confirmed Peattie's account in her 1909 narrative The Underworld Sewer. *Young girls became prostitutes, according to Washburn, by "two broad ways, men's double-dealing, deception and lust; and by deprivation, poverty and abuse" (qtd. in Bristow 204). For single mothers in the 1890s trying to survive on servants' wages and to keep their children out of orphanages, prostitution was often the only choice.*[7]

❧ Leda, in spite of her poetical name, was only a clerk in an Omaha store. No one paid much attention to her. That was partly because she was never in the way of any one. She had no ambitions – no, not even to be at the head of a department and "'take' count of stock." Her parents – well, there are some

Unidentified girl in white dress with flowers, ca. 1895.
(Douglas County Historical Society Collections, Omaha, Nebraska)

children who are not sufficiently cautious in their selection of parents. Leda had been one of these. Her parents had only given her a name, which she was never able to live up to. Life had been very dreary back on the Nebraska farm. Leda was never permitted to have any amusement, or even to buy clothes such as maidens love to wear, because there was always a harvester to pay for or the interest to meet on the farm, or a new cow to be got. None of these things ever appeared to improve the condition of the farm; however,

Leda used to think that the more "improvements" the farm had the more abject did it become. One day she said she was going away.

"I want to be independent," said she, with a little swagger. She swaggered because she knew she would meet with opposition. If she could have counted on sympathy she would have wept. But hardness begot hardness.

Her mother called her ungrateful. Her father said nothing. He did not speak to her again, even to say good-bye. That was his way of "taking it out of her." Leda, who had good luck, got a position in a store without much difficulty. It was partly because she had a way of seeming able to take care of herself. And then she was very comely, and her voice was sweet. These things count, even with managers of dry goods establishments.

Young gentlemen came to her counter sometimes to buy handkerchiefs. She was very much interested in them because she had never before seen any men except farmers, and they are different in their manners from young gentlemen. The young gentlemen were also interested in her. One of them asked one day if he might call. She had never received any lessons in social etiquette. She did not know there was such a thing. She told him he might.

Two weeks later she was calling him "Harry."

Every one who came to the store began to notice her now. She had become beautiful, and she sold goods with a marvelous dexterity. She could not take pains enough to please those who came to buy. Although she had not aspired to it, she was given a better position, with three girls under her. Her employers said she was "smart." They were mistaken. She was merely happy. But in women it is always hard to tell the difference.

She developed a sudden knowledge of dress, and added style of costume to her beauty of face. She read books and talked about them.

One day she came down radiant.

"In a month I shall be married," said she to the girls in her department.

"To who?" cried the girls. They were very enthusiastic, but not grammatical.

"To Harry," said she.

"I don't believe it," said Christine, who was 80 and a trifle sour.

"What will you wear?" cried Mame. Mame was only 16 and she was a lover herself.

"Why don't you believe it?" asked Leda, faltering.

"Because," said Christine, "Harry belongs to the swells. They are not marrying shop girls. Not this year. Some other year, maybe."

Leda said nothing. She stroked the leaves of the red rose in her bosom. She always wore roses now. This lasted a fortnight longer. Her wedding dress was made. All of the girls came to her room one evening to see it. Only Christine shook her head.

"You should have got something you can wear at the store," said she, "for that is where you will need it." The tears came into Leda's eyes. She grasped Christine's arm: "You do not think he would break his word – not now?" Christine put her arm around her.

"I think some men would break their word any time," said she gently, "but of course I know nothing of your Harry."

That night Christine prayed for Leda. She knew that Leda needed the prayers.

Two weeks later Leda stopped wearing roses.

"Harry is gone to New York," she said. The time for the wedding day passed. None of the girls laughed, however. Something in Leda's face kept them from it. She became ill and fainted one day. She no longer took a pride in selling goods. She got slovenly about the "stock" and was reprimanded. But this, which a few weeks before would have humiliated her, seemed now to make no difference. One day she left the store. She dared go there no longer. She had a frightful secret from which she never escaped. She was imprisoned with pain, harassed with a loathing of herself, terrified by wild struggling emotions, which threatened to be almost happiness, but became madness.

In all the world there seemed to be no seclusion. There was no place where a girl might hide – no place where cruel eyes would not be on her. She stayed in her room for a week, almost always on her knees. No words came from her lips. She did not know how to form her petition. She was only silently suing for mercy.

To return home was impossible. She would have been cast from the doors. She dared no longer go on the streets in the daytime lest she should betray her secret. She found there was no hospital in all the city for such as she. One night she went after the darkness had fallen and walked the street in her despair.

A painted woman, alone, with sparkling trimming on her dress, hurried by. Leda knew what sort of women dressed like that. The girls at the shop had told her. She caught at her gown.

"I must speak to you," she said. The woman stopped. Leda leaned against a gate and panted.

"Go on," said the woman, "I won't bite you." Somehow Leda told her story.

"Where can I go," said she; "what must I do?"

"You can go to a hundred places," said her companion, "that I could show you. And you will be cared for well enough. The baby – well, that is always taken care of." She laughed.

"You mean – " gasped Leda.

"I mean you do not concern yourself with these matters. It is enough if you get off scot free."

"My God!" gasped Leda under her breath.

"Oh! That's nothing. There's worse than that! You have to stay there then, you know. They expect your services." Leda started. The wind blew strong from the west and it tossed away the wrappings from about the woman's throat. Under some laces her bosom showed. Leda caught at the fence. . . .

"You've had plenty to eat, haven't you? Because here's a dollar or two – "

"Thank you, no!" cried Leda. "I've more than enough to eat." She ran down the street in the darkness, weeping as she went, and sobbing aloud. It was in that way that Sam McCarthy saw her. He wears a star, and has a chest measurement the greatest of any man on the police force in Omaha. He caught Leda as she flew by him. He thought she was insane. That is how he came to take her that night and place her on a bench in a cell. Leda hardly noticed. The horrible ribald visions keeping their mad dance in her brain made her forget all else. In the morning the policeman talked with her awhile. She was not taken before the justice. No one in the outer room saw her.

That next night she laid her head down in the safe shelter of the Open Door.

Do you know what that is?

It is the only place in the state where, without certificate, or application, or red tape, a woman may go when friends have deserted her, when honor is gone and despair is faced.

Here it is not presumed that the soul is black because the body is defiled. Here the sins of a woman are not counted greater than those of a man. Here alone, common humanity wipes out differences of life. Here the innocence that springs even from the vilest mother, in the life of her babe, is counted holy. Here life is considered a gift of the Lord.

There are no reproaches. There are only prayers. There is no questioning, except that which may lead to final happiness. Tenderness, courtesy, love, these are the things that the broken heart can find.

Leda stayed there. She went out saved from suicide. Her life is pure in heaven. It is devoted to others – and in no lowly way. For fortune had followed her. She is respected and loved in this city by hundreds who do not know her story – and who will never know it.

And the little one has found love, too – an abundance of it – and will grow up to bear an honorable name, never guessing that shame has even remotely touched it.

If the heart of the mother sometimes hungers for him, she is consoled by the thought that now honor is his heritage, while she could have given him only shame.

This happened long ago. And yesterday the 101st baby was born at the Open Door. That means 101 women saved to lead better lives. One hundred and one women saved from crime by suicide or by worse than suicide.

This is the institution, which some good persons – and some bad ones – do not think it worth while to encourage. Perhaps they are afraid they will compromise themselves. They are afraid that by being lenient to the sinner they will encourage sin. It is not the view that Christ took of such matters – but a great many persons have improved on the methods of Christ.

"Lovely Woman and Indians"
4 January 1891

Native Americans, too, found an advocate in Peattie. She looked behind the rhetoric of Manifest Destiny, questioned the negative stereotypes, and respected the customs, religion, and rights of the first Americans. Although she was not a lone voice in their support, most news stories of the day did little to foster positive attitudes toward them.[8]

In January 1891, shortly after the slaughter of the Lakota Ghost Dancers as well as women and children at Wounded Knee, Peattie wrote two editorials in support of Native Americans. Influenced by her friend and associate Thomas Tibbles, an editorial writer and reporter for the Omaha World-Herald, *Peattie had firsthand information.*[9] *On 30 December 1890, the day after the Wounded Knee tragedy, the* World-Herald *published Tibbles's eyewitness account, which called the event "a war of extermination." He reported that Native American casualities totaled 106 men and 252 women and children. Only 56 Sioux survived, mostly women and children, and all but 2 were wounded (Limprecht 10–11).*

With emotions running high among Nebraskans, Peattie first chose a logical appeal, urging her readers, especially the women, to learn the facts rather than relying on emotion in trying to understand the situation. She provided a comprehensive list of historical and contemporary works about Native Americans to educate her readers out of their barbarism.

❧ There used to be every reason why a woman should be governed by her heart or her prejudices, instead of her brain. But there is no longer such an excuse for her. Whatever the colleges, practical experience in life, fiction, reading and opportunity for comparison of ideas can do for her,

Soldiers and Hotchkiss guns of the famous Battery E of the First Artillery at Wounded Knee, 1891. (Library of Congress, Prints and Photographs Division, LC-USZ62-11974)

has been done. Therefore if she now shows a mental passion in the place of mental judgment she confesses to a defect, which may be temperamental or a part of her femininity, as one chooses to believe. Of course, I hope it is temperamental.

Concerning the Indian troubles, which are now reaching their tragic climax, I have noticed that the women have used less judgment in expressing their opinions on the matter than some of the men. They choose to indiscriminately pity or detest the Indian. Those who pity appear a great deal lovelier than those who detest because pity is a womanly emotion and detestation is not womanly – though, perhaps, it is feminine enough.

I am sure there are plenty of exceptions to this rule, but I fear that few women think nothing about the abstract justice of this affair. The maintenance of an abstract sentiment is of more importance than the exercise of mercy in some specific case. What I mean to say is, the reason why the United States government should treat the Indian with justice has nothing to do with the deserts of the Indian. I heard a lady say the other evening after the news of the Wounded Knee massacre had reached this city:

"The dirty wretches! They ought to be killed." She used the word dirty in the sense of uncleanliness. I suppose she thought they were worthy of extinction because they were not intimately acquainted with perfumed soap. As a matter of fact the government has chosen to give them very limited rations of soap. No one could keep clean on it. However, not to digress, I will admit I heard a gentleman say something almost as ridiculous.

"The treacherous dogs!" cried he, "after they had surrendered, to turn and fire. That is always the way in Indian warfare. In civilized fighting such an occurrence would have been impossible."

He had not chosen to understand the situation. Most persons seem to prefer misunderstanding every Indian situation. The gentleman must have known that the Indians at Wounded Knee could not have surrendered, since there had been no engagement. They saw themselves surrounded by soldiers, with four frightful guns looking down at them from the tops of the dunes and they in the hollow; about them were their teepees with their wives and children. It looked like the last act of a long tragedy. They were weak with hunger; they were fearful of involving all those they loved in their own disaster; yet they fought, with a grim heroism that in a less despised race would be the subject for a hundred songs.

These are the facts. How can they be perverted? There is no use in calling this statement of facts sentimentalism, because fact is not sentiment, however pathetic it may be, any more than fact is fiction. What I started out to do in this article was to recommend to every woman who intends to take up a course of reading for the winter a study of the Indian history of this country. They need not imagine the subject to be a dry one. It is like an epic. It has the slow stateliness of an old Greek tragedy. It goes from woe to woe with solemn march, and such gladness as it contains is but the contrast which makes the darkness blacker. The proud six nations that the Puritans and the Dutchmen knew; the stately and wealthy savages of the southern coast; the gay and poetical hoards who welcomed Francis Drake on the shores of the Pacific; the grave sun worshipers of the Mississippi; the long conflict between French and English for their friendship; all the gallant tales of the fierce fur companies in their interminable fights; the beautiful histories of the missions; the hideous revenges, first from Indian and then from white man, all unite to make up a history beside which the conquest of the Gauls and the fights of the Goths are dull and tedious.

To the perusal of the books which set forth these things might be added the later ones of Helen Hunt Jackson, but these should be left till the last, because they deal especially with the legislative side of the question. I do not suppose the women can have any influence in the matter of bringing about an adjustment of this terrible question, because it is quite beyond even men who are in power; but I do suppose that good feeling is always beneficial in some subtle way and makes itself felt. Those women particularly who live near the agency may be able to do deeds of kindness to women of that other race, who by their faint fires, sit gloomily watching the closing in of the foe. They chant the death hymns of their nation. They wail for the lost freedom of the Sioux.

If all this seems foolish to you, then I will tell you it is because you are provincial – because you are not yet learned in the art of thinking – because you have not passed beyond prejudice, which is barbaric. You are savage yourself if you cannot see in the decay of a nation, or the destruction of a race, a great historical fact, and a gigantic crime. But I feel sure after the completion of the course of reading which I recommend to you, you will be able to see both sides of the question, and will feel moved to subdue anger and impatience whenever you meet with it, and to advise reflection and mercy. Here are a few of the books which might be read with profit. I may not have all the titles exactly right, but as nearly as I can remember they are so. At least they are near enough for you to procure them at a library or book store. Buchanan's "History, Manners and Customs of North American Indians"; John Smith's "True Relation of Virginia"; Campbell's "Virginia"; Doyle's "English Colonies in America"; Thompson's "Vermont"; and Williamson's "Maine"; Lodge's "English Colonies in America"; Parkman's "The Old Regime in Canada"; Clute's "Annals of Staten Island"; Barnes' "Early History of Albany"; Palfrey's and Elliott's "New England"; Spark's "Gorton"; Penshallow's "Indian Wars in New England"; Abbott's "History of King Philip"; and I think that it is in Broadhead and O'Cailaghan's "New York" where one reads of the awful massacre of Indians [lines missing] . . . Parkman is always good. His book reads like a romance because he tells the whole truth. It is only those historians who see a part of the truth who are so stupid. I have not mentioned the dozen of novels, poems, and dramas which accompany the histories relating to each period of the long Indian struggle, but there is no trouble in finding them. To resume: There is Parkman's "France and England in North America"; LaSalle's "Discovery of the Great West"; Curtis' "Children of the Sun"; Help's "Spanish Conquest of North America"; Kip's "Early Jesuit Missions in North America"; Ramsey's "South Carolina"; and Williamason's "North Carolina"; Drake's "Indian Wars"; Parkman's "Pontiac"; James' "Ticonderoga" – which is, of course fiction, but which can be read with reliance – and it is even worth while to read Cooper's "Last of the Mohicans" if there is any one who has not read it.

Then there is Flint's "Indian, Wars of the West"; Drake's "Life of Tecumseh and the Prophet"; Abbott's "Life and Adventures of Davy Crockett"; "Black Hawk's Life of Himself"; Moncrieff's "Men of the Backwoods." I know of no history relating extensively to Oceola, so suggest the reading of Mayen Reid's novel of that name. There should be something about Sam Houston too, and no doubt there are plenty of biographies of him. Jones' "Republic of Texas" and Urquhart's "Annexation of Texas" no doubt contain much.

General Miles has an article in the last number of the *North American Review* well worth reading – a very judicious article, which takes cognizance of both sides of this question, as do the books I have mentioned. I sincerely wish that the women of Nebraska would read a part of these books this winter, and fill their minds with the truth of this matter, and not cover themselves with disgrace by making petulant and ignorant remarks on the subject. The outlook now is terrible. This long winter may see many frightful battles on those bleak western plains. The soldiers and the Indians are alike the victims of a conspiracy. Remember that always. The Indians have done nothing to deserve their present treatment. War has been thrust upon them.

For what reason?

It is possible to surmise. It would not be safe to definitely affirm the reason. But it is none for which the department of war is responsible. There is greed and dishonesty behind all this.

Therefore, if it comes in the way of any of you to feed a hunted woman; to care for a child dying from a United States bullet; to nurse a baby whose innocent lips hunger for the cold breast of its murdered mother; to speak kindly to a man whose eyes gleam with the savage despair of the condemned, it will be counted for so much glory to you in the day of the future reckoning which all of us believe, even in the midst of our doubt, will surely come.

"The Triumph of Starved Crow"

4 January 1891

After appealing to her readers' intellect, Peattie penned a sentimental sketch titled "The Triumph of Starved Crow" to add pathos to her argument. Using a fictional Indian character she named Starved Crow, she narrated the events of Wounded Knee from the perspective of Native Americans and a priest, Father Francis M. J. Craft, a dedicated Indian missionary who may have been of Mohawk heritage (Finnicum). Father Craft wanted to be of service, "as malicious whites on and near all agencies, during the present excitement have, by misrepresenting the intentions of the army, caused such a state of alarm and suspicion among the Indians as to make it possible for the least excitement or misunderstanding to [precipitate] serious trouble." As a result of his compassion, Father Craft suffered a severe knife wound that punctured his right lung; however, he survived the battle, whereas most of his Indian friends perished (Jensen, Paul, and Carter 136).

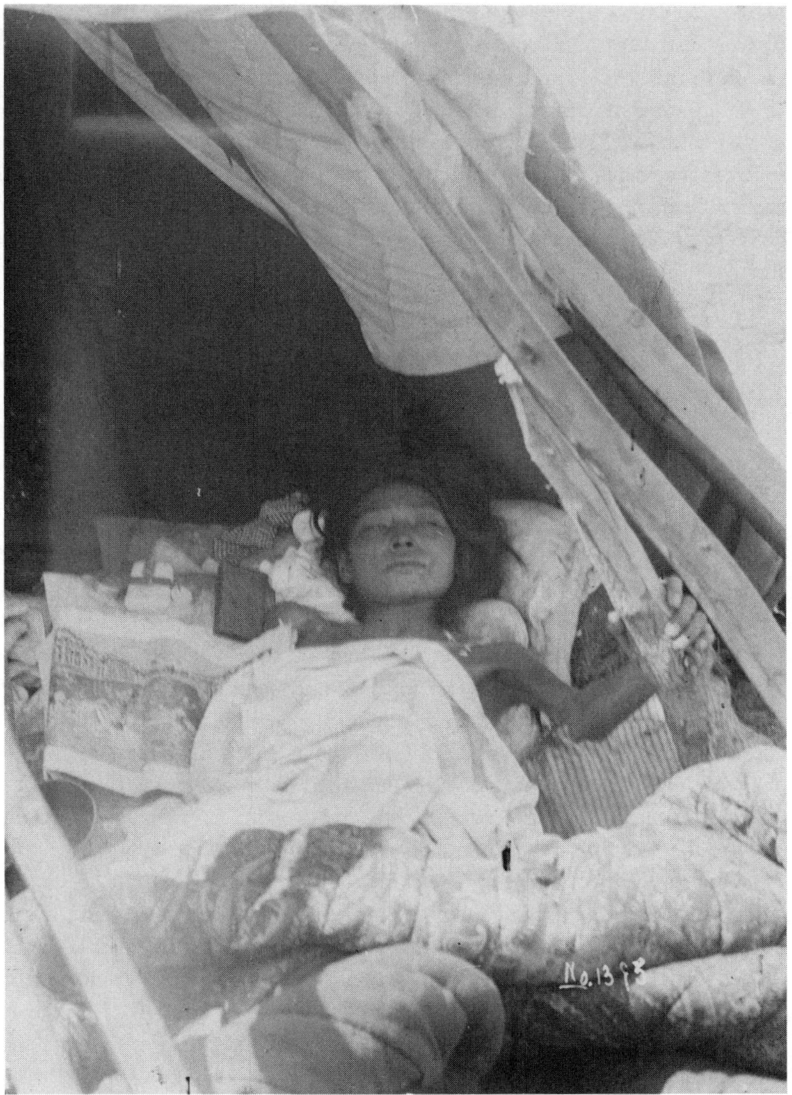

A starving Indian woman survivor of the massacre at Wounded Knee, 1891. (Nebraska State Historical Society Photograph Collections)

❧ A place where the hills and the hollows seem made by the devil and not by God – stretch of unfinished earth where the fires of the innermost globe search to the surface and smolder hideously; a land where the trees writhe as if they were in torment; where the buttes rise bare and brown in shapes fantastical, and the treacherous ravines drop with malicious suddenness – such are the Bad Lands of the Dakotas. The cayuse can barely follow the wild paths; there are places there where even the rabbits can die of hunger, and the scoria of dead fires here and there poisons the bunch grass with noxious slime.

There is only one thing which can drive a white man there. It is greed. An Indian can be driven there only by fear. For an Indian likes pleasant pastures for his herds, and streams where the fish are and where the cattle love to drink.

It was fear that drove Starved Crow there. And he took his wife with him, and the two little ones. The baby had died the week before because the milk in her mother's breasts had dried up. Father Craft, who spoke only blessings, muttered something that sounded like a malediction when he looked at the dead baby.

"But you gave what you could," said he to the mother when she wept. "The crime is not on your soul – not on your soul, my poor daughter."

The Bad Lands are no more terrible than a teepee when the cupboard is bare and there is no fire where the children may sit at night. Even when the frightful dunes, with their split tops and windy caverns, rise all around one, and strange shapes seem to glide out of them at night to stir the blue flame of the lignite beds and dance unholy dances, they are no worse. But neither hunger nor cold firesides had driven the band of Sioux here when the cutting ice storms blew from the bleak northwest, and the moon was ringed at night.

It was the soldiers, down at the camp, come for murder as surely as the moon wanes to wax again. Come for murder and land. Every Sioux knew how it was done. Perhaps if they could stand the cold a while out there in the wilderness the soldiers would leave or forget them and they could return in safety. Father Craft every night, when the young braves talked together, walked among them and preached: "Patience! Peace!" And he was more than preacher. He was friend.

"What can you do against so many?" said he, when one, wilder than the rest and younger, said they had a right to return to the land which was theirs and the houses they had built. "Better wait awhile here, harming no one. Perhaps there has been some mistake."

At last Sioux came riding hard on their cayuses.

"They say you are at war, hiding here from the soldiers. You must get back or they will come out to battle. You will all be killed. They will surround you. And you cannot fight, for you are hungry. You must come back." Father Craft looked puzzled.

"Do they say these are turbulent men, these who have left their homes for the sake of peace?" said he. But every day new messages came. There was a council. They feared that other Sioux would suffer for their sakes. They determined to return.

When a snow has fallen, so that the paths are treacherous, it is terrible to walk the paths beside the canyons, especially for the children. And the children – they have not yet learned what it is to be a Sioux. Some of them are not ashamed to cry when they are hungry.

By and by the band reached Wounded Knee. Here they rested. "Patience and peace," said Father Craft continually. "Who knows but some good will come of it all? The good father at Washington will hear how hungry you all are and will send you more food. He will learn how your crops have failed; how the corn burned up at ripening time; how poor is the land that has been given you, and he will see your wrongs righted. Remember, patience and peace," and he walked continually among the Indians, and even let little White Bear, the baby, play with his ebony crucifix. "Thou wilt learn to love the cross, perhaps, if it serves thee for a plaything," said he quaintly. Sometimes he spoke in English of the old fashion. Oftener he talked in Sioux. The day the band reached Wounded Knee the chief came rushing to Father Craft.

"Do you know what is to be done?" he cried. "We are to be taken somewhere, I know not where. We are not to go back to our homes. The railroad is to take us to some strange place. These white dogs are to take our lands from us. They said they wanted to talk. That is not what they want. They are always liars." All the band heard of this. They talked together. No one could tell what to do. They could travel no further; they were too weary. They must at least rest for the night. The next morning very early they gathered for council. The soldiers were already there. They came down and counted the Sioux. Starved Crow saw them wheel mighty guns up to the tops of the hills. There was one to the east and one to the west. There was one at the north and another at the south. This was while the Sioux sat in a circle, shivering in their blankets. All about them were the soldiers. Starved Crow looked at them closely. Some of their faces looked familiar. He put his hand to his face and whispered to the man next him:

"Do you know who these men are?" said he. "They are 'Custer's Avengers.' They are the men who swore to revenge Yellow Hair and Rosebud."

The soldiers were still counting the Indians, who sat with immovable faces. But in a moment every Indian knew the truth.

They were told to bring their guns. Starved Crow smiled. He found his wife and drew her aside for a moment. No one heard what they said. Then he began the death song. He knew – all the Sioux knew – that they were to be murdered. They were 150, not counting the women and children. The troops were more than twice that number. Two of the men went up to deliver their arms. It was a feint, that the death song might be finished.

"Why should we wait to die?" said Big Foot to Starved Crow. "Let us die now. Do not let our wives call us cowards."

"So!" said Starved Crow. He looked back at his wife. The children were clinging to her poor skirts. Her great eyes were fixed on him. He threw himself on the ground and pulled the trigger of his rifle. The bullet went whizzing up through the bunch grass. Then, a moment later, the red fire poured out of the guns like a molten streak from hell.

The Sioux fell in their tattered garments, their faces proud, still, and fierce, and untamed. The men in blue fell, too. Some of them, wounded and bleeding, fought there in the brown grass with those other men, and the old hereditary hatred burned up, consuming both.

Father Craft ran between the lines of hideous fire. His strong limbs rent his black gown in twain as he leaped forward. He held up the crucifix high over all.

"Peace! Peace!" he cried. "They know not what they do!" No one heard his words save Starved Crow. He had aimed at the heart of a gay young Irishman. The bullet struck instead the breast of Father Craft. The cross, the symbol of peace, fell in the dust.

Hours after the men came to carry away the dying, Little White Bear, though only a baby, lay with a hole in his throat. When they gave him water to drink it ran out of his neck. But his feverish hands held the crucifix that had fallen. He was still playing with it and babbling inarticulately. There were so many dead that it was easy to care for the wounded. Someone stooped over Starved Crow. He rolled back his eyes and lay perfectly still. They passed on. He wanted no care from his foes. He would not be nursed back to life only to be killed again.

That night a storm of ice came with wind, cutting and killing.

Two days later someone visited the field where the men had fought.

Three of the dead men sat with their arms about each others' necks. One of them was Starved Crow. They had been frozen so. But at least they had conquered. They had not again been driven from their homes. They had chosen their own fate. No one had coerced them.

"A Word with the Women" – Francis Schlatter, Faith Healer
18 November 1895

One man who dominated the headlines for weeks was Francis Schlatter, an 1884 immigrant to America from Alsace, France. Raised a Catholic, he was supposed to have been born blind, deaf, and ruptured but had healed himself by faith in "the Father." After working as a shoemaker in New York, he went to Denver in 1892. The next summer, compelled by Providence, he began a barefoot pilgrimage of self-denial and healing. In 1895 he reached the Hispanic Rio Grande villages south of Albuquerque, where he began herding sheep and quietly healing the Navajo Indians. He became known as the "New Mexican Messiah" and the "Second Messiah."[10] *In mid-September, following a fast of forty days, Schlatter was called by "the Father" to return to Denver to open his healing ministry at the home of E. L. Fox, who had visited him in Albuquerque (Mayfield 2).*

On the night of 13 November, after fifty-eight days of public treatment, Schlatter suddenly left Denver. He was last seen in Hastings, Colorado, traveling south along the railroad tracks, riding his big white horse, Butte. After he left the railroad lines and entered New Mexico, he disappeared. With her typical wit and candor, Peattie drew a perceptive psychological profile of a man (indeed of all men and women) who becomes deluded with power.

❧ One cannot too much admire the adroitness of Schlatter, the healer, in disappearing mysteriously. It was really the most histrionic thing he could have done, and is calculated to pique into acuter interest the curiosity of the people. A mysterious disappearance is a part of the dramatic unity of such a role as this powerful young man is playing. And it is, by the way, a role well worth the playing. People of dull imagination can see nothing but disinterestedness in his work, because he will not, forsooth, accept money for his services. But money – bah! What stuff it is compared to other things! Could money buy such elation as Schlatter feels when he sees hundreds of people awaiting his touch, believing in him, loving him, almost adoring him? Could money buy the sense of power which exalts him when he sees the crutches of the lame dropped and hears the suffering declare that their pains have ceased? May he not well be forgiven for believing in himself?

I once knew a man who had failed at everything, and who thereafter became a Christian science healer. He was an amiable but useless member of his own household, without any particular authority over his own children.

Francis Schlatter in 1895. (Courtesy of Colorado Historical Society, 10029143)

His wife observed her marital obligations by studying his taste in cooking, but she shed no tears when he went to Kansas on a healing expedition. The man, though commonplace enough under ordinary circumstances, came suddenly to believe in his power to heal the afflicted. And did he do it? Why of course he did. All the people who had gone grumbling around in the outlying districts of the Kansas towns, came, listened, believed, and recovered from their nervous dyspepsia, their hysterics, their headaches, their backaches, their rheumatism and what not. Some of the believers were even cured of their selfishness – truth to tell, 10 per cent of the sickness of a chronic sort is only a form of selfishness anyway. But one day the healer lost his grip. He ceased to believe in himself. Perhaps he was bored. Anyhow the fizz got off his champagne and he came home and resolved himself into amiable uselessness once more, and has since become himself the victim of dyspepsia.

Schlatter has, however, played a stronger part and amid more inspiring scenery. He is, very likely, honestly self-deluded, which of course makes life all the more interesting to him. The self-deluded are among the world's greatest leaders. It takes such a one to lead to the greatest victories, whether they are on the field of battle, or in the field of morals. Sanity dare not attempt what insanity will attempt and carry to success. Men will not follow a sane leader where they will an insane one. It takes a vision – seeing Joan of Arc to lead a hopeless army to victory. It takes a Mohammed to penetrate the dull and selfish intellects of an indolent race. It takes an opium-eating Poe to make the art which redeems American letters from mediocrity. Vive la Schlatter! May he play his passionate role down upon some pretty martyrdom, which will save him from the humiliation of an anticlimax!

"A Word with the Women" – For the Sake of Love
26 October 1895

When the division supervisor of the Union Pacific believed that faith healer Francis Schlatter had cured him of injuries he suffered in an accident, the railroad offered free passes to all employees and their immediate families ("Denver the Mecca"). More than two hundred people daily took advantage of the twenty-four-hour round trip by way of Cheyenne, Wyoming, and the offer raised havoc with the railroad stations and engine yards ("Steady Stream").[11]

Omaha pastors were divided in their opinion about Schlatter. Dr. S. Wright Butler believed that the man was sincere, a little unbalanced mentally but morally alright; Rabbi Leo M. Franklin did not believe the man was endowed with divine power, but he did consider him basically honest; and Rev. F. H. Sanderson, pastor of Trinity Methodist Episcopal Church, believed that Schlatter was sincere but had some sort of hypnotic power over people, adding, "People have been humbugged and always will be from now until the dawn of the

A crippled woman waiting to be healed by Francis Schlatter in Denver, 1895. (Library of Congress, Prints and Photographs Division, LC-USZ62-105413)

millennium" ("Who Is This" 2).[12] *Although Schlatter accepted no gifts or money for his curative powers, others were not so scrupulous. As a part of Schlatter's healing process, each person would leave a handkerchief, which he would take into his hands, bless, and distribute the next day for "home treatment" (Magill 76). Soon after his disappearance, the Boston Store in Omaha offered for sale, at twenty-five cents apiece, handkerchiefs that a man named W. H. Levy said were blessed by Schlatter. In fine print, store owners noted that these handkerchiefs were to be sold only as mementos and souvenirs ("Schlatter Blessed Them"). Peattie likely penned this sentimental tale to warn her readers not to be duped by rumors.*

❧ If it had not been for Ben she would not have minded. She had grown used to her drooping arm and her weary limp. She had given up expecting to play any active part in the world, and bore the long, idle days with patience. Other women had homes, husbands, children, but these had come to seem to her the most marvelous attainments. She regarded the accumulations of such possessions as beyond her. She could not even imagine what it would be like to have a man say: "I love you." At least, she could never have imagined it before she met Ben. After that, it was different – very different indeed. Ben was a young telegrapher who held a railroad position in the town where Janet lived, and at the invitation of her stepfather he had called at the house. Janet had not the least interest in him before he came, and did not think he would more than look at her, to pity her affliction. But on the contrary, he spent most of his evening near her chair, in the corner where the geraniums were, and the goldfish, and the canary. Janet gloried in color, and the scarlet of the flowers, the bright breast of the canary, and the iridescent gleams of the fish were her delight. Her own hair was a reddish gold, which lent a splendor to her pallid face. She blossomed out into happiness that evening, and talked of the subjects which were her delight, but which she was usually too shy to mention. So Ben came often at night, when the last train was out and the telegraph office closed. He brought her books which they read together, and he added growing plants to her window garden. They were very happy till one day – well, one day their eyes met with a new meaning. For a second they gazed in rapture. It was as if they had seen the apocalypse. Then the rapture faded. Their young faces grew white and cold. Neither spoke. Their misery was beyond speech. Ben got up and left the house, stumbling as he went. From Janet's eyes the tears fell slowly on her withered hand.

In the days that followed they kept apart, yet watched for glimpses of one another – yet, looking, would not speak, and grieved at the silence, longing as lovers long, piqued as only lovers can be piqued, and full of transient suspicions, which melted in the sun of their love. In the midst of all this trial she read of a strange man – a mystic mendicant, with power beyond that of most living men, to bless the spirit and make whole the body. All day, in the city's common streets he stood, without food or sustenance, with soul intent on others' good, healing by touch and word those who came to him. Simple and sweet, they said he was, taking no pay from any man, living only to use the power which God had given him. Janet read and was fired with an idea. Once, when Ben went by, watching her from sidelong eye, she summoned him. He came reluctantly, because he dreaded the torture of their meeting eyes. But he came. She gave him the paper to read. He said nothing then, but at night he came and laid a roll of money in her lap.

"It is all I have in the world," he said. "Take it and go." She looked back her speechless gratitude, and he, stooping, laid his trembling lips on hers for the first time.

The journey ended, Janet stood with the throng in the city street. The line of waiting people reached far down the street, carriages were there in numbers, with the rich in them, yet to reach the simple friend who stood there to bless them, these must dismount and mingle with the rest. No respecter of persons was he, but a man who stood as one bearing a message. For half a day Janet rested wearily on her crutches, faint with fatigue, and at last she came to the healer.

"For the sake of love, help me," she said.

"For the sake of love," he answered, lifting one hand in reverence, "I pray you may be helped." He held the withered hand in his, and Janet felt the magnetism of his spirit spread over her like a balm. He touched the helpless knee softly with his finger, then, serene, and simple, motioned her on. Before Janet was a woman who shouted out that she could see, although she had been blind. Near her was a man who in awe stricken tones whispered that all his pain was gone. Janet went back to her room, gathered her things and started for her home. She laid down in the whirling train, expecting to awaken in the morning, healed. She never doubted. And so she slept, dreaming a dream.

Ben, in the morning, heard the train coming, far, far down the track, and hastened out, half blind with fear and hope. It stopped but a moment, and Janet did not appear. He leaped upon the train, then saw her at the other end. She was not using her crutches, because she and they were being carried. They laid her in the station on a couch. She looked at Ben, but she could not speak. The curse of living death had enveloped her whole frame. Her eyes looked their despair, but tongue could not speak, and both sad little hands lay helpless now. Ben stooped again before them all, and laid his lips on hers – this for the last time. A week of waiting and the end! Ben was transferred to another station, and as he left, looking at the cemetery on the hill, he saw the fires had got in and charred the grass, and out of the blackness the headstones rose like ghosts.

"The Law and the Lynchers"

18 October 1891

In February 1890, Ed Neal, a white man, was convicted of murdering an elderly farm couple, Allan and Dorothy Jones, stealing horses and cattle under their care, and burying one body in a manure heap and the other in a millet stack. Neal was sentenced to death. After two appeals, the Omaha Supreme Court upheld his guilt. At about 8:30 on Saturday morning, 10 October 1891, approximately 250 people, who had obtained from Sheriff Boyd tickets to watch the hanging, began to arrive.[13]

Meanwhile, Joe Coe, alias George Smith, a black man and alleged rapist of five-year-old Lizzie Yates, was awaiting his preliminary hearing in the city jail. Word circulated that he would serve only three years for his crime – only twenty years even if the victim died. Rumors escalated to a false report that Lizzie had died. Soon, one hundred men broke into the jail, dragged the alleged rapist into the street, kicked him to death, and then lynched his mutilated body.[14]

Peattie did not let the issue rest. As the legislature convened in January 1893, Peattie lobbied against the death penalty.[15] *With the issue still pending in 1895, Peattie took the matter before the Omaha Woman's Club, where she proposed that Omaha women "express their hearty approval" of the removal of the statute condoning "legal murder." The resolution passed, but only by a small majority. An unsigned newspaper account of the meeting voiced the disappointment of the "small majority": "They wouldn't let a citizen smoke a cigarette, but were perfectly willing that one citizen should take the life of another – so long as he had legal sanction" ("Is Opposed").*

❧ A few days ago a man was murdered for murdering. The first crime was committed by a mysterious man, with an unconfessed identity, who, though he seemed to have some brains, was so stupid as to make a criminal of himself. The second crime was committed by the law.

On the day of the commission of the second crime the *World-Herald* said: "For two days the consciousness of the crime about to be committed has poisoned the moral atmosphere of the city." And it added: "A city which sees its judiciary sanction statutory homicide cannot have high ideals."

A sensible man going down in the street car that morning read these remarks and smiled.

"I get tired of this occult twaddle," he said. "What is meant by moral

Crowd awaiting the execution of Ed Neal outside the Douglas County Courthouse, 1891. (Douglas County Historical Society Collections, Omaha, Nebraska)

atmosphere? We're too sentimental nowadays. It's a matter of common sense and of economy to hang a man like Neal. He deserves the worst he can get."

There was a man sitting behind him and he rattled the chains that made a jingling guard along the side of the car.

"It isn't a question of what Neal deserves," he said, "it's a question of the right of the city to so degrade itself. Economy is that which brings the greatest good to the greatest number. I think every man and woman in Omaha has been injured by Neal's sentence. Neal's punishment is not worth that much to the community. It has cost $10,000 to bring him the gallows. That $10,000 would better have been spent in caring for him in the penitentiary. Then the state would have been protected and it would not have red hands."

"But it's the law," said the other.

"My friend," the other man said, "the law is an experiment. And every citizen is more or less the victim of it."

The car had reached Harney street. Two blocks away a grim little brick structure stood in the shadow of the picturesque county building. About it, moving here and there like a flock of crows, were black-coated men and boys. A fresh pine stockade shone in the morning sun.

Behind the stockade was a gallows.

A woman with a baby in her arms got off the car and walked toward the stockade. Three young fellows had started before her.

"It's curious," said the man who did not believe in a moral atmosphere, "the morbidity of some people."

About noon the men in their offices began to feel restless. There was a sense of oppression, although the day was so fine. The Missouri was beautiful for once, and blue as the Columbia. On the distant bluffs the mists slept in rich autumnal languor.

The women at work in their homes wondered why their hands trembled as they kneaded their bread or fed their children.

At twelve of the clock a young reporter staggered out of the grim little building on Harney street, and as he made his way blindly through the dense crowd about the building, he saw only the convulsive strugglings of a man who had just been strangled in the name of the law.

There was something peculiar about this crowd without the jail. It was dissatisfied. It looked baffled.

"The people have smelt blood and they haven't been fed with raw meat," said he to himself. "It isn't safe to rouse a hound's appetite unless you can gratify it."

One hundred thousand men and women at noon of Friday, October 9, were thinking of a man who was being murdered. Out of the 100,000 less than 100 saw the deed done.

It was in that crowd of ungratified men about the jail that one man, laboring under a misconception, started a terrible rumor.

It was only a rumor that a baby was dead. That was not much in itself. But within that jail was the man who was responsible for her death – and not by means of common murder.

Fancy this! Here in this populous and safe city, a lassie, barely 5, goes to play in the familiar precincts of her father's doorway. Fifteen minutes later she comes in to her mother blighted – shamed and wounded at once – suffering strange, nameless perplexity and unspeakable disgust – degraded by a sudden meeting with hell!

The men around the jail talked about it.

"We have children ourselves," they say.

"It's his fifth victim."

"They tried to punish him for his last damnable crime," cried another, "and why didn't they do it? Because no one could tell whether the ground on which the crime was committed lay in Nebraska or Iowa."

"That's what the law does for you."

"What's the penalty?"

"Twenty years if the child dies."

"That leaves the rattlesnake plenty of time to do more biting."

"It's only three years if the child lives."

"Good God!"

"That's good sense! Oh! He'll have a chance to kill more babies."

It was then that men began to look at each other in a strange way, and that something happened which it would be impossible to put in words. It was the sudden growth of a terrible mental disease. It germinated in the stockade where the gallows was, and it spread over the city. Men passing each other on the street, or leaning together at the bars, or dealing with each other over counters or through bank windows, or lunching about the shops said:

"Do you know that little girl is dead?"

"Where's the nigger?"

"Oh! He's in jail."

"How long does he go up for?"

"Twenty years, if he can be proved guilty."

And then again the men looked strangely at each other, and the infection spread like the black plague.

It is in incontestable fact that women working in remote parts of the city, who had conversed with no one for hours, began as the afternoon wore on to think strange, angry thoughts, and they all whirled in a sort of red tumult around that loathsome creature in the jail. And as they looked at their own little daughters at play, thoughts foreign to their humanity took possession of them.

This fever raged in every vein and artery of the city.

A few were not stirred. They were apt to be men of large affairs who have ceased to care for individuals in caring for classes. Or they were gentlemen belonging to the profession of the law, who had got in the habit of thinking very highly of the law – and who had forgotten that it is the people who make it, and that one of the ways of making a good law is to break a bad one. These men look at things in a very dispassionate way. They are the accomplished advocates of a vast perplexity. The common public sometimes has difficulty in finding out why it takes such learning to secure justice, and now and then some ordinary fellow who has time to think a bit as he cobbles his shoes or sews at his harness, gives it out as his opinion that where there is the most law there is the least justice. And there are others who say that when any expression of the mind, like religion or literature or law, becomes complex then it ceases to become effective in proportion to its complexity. And the women – who have no power of reasoning – say that a device for the securing of just punishments and exculpations which will permit a man to escape because of a technicality is only a great miscarriage of justice – it is an obstacle, maintained at enormous expense and so involved as to require libraries for its explanation, and the most brilliant men of all ages for its exposition.

The afternoon wore on, and even a stranger walking the streets would have perceived that the men on it were not in a normal condition. At dinner that night there was only one thought on the minds of the masses. It was this crime which was several days old, but the enormacy of which seemed only to be just appreciated. And after dinner the men began to leave their homes.

The women said at parting: "There is nothing too bad for him."

"It cost $10,000 to hang Neal," they said, "and a little economy is not bad, is it?" None of these people felt like anarchists. They were for the most men and women who had never knowingly committed a crime in their lives. None of them could have explained the hot throbbing in their brains.

From every part of the city the men began to hasten toward a common focus – the little jail, above its stone steps. This was the magnet, and the men were drawn to it like nails.

Early in evening, the people in the theater began to hear a formidable noise. It was far more tragic than any miming. Among them was a lady who had never seen an act of violence. She had never even stood at a death bed. She had never injured any living creature. All her life she had lived in a sort of delicate seclusion, such as women of fine tastes are happiest in. She was young and beloved and prosperous – the last person in the world to sympathize with violence or crime or cruelty. She stood at the window at the second story of the theater and looked out on the mass of men below her. These men now numbered many thousand. They thronged the high terrace, they filled the street, they blocked the walk. Sometimes a frightful silence fell on them. Sometimes their words had a fatal significance. And always there was the hollow hammering of the sledges and the axes against the steel bars of the cage within the jail where the ravished was. Now and then, when these blows ceased for a moment, the lady knew that the men who had been working were relieved by other men. None of them had weak muscles or were novices in the use of the hammer. They came, doubtless, from the machine shops. All about them were men with arms less trained to toil who would gladly have assisted. Jammed up by the door was a reporter writing his notes on the wall. So closely was the crowd welded about him that sometimes he could not even move his elbow. The office boy, a fine fellow, made his way back and forth between the reporter and the office carrying copy. He made his way through the crowd when no one else could.

"Make way, make way!" he cried importantly. "Here comes a man with a battering ram. Here's a man with a rope!" The crowd made way for him obediently, and he slipped through like a snake.

A great deal had happened before this. The sheriff had been silenced after his half-hearted appeal and taken off at a convenient distance – which was really a kindness and saved him a great deal of embarrassment. The deputies were half drunk, and not inclined to make a stalwart resistance. The mayor had sent down a hose cart with the intention of quieting the public fever with a cold water application.

When a fireman went to connect the hose with the water plug a man with a hatchet in his hand went up to him and said with easy jocularity:

"Sonny, you don't want to put that hose on there, do you?"

The fireman looked at the man. The man was smiling and toying with the hatchet. Then the fireman smiled too.

"I'm not very anxious," he said.

"I thought not," said the man with the hatchet.

The hose, meanwhile, was cut in many pieces. The cart was run far down the street.

"We're busy," said a man to the driver, who was looking after the horses, which had been cut loose, "Don't interrupt us."

It was marvelous, the appearance of preconcertation. Someone was found willing to take up every necessary task.

There were two distinguished Englishmen in the crowd, and they looked at the goings on through their eye glasses.

"What do you think of this?" said an American to them.

"Ah! my dear sir," said one of them courteously, "you know we are always interested in the institutions of the country."

Men of all classes, in every walk of life, of all shades of religious belief and unbelief were in the crowd.

The lady up in the window saw hundreds of men she knew – men she had met only in drawing rooms or in their homes. Now she hardly recognized them – not because of any change in face nor because of any alteration of manner, but because of the fierce determination that seemed to reach from them to that trembling wretch behind the steel bars – the bars which were giving way as the iron doors had given way before she began to watch the tragedy. This office boy who was carrying the copy was amusing himself. Every little while he leaned out of the window and entertained the crowd with fictitious bits of news, always sensational in their nature.

"Five minutes more and they'll have him out."

"Get the rope ready – you'll soon need it." As a matter of fact he was only trying to keep in the good graces of the crowd. He wanted to be allowed to convey the sheets of paper that the reporter was filling with straggling words. An old scout with white curls on his shoulders, his breast covered with badges, his face bearing the peculiar beauty of the half-breed gave out equally sensational scraps of intelligence.

The woman up in the window wondered if those bars would ever give way.

She wanted the negro out! What for? Why to be hung! To be killed – no matter how. She quivered with a sort of hatred. A loathing of the monster shook her. The pitiable innocence of the wronged baby came to her like a passion. She had become infected with this strange disease which was swaying the men below her. She hated the men who tried to save the negro after they got him out on the open terrace. She saw the crowd lose sight of their victim and hunt for him this way and that. Little knots of men ran hither and thither. They tore open the door of cabs to look within. They cried out that he was escaping. Then she saw them fight him. They kicked his body, they wrenched his arms. They struck at him with clods. All of his clothes were torn from him. They cried out derisively that he said they were killing him. He had a rope around his neck minutes before he was hung. Someone bound his old blue shirt around his loins. By this time he was dead. His terrified heart had stifled him.

A man climbed the motor pole and threw the rope over the cross-wire. The action aroused a terrible apprehension.

"We will all be electrocuted," said one.

It is quite true that the crowd was so closely packed that if one man had been killed with electricity, all would have been injured. Then suddenly, before the lady realized what all this meant, a brown, limp body, with legs dangling like those of a rag baby, hands bound, head inert, shot up above the crowd. For a moment this lady was dizzy with exultation. A sentiment primitive as anything a cave-dweller ever knew made her shut her teeth together. The disease had reached its height. And the rattlesnake had been killed.

That's all there was to it. From that moment the disease began to decline. The following night a fainter delirium showed itself when the people tried to free from the jail the men who had been arrested for participating in the lynching. But the deputies had recovered their senses. The police had become re-embodied – the night of the lynching they were nebulous as air. The offended chief of police, who had not been invited to the first hanging – that conducted by the sheriff – had forgotten this breach of etiquette and was on hand to do his duty. No one was sorry that the negro was dead. A few feared that Omaha had been hurt – they looked at the thing from a monetary standpoint. Some others – mostly attorneys – thought the whole occurrence shameful. They forgot that even had the man been innocent and been wrongfully executed the people would have committed no worse a blunder than the law has frequently done. One attorney who is an American citizen, though only a little while in this country, gave it as his opinion that no man should now be safe in Omaha. He has forgotten that it was in defense of innocence that this avenging crowd congregated. He had seen only European mobs, which make riot for a holiday. In America men are very busy, and they only pause to fight for a principle. This man had not the emotional quality. He did not catch the spirit of the crowd. He thought it was always wrong to break the law. He forgot that some of the greatest heroes of history had proved their heroism by breaking laws. There is no use in imagining that this crowd was working according to a theory. It was confronted with a fact – a condition.

As for me, I am glad the man is dead.

Is there anyone who is sorry?

But I wish he had died by act of providence.

It is because I think so much of humanity that I think so little of law. Law should be obeyed, not because it is law, but because it is intrinsically right. Besides, it is changed more or less at every setting of the legislature.

That which makes a moral community is not law, but education.

Omaha had just given her citizens an object lesson in hanging. They were quick to imitate it.

The moral tone had been lowered.

Capital punishment has never done anything but harm in this state. It has secured the escape of notorious murderers. It has turned temperamental criminals loose upon the public. The present law makes a jury find a man or woman innocent of murder absolutely, or else it forces them to hang him or her. There are few men who, in cold blood, will consign a fellow being to death. Because only very hardened or egotistical men forget the mandate, "Thou shalt not kill."

The interference with punishment is also intolerable. One is never sure when a man is safe shut in the penitentiary that he will stay secure.

Sentimentality and cruelty are equally degrading. A man with a natural tendency to rape or murder should never be allowed his freedom. Nine-tenths of the men in the penitentiaries should be in the insane asylum. Crime is generally a disease. It wants the services of a physician. Continued safely, the public cannot be harmed, but a criminal should no more be let loose than a tarantula.

Such treatment would be at once merciful and severe. That is to say, it would be just. But the state [must] remember that in punishing one man it has no right to injure others. Every time it stains its records with the blood of a man it directly injures the public morals. It confirms the disgusting tendencies of diseased minds. It makes temperate citizens delirious.

Capital punishment is wrong because it is founded upon and inculcates the desire for revenge – an eye for an eye. The law is degraded when it takes this attitude, and legislators are ignorant when they advocate it. Only very short-sighted men who have thought little about the question of moral responsibility advocate such a theory. It belongs to the age when men were governed only by force. In a country where men govern themselves it is different. To restrain, to educate, to treat, to cure – that is the purpose of the state with high ideals. It is the physician, not the hangman, who should be employed, very frequently.

Do you know who should be indicted of the killing of the negro ravisher?

It is the state of Nebraska.

If Neal had not been hung Smith would not have been lynched.

The day after the double tragedy a little boy in our neighborhood was playing with his dog. Is it necessary to say that he loved it?

Every boy loves his dog. That day he put a rope around the dog's neck. He threw the rope over a taut clothes-line.

"What are you doing?" shouted a man who was passing.

"I am going," cried the little boy, looking at the man with his pretty blue eyes, "to hang my dog!" He had learned the lesson of killing.

That was the moral atmosphere of this city after the legal hanging.

The act of a private individual or any number of private individuals, however culpable, can never be as degrading in its effects as a crime committed in the name of the state.

Law is valuable only when it expresses the best instincts of man. When it represents his worst tendencies it becomes a drag on progress.

CHAPTER 3

Community Concerns

"All really interesting occasions of a social nature are more or less associated with good coffee."

In Omaha in the 1880s and 1890s, hordes of entrepreneurs took advantage of the lucrative opportunities available in the adolescent city. Elia Peattie was especially aware, and often critical, of the materialism of these newly genteel families who participated greedily in the excesses of the Gilded Age, a time when society worshiped wealth and celebrated leisure, when prosperity provided a veneer of respectability for the new moneyed classes, and when immigrants thronged to the cities, causing the upper class and the new middle class to spread to the suburbs.[1]

The effects of "big business" trickled down to Nebraska. The telegraph and the Union Pacific Railroad, which passed through Omaha in 1866 and linked the east and west coasts by 1869, played a key role in the economy and politics of Omaha. The city became a thriving railroad and meatpacking town, and many entrepreneurs of trade and commerce profited from the influx of middle-class professionals, businessmen and their families, and working-class immigrants. Quickly, a class of affluent capitalists surfaced in Omaha, their Victorian mansions towering like monuments to success on a prairie once blanketed by big bluestem.[2] *The urbanization of Nebraska had begun, and with it the problems of large population centers everywhere.*

Always questioning the moral, ethical, and political foundations of American society, Peattie encouraged her readers to reflect on the world around them. Her comments about the people and events in Omaha frequently ruffled egos, and critical feedback – quite often from rival columnists and editors – littered the editorial pages of Omaha newspapers. No one could ever accuse Elia Peattie of not having opinions, and no matter how controversial the issue, she took a stand – often against the current of popular sentiment.

Even if Peattie disagreed with some of the social, political, and religious leaders, she believed they had a right to voice their opinions, even if they were extreme. In a comment about Frances Willard, president of the Women's Christian Temperance Union and a leading educator, Peattie argued, "It is always

Omaha residence of Christian Hartman, founder of the Omaha Lead Works and city treasurer, 1891. (Douglas County Historical Society Collections, Omaha, Nebraska)

best for any leader of any cause to stand identified with that cause exclusively and absolutely. A leader must be extreme in action, passionate in proclamation, single in purpose and with a capacity for martyrdom. The followers may modify, amend and compromise. But the calm, critical, well-rounded natures who believe in many things, advocate numerous ideas of reform, and temper their views with policy, can give no inspiration to others."[3]

Peattie herself became politically involved in one of the only areas where nineteenth-century women had the right to vote – for the public school board candidates. So concerned was she about education in Omaha that she accepted the nomination to run for the school board in 1894. Peattie was endorsed by the Democrats, the Populists, and the Omaha World-Herald, *of course, and supported by the Omaha Woman's Club. The campaign became contentious, especially concerning the issue of women voting. Although women had not been granted universal suffrage, any woman in Nebraska who had school-age children or owned property assessed in her own name was entitled to vote for the school board. Many assumed that Peattie would win easily; however, when the votes were counted she came in sixth out of ten candidates. Most people, even the women, voted a straight Republican ticket. In a concession editorial, Peattie, although disappointed in the lack of support from women voters, urged women not to be discouraged and to continue to try to elect a woman to the school board. "In no one branch of civic work," she declared, "is woman so much needed as in that which supervises the schools. It is fitting and appropriate that she be there. Her duties will not be of the same sort as those which the men assume. The men may attend to the finances in a general way, and dole out the janitorships to their political henchmen." Thanking everyone who "fought for the cause of woman's representation," Peattie, always the gladiator, concluded with this retaliation: "To those who have misrepresented my words, who have distorted my actions and who have repaid favors received at my hands with treachery, I also return thanks. My knowledge of human nature has been enlarged – and that is an invaluable thing to a person who turns a penny by the writing of fiction" ("Was Not a Partisan Fight"). Although Peattie's attitudes about social, religious, and political issues would not be considered "extreme" by twenty-first-century standards, she voiced her opinions clearly and strongly in her editorials, and when the need arose, followed up her words with action.*

"Stand Up, Ye Social Lions: Mrs. Peattie Arraigns the Sickly Forms That Sin from Nature's Rule"

7 January 1894

With industrialism and the rapid growth of trade and service industries, many Americans, including newly arrived immigrants, found very different occupations from those of their working-class parents. Because late-nineteenth-century America was an especially "open society" with considerable mobility between classes, opportunities to rise abounded for those wishing to gain social prestige along with their new wealth. Even in the egalitarian cities of the West, a class-based, not classless, society emerged, although it was not as rigid as in the more established East. Competition for acceptance into the elite class became an all-consuming preoccupation for many of the nouveau riche; in America, very simply, money determined status.

Although both Robert and Elia came from working-class backgrounds, they began to wedge themselves precariously, through industry and risk taking, within the middle class. However, Elia had no desire to follow the rules necessary to ascend socially, for she scorned the wealthy class as superficial, spendthrift, conventional, and consumed with public appearance rather than intellectual or ethical development.[4] *The following article began with a long excerpt on manners in London society from the* San Francisco Argonaut *that has been omitted here.*

Emma Schaper dressed for a social gathering, 1908.
(Courtesy of author)

❧ When one touches upon Omaha society, one touches a tender point. There are so many persons in it who are there almost by force of circumstances, and whose hearts are warm, and their lives pure and useful in spite of their connection with a body that aspires to be purely fashionable, that one hesitates to relapse into unkind generalizations. Omaha society, for the very reason that it is as yet new, flexible and uninformed, is not confirmed in the worse vices of its kind. But it already possesses much of which there is cause to be ashamed.

. . . It is a well known fact, and one hears it whispered everywhere, that hardly one of the parties and balls of the winter has been a success, owing to the fact that the young men would not dance, nor talk, nor pay attention to the young ladies, nor do anything that a gentleman is expected to do on a gala occasion. They have stood around the doors in stupid groups, looking cynical – or trying to do so – and discussing, without much interest, the relative charms of the young ladies, who, arrayed for their approval, and launched out into society for their allurement, have endeavored in vain to make themselves attractive.

Perhaps it is not the young men, so much as society that is wrong. There has always been, and always will be, something almost shameless in the cold-blooded putting up of a young girl into the matrimonial market. The coarseness of it is disguised, to be sure. It is an immemorial custom, to begin with, and most folks are apt to think a thing venerable because it is old, because it is surrounded by a glamour of elegance, happiness and youth. But if the facts are plainly presented they show that the entrance of a young girl into society is the formal admission of her readiness for marriage. The young men certainly think of it so. They have the arrogance of sultans, the cynicism of rogues – although they are not such – they know they are expected to compare, examine and select. They know that the money so prodigally spent, the dinners, balls, costumes, carriages, flowers, wines, ceremonies and all the nameless elaborations of society are for their benefit in a way. And it is little wonder that they become rapidly spoiled, or that they do not show proper respect for the mothers who thus flaunt their daughters, or the daughters who prink and pose for their benefit.

It would seem as if any woman who possessed so beautiful and dear a charge as a daughter – a girl woman – would spend her best efforts in trying to protect her daughter from the inquisitorial glances, the degrading frivolity, the envy, malice, treachery and contentions of society. One would think that pride would insist that the daughter should be sought, and not that she should be set up in the public place for view. One would imagine that the more a mother had traveled, studied and possessed, the more refined would be her heart, and the more desirous she would be of teaching her daughter to put humanity before society, the delights of learning before those of flirting, and the preservation of health before gayety. Think what a pitiful exchange all this is for happy home life. I do not want to be sour and absurd. I would not think of denying any wholesome pleasure to the young. I think young men and women should be much together. But when society interferes with them, when it introduces the chaperon in the peculiar way that it does, when it throws young men and women together under such conditions that both are forced to think of the materialistic side of a matrimonial union, then it seems to me that the sweetness of youth, and love, and life is deliberately taken from them.

No one supposes for a moment that these young men and women want to be competitors in expenditure, or that they desire to be meanly critical, or to give up the best things of life for the tiresome round of noisy gatherings where people clamor like peacocks and eat half melted ices and oily salads. Not at all. They are forced into it all, and only now and then is there one who, having the money and position which enables him or her to enter society, has the courage and peculiarity to renounce it all and to live the unselfish instead of the selfish life.

The idea that society polishes the manners of the young is only true to a very limited extent. I have seen it replace modesty with bravado, truth with deception, kindness with pertness, gentleness with bluster, and politeness with arrogance. Society, so far as I know, does not teach veneration for the aged, love of parents, love of learning, love of humanity, sympathy for the unfortunate, beauty of thought, or the brotherhood of man. I have seen all the graces of manner possessed by the home-brought-up boy to an equal extent with the society-developed boy. And I think the training and the manners of the home have a much more formative effect than society upon the manners of the young, so far as the improving of them goes. . . .

Society must, if it would show a reason for existence, have some dignity about it, and some brains. It must have other things in common besides champagne and jack pots. It must not ask guests to its houses to fleece them out of their money at the beguiling poker table. It can never lay claim to hospitality while it does this. It must not permit its young girls to drink so much champagne that they have to be cared for by their friends. There is no use in pretending that society has elegant ladies while some of them disgrace it like that. It must not have in it persons who owe their grocers while they buy diamonds, and who freeze the grocer's collectors with frigid stares and rebuking voice till the poor man cringingly apologizes for existence.

All this sort of thing may do over in Europe, but it isn't what we want here, in the country we all love, and would beautify with fine acts. We do not complain because society is elegant, or rich, or refined, or well dressed, or courtly. So far as it is these things it is to be commended. Would we all possessed these good things. But in so far as it is coarse, stupid, dishonest, of low taste, mercenary, selfish and ill-bred, we do condemn it. We condemn the young men here who do not even thank their hostesses for the money and effort they expend in entertaining them, and warn them that the edict has already gone forth from some of the really best houses in town that they will be punished for their boorish manners by not being entertained there any more. We condemn the young girls for their ridiculous affections, their utterly inane exchange of flatteries, and their belittling conversation. We condemn the men for their pretension – which they cannot afford, and for which the tradesmen suffer. We condemn the women for the rivalries to which they incite their daughters, and the coarse ideas they implant in those young minds. We condemn them for not impressing upon their daughters any of the responsibilities and duties of life – for not looking after their hearts and minds as well as their bodies.

Society – the more leisurely part of us – could help us all if it would. Why is it false to its trust? Why does it set us poor examples? Why are its manners bad and its tongue sharp, and its acts selfish?

"What Women Are Doing" – The Art of Shopping

8 February 1891

Peattie frequently upbraided the wealthy people of Omaha for their materialism, their superficiality, and, in this 1891 column, their lack of economic support for their own Omaha businesses. By 1890, Omaha had become the nation's second-largest city – between Chicago and San Francisco – with a population of 140,452 and boasting more than 186 manufacturing firms, a wholesale trade of over $42,000,000, and internal revenue collections of over $3,166,000 (1890 dollars). If Omaha women were going to spend money lavishly, she insisted, they ought to help their "Western Metropolis" continue to prosper (Omaha Board of Trade, Omaha *21).*

❧ The women of Omaha have one foolish habit. They insist – a shamefully large number of them – on buying their dry goods in eastern cities.

Now every cultivated and thoughtful woman will feel as much pride in the city she lives in as a man of cultivation and thoughtfulness. She will have public spirit. She will reason about the effect of her acts on her neighbors.

An unidentified woman shopping near Albert Edholm's jewelry store, Omaha, ca, 1890s. (Nebraska State Historical Society Photograph Collections)

She will perceive that she is a moral force, and that morality has a great deal to do with commerce. Give a man a way to earn his dinner and he will not steal it. This applies throughout all the vast system of commerce, often in complex ways, but unfailingly, all the same.

It is wrong for a woman to send to New York or to Chicago to purchase anything that she can get in Omaha, if she can buy in Omaha as advantageously to herself. For by sending her money, earned in Omaha, to be spent in Chicago or Philadelphia, she impoverishes the city she lives in to just that degree. The industries of Omaha are still young. The system of credit is large – too large – for various reasons, but principally because as yet the industries are in what may be termed an experimental state. If women will think a little while they will see that they themselves are a part of that extensive plan of reciprocity which exists in every community. They themselves are injured if a merchant in the city fails, for the reason that that merchant gave his money in turn to other men – to the husband of the woman who sends her money away, thus defrauding her own husband, as she can clearly see, if she pauses to reason it out.

The men of a community cannot afford to ignore each other. They must assist in sustaining local enterprises, not alone for the good of their neighbors, but for their own good as well. But though all women with brains in their heads must have perceived this fact, yet it is a lamentable fact that thousands of women in Omaha send east for everything they wish to buy. The heaviest purchasers do this. And then they unreasonably complain that the merchants do not bring fine enough goods here. Pray what encouragement can the merchants have to import extraordinary wares when they know that the women who can afford to buy these novelties will send to Paris, New York or Chicago to purchase their supplies?

But, as a matter of fact, there is nothing that cannot be obtained in Omaha. There are houses which import unique dress patterns from Paris, every sort of lace can be procured here, every kind of underclothing, the very latest things in wraps. What is more, they can be obtained for the same price that they can in other American cities under similar conditions. It is true that occasionally there may be a large sale of rare fabrics in some of the larger cities at which bargains can be made, but there are also opportunities for bargains in Omaha, for those who want them.

I do not think much of a bargain myself. I know that in some way or another the profit rejected on that article by the merchant will be extracted from me on some other article, and though I am perfectly willing he should have that profit, I prefer to know where he is making it. I always feel better satisfied when I buy an article at its real value allowing a reasonable profit to every person who has assisted in its manufacture, its importation and its final sale. In a simpler form of domestic economics it might be well to dispense with middlemen. Perhaps there might be some saving of energy by direct dealing. But as things are now it is better for the whole community that many small profits should be made by many persons. It equalizes things better. It gives men and women bread and butter. One of the strongest arguments against a market in Omaha is that an army of middlemen will find their occupations gone. I would rather pay more for my butter, my eggs and my vegetables and have the consciousness that these other men who buy and sell are making their livelihood than get my wares cheaper and have to feed tramps at the door – tramps who were once these middlemen, or who, engaged in other occupations lowlier in their nature, were crowded out of their places by men of greater capabilities.

But this is a digression.

The gist of the matter under discussion is here: every citizen feels the benefit of a prosperous condition of a city. Perhaps it would be safe to say that in America at least, women experience the direct benefits of prosperity quicker than men. An American man desires wealth because of his family, and no sooner does he reach a state of financial comfort than he enlarges those advantages which his family enjoy. Therefore, the least that women can do is to assist in bringing about the prosperity of which they would be the greatest beneficiaries. They hinder that prosperity when they take the husband's money or their own money to send out of town.

If they cannot find what they want in the stores, it is their own fault, for there is not a merchant in town who will not be glad to send away and get what they desire. The merchants are entitled to this much consideration. No one knows better than the women that if money is desired for any charitable purpose, or any social purpose, there is an immediate cry that the "business men" must respond. Yet, the women who so carelessly ask favors of the same "business men," are the first to forget that those men must be sustained. As a matter of fact they overestimate the capabilities of these men. Very frequently the typewriter girl on $8 a week is better able to spare a little from her earnings than the man of business whose wealth is counted by hundreds of thousands of dollars. For nine times out of ten that man has responsibilities which make it a moral responsibility for him to be cautious. He is furnishing perhaps, employment to 100 men. Each of these men, at a low average, is supporting two persons besides himself. Upon the continued success of this rich man depends the comfort of these 300 persons. Therefore do not be too ready to ask this man to part with his money unless at the same time you contribute so far as you may to his continued success.

It is quite the fashion to talk about the sufferings of the poor. I fancy the sufferings of the rich are quite as bad. I notice often the perfunctory work of the employed. He drops his task the moment his hour of labor is up. He has his salary, and can count on it definitely. He has only to arrange his living expenses so that they will be met by this income and his financial troubles cease. But the man of affairs sits for hours after his workmen have gone home, laboring, arranging, thinking, planning. He belongs to no protective association. No one utters a word of pity for him. No one believes that he feels deeply responsible for all these men he is employing. No one knows how the blood hammers at his brain, and how sick with dread he often is. He is accused of lacking public spirit when he exercises the instinct of self-preservation and refuses to give to everything that every one else thinks he ought to give to. He is always supposed to be soulless.

I have often thought of the woes of the down-trodden capitalist. I have often sympathized with them.

All this sounds as if it were not to the point. But it is. It all comes back to the same thing: Why do the women send east and go east to buy their household supplies? Why do they wait till they are on the way to the seaside to purchase their summering dresses at Philadelphia and Boston? Are they so dull that they do not know a good shop when they see it? Can they not recognize fine goods? If they can, they will buy in Omaha, for they will find shops here at which they can buy anything – if they only understand the art of shopping.

"All Fuss and Feathers: Wedding Ceremonies Which Are Almost Grotesque Because of Their Flummery"

21 April 1895

Peattie was irritated at a 1895 wedding account that described "the maid of honor, bridesmaids, flowers, palms, white prayer book, veil and 'a diamond star, the gift of the groom.' The groom is mentioned most incidentally and casually. The description of the gown of the bride fills a quarter of a column. Is it a marriage – or only a wedding" ("Word with the Women," 10 March 1895). The bride's gown, flowers, food, and refreshments all attested to the family's economic stature and social aspirations. Moreover, argued Henry Ward Beecher, the display of wedding presents on the marriage day promoted guests to exhibit their own status rather than give practical gifts (Green 25). Weddings, once a family affair, were becoming pageants that advertised the social status of the bride's family, celebrating wealth, not love and commitment, and putting the bride in the center spotlight. Peattie, however, sympathized with the upstaged young grooms and favored elopement.

❧ The following dispatch appeared in the papers last week:

"Edward Howard, son of ex–County Recorder Howard, and Miss Etta Garceau, one of the most beautiful young ladies of South Bend, were to have

"The Wedding March" from *Good Manners for All Occasions: A Practical Manual* by Margaret E. Sangster, 1904.

been married this morning in St. Patrick's church. At the appointed hour the church was filled with prominent society people, when the priest appeared and announced that no wedding would occur. It develops that the bride and groom-elect left the city last night and were married at some place out of town. It is believed they were married by a squire at Niles, Michigan. The act of the young couple created a great sensation. They were to have been at home May 1 at Pittsburg, Kansas."

Now, that strikes me as being one of the most interesting newspaper paragraphs I have read for many a week of yesterdays. Of course, the "prominent society people" must have been annoyed. They must have accused the beautiful Miss Garceau of inconsideration, ill-breeding, selfishness and several other bad qualities. No doubt a great many persons thought it unbecoming; the priest was probably much pained at such intemperance of action and – the young men laughed to themselves and sympathized. For, as a general proposition, it may be said that all men would like to run away to be married. Man has never entirely got over the love of capturing his bride. Moreover, man never becomes addicted to the wedding of civilization. He may submit to it. But he does not like it. It not only bothers and mortifies him, but it actually offends something fine in his nature. He does not like to have the weeks which precede marriage given up to a great extent to the overseeing of flummeries. Only a very few men have I known who desired any display at their weddings. These were all young men who were making an excusable but not very picturesque effort to rise in society, and to develop business. They each appeared to think that business would be assisted, and social standing more or less assured by a large public wedding, at which there should be many people, many flowers, a variety of classical music, endless millinery and, incidentally, a wedding ceremony.

There must be a bit of nature of the squaw left in the civilized woman, that she should so run to the decoration of herself at an hour when one would suppose that it would be natural for her to be consumed with thoughts which left material display far in the background. I shall never forget one personal experience in my life. I knew a lovely woman, with a fine and well-trained mind. She came, in course of time, to select from many lovers a man of much firmness of character, who was nobly and devotedly attached to her. Their love was of the lofty type, and I doubt if trifling words of any sort passed between them during their courtship. Now, I fully expected the wedding to be the climax of all this, and looked to see this ceremony ideally conducted. But what was my amazement to see this woman suddenly drop all her dignity, all her beautiful love-making, and become a flurried, nervous creature, flying from milliner to dressmaker, rejecting twenty samples for a gown to telegraph for more bunches of samples, weeping over bonnets which she thought did not become her, and quarrelling with dressmakers over the fit of her gowns! It was as if Ariel, on being released from the cloven pine tree should have asked if she could have pancakes for breakfast.

The wedding was stupid. It was an anti-climax. She thought all during the ceremony that the back of her dress did not fit; he had a boil on his neck, and one of the maids tipped a tray full of water glasses over the heads of the guests – that was really the only enlivening and perfectly natural thing about the occasion. The Ideal of love sat weeping somewhere on the back stairs; and the milliners and dressmakers were with us in our thoughts and even I believe in our prayers. I am almost sure the bride prayed that no one would notice the wrinkle under the arms of her gray-blue velvet gown. I have forgotten the exact tint of the dress, or what it was called, but I expect she mentioned it accurately in the prayer. . . .

In one of his books Hamlin Garland, in his regard for the spirit of things and his disregard for form, chanced to neglect to mention the circumstances of the wedding ceremony of two of his lovers, merely speaking of them as being united in their lives. The prunes and prisms readers wrote frantically to the *Arena* to inquire if a wedding ceremony was really performed. They had to know before they could approve of the story. Garland apologized. He said the ceremony had been performed. He had not supposed that his characters seemed so grotesque that anyone would suspect them of disregarding a wise law, but he had considered a ten minute ceremony of too little consequence, in view of the purpose and passion which united his lovers, to consider it worthy of mention. His readers still could not understand. They requested him to mention the fact of the ceremony when he published the novel in book form. And he did. It may be that he also mentioned the amount of the fee and the kind of flowers the bride carried – but I am not sure.

There used to be a tradition that runaway marriages did not turn out well. So many marriages turn out ill that it would probably be fair to suspect marriages of any sort of not being absolute perfection. But there are many runaway marriages which are ideal. The Brownings fled together – Mrs. Browning gathering from her elation of spirit, and her sense of power and love, the strength to walk which she had not possessed for years. Her happy heart healed her weary body. William Henry Stoddard and Elizabeth Stoddard, both of them poets, fled together and tell of it now, even when their heads are white, with enthusiasm.

As for Gretna Green, ballad and story has made it famous and dear.

The one great objection to a runaway wedding is that it may bring much anxiety to some one who is deserving of every consideration. A mother wishes to see her daughter decorously betrothed and married, with her proper trousseau packed in new trunks, and a stock of table clothes and drawn work doilies laid away, in proper piles tied with blue ribbons. Respectability becomes a passion with the happy matron and mother. She is nothing if not seemly. And it really is a shame to view her loving heart. That is the head and front of the offending in matters similar to the historic Lochinvar incident. But the young couple at South Bend must have looked more or less after the doilies and all other evidences of respectability. Probably they meant to be proper up to the last moment. The evening before their marriage it was only natural they should be together. They went walking, of course – one talks much better under the stars, than by gaslight.

"Tomorrow," he probably said. "I ought to be the happiest man alive, and I would be if it were not for that dreadful wedding in the church. Do you think there will be many there?"

"The church will be crowded," she very likely replied, "to the doors. They will talk about my veil. They will say you looked awkward – if they notice you at all. I shall carry a white prayer book in my hand and look as stiff and uninteresting as a portrait of a lady on the walls of a picture show. I shall not think of you at all. I shall forget all about loving you, and wonder if the bridesmaids will remember how to stand, and if you have got the ring in your pocket. I should like to think of the words of the marriage, and be very happy remembering that after this I can always stay with you and be your wife. But I shall be forced to notice that papa tripped over mamma's train when he gave me away, and that the girls were giggling in the front row, and Aunt Bessie's nose was getting red from weeping."

"That's just it!" he probably cried, enthusiastically. "And then we will have to be congratulated by hundreds of people, whose names we can hardly remember, and you will be kissed by people who are not fit to touch the hem of your garment, and we will eat – we who have meat they know not of – and hours and hours will pass, with people around crying and bothering, when we ought to be at our best – when life ought to take on its highest meaning. But in that chatter we shall only be able to think about the refreshments."

"It's sacrilege," she may have said.

"It's unholy and barbarous! We are fools to submit. We were fools to consent. I've half a mind to leave it all now. If I could take you away tonight under these stars, and we could be married by some clergy man while we stood alone with none to interrupt our thoughts, how much better and lovelier it would seem."

Then there may have been a long, long silence. Then, perhaps, he kissed her. And it is possible that that was also long – long! Then he said – at least, maybe, he said:

"Why not?"

"Anything you say – anywhere with you!" is perhaps what she replied.

And so it was done – and society was cheated of a pageant, the caterer had his horrid little paper dishes of sweet breads left on his hands, the mother grieved honestly, society whispered and marveled, not understanding – and the young men laughed.

"The Mockery of Mourning: Thoughts upon Outward Signs of Inward Grief Prescribed by Convention"

30 April 1893

By the late 1800s, mourning had become a national obsession. For many Americans, influenced by Darwin's new scientific image of humans as evolutionary animals rather than creations of God, death was no longer considered sacred but simply a part of the natural selection process (Stephenson 26–27). The drift away from the religious aspects of the funeral was also reflected in the ritual itself, with more emphasis on public display, not only of wealth but also of grief. The rules of mourning for women were elaborate and strict, normally requiring wives to mourn their husbands for two and a half years, remaining in deep or full mourning for the first year. During that year, a widow's entire wardrobe had to be constructed of dull, black fabrics, including her "weeping veil," which often reached to mid-calf, her parasols, and the edges of her handkerchiefs. Nothing could shine or gleam. The blackness of her clothing symbolized her desolation within (Morley 64).[5]

The deaths of siblings and other relatives each demanded some period of public mourning, including eighteen months for a parent, twelve months for children, six months for grandparents, brothers, and sisters, three months for an aunt or uncle, and four to six weeks for first cousins (Taylor 133). Women often dressed in black for years, mourning one relative after another (see Mescher and Douglas). Children wore mourning, too. Men, however, were only required to wear plain, black suits with a black crepe armband or hatband: the wider the band, the closer the relationship to the deceased. Furthermore, they only needed to mourn their wives for three months and could remarry as soon as they pleased. Peattie, perceiving death as a personal and spiritual experience, did not commend the conformist attitudes of most mourners or the sexist expectations of mourning.

Woman in mourning, 1899. (Douglas County Historical Society Collections, Omaha, Nebraska)

❧ Why do women wear mourning?

They will reply, without a doubt, in order to make some outward evidence of their inner grief.

But the question arises, if this is so, why do not men also wear it? No one will maintain that they suffer less than women. Their hearts wear black much oftener than their hat bands do. They used, it is true, to wear it much more in former years than they do now. But at present mourning is almost exclusively a feminine demonstration, and it is rather interesting, psychologically speaking, to inquire why women should still cling to this ancient custom, while men have almost abjured it.

Anyone who stops to think on the subject for a moment or two, will perceive that men have been the ones always to make progress toward greater spirituality in matters concerning death and burial. For example, it is the men, almost without exception, who are in favor of cremation, that hygienic and economical method of disposing of the dead. But women will have no crematories. They want a grave to weep over. They want a palpable, cold, long, grass-grown grave to put wreaths on, and at which they may sit and remember the virtues of the deceased.

It may be that this is not materialism, but it looks very much like it. Men seldom visit graves, except in the novels of Mrs. Augusta Evans.

They find no solace for their woe in the purchasing of cheap flowers – for women are very apt to exercise economy in these melancholy purchases and generally choose white carnations in preference to roses. It is difficult, always, for a woman to be so prodigal that she will forget the limitations of her purse, and even when she purchases the flowery emblem of a broken life, she will pause to inquire the price, and to calculate whether or not she will have enough left over to buy the week's groceries. Of such details must the life of woman be compounded.

Mourning is a hard thing to reconcile with the sense of fitness of a woman who has really loved the person whose death she celebrates in the wearing of her solemn garments. Supposing, for example, that you had loved one man all your life – loved him from the first time that you saw him – and that you had married him, and that he was the father of your children and your constant companion, and, withal, your heart's dearest possession. And suppose that suddenly some day he should die. And that you would have to face the fact that henceforth your soul must remain silent – that it was stricken dumb – that you must simply wait, through the rest of life, for the day of death, which might – just possibly, might – reunite you. And supposing, then, that you swathe yourself in black. You drape your garments in folds suggestive of woe, yards of black hang from the bonnet on your head, you see that every letter you write bears its silent evidence to your life's disaster, and even the pocket handkerchief with which you wipe your nose proclaims the fact that your condition is a sorrowful one. You regulate all these signs with a fine nicety. The width of the hem of your veil is regulated by inexorable fashion; so is the size of the border of black on your handkerchief and your stationery.

The days drag on. Six months pass – six little months. And what happens? You buy new writing paper with a border of black but half the width of that on which you wrote in the first dread days of your sorrow; you let out the hem of your veil, and divide its width, and you hasten to wear out the handkerchiefs with the wide border and to get some with a smaller edging of black. For it is unnecessary to say that no woman, however rich, would think of setting aside or throwing away her handkerchiefs, even to oblige the tradition which has set its limit upon the sharpest hours of her grief, and told her when she ought to begin to appreciate the law of compensations. No, no woman, in any transport, would throw away good handkerchiefs.

Very well; six more months pass. And, by Niobe, but gray and lavender take the place of blackest black! There is a flower in the button hole. One even wears a diamond or two. And a little later, the costume of delicate or rich tints tells the world that your heart is mended and that you are ready once more to take part in the world's gayeties, and to laugh when others laugh. It would be very well, if your heart had really grown light in the same ratio that your garments have. But it's all a ghastly lie. The heart awakes at night to cry for the love it has lost. Through all the world it goes, alone, and the cancer of loneliness eats at it always.

Or, on the other hand, suppose that one nearly related to you – perhaps, even your husband – dies, and that you did not care in the least for him, and were secretly much relieved, though, of course, shocked, as we all must be at the fact of death. You were relieved to know that you were to be spared from possible shame, or from a life of lowering discontent, or from wranglings and deceits. Such things happen, it is said. Then what a horrid, revolting, contemptible sort of a lie, to pull your mouth down to the proper angle of regret, and hang yards of nun's veiling around you!

Whichever way you take it, it seems to be artificial, foolish, insincere and repellant. I don't say that every one of us might not do it. But I insist that it is a bad thing to do.

Along with this wearing of weeds goes the tradition that the person thus afflicted absolutely must not enjoy herself. She cannot go to hear beautiful music. She must not attend any sort of a public gathering. She can meet only a certain number of her friends at one time. In short, she must apply no balm to her wounds. She must steadfastly refuse to drink of the waters of Lethe.

It's all nonsense. If there is ever a time when music has a message for one it is when the house has been made dreadful by that awful Absence – it is when the yearning imagination hears in fancy the familiar foot on the stair, and shudderingly discovers the lie, and then recurs, with maddening mechanical repetition, to the same fantasy.

If ever the mimic life of the stage is really calculated to help one, it is when one is most anxious to forget the real life in which one is forced to live. If ever human companionship would be stimulating, it would be at a time when solitude was haunted with its newly made ghost, and when, in the persistent laughter of the rest of mankind, could be found life's grim, but wholesome philosophy.

I do not suppose that it is very surprising that women, even the most original and independent of them, come under the thrall of this imperative fashion and yield to it, when I consider that their failure to do so would lay them open to be suspect by other members of their sex of lack of affection for their dead. And that would be the one thing that no woman could endure patiently. A woman likes to be thought to be crushed by grief, even when she is not. She cannot bear to be thought disloyal, and she seems to think it a form of disloyalty not to love everyone that she might be expected to love, because of the accident of their connection with her. Woman insists upon having the world believe in her affections. She would rather be suspected of wantonness than of hard-heartedness. And the world itself always receives with reluctance the idea of a cold-blooded woman. Indeed, the world consents to be rather interested in her when she weeps. It considers her very feminine when she is bathed in tears.

No one, I hope, is so dull as to inveigh against the sentimental. But there is a good deal of sentiment that is really of a very low and commonplace order, and that we would all be disgusted with if it were not familiar.

But some day I really hope to meet a woman, who, when she loses her best beloved, will say:

"He is dead. And he is immortal. Burn that putrefying mass of flesh. It was dear to me once, for it held his soul. It is repulsive now, for it is vacant, and it is changing. I cannot weep over that vacant and repulsive tenement. What I remember is his soul, and that is not beneath the ground. If I shed tears of loneliness, it will be when I am looking at the stars – beyond which I prefer to imagine that he is. As for my dress – black or scarlet, what is it to me? I have not thought of dress. How could I pause to think of my bonnet when my love was making his way through space and the silence up to God! No, I shall tell the world nothing about my sorrow. It could not understand. It did

Four-year-old girl in full mourning, ca. 1880s. (Courtesy of author)

not share my sacred joy while he lived. It shall not share my sacred grief now he is dead."

Some day, perhaps, I will know such a woman. But I never have yet.

As for funerals!

But the subject sickens one!

Carbolic acid and tuberoses, lachrymose hymns, and insincere clerical panegyrics! A ghastly room, round which the live Things sit, looking with hot eyes at the dead Thing! Whispers going on in the room beyond, the house chilly for want of fire, nothing much to eat, everyone as faint with hunger as with grief, all sorts of people daring to try to console you with commonplace words, all sorts of lies circulating, amiable and otherwise – Oh, most desolate, repulsive, wretched, material time, in which one has no pause to stop to hear the song of the liberated spirit who sings his song of victory above the bowed heads of those who weep!

Think of going down to hang over the coffin of your dead before the curious eyes of casual neighbors, to whom you may lend your flatirons, but to whom you certainly would not lend your soul's secrets! Think of having them talk over, afterward, all your blind, incoherent utterances, and to know that they enjoyed your misery in proportion as it was demonstrative. Not that they are cruel – far, far from it. But some persons cannot help their morbidity. They like superlative conditions. If they hear of a cyclone they want it to blow down all the houses in town; if they hear of a fire in a mine they want 200 miners imprisoned just where the sounds of their voice can reach those who are making futile efforts to liberate them; and if you lose a friend, they want it to wreck your life absolutely, and want you to let them see that it does!

No, no! It is all hideous, this public show of grief; this cant of the preacher who has to praise a man for qualities of which he knows nothing; this deliberate laceration of the tortured heart by the singing of mournful songs!

But when will we outgrow it? When will we go alone with our dead to some place where their perishing mortality may most quickly be made innocuous, refusing to make a spectacle of our grief for the inquisitive and the vulgar! When will we wear our grief in our hearts instead of on our bonnets? When will we take the money we spend on wreaths for the dead, to buy bread for the living? When will we forget the material part of death to remember the spiritual part of it?

Truly, only when we have fewer superstitions and more culture than we have now.

"Want to See a Knock-Out: Americans Seem to Feel That Way in Spite of Their Civilization"

4 September 1892

For most of the nineteenth century, prizefighting was considered illegal, and by the 1890s few cities and states had legalized the sport.[6] *In the 1892 match between John L. Sullivan and Jim Corbett, the two men, both sons of Irish immigrants, presented opposite public images. Sullivan, the last of the bare-knuckle champions, was the stereotypical brawling prizefighter who gave Americans their first sports idol. At five foot ten and a half and weighing from 190 to 229 pounds, Sullivan was respected for his exceptional strength and his ability to take punishment. Corbett, six foot one and a half and weighing from 173 to 190 pounds, was an educated man who practiced the scientific methods of boxing. Called the "Father of Modern Boxing," he introduced fancy footwork, fast jabs and hooks, and slippery movements of his head and body ("'Gentleman' Jim Corbett").*

With so much controversy surrounding boxing, both legal and moral, the subject proved a perfect sparring partner for Peattie. Four days before the big fight, she questioned the reasons behind such exhibitions and went to literature and history to try to understand boxing's appeal. The day after the fight, the Omaha World-Herald *published a blow-by-blow account. In the twenty-first round, Corbett knocked Sullivan down – for only the second time in Sullivan's boxing career – winning thirty-five thousand dollars and the Heavyweight Championship of the World.*[7] *In the end, Sullivan defeated himself, both inside the ring and outside of it.*[8] *Peattie's questioning of the moral effect of battle ironically anticipated the downfall of America's first sports hero.*

❧ Within the last few days I have asked fifty gentlemen – well-bred, quiet, kindly gentlemen – if they would like to see the Sullivan-Corbett fight.

Forty-seven of them enthusiastically said "yes."

Three of them said "no."

There is nothing like getting at the truth of things. Facts discount theories every time. And it is a fact that Americans like a "knock-out," and that though there might be a good many who could not tell you who Peter Cooper was, there are none who could not tell you who John L. Sullivan is.

Now, I find this very interesting. Any woman must find it interesting, because it is rather out of the way of her imaginings. Women like to imagine a great many things they can never experience, and there are few of them, probably, who have not thought out in some hour of the night how it must be to go rushing on in the thick of battle with the blur of pungent smoke all about, and the little wall of the bullet above; the long yell of the shell; the slipping on the trampled ground; the bolt of a frightened horse; the half-heard, fateful orders; the surge of blood to the head, and in the heart the battle of pride and fear, of humanity and hate, of despair and courage!

Women understand that because they can always understand sacrificing themselves for a principle, and they have a theory that there is always a principle involved in war.

But they can't quite get at the reason why men enjoy a fight which is done for the sake of fighting. They haven't much confidence in the talk about "science," and do not believe science is what attracts men in a prize fight. They

John L. Sullivan (*left*) and "Gentleman" Jim Corbett, ca, 1892. (Courtesy of author)

are inclined to think it is something quite different and apart from science. It is the old, primitive, natural masculine love of strife. It is the cave dweller coming up in the civilized man. It is the love of seeing strength matched against strength. It is the delight – a strange, wild but undeniable trait – that men feel when they see blood.

But even so, there is yet something to explain. It is the element of effeminacy which has to be taken into account. For while the cave dweller did his own fighting and stood first among his fellows when he had proved himself strongest, the American is willing – nay, anxious – to have his fighting done for him.

The newspapers have done marvels in the way of descriptions of prize fights, and some of these are as good bits of realism as are to be found. Some of them are written with a conscious moral showing itself through the mesh of words; some are deliciously humorous. But in literature proper there is, so far as I know, only one description of a prize fight as it is conducted in America since Sullivan instituted the present school. It is in "Gallagher," that best of Mr. Richard Harding Davis' good stories. The fight he described must have been suggested, I think, by the great fight between Paddy Ryan and John Sullivan – the one in which Sullivan clinched his reputation.[9] . . .

It will be noticed that in this very excellent sketch Mr. Davis makes reference to the days when brave knights threw their gauntlets into the tourney field in challenge. But does not the bravery of those men compare favorably with that of any knights who ever lived? Could anything be braver than the meeting of the two men to fight until one or the other is "knocked out," perhaps forever? It does not appear to be a question of comparative bravery – the fighting of knightly days, and fighting of these commercial ones. The difference seems rather to lie in the fact that fighting was once fashionable and that now it is not so. "Fashionable" is not the best word, perhaps, but it is a convenient one. Gentlemen used to fight. And they fought for glory. Sluggers now do the fighting. And they fight for money.

The pursuit of "honor" is too vague a following for a gentleman of the present age. He would lay himself constantly under the danger of being "run in" for lack of means of support. Honor may sometimes be used as an accessory of some other business nowadays, but it has no marketable value by itself – and things here are judged mostly by their marketable value. That is why certain men with a great deal of muscle and not any too much industry have found it convenient to make a specialty of fighting. They have forced their sort of fighting to have a marketable value. They have taken the American commercial view of the matter. That is what has taken away the picturesqueness and the romance of fighting. It is what has destroyed the sentiment. But it has in no way destroyed the bravery. Sullivan, Slade and Corbett, Joe Goss, and Jem Mace, and the rest are brave enough. But they are not fighting for a lady's love. If they were they might fight just as hard as they do now, and nobody would complain of the brutality. On the contrary, poets would sing of them, and women would wear their colors, and great men would give banquets in their honor. It's a question of sentiment.

Right and wrong are only relative. The age makes a difference, the condition makes a difference, the very climate makes a difference.

Down in Lima, where it is safe to suppose that women are just as modest, as maternal and as sweet as they are here, they think nothing of going to bull fights. Life would, indeed, seem very dull to them without this diversion, which makes their pulses leap as nothing else, except, perhaps, the first kiss of their favored lovers, ever can do.

They carry the pictures of the matadors and the toreadors on their fans. They look upon them as the popular heroes; and though no gentlewoman would be seen in the company of one of these fellows, she, nevertheless, feels proud if by chance he picks up and wears the flower she flings at him.

In Australia the men appear to get a great deal of amusement out of rat baiting. They tie the hands of a man, put him in a pit with a lot of starved rats, and he fights them with his teeth. It is said that Australians are very fond of this "amusement." The Puritans were fond of bear baiting – perhaps because it was such a serious diversion. Americans enjoy pigeon shoots, in which they use live birds as the targets for their bullets. The Indians used to prefer shooting at captive white children. It is, of course, all a question of taste, or, as I have remarked before, of fashion.

It has always been my way when I found that a great many people were enjoying a thing, to believe that there must be something in it. So I have just been reading the alleged autobiography of John Sullivan. This book bears the really inviting title of "A Nineteenth Century Gladiator," and inquires piquantly on the title page: "Why don't you speak for yourself, John?"

Within are very exciting descriptions of how Sullivan sent Slade to the ropes, and of how Mace, who was somewhat groggy, managed to struggle to his feet and aim one at Sullivan's jugular. When I had read a little way I perceived that my vocabulary was likely to become materially increased. I also found that certain words which I had always used with confidence, seemed to possess a different meaning from that which I had always attached to them. Mr. Sullivan – or rather, the man who wrote his reminiscences for him – has made the most of the newspaper work which has been done in connection with him; and as good reporters are always put on anything with which Sullivan is connected, some of the work shows excellent character sketching. Not infrequently it preaches a fearful sermon in a jocular way. For though newspaper men may professionally take a keen interest in slugging matches, personally they may have many objections to it. Here is such a piece of work by some New York correspondent:

"If John L. Sullivan had received the necessary majority of electoral votes to proclaim him president, the homage paid by the successful party would have been scarcely less than that accorded him by the multitude of people of all classes who gathered in and about Monico Villa, at One Hundred and Forty-sixth street, November 9, 1884, the day previous to his fight with Laflin. Such a crowd had never before been seen in the locality. They came in buggies, dog carts, barouches and sulkies; Sullivan's constituents from Boston were present en masse, and all were willing to back their pugilistic townsman to any amount – from $1 to the Bunker Hill monument. Two Boston brokers expressed a solid admiration for the champion by offering to bet any part of $20,000 that he would defeat Laflin the next evening.

"There was nothing in the fight between the pugilists, Sullivan and Laflin, which seemed more intensely interesting than the smile on Laflin's face right after Sullivan had hit the countenance squarely in the middle. Laflin is a coarse and burly, yet good looking, man, and from the beginning of the encounter there had been an air of lofty condescension on his part, as if to say: 'I am letting myself down to this fellow's level for this occasion.'

"You probably have seen accounts of the match. This particular blow was struck straight from the shoulder with all of Sullivan's might, and it was easy to imagine that the gloved fist sunk so far into the face that the nose was flattened. However, the visage rebounded into place, like a hollow rubber ball when you stop squeezing it; but it was left for an appreciable moment in a terribly distorted condition, then shaping itself into the sickliest smile that human features ever conformed to. The grin of the ballet girl, whose toes are excruciating, gives a very faint idea of it.

"In spite of hugging and crawling, Laflin was knocked out."

Here is more concerning the same fight:

"The pilgrimage to the wayside inn, just outside of the city limits, where Sullivan makes his headquarters, is made by hundreds every day. The lamentable feature of these gatherings of worshipers at the shrine of the slug-god is the presence of boys in throngs. Imagine the burning desire of the little rascals to grow up into prize-fighters! They have gone into training, every one of them, as shown by the striding, rapid gait, with which they walk to the tavern from the nearest street car line. Yesterday about noon a stout, rosy-faced young fellow, with evident sporting proclivities, was seen rushing in the direction of the inn at a 2:12 gait.

" 'Johnny, are yez going to dinner?' asked a passer.

" 'Dinner be d – d; I'm going to see Sullivan,' was the characteristic reply.

"An audacious urchin asked Sullivan what he ate and drank.

" 'Blood, nothin' but blood,' was the reply. 'I drain a boy about your size three times a day.'

"The anxious inquirer escaped with no delay, but the words of the illustrious man spread among the lads with pugilistic aspirations and they got the further belief somehow that beef blood from a neighboring slaughter house really composed most of his diet. A consequence is that they go in numbers to the abattoir in question, where the butchers provide all the blood called for. The boys take it from a tin cup while it is yet warm from the slaughtered beasts, and some of them are able to gulp down half a pint without stopping for breath."

Now, there's a sermon for you, and if you don't think it is pretty reading, why see to it that your tastes and the expression you give them are not such as to lead your boys to try the same experiments.

You've got to get over the cave dweller habits of thought if you want to be a gentleman. A fight without a reason has no place in civilization. The reason of it is that such a fight is of no use. It has no value. And if civilization is anything, it is the understanding of utility and the conservation of value.

Here's the description of another sort of a "knock-out," just by way of contrast:

> And anon
> The Trumpet blew, and then did either side,
> They that assail'd and they that held the lists,
> Set lance in rest, strike spur, suddenly move,
> Meet in the midst, and there so furiously
> Shock, that a man far off might well perceive,
> If any man that day were left afield
> The hard earth shake, and a low thunder of arms.
> And Lancelot bode a little, till he saw
> Which were the weaker; then he hurled into it
> Against the stronger: little need to speak
> Of Lancelot in his glory! King, duke, earl,
> Count, baron – whom he smote, he overthrew.
> But in the field were Lancelot's kith and kin,
> Ranged with the Table Round that held the lists,
> Strong men, and wrathful that a stranger knight
> Should do and almost overdo the deeds
> Of Lancelot; and one said to the other, "Lo!
> What is he? I do not mean the force alone –
> The grace and versatility of the man!
> It is not Lancelot?" "When has Lancelot worn
> Favour of any lady in the lists?
> Not such his wont, as we, that know him, know."
> "How then? who then?" a fury seized them all,
> A fiery family passion for the name
> Of Lancelot, and a glory one with theirs.
> They couched their spears and pricked their steeds, and thus,
> Their plumes driven backward by the wind they made.
> In moving, all together down upon him
> Bare, as a wild wave in the wide North-sea,
> Green-glimmering toward the summit, bears, with all
> Its stormy crests that smoke against the skies,
> Down on a bark, and overbears the bark,
> And him that helms it, so they overbore
> Sir Lancelot and his charger, and a spear
> Down-glancing lamed the charger, and a spear
> Pricked sharply his own cuirass, and the head
> Pierced through his side, and there snapt, and remained.

It makes a difference, very obviously, how things are put. If in this episode, for example, Mr. Tennyson had chosen to describe Lancelot as being knocked clean over the ropes, and being picked up in a groggy condition, it is very much to be doubted if his wounds would have interested us, or the tender ministrations of Elaine, the Lily maid of Astalot, appealed to our sympathies.

Personally, I do not believe that these encounters of the Table Round had any better moral effect than the engagements of Mace and Sullivan. But they certainly read better. And they were of a savage time – a simple, stalwart time when men reasoned with their brawn and not with their brain.

But now, surely, the day is past – but no, that is a theory! After all the moralizing, the theorizing and the protesting, we are still confronted by the relentless verities.

And forty-seven out of fifty men wish they might see Sullivan when he puts on the gloves with Corbett.

"The Work of the Worker: Qualities in Evangelist Mills That Give Him Success in Soul Winning"

15 December 1892

As families moved west during the homesteading period, and trainloads of new immigrants arrived daily, families scattered across America. A great surge of Protestant nondenominational evangelists followed after them to win converts and to provide order, stability, and community in the bursting new cities of the West.[10] *The wide assortment of religious beliefs imported to Omaha by foreign immigrants as well as the revival of evangelism at the turn of the century intrigued Peattie philosophically, and she studied each with the objectivity of a reporter. Omaha in 1891 boasted ninety-nine churches: twelve Baptist, ten Catholic, two Christian, ten Congregational, ten Episcopal, three Jewish, one Latter Day Saints, fourteen Lutheran, sixteen Methodist, seventeen Presbyterian, one Adventist, one Unitarian, one Universalist, and the City Mission (Omaha Board of Trade,* Omaha *15).*

Benjamin Fay Mills, who preached in Omaha in 1892, began his mission in 1886 and continued uninterrupted for the next thirteen years, speaking to five million people and converting two hundred thousand of them (McLoughlin 335). Mills, known for his deliberately orchestrated revivals, never entered a city until the ministers who had invited him had established an elaborate committee system, which raised funds, spread publicity, procured ushers and musicians, invited guest ministers for invocations and benedictions, and organized prayer groups.[11]

Successful, honest, and humanitarian, Mills was one of the few professional evangelists who emphasized social responsibility and action rather than strictly individual reform.[12] *His socially conscious message was one that Peattie could wholeheartedly endorse.*

❧ The extraordinary series of meetings conducted by B. Fay Mills, the revivalist, is almost at an end. Next Sunday evening he will hold his last meeting.

The effect of this young man upon the community has been very peculiar. He has been able to call together, at any time of the day that he might designate, and as many times a day as he would, a crowd of 2,000 persons. And it is no inaccuracy to say that his listeners have been limited to this number only because that was the limit of the Exposition hall in which he has been holding these revival meetings.

There is nothing in the appearance or in the manner of Mr. Mills which would immediately arrest and hold the attention of a casual observer; as is, for instance, the case with Edward Strauss, that tense, alert and most magnetic of orchestral conductors. This comparison may seem peculiar, but when it is remembered that both men have the ability to produce any effect they may desire upon an audience, the reason of the comparison will be perceived. Mr. Mills is exceedingly magnetic, but it is a subtle magnetism, and wins the attention of an audience instead of commanding it. It shows itself by means of intense concentration. And this, beginning to make itself gently felt when Mr. Mills first comes upon the platform, increases minute by minute, until it reaches a fine and palpable climax as the meeting nears its close; when Mr. Mills is the center of 2,000 invisible currents of sympathy, which are sent from every individual within sound of his voice, and converge upon him.

The young man is fully alive to the pleasures and elations of this marvelous correspondence of emotion. His blue eyes acquire electrical light; his face, which is distinctly that of the born orator, is mobile with delicate emotion; and his voice, a finely modulated instrument, suits itself to the humor of the moment and leads the responsive listeners into whatever emotional fields that the possession of it may select.

Mr. Mills could not be better described than by the remark, casually made, that his face is that of a born orator. In repose it is not particularly significant. But it is facile; has strong muscles, which only show themselves when he is speaking; the mouth is large, the lips thin, and the whole lower part of the face capable of lending itself to the expression of any sentiment or passion; while the eyes have the penetrativeness before referred to. In short, Mr. Mills has a face which would do a good actor fine service – and it must be understood

Poster announcing Benjamin Fay Mills and associates at an evangelical gathering, 1895. (Archives of the Billy Graham Center, Wheaton, Illinois)

that this is meant only in the most complimentary sense. For the good actor, above all other men, has an educated face.

Mr. Mills must be aware of the fact that he employs, with excellent results, well-known laws of acting, such as a most discriminating and delicate intonation, and that form of mental bravery and physical imperativeness which is known as "presence." Like the good actor, he is not upon the stage at the opening of the performance, but appears after the people are all seated and amalgamated sympathetically by a fifteen-minute song service. He knows the value of pauses. He knows that "the silence that follows is half the song." And his understanding of oratory is so good that one does not even perceive that he is an orator. To exercise an art so consummately that the art seems to be nature, is the warmest thing that can be said.

In employing all of these agencies Mr. Mills shows his singular good sense; and his adaptability to the demands of the time and the general temperament of the people. It marks him in short a man of cultivation; one who is eager and willing to bring a well-trained body and mind to the service of his Master, and who does not make the mistake of supposing that in order to be sincere one must be rude.

But even the intelligence of Mr. Mills might sometimes fail to adequately serve the commands of his devout soul if it were not for his alert perceptions. He has the ability – and this is one of his most conspicuous characteristics – of perceiving the quality of an audience immediately upon standing before it. And he suits his discourse to the requirements of the occasion. He knows how to address himself to an audience composed of men and women of the middle class – of the "great average" – he is acquainted with the form of phraseology which best suits the business man; he knows how to adapt himself to the more alert and lofty perceptions of a congregation of gentlewomen; he can make himself companionable and understandable to the despairing wretch, who, debauched with loathsome vices, cries out to Christ to save his diseased body and putrid mind from the hell in which they are engulfed. Mr. Mills' greatest power, not taking into consideration his spiritual self, lies in his genius for sympathy.

But his sensibilities, unusually developed though they undoubtedly are, have not mastered him. A well balanced head, a great deal of good sense, and good breeding in the bargain, have enabled him to conduct a revival which has won more converts than any other ever conducted in this city, without one unseemly demonstration, or one outbreak of surcharged emotion. His will is intensely strong, and as he has no hesitation in showing his disapproval – though in a most kindly way – he has kept his vast audience within bounds.

When they have wept it has been in silence, when they have cried to God it has been with the heart, not the voice. When they have rejoiced their joy has found expression in their eyes, but not by their tongues.

Perhaps it has been the good breeding of Mr. Mills, as much as any one thing, which has kept down any intrusion of individuality in these meetings. The methods of the Methodist camp meeting would seem very crude and distasteful if introduced into his meetings. Such excitement must always be the result of the unrestrained primitive emotions, and they are awaked by an unrestrained and primitive man, such as Sam Jones.

It has generally been a fact – though there are great historical exceptions – that religionists who have had the power to greatly move men have been men of uncultivated speech and the rude manners. Their appeal has been to the intemperate passions of the heart and the fact that the motive was good hardly redeemed the offense, for the reason that it made religion, which should be the daily inspiration of the calm and peaceful heart, a sort of frenzy, which exhausted the body and threatened the sanity of the mind.

Mr. Mills, it is but fair to say, resorts to nothing so cheap, and would, undoubtedly, have strong conscientious scruples against inflicting any such injury on any living creature.

It is not what things seem, but what they really are, that he has concerned himself with. To adjure Christians to more earnestness; to compel them to live in the spirit and not according to the letter of Christianity; to convince the un-Christian that Christ alone was happiness, and chance for growth, and the giving of significance to life, has been his object – his mission.

That he feels it to be a mission no one can doubt.

"Why did you leave the pulpit and go into your present work?" I asked him yesterday.

"I felt compelled to do it," he said, brightly and without any affectation at all.

That he believes in himself there is not a shadow of doubt, although no one, however critical of him, could call him an egotist.

Yesterday afternoon a large number of the shops, stores and offices in the city were closed that employees might have an opportunity to attend the service of what Mr. Mills quaintly terms "the midweek Sunday."

"I suppose," said Mr. Mills in the course of his remarks yesterday afternoon, "that this city in all its history has never seen a day like this, when men on the street want to stop and talk about God and nothing else, and when merchants, in the thick of the holiday trade, have been willing to close their stores that they might come here and participate in the blessings which God is pouring out on us."

But he said it without any particular consciousness of self, and while he has no cant about being nothing to himself, and being the mere instrument of God, yet he undoubtedly feels that such is the case. Not that he thinks that he is inspired, but that he cannot but be aware that he has the ability to tell the Christian story so that it will not only reach their heads, but their hearts.

The text yesterday afternoon was: "We stumble at the noonday as at the night," and Mr. Mills made especial application of it to men living surrounded by the influences of Christianity, and the great object lesson of Christendom and civilization, who could not see what it signified, and would not openly acknowledge Christ. His talk was very conversational, and his graver talk was interlarded with simple and homely stories which he applied in a graphically allegorical manner.

Some of these stories were certainly rather startling, but since nothing is so startling as truth, there is no reason to question Mr. Mills' accuracy. But at any rate, fiction is but the modification of fact for use, and it was therefore perfectly permissible if Mr. Mills employed it.

These stories were carefully selected. They pointed out the significance of his remarks as the mile post points the road to town. They gave a distinctively American flavor to Mr. Mills' remarks, making them graphic, pictorial and personal.

The attention of the audience was as undeviating as if the young preacher had hypnotized it. Many took notes, that they might preserve his words for future reference. Some of the women wept – not wild tears of excitement, but gentle ones of sensibility. When Mr. Mills made any request of the audience, there was instant response.

Every seat was taken; many were standing; up the narrow stairs leading to the gallery sat a line of people – a round-faced old woman, with her face framed with a black hood; a middle aged woman, with a widow's bonnet, who sat with her head bowed; a couple of intent little boys; a gray-headed man, who rested his head on his hand, and a group of young girls. Now and then a baby cooed in the audience, or gave a little cry. Down at the front sat a woman who was partly deaf, and who closed her eyes that she might concentrate all her power upon her one deficient faculty. On the platform was the phalanx of clergymen. Dr. Duryea, with his scholarly face; the Rev. Mr. Savidge, with his emotional one; Mr. Crane, handsome and boyish; a young Swede clergyman with his nationality indelibly stamped on his face; Rev. Clark of the City Mission; the Rev. Dr. Gordon, that clerical cosmopolite and many others.

And of course there was Mr. Hillis, the singer, whose art is very good indeed, and who understands the dramatic [conventions] quite as well as does Mr. Mills, and who, in addition, seems a very sincere young man who is most eager to win people to the happiness to be found in Christianity.

One of the incidents of the afternoon was the rising of a very old man, with bounteous silvered hair, to express his desire to become a Christian – hundreds arose to express this desire, but among them he was the most venerable. The incident was all the more remarkable as Mr. Mills had just been demonstrating by inquiry that five-sixths of the persons who "confessed Christianity" did so before they were 20 years of age.

Today there will be a meeting at 3 o'clock and another in the evening.

Tomorrow the program will be the same. Saturday there will be no meeting except one at noon for men at the Y.M.C.A. hall.

This suggests the extraordinary organization which has characterized this fortnight's run of meetings. I believe that at the beginning, before Mr. Mills came, but of course according to his direction, the city was divided into districts, each district having a complete set of committees, and then there were held special services in these districts for a number of days; all these meetings, when Mr. Mills came, in the union meetings at Exposition hall, under a set of central committees, made up of the chairmen of the respective district committees.

Thus a large machine was set in motion, which has noiselessly operated at every one of the great meetings. It is so arranged that one assistant sits in the midst of every twenty-five persons. These assistants are composed of the best men of the community – they are men of affairs, who have decision and brains enough to act in an emergency, and Christian enthusiasm sufficient to let them perform any service that might be required – even of a spiritual nature. In the center of the platform has sat at each meeting, Colonel Bird of General Wheaton's staff. Under him have been two messengers, who, standing just beneath the platform, have executed any orders that the colonel has given them. He has seen to it that the people were seated in blocks, thus filling every seat from the front backward as the assemblies gathered. He has kept the temperature regulated by a thermometer; he has directed the dispersing as well as the gathering of the crowd and overseen a thousand trifling details.

Thus, under this fine management, the crowds have met day after day, with the greatest quietness, orderliness and precision. And a revival has been conducted which has defied the censure of the most critical, and has won praise even from those opposed to this method of religious work.

As to the spiritual regeneration that it has brought, or the assurances that it has given to doubting men of the living power of Jesus of Nazareth, or the despairing that it has given hope and promise to, who can say? Deep in the hearts of men lie hidden these things.

The nightly mission meetings which will be held at the People's theater, the beds placed there for the use of wayfarers, men or women, is one of the large, palpable results.

The still larger, but the impalpable ones, which effect the inner lives of men and women, he who hears the voiceless cry of the soul alone can judge of.

"A Salvation Army Funeral"

18 March 1891

Whenever possible, Peattie championed the work being done by women in religion. In 1891 she commemorated the life of Stena Glassman, an Omaha Salvation Army soldier who asserted her beliefs despite public derision.[13] *Omaha city records show that Stena Christensen was born in Denmark and was a resident of Chicago until 1889, when she married John H. Glassman, a salesman at Shook, Summers, and Co., an Omaha watch, clock, and jewelry store. The couple had a daughter ten months later. Stena died at age twenty-two of septicemia, or blood poisoning. After a service at her home at 1036 South 18th Street, she was buried in Laurel Hill cemetery.*

Three years later, General William Booth, who had founded the organization in London in 1865, visited Omaha to lend support to his army. He declared, "What we wish to do is to get hold of the submerged classes. They must be helped – they have not strength to rescue themselves. They are to be found in every country" ("General Booth in Omaha").

By 1896, Peattie, lamenting the loss of other "rescue homes" in Omaha, reported that the Salvation Army had just secured a house at 2015 Pinkney Street and asked for contributions from the community. Noting that the Salvationists had been trained to work among the poor and the outcast, she remarked, "They are the scavengers of the world, gathering up those cast away souls for which others have no use." Trusting that they would continue the necessary work among the poor of Omaha, she added, "There is one characteristic of the army which is famous, and that is its tenacity. When it takes up a thing it carries it through to success" ("Word with the Women," 10 October 1896).

❧ Yellow, purple and red is the flag of the Salvation army.

Yesterday two other colors were added. One was black; that was for grief. One was white; that was for innocence. Sister Stenie Glassman was dead.

Who was Sister Stenie Glassman?

Unknown Salvation Army sister, ca. 1900.
(Courtesy of C. Richard and Nancy B. Johnson)

A woman, young, plain of face, decisive of speech, simple of manner, who could kneel in the mud of the street and pray while the crowds jeered at her, a woman who could enter a saloon and wage there fierce battle against what she considered sin; a woman who could swing the cymbals in metallic clangor in the street march of the Salvationists and call on the ungodly to fall in and march with the army of the Lord.

Such women are generally counted a nuisance.

But it is very difficult at times to tell the difference between a nuisance and a hero. Besides, public opinion holds up but an illusive mirror. Sometime, centuries from now, when men are permitted in that dim and doubtful resurrection to look in the mirror of truth, it may appear that many of the figures which seem dwarfed now, will tower then among their fellows, while many that stand tall and straight will be shrunken and strangely deformed.

Stenie Glassman, with those mud stained garments and the strap of the Salvation army on her sleeve, may stand then above some white cravatted clergyman, who discoursed to his followers in English, and the faultlessness of which the girl who marched the streets could not even appreciate.

However this may be, she was buried yesterday in the new cemetery and services which were attended by 500 persons were held in the Salvation army barracks at the corner of Davenport and Seventeenth streets. The flag under which she had fought her own peculiar and daring little fight drooped above the coffin. On the platform sat five officers of the army, young women, all with broad white sashes soldier-wise over their breasts, and gloves of white. Back of them were a group of girl cadets in the uniform, but without the sashes.

Concertinas, violin, cymbal and zither accompanied the singing. There were no dirges, but instead songs of triumph. Why mourn when a soldier had marched to victory? That is the way the Salvationists looked at it. Ensign Eddie Parker, Lieutenant O. Leyres, Cadet Woodhouse, and the Rev. J. B. Phillips sat together in a row where the pulpit would have been, had there been one, and all but the Rev. Phillips made a few fitting remarks. He said Sister Glassman had died in the service, and that while her death was mourned, her fearless life would serve as an inspiration to those who knew her.

Have you ever seen that little man with the piercing voice, all nerve and fire with the eyes of an enthusiast and the graphic speech of the born leader, who leaps and dances before the processions of the army on the street, and who harangues the congregations with hectic eloquence?

"We do not come here to mourn," said he, "although we loved her who lies there in the coffin. We can mourn in our homes better than in a public place like this. We come here to say to those who are dead in trespasses and sins; to this will you all come at last. However fine and safe you may think yourself now, the day will dawn when the cold hand of death will be laid on your shoulder; you will be pushed to the brink of the dark river and from you will be washed all this that hides your true self. Therefore, today, while you see what death is, how suddenly it comes, how inevitable it is, whether you be four-scores or only a child, kneel beside this coffin and swear to be ready against the day which waits for you."

He told how this lamented sister died, smiling and saying her house was in order for the coming guest, and some of the girls in the congregation wept.

Meanwhile the air within grew heavy and foul; but the motley crowd – English, Welsh, Irishmen with the green in their button holes, Negroes, Swedes, companies of men out of work, other companies of the curious who had nothing to do with the army, children, who love to hear the noise and rough display of the Salvationists – seemed not to mind, and kept their eyes on the scarlet waistcoat of the little man on the platform, who seized his concertina and sang to them and then laid it down to beseech his listeners to enlist under the banner of the Lord. Much singing and talking in the open air had given his tones their strident qualities; much suiting of words to vice-befuddled brains had given him his simple eloquence; much need for bravado had given him his almost belligerent earnestness.

A very valuable man to the Salvation Army, this little, tense, nervous, electrical, alert creature in the scarlet waistcoat.

The sisters with the white sashes sang more songs after he had finished his talk, all of them glad songs. Meanwhile some boys called from the street without, a baby cried in the audience, and the undertaker hovered in the rear.

Meetings were announced and then the little man asked "The dear undertaker to do his duty," which the dear undertaker promptly did, and all the congregation marched around to look at Sister Stenie Glassman – not so much because she was Sister Stenie Glassman, as because she was dead.

A crowd always likes to look at anything that is dead.

They filed past the be-sashed and still singing sisters, and past the wonderful picture on the wall, where a moon, a star, a shaft of lightning and a setting sun are all contending together to see which can shed the most light upon a wobbly cross, decked with ivy and standing in the midst of the most precipitous mountains ever designed by nature or painted by artist. Reaching the open air the congregation waited while six sisters brought out the light coffin. Before them marched the color bearers and six young men; behind them followed the mourners, including the husband of the dead woman; and then came the soldiers of the army from Omaha and Council Bluffs. A long procession of sympathizers closed the rear. The muffled drum set the slow pace of the march; and on the coffin were the American flag and the military bonnet of the dead captain. For six or eight blocks the procession marched before the empty carriages, then, near the viaduct, the coffin was placed in the hearse, officers and soldiers got in their carriages, and the crowd dispersed.

At the grave the services were concluded, and Sister Stenie Glassman was laid to rest to the sound of cymbals and songs, zithers and triumphant cries, sounds long familiar to her ears as she marched the streets of Omaha with the little band of friends.

Do you think it was vulgar, you fine conservative?

The vulgar thing is the false one.

This funeral was honest.

"Brains in the School Room: Some Pertinent Remarks Regarding the Needs of the Public Schools"

8 November 1891

Because Peattie's own formal education halted in the sixth grade, she realized the handicaps caused by a lack of schooling and parental support. As a result, she did not want to smother any child's desire to learn or thwart his or her chance in life, so Peattie remained one of the staunchest supporters – and harshest critics, when necessary – of the Omaha schools. Peattie criticized not only the school system, the school building, the school board, and the teachers, but the voters as well, urging much needed reforms and offering suggestions for improvement.

When credit was due, on the other hand, Peattie did not hesitate to lavish it on deserving teachers and institutions. On 16 April 1893 she lauded the Hanscom Park school, established in 1887. Since then, its five rooms and 240-pupil enrollment had grown to twelve rooms and nearly 600 students. Peattie described principal and fourth-grade teacher Lillian Littlefield as "a teacher who never gets tired of children; who has a sense of hearty companionship with them, and whose patience is exhaustless – largely, no doubt, owing to her buoyant sense of humor." After listing the faculty members and the curriculum, Peattie concluded: "In fact, the school is an example of the American public school – absolutely democratic, giving equal chance to all, mixing all nationalities, giving preference to no interpretation of religion, binding in good fellowship children of all races, religions, and colors – thank heaven!" ("Successful Public School").

❧ Nine women – nine very quiet-going women, used to staying at home and admiring their husbands – decided the other morning to exercise the limited privilege granted them by a grudging legislature, and cast a vote for their five favorite candidates for the board of education. Most of them wore veils. Some of them felt as if they were about to commit a crime. All of them tried to look as if they were only going over to order the morning groceries.

Miss Mary Reid's seventh-grade class in Omaha, 1893.
(Nebraska State Historical Society Photograph Collections)

They weren't anxious to vote. But it had to come to seem as if it were a duty for them to do so.

As they walked up to the polling place the men who had taken the day off to do five minutes' voting looked at them and smiled mechanically. Some of the ladies blushed [lines missing] . . . The little voting booth with its corrugated iron walls looked very cold, but it was not. It was warm, not only because of the brisk fire in the baseburner, but also because of the discussion which was going on within.

A pleasant policeman stuck his head out of the door and told the veiled ladies that they could not come in till the judges decided whether or not they were entitled to vote. So they waited and smiled back at the policeman, who was really very nice, and who wore a new uniform. A moment later this affable guardian of the law said six might enter. Six did, feeling so small that they wondered if they were only three. The men took off their hats, and stopped squirting tobacco juice. Then one man arose and swore them, and the women took oath that they had, so help them God, taxable property in the district, or that they had children of an age permitting them to attend public school. Then one of them announced that the women would not be allowed to vote on the school bonds, and that if any did so their votes would be thrown out.

"Is that the law?" said one, unconsciously quoting Shylock. The law was read aloud. There was no doubt about it. A woman could buy property and pay taxes, but had no right to say, even in the smallest particular, what should be done with the taxes thus levied. Men would have headed another revolution under such circumstances. The women smiled. Then they took their tickets and retired to the little stalls at the rear of the building.

"Gentlemen," said a voice, "I 'rise to a point of objection. Kin these here ladies be trusted to vote fur members of th' board without votin' fur th' bonds? What means hev we fur knowin' whether they will vote fur th' bonds ur not? There is nothin' to distinguish their votes from th' votes of anyone else."

No one said anything. The ladies in the little stalls lifted their heads from their oats – otherwise their tickets, and listened. They were not exactly used to having their honor openly impugned, but they concluded that such customs must obtain in such masculine affairs as voting. Probably it was political etiquette to insinuate that a person was a liar and a cheat. Finally one of the women suggested that the ballots be designated as feminine by a line from the judges. This could be written on the back. It was decided that this would make the ballot illegal. One of the ladies gently remarked that the word of honor of the women ought to be sufficient.

The challenger said he didn't know about that.

"I don't take th' honesty of no man fur granted," said he, "an' why should I take it fur granted that these here ladies is honest?"

One of the men protested that if the law took their honesty for granted the judges could afford to do so. And the ballots were then accepted by a gentleman who performed the onerous feat of dropping them in a box. The perplexed challenger was still in the slough of despond.

"There ain't no places on th' books fur these ladies' addresses," he cried. "If it had been intended that these here votes should be taken th' books would hev bin fixed fur 'em."

It was suggested that it was not the fault of the ladies that the books had not been properly prepared, and that their votes should not be discounted on that account.

"Now look here," went on the man who was hired to make objections, and who was trying to earn his salary. "What is there to keep these here same ladies from votin' in every pollin' place in this city? There ain't nothin' to prevent 'em."

Again the women wondered if it was usual for men to insinuate to each other that ballot box stuffing was likely to be one of their habits. They said as much. And again the paid cynic responded that he "didn't trust no man," and therefore he wasn't supposed to trust no woman! And then he thought of something else. He raised the point that the ballots might not be legal because they were not complete – that is to say, because the spaces opposite the bond question would be left blank. This point was often raised at many precincts, and was sufficient in several cases to make the judges decide against the voting of women.

This was very stupid. No man feels obliged to vote for a candidate for every office represented on his ticket, yet no question has ever arisen concerning the validity of masculine votes on that score. However, on this trifling excuse dozens of women were kept from voting this last election. The women referred to said all this and more, and a moment later they were let out of the little iron shed by the policeman in the nice fitting uniform, and returned to put lunch on the table before the children got home from school.

When the children did get home from school they had a headache. They couldn't tell why. They didn't care about eating anything. And they said their lessons had not been good. It is a noticeable thing that the children do not feel this way in warm weather. It is only after the windows are closed. The children are that way all over the city. And the reason of it is the bad ventilation. And it was the reason why dozens of women who have no sigh to heave for the privileges of the ballot were willing to go out the other day and vote for men whom they believed could look at the matters under their charge in the most intelligent way. They wanted men who would realize that the importance of a school depends upon the condition in which the body is kept. There is nothing that simplifies a problem in fractions like plenty of fresh air.

A school which is held up above all others as having good ventilation is the model school. This school is heated by a fan. And it has a fan which belches up frosty cold air through a yawning black register. When the children wish to amuse themselves they stand before these registers to get their clothes dusty. Now those unhappy little fellows who sit near this are congealed; and the equally unhappy fellows who sit by the steam radiator are roasted, and it is only a few fortunate little fellows at the extreme opposite end of the room who get air properly modified. And they must find it laden with dust. [lines missing]

Children are forever complaining that they have too far to walk to their readings. This is rankest nonsense. It doesn't hurt children to walk. There is nothing that enervates a child more than to keep him in that sedentary state where he thinks he must have everything prepared for his convenience. The days when lads and lasses had to trudge two miles to school along the country road were the days when school was most appreciated, and it was also the time when the school turned out the finest, most stalwart, patriotic men and women. I don't think it necessary that the state should provide conveniences or luxuries for school children, and the children are very lucky, indeed, to get free instruction. But the state has no right to poison the children after it gets them in the school room. And that is just what it is doing. It is giving them consumption and indigestion, and worn-out brains and stunted bodies and weak hearts.

Are the new members of the school board going to remedy this condition of affairs? Or are they going to spend the year talking about nothing and jangling with each other? There appears to be an idea that these matters are no one's business. But this is a mistake. They are the business of everyone who has children or expects or hopes to have them.

When one speaks to the teachers about the bad condition of the schools they say: "Why do the parents not insist on something better?"

The parents are as powerless – no matter what support they give to the schools – as they well could be. They have not even the ability to secure for their children the right to enter the school house before the call of the session. Indeed, the youngsters are even prohibited from standing in the vestibule under shelter before the sounding of the gong. The snow may be flying or the rain dripping. It makes no difference.

"It toughens them," a teacher remarked when it was suggested to her that it was inhuman to keep the children standing out in the storm.

Again, there is where the country school is better than the city school. In your little board or sod school house the teachers will not only let the children in when it is uncomfortable or unsafe for them to be without, but she will hold little aching fingers in hers, she will take off obstinate rubbers, she will let the children study their lessons around the stove. There is no use in saying that discipline would be destroyed if that sort of thing were done in city schools. I have been hustled with 1,000 other young ones through a city public school and I have toddled up a lane to a country school house. I know what the comparative drains were that were made on the teacher. I know, too, that the instruction we got in the country school house stuck longer and had in it truer elements of culture than that which we got in the city school. And the reason of it was that there was more humanity in it and less clock work.

There is too much routine in the public schools. Too many things are attempted. The scheme is too rigid, and the teacher is not allowed to sufficiently assert her individuality. In many cases the teacher has none – and such should not be allowed to teach. No teacher should be permitted to stand on the rostrum of our schools who has not intellect enough to perceive something of the personality of each child. It is no exaggeration to say that there are teachers employed in these schools who have never read anything to speak of beyond the text books from which they drearily teach. They have no vitality, either physical or mental. They are at low ebb in every respect. They look forward to vacation from the day that the school year begins. Their work is absolutely perfunctory. And it is the duty of every principal to report such cases to the board of education. In contrast to these dry-souled creatures, who are incapable of any emotion stronger than a dull irritability, there are some magnificent young women in the schools – young women who have curiosity, energy, hope, love, ambition and the love of competition. These women know how to shine on a child so that its soul will grow as a flower would under the actinic rays of the sun. Such a teacher has this week given up her work in the public schools and has left for reasons which are very interesting, and for which she is to be congratulated. This is Miss Stall, who taught the primary department in the Park school. She was a teacher who thought and who understood the philosophy of teaching. She taught the children a thousand things which were not in the text books. She taught them courtesy by being courteous; love, by loving them; esthetics, by showing them what was beautiful; optimism, by always wearing a smile.

"She is going to be married," said a little boy who learned his letters under her instruction, "and I am sorry, because I was thinking I might marry her myself when I saved up enough pennies. It will be so hard to find anyone else that smiles so nice as she does," and he had to be allowed to purchase thirty little "nigger babies" made of liquorice before he could forget his first love disappointment.

A year ago a timid, nervous, and apprehensive little girl was sent to school to this teacher. She trembled as she left her home, and the mother who kissed her goodbye trembled, too, with that nameless pain that every mother feels when she sees her baby toddling out with such pitiable ignorance to meet the world. It is like sitting by while your baby runs laughing into the tentacles of an octopus. This little soul crept into the big school building – grown-up folk simply have no idea how big a school house can look – sniffed for the first time that indefinable scent which clings to all school houses, and looked with terrified eyes at the rows and rows of seats in which she was to work out what seemed to her a term of penal servitude. By and by along came the Teacher, that dreaded creature made for the misery, so the little girl thought, of wretched girls and boys. Again, there is something that grown-up folks know nothing about – the terribleness of the teacher in the eyes of the boys and girls. This teacher came along and looked at the new pupil – such a tiny, miserable new pupil. She stooped over and lifted her up in her arms, and smoothed back the soft brown hair.

"So this little woman is coming to school, is she," she said. "I hope she will be very happy here."

It was enough. The apprehension was gone. The baby felt safe. She ceased to tremble. Her heart stopped fluttering.

There were wonderful blocks to play with now and then after one had got tired trying to understand those phonetics. And these blocks had names, so that in a little while one could easily tell a rhomboid from a triangle. And there was clay out of which to make beautiful vases, and little figures of boys, and cats and other interesting things. And now and then when one was very tired indeed, this teacher would sing about how the birdies chattered when twilight came, and got into their sociable nest with all the bird family, and dropped their lids over their bright eyes. And the children suited action to each word, and when the song told how the birdies rested their little heads on the desk, stayed there for a time – five full minutes sometimes. And the little fellows returned to their work decidedly refreshed.

What this teacher did every teacher can do. It makes no difference what grade she is teaching in. She may say she cannot do these things – cannot look after the happiness of the children and their health, and the development of their sense as well as the development of their memories. Then, if she cannot, she is behind the age, and does not belong in the public schools.

In nothing did Miss Stall show her wisdom more than in teaching the children to rest. A person has arrived at a stage of high culture when he understands the art of relaxation. The nervous tension at which pupils are kept is one of the several things that makes them leave the schools to enter homeless invalidism. On both boys and girls it is hard, and particularly so when they approach maturity. If vices are found in the schools – as they certainly are, though every one seems to be afraid to say so – it is more the result of the nervous disease engendered by the unrelaxed strain of the school hours than any other one thing. A child depleted in nervous force will take to evil habits as naturally as smoke will fly upward. Those who will be most shocked at the statement that noxious vices do exist in the public schools are probably the very ones who have most need to find out what their children are doing after school hours. It is with absolute knowledge that I speak when I say that in some of the finest families in this town the children are given over to vices of the most shameless character. The teachers – some of them – know of it. But any word from them to the parents is apt to be regarded as insulting, and so they keep still.

Now, get fresh air into the school rooms and cease making the lessons a burden, and these vices will disappear in the majority of cases. They are the result of wearied brains, of exhausted nerve force, of unbearable irritation.

The mind is of no account for any earthly purpose unless it is housed in a body. And for this reason the body should be cared for first. The care of the bodies is not provided for in our public schools. Mr. Lewis of the High school feels this, and has tried to do what he can toward mitigating the evil by encouraging out of door sports and athletic exercises. He thus not only helps to preserve the physical health of his pupils, but substitutes for a pernicious curiosity a healthy friendship in his classes, and fosters a strong class feeling, which, during the last year or two, has become almost as strong as that felt in colleges. This heightens ideas of honor, it increases self-respect. It keeps the boys and the girls high-minded and above board. If it were not for this, one shudders to think what the pupils might degenerate into by the time they had been preyed on by the exhausting school course through all its grades.

The board has in a way observed the danger of this failure of health, and has introduced into the school a system of calisthenics designed as a remedy. It is a system intended for use in gymnasiums – the Sargent system. It strains the muscles a great deal more than it develops them. It is not beautiful and it destroys what natural grace a child has, and some of the exercises are of such a nature that it is a marvel that the teachers do not have to put themselves under medical treatment after practicing them.

It is a well-known fact among the teachers that the children hate calisthenics. If the proper system were introduced the children would enjoy it and look forward to it. It is only fair to say that this instructor is, in his own field, that of the gymnasium, considered a competent teacher, and that he is popular among the turners in this city. But the calisthenics which the children repeat at home when they are asked to do so, resemble nothing so much as St. Vitus' dance.

That is the truth. It is unfortunate that it is unpleasant.

All this is but a way of saying that what is needed in the school board is brains. What is needed among the teachers is brains. What is needed with the superintendent is brains and moral courage – and doubtless it exists there. Since Mr. Fitzpatrick came into charge of the Omaha schools he has had little opportunity of showing what is in him. But he will soon have that opportunity, and then every thinking citizen in Omaha hopes that he will make a determined stand for improvement in various matters. Omaha is behind St. Paul, Minneapolis and Kansas City in her school system. At least, so it is said by those who understand educational matters and who have thought much on the subject. New school houses are all very well, but improved methods in those we have would be better still.

Undoubtedly the conduct of the schools is of more real importance than any other public matter in the city. It is very well to put down miles of pavement – but paving will rot. It is a good thing to have a new library – books are sometimes good things and worth preserving and collecting. It is well to have beautiful parks. They help a city in many subtle ways, as well as in material ones. But that which is done in the schools is done for eternity. For souls are educated there as well as minds.

Therefore the responsibilities of the school board are incalculable. Therefore every teacher should see to it that she does her best, and that her best is a little better each year.

This is dull, isn't it? But it's not nearly so dull as the next generation will be if the schools are not placed in better sanitary condition and the teachers selected with more care.

No teacher should ever be appointed because she needs the place. The state can better afford to take care of her in the poor house than to have her warping the spirit and misleading the minds of its future citizens. No teacher should be retained because she has been long in the service or for any other sentimental reason. Ability is what is needed, and it should be the only criterion of appointment. It is here, in this culling out, that Mr. Fitzpatrick can do his good work. These words can give no offense to those who do not deserve them. Those honorable and aspiring women who teach with a full consciousness of their responsibilities, and with a delight in the importance of their trust, proud to live in an age when instruction is made a fine art and the occupation of teaching a poetical one, will know they are not meant.

CHAPTER 4

A Word with the Women

"A modern woman who respects herself and the fact that God made her and expects her to be accountable for herself, does not yield one particle of her individuality when she marries."

With intellects and personalities well suited to each other's needs, an abiding faith in God, and a deep responsibility toward their children, Elia and Robert Peattie formed a companionate and loving partnership throughout their lives. Reiterating the importance of woman's role in the home in her writings, Peattie preached, "Home is the place to be happy. Riches cannot make a home, nor can art do so, nor intellect. It is the heart that makes a home" ("What Makes Home Home," 22 May 1892).

However, as much as Peattie gloried in the roles of wife and mother, she was also realistic about the tedium and the demands made upon her. She explained her viewpoint in her 3 July 1895 "A Word with the Women" column: "It is quite true that it is best for the human race, best for the state, that nearly all the women stay at home and raise children. But let no one say that such women are necessarily happy. There are more drudges, more broken-hearted women, more mere human vegetables, more women who 'weep in the nighttime,' in the homes than anywhere else. It is very irritating to hear the home celebrated as the one place where women are in a state of blissful serenity, when anyone can look around over neighborhoods where domestic unhappiness spreads like a deadly mildew, and the women slave like men in the trenches."

The 1880s and 1890s were turbulent times for women. Not only had the opening of the West for homesteading isolated women from one another and their families by distance, but immigration, industrialization, and urbanization separated them into disparate social classes. They became further divided in their notions of women's status. The traditional nineteenth-century Victorian belief in the exalted role of the self-sacrificing, socially isolated housewife, the True Woman,[1] was being displaced during the 1880s and 1890s by a modern ideal, the New Woman.[2]

According to nineteenth-century ideals of True Womanhood, a wife's attributes comprised the four cardinal virtues of piety, purity, submissiveness, and

Elia Peattie, 1904. (From *The Reader* 4 [June–Nov. 1904]: 455.

domesticity. Guided to patiently and passively submit to God's will and that of her husband, a woman was to surrender her own ambition and opinion to his. The home was her world, and she was advised to make it as comfortable and cheerful as possible so that sons and husbands would not go astray. Her duties centered on ministering to the needs of her family, both physical and spiritual, and perfecting the science of housekeeping (Welter 21–41).

On the other hand, the New Woman, found predominantly in the middle and upper classes, asserted her independence by insisting upon equal education and employment opportunities, by strengthening her body through physical activity, by freeing herself from social restraints, and by attempting to influence the political system.[3] Although some New Women rejected conventional female roles, many did not seek to undermine marriage but rather to reform it, replacing bondage with independence (Ledger 20–21).

If one were to read only Peattie's editorials and columns concerning her family and home, she would appear very much a True Woman whose life centered around her home. She loved her husband and children with a fierce passion and pride, and she believed that maintaining a beautiful, healthy, and happy home was a creative and spiritual act. "The quality that makes a home is not describable, any more than poetry is, or love, or art," she maintained. "But just as sure and distinct as all these things is its existence, and no sooner does a stranger enter the door of a house than he can discover whether that house is a home" ("What Makes Home Home").

By entering the male-dominated newsroom, however, Peattie not only broke from woman's domestic domain but deviated from conventional women's occupations to enter into the masculine public realm.[4] Although Peattie's job was a necessity for the family's economic survival, writing was more than a vocation for her – it was her ambition. Her biography in A Woman of the Century *emphasized the importance of her career: "Nothing could have prevented her entering upon her career as a writer, but a happy marriage, with one who sympathized with her ambitions and who also was able to give her much important assistance in the details of authorship, was to her most important" ("Mrs. Elia Wilkinson Peattie" 562). Being a career woman was crucial to Peattie's intellectual and emotional well-being. Determined to be viewed as a professional, she listed her name in the Omaha* City Directory *alongside her husband's with her occupation, "Editorial Writer," in boldface type. Robert's job as managing editor, interestingly, was listed in regular type.*

During her years in Omaha, Peattie grew from a woman with a personal belief in the equality of the sexes to a strong advocate of women, and her outspoken editorials in the Omaha World-Herald *campaigned for their rights. She had vitality, intellect, and passion, and her work to enhance women's lives, especially her leadership role in the Woman's Clubs, had an impact on many.*

"Ties Which Do Not Bind: The Matrimonial Knot and the Ease with Which It Is Broken"

1 April 1894

Peattie championed the primacy of marriage, family, and home all of her life. Believing that marriage should be viewed from a sacramental standpoint, not as a "selfish pleasure," she emphasized that marriage was an awesome privilege: "To be permitted to create other humans, with bodies which will house souls, to train these souls for immortality – this is the highest happiness which God has devised for man."[5] Marriage, Peattie avowed, was not so much a question of happiness but of duty.

Many late-nineteenth-century women still living within a world governed by their husbands and bounded by their home and the church would have shared Peattie's philosophies of marriage and child-bearing. In much of middle- and upper-class America, the "True Woman" persisted, her life one long act of devotion, not only to God but also to her husband, her children, and all of humanity (Fowler xvi).[6]

❧ Popular opinion, based upon the lucubrations of the jocular paragrapher, has come to hold the view in a casual way that divorce is easily obtained in this country. But anyone who has had direct or indirect association with a divorce case, or who has reported them in the courts, or by any other means become acquainted with the facts of this subject, knows that, on the contrary, a divorce is a difficult thing to obtain. The law places many obstacles in its way. The court insists upon a strong reason. And many are the disappointed applicants for separation from marital responsibilities, who leave the court room impressed with the severe scrutiny of motives which the law exercises in such cases.

To anyone interested in the social questions, the query must often arise why marriages, which are so much more important, considered from an economical point of view, than divorces, should be so easy to obtain. Such a moralist must often feel that there is nothing more astonishing among all the incongruities of our civilization, than the lightness and ease with which men and women marry. In at least one-half the cases it is safe to say that neither are acquainted with the past life of the other. The family is not known. Questions of heredity are not considered, and the young persons who desire to get married would probably feel very indelicate if they undertook to discuss them. The old fashion of having parents arrange marriages had

An unknown family, ca. 1890. (Courtesy of author)

its advantages, perhaps, but it cannot and should not exist in a country where personal liberty is the fundamental principle. An American would rather make his own mistakes than have some one else make them for him. And being an amorous creature with strong domestic proclivities, he prefers, above all things, to attend to his own selection, love making and marrying. For these reasons it is necessary for him to proceed along the path which he instinctively chose for himself as a lover of women and liberty, and to do his courting without the intercession of parents or anyone else.

But this reliance upon the impulse of love, this deliberate apotheosis of instinct, has led to a degree of carelessness which can be considered as nothing less than criminal. If the results of this carelessness were felt only by those two persons who had indulged their young happiness, it would not be so bad. But the thousands of children who are bereft by one or the other of their parents, who are acquainted with the miseries of a home rent by quarrels and scandals, who come to a too early knowledge of the brood of passions that grow out of unhappy marital relations, and who are cast practically adrift upon the world through no fault of their own, makes the carelessness inexcusable. In fact, it is not too much to say that the sacramental idea of marriage seems to be almost lost sight of amid the adventurous philosophy of the age. The radical ideas which impregnate our society in every direction have reached into the home. Men and women maintain, not without show of equity, that marriage without love is but a legal prostitution, and that one performs the better part by securing a separation from ties so loathsome, and which can not but lower the tone of life and rob the soul of the development to which it is entitled, and for which, possibly, it was created.

But the question is not so much one of happiness as one of duty. If marriage is looked upon as a sacrament, if it is entered into as the result of the most earnest thought which can be given to any subject, and if its obligations are lived up to – its natural obligations – there will not be so much marital misery.

When marriage emerged from the condition of a mere domestic convenience, and the imagination of mankind began to clothe it with the splendid idea of soul-companionship, and when this idea became popularized, and every man began to aspire to an ideal home, then for the first time a consideration of all those psychological details entered into the question of marriage, which are now such a menace to its durability. Men came to regard their wives as their mistresses, in a fine and beautiful sense of the word. They wanted them to be a constant delight, they desired to get their best inspiration from them; and no sooner did they become bored than they were alarmed, lest they had missed their soul's companion, and began to look about to discover where that longed-for creature had concealed herself. It was the same with women. They resented the absence of congeniality. They wanted a man who would match their every mood with one in kind. They became jealous of a man's occupations, of his absorption, and they bitterly resented any lack of appreciation of their finer capabilities. Thus it came about that from the very development of the finer faculties, men and women became conscious of incompatibility, and the law was forced to recognize it as a reason for legal separation.

But now that these dangers have come to be well-known and that they are perceived to be the inevitable condition of a society manifestly imperfect, yet haunted with ideals which are a vital part of life itself, the only sensible and practical thing that men and women can do is to consider how the abuses of marriage can be remedied. How, in short, can divorce be decreased?

It seems to me that the reply must be, by exercising control over marriages.

There is almost nothing that public opinion cannot do. It can overthrow a government, or make a law, or render one inoperative, or control a people without any law at all, or free 1,000,000 slaves, or keep a man out of office in spite of the most effective working of the national political machine. Public opinion could, if it would, surround marriage with safeguards. And this reform could be appropriately begun by the clergymen, who have control of the marriage ceremonies of the greater part of wedded couples.

If anyone were to investigate he would find that few clergymen make any inquiries whatever of those who come to them to get married, beyond asking to look at the license which has been procured with perfect ease from the clerk of the county. Yet, if the truth were known, the most important impersonal act of a clergyman's life is when he unites a man and woman in wedlock. The potentialities of his act are greater than those of any other service which he can be called to perform, either as clergyman or man. Yet what does he do? Reads the license, performs the service, takes his fee, and thinks no more about it.

There are, it is only just to say, exceptions to this rule. There are clergymen – a very few – who insist that one or the other of the parties to a marriage contract shall belong to the church, and that one or the other shall be known to him personally. There are those who make inquiries into the health, the habits and the ancestors of those about to be united for purposes of mutual happiness and the incidental propagation of society. Such do not perform a marriage ceremony without endeavoring to determine the motives which prompt the man and woman to enter into the marriage relation, and there is at least one clergyman living today who will not perform such a ceremony if he perceives those motives to be other than the sort he deems to be fitting and sacred.

This course of conduct must of necessity be confined to those who are of the Christian faith and would not apply to all good persons in this county who desire marriage from high reasons. But, over all, whether high or low

Christians, or of other faiths, or of no faith at all, some sort of scrutiny could be, and ought to be exercised. Though temporary inconvenience might be entailed, or the transient suffering involved, or even the life disappointments incurred, it would be as nothing to the misery and shame entailed by our present system.

The hard drinker, the scrofulous persons, the person with epilepsy, the consumptive, the person with taint of insanity, the constitutionally poor – those who are doomed to poverty by laws of nature – those of dangerous passions, and those of deficient physique, especially in certain vital directions – should be debarred from marriage so far as possible. It is to be admitted that very often such interference or advice would fail of its object. But on the other hand it would occasionally succeed. And public opinion could, in time, make it seem as much of a shame for some persons to marry as it now is for other persons to be divorced. For, let the lighter part of society say what it may, the man or woman who is divorced is much pitied, and is looked upon, more or less, as one who has met with a terrible misfortune and made a failure of a part of life. One is always prompted to inquire into the circumstances before taking a divorced man or woman into one's home or into one's friendship. Divorce seems like an avoidance of responsibility; it seems selfish, and the divorced persons stand suspected until he or she has told the tale of the tragedy.

If marriage were a mere legal contract it would be different. There would then be no reason why it should not be undertaken with comparative lightness, and dissolved whenever it became objectionable. But the fact that children, incontestable, palpable facts, with a possibility of futurity, and a certainty of the power of living, are born as the result of such union, and that men and women are thus put in touch with the whole scheme of God's creation, gives to the marriage relation a loftiness and holy dignity which the utmost human puerility cannot destroy. As all men are made dignified by death, so all men are made dignified by the kiss of love, which is the beginning of the great mystery of life, and they cannot escape from its godlike responsibilities, try as they may.

One sometimes hears complaints made that marriages are not common enough. There is something to be said on this question, but on the other hand it may be urged with equal force that marriages are too frequent, too light, too profane. The immorality that might be the result of too few marriages cannot equal in its consequences the immorality certain to be the result of mistaken marriages. And, indeed, it is very well established that the grossest immoralities of city life are not sustained by bachelors, but by men with domestic establishments, who are coarsened and made reckless by the unhappiness they have encountered where they expected to find life's best consolation.

As the century grows old, and the cumulative ideas of the great cycle fuse themselves into a passion for liberty which is shaking the world, and amid which old ideas and superstitions, old governments and old faiths fall with a mighty noise, there is danger that the home will feel the jar. There is no way in which this can be prevented except by educating society to perceive the physical and philosophical responsibilities of marriage. It is futile to say that society cannot be educated to this. It can be educated to anything good. As patriotism is ground into the consciousness of the young till they accept the idea of the indivisible republic, and its sign, the flag, as something for which to die without question if the necessity arises, so can they be taught the sacredness of marriage – a fact which can never, by a sophistry, be made to seem to the sane, as a mere theory – which cannot be discounted by any whim of society, or belittled by any perverse generation of men.

In this age men are beginning to discover that nothing is so expensive as crime. We are reaching a toleration for socialism, because it is cheaper than selfism, with its wealth, and its poverty, its crime and penal institutions. To prevent crime is the philosophic thing. To prevent bad marriages would be much cheaper than divorce considered from every point of view. The individual and the state would find it economical. And posterity would not be so sinned against. Parents, the church, the schools and the press can array the barriers of public opinion against the light making of marriages if they will.

"How Not to Treat Babies"
20 April 1890

In 1923, when Peattie returned to Omaha to lecture, she told a reporter that babies had always been her "chief amusement. And over and above this, and under and around it, is that sense of satisfaction and joy which only children can give" ("Writer"). Peattie enjoyed her children throughout all of their developmental stages, encouraging their imaginative play, supporting their individuality, and promoting their sense of self-worth. Typical of Progressive Era parents, the Peatties encouraged extended educational opportunities, enhanced recreational activities, and the development of moral, ethical, and religious ideals (D. Macleod 101). And, like many other American families reacting against the materialism and corruption of the urbanized and industrialized Gilded Age, they romanticized childhood, idealizing children's innocence, beauty, freedom, and closeness to God and nature (A. S. MacLeod 117–18).[7]

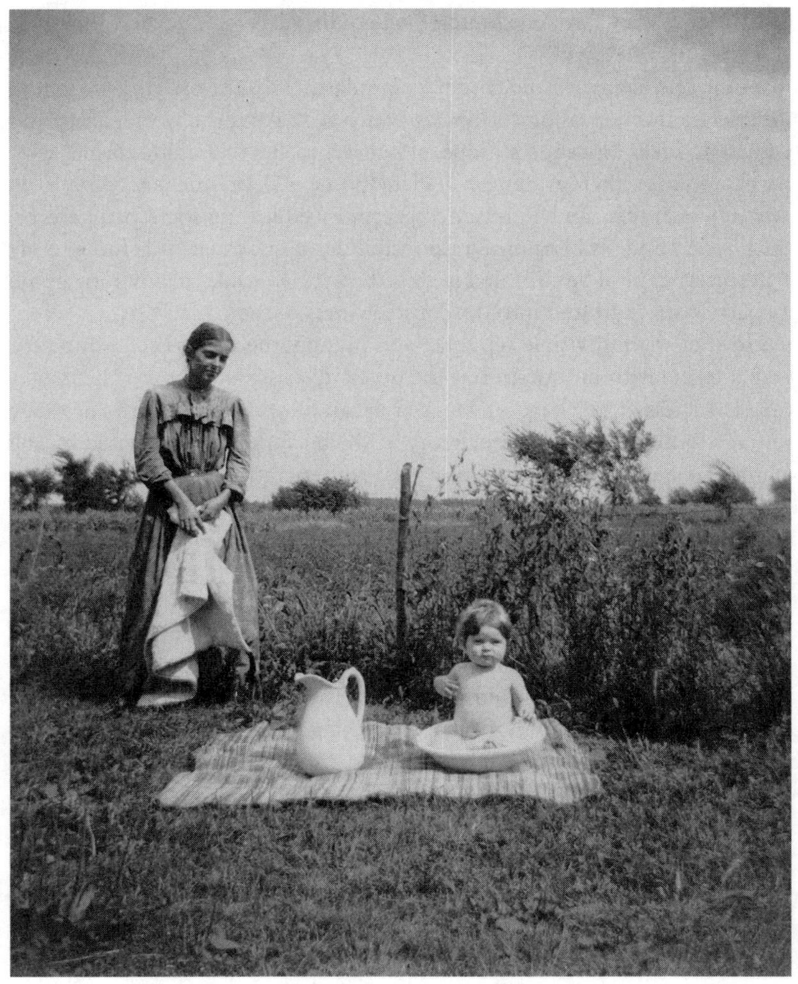

A young rural mother and child, 1910.
(Stuhr Museum of the Prairie Pioneer)

As the twentieth century neared, society began viewing the homemaker as a professional whose job required training and scientific knowledge. "Experts" wrote child-rearing manuals with strict rules for raising the young, and these became bibles for late-nineteenth-century mothers.[8] *When Nell Nelson, a former Chicago reporter, wrote an article for the* New York Sun *on raising children, Peattie disagreed with her "scientific" child-rearing advice.*

❧ Nell Nelson has been telling the readers of the *New York Sun* what not to do with babies. This is what she says:

Don't rock the baby.
Don't let him sleep in a warm room.
Don't let him sleep with his head under cover.
Don't let him sleep with his mouth open.
Don't "pat" him to sleep.
Don't try to make him sleep if he is not sleepy.
Don't let him nap in the afternoon.
Don't let him be kissed.
Don't let him wear any garment that is tight enough to bind his throat, arms, waist or wrists.
Don't have ball buttons on the back of his dress.
Don't have clumsy sashes on the back of his dress.
Don't cool his food by blowing it.
Don't feed him with a tablespoon.
Don't use a tube nursing bottle.
Don't change the milk you started with.
Don't bathe him in hot or cold water.
Don't bathe him more than three times a week.
Don't allow a comb to touch his head.
Don't let him eat at the family table.
Don't let him eat meat until he is 2.
Don't let him sleep on a pillow.
Don't coax, tease, torment, mimic or scold him.
Don't whip him.
Don't make him cry.
Don't notice him when he pouts.
Don't frighten him.
Don't tell him about ghosts, bugaboos or bad places.
Don't shake him.
Don't put him in short shoes.
Don't dance, jump or dangle him.
Don't overfeed him.
Don't let him sleep with an adult.
Don't place him face to face on a bed or in a carriage with another child.
Don't let him swallow things or eat ashes.
Don't let him roll down stairs.
Don't let him fall out of windows.

Don't teach him to walk.
Don't wash him with lye soap.
Don't let him chew painted cards.
Don't expose his eyes to the sun unless protected by a peaked hat or veil.
Don't scream in his ear.
Don't rap him under the chin.
Don't take him by the wrist or arms.
Don't starch any of his clothes.
Don't allow him to wear wet bibs.
Don't worry him.
Don't give him anything to eat between meals.

Now Nell Nelson, as she is known to the world, is a dear good girl. I have known her these many years. We have been to weddings together, to conventions together, to races together. We have, in short, met everywhere that the two busiest women in Chicago, employed on rival newspapers, would be likely to meet. We have hired cabs together to save cab hire, and lunched together at gruesome hours of the night, after hours, for mutual protection. We have helped each other out in all sorts of ways, and after an acquaintance of this sort, I am bound to say that for a friend in rainy and sunshiny weather, in work hours and out of them, Nell is about as sensible a woman as one finds. She used to teach school all day and report half the night, to keep her mother and a band of sisters and brothers in food and clothes – not common, every day food and clothes – but a house on the avenue, moquette carpets, the latest thing in spring wraps, the best sort of an education, theater tickets, carriages for the opera! That was the way Nell Nelson took care of her family. And she always looked like a queen herself. Physically, she is superb. She has magnificent gray eyes set in an intellectual face, a fine carriage, and a trick of looking well dressed always. The boys on the papers – well, most of them, went the same way. The new ones usually fell in love with Nell, and the old ones sat by and smiled. The day had been when they had also been in love with her. It was no use, though. Nell was and is devoted to journalism and her family.

But when it comes to the question of babies, I object. She doesn't know anything about them. She has been consulting some old maid who lectures on the bringing up of children, and has taken notes on the remarks of the old maid. If Nell ever gets heaven, and St. Peter asks her any questions, she will be sure to take notes on the subject, and after she gets in the gold gate will mechanically write up a fashion report on the latest fads in angel wings. So I am sure she has been taking notes about babies.

There are a number of things in this list of negations with which I do not quarrel. There are others that are superfluous. For example, it is not customary, so far as I know among mothers in any class of society, to let their children roll down stairs. One may say that there is a fixed prejudice against this sort of thing, which the onward sweep of the ages cannot eradicate. Neither is the eating of ashes considered good form among mothers of high degree. The ladies of the Vere de Vere family are said to have a dislike to having their children fall out of windows. It lacks repose. But there are a number of things to which I must object. Nell says the babies are not to be kissed. I once had a nurse whom I disliked, without being able to tell why. She was the soul of neatness. She never neglected her charges. She was a good Christian – so she said – and used to read the Bible while I dusted the nursery. One day my little girl fell down. I hadn't time to kiss her myself, so I asked Lena to do it. A kiss with my babies has all the curative qualities of patent medicine, and is warranted to cure broken heads, pricked fingers, smashed dolls, lost drum sticks, rainy days and bleeding noses.

"I never kiss children, ma'am," said Lena with a superior accent. "It is not hygienic."

I stopped to kiss Barbara so that she would stop crying and I could talk.

"Lena," said I, "do you mean to tell me that you have never kissed the babies since you have been here?"

"Certainly not," returned Lena, lifting her colorless eye brows. "There is no manner in which contagious diseases can be more readily transmitted than by kissing."

Those are Lena's words. She had taken a course at some kind of a place where they taught massage and grammar.

"My dear girl," I said, "I am really very sorry, but could I trouble you to go out this afternoon and look for a new place? Stay here till you get one but please make a strong effort to get one soon, for I feel that we can not live up to your standard of hygiene."

Then I got a good fat Irish girl who would not sew on the children's buttons, but who kissed them as naturally as she took a drink of water when she was thirsty. And I felt a great deal better.

A distinguished physician who had had experience in the hospitals of London, New York and Chicago, once told me that the babies at the asylums die for want of love.

"They have healthier surroundings," said he, "than the children in the majority of the homes. They are fed more wholesome food, and in more judicious quantities. But they die, die, die! Do you know what they want? They want to be loved. They want to be cuddled and played with. They need to lie at night in a mother's arms. They want the inspiration of a mother's eye."

Allow me to ask Nell Nelson where she can find healthier children than the little dirty rascals who run about the cottage of a day laborer? And as for kisses – why, they get them from a whole neighborhood. It doesn't seem exactly polite to suspect your friend of harboring microbes, and germs, and animalcule and things, which they will bestow upon the baby. And your friends do not do it once in five thousand times. Of course, I do think a baby's feelings ought to be respected. There are some persons that a baby objects to and resents being kissed by. When such a person comes the best thing to do is to say you think the baby has scarlet fever.

Then Nell says that we are not to rock or pat our babies. Perhaps she is right. I have seen well brought up infants who were laid away on the bed like a cold fish on a platter. And they went to sleep after the first few nights of bitter crying, like majors, and behaved in a sensible way ever after. The mothers were very proud of it. I am not sensible myself. I used to like to undress the baby by the fire, toast its blessed toes till they looked as if they had been tipped with cherry lip, and then rock them to sleep with an accompaniment of melodies and yarns, adult "sleepy town" and "baby land" and "Willie Winkle," and all that sort of trash. I'm afraid it wasn't hygienic, or progressive. Then after they were asleep I used to lay them down and pat them till I was sure they were quite over the border into "the pleasant land of sleep." When they first touched the pillow they used to look up with a reproachful glance, but when they saw me there they would break into that bonny smile that only children can summon, and so fall asleep with it on their lips. And I would go away feeling as if I had been sanctified. It was a great deal better than being hygienic and sensible.

Then Nell does not want us to let the baby sleep with his mouth open. What does she expect us to do? And if the child has a cold, what does she expect the child to do? Die of strangulation?

She also says that the baby is not to have a nap in the afternoon. But there is no call to talk upon this subject. The babies will settle it. They will not ask permission to take the nap – they will help themselves to it. She also says we are to give him nothing to eat between meals. As a penalty for this I would like to make the dear girl take care of a teething baby about 2 months old, who had nothing to eat between meals. Still, perhaps the punishment would be too severe for the crime. But Nell is absolutely wrong here. The tender stomach can not do heavy work, nor digest great quantities at one time. The work should be judiciously distributed. Nature demands that. Any mother knows that who has watched the expression of a child's face. About midway between meals, they begin to wear a look of dejection, and even if they do not ask for food they need it. The child who goes to school needs it also, and every little youngster during the first few terms ought to have a bowl of bread and milk waiting for him when he gets home at half past 3. There is no hunger on earth like the gnawing of this after-school hunger. In my earlier years I was once in a journey across country without food for twenty-four hours. It was disagreeable, of course, but it was not [as consuming as] the hunger I used to feel as I let myself in the barn yard bars at night after school when I was a little lass, and made for the pantry. But I had a mother who was not advanced, and I used to find a bit of bread and honey or a ripe peach and a cookie or some other delicious morsel laid on the broad pantry shelf along with a pitcher of water fresh from the well. Perhaps mother would come along and set me on the shelf – which of course was not nice, and would not have been done by a well brought up mother. But I remember still the scent of the apricot tree just outside, and the shadows its long pointed leaves cast on the floor, and the tingle of my feet when I leaped from the shelf to the floor, and as I remember it my eyes fill – thinking of the mother. And as soon as I finish this article I will write her a letter and tell her how nice she is! And that is what the absence of hygiene and things has done for me! If I had had a really progressive mother, who objected to meals between hours, there would not be these tears in my eyes now at memory of her thoughtfulness. Not a bit of it.

Nell says we are not to blow in the baby's food to cool it. It would be good fun to see Nell some afternoon with a very impatient, assertive baby, and a bowl of hot gruel. It would indeed. It would not work well with her injunction not to shake him nor let him cry. For both things would happen, sure as guns. Then we are not to dance, or jump or dandle him. Well, certainly no considerate parent jumps a baby immediately after dinner, or teeters a youngster till it barely escapes nervous prostration, and no mother who knows what is good for herself gets a baby in the habit of thinking that it must continually be kept in motion. But as to never dancing or dandling a baby! Well, positively I lose patience with this excellent but inexperienced young woman when I think of it! I am in the habit myself of all but tearing my babies' limb from limb, and if I did not they would suspect that there had been a falling off in my affections. Besides, it is natural to dance a baby. There is an instinct that tells one to do it. The cave dwellers used to do it, I know they did. You can't help doing it. You want to feel the little legs gain control of themselves; you are electrified by that strong feebleness as the feet strive to take their right position and do their right work; you are more charmed with the look of exaltation that comes into baby's face when he first learns to take a leap himself, and spring on your knee, than you ever will be by the most glorious music made by a prima donna.

I like the idea of only bathing a baby three times a week. Some mothers bathe far too much. It is very exhausting with some children and I think friction should always be got up after a bath. I am very certain that I like the idea of not frightening him in any way at all. Neither would I have him shown anything or told of anything that is not good and beautiful. I like my children to hear pleasant stories, see pleasing pictures and then I firmly believe they will speak pleasant words, and have pleasant faces.

And they have, bless 'em.

Poor Nell Nelson! I can afford to disagree with her. She has no babies.

"Where Are the Children? A Lay Sermon Suggested by Chief Seavey to Colonel Hogeland"

20 March 1892

As children matured, Peattie believed, parents' duties expanded to governing their children's actions outside the protection of the home. She responded with alarm to the Omaha chief of police's report on the number of truant boys in the city. Because of the influx of immigrants and rural families to the cities at the end of the nineteenth century, neglected, destitute, and delinquent children were becoming a major concern. They faced not only the complexities of city life in a country foreign to them but also debilitating poverty and cultural clashes with their parents' old-world values. When they succumbed to vice, not a single institution in the United States existed for their reformation; juvenile offenders convicted of crimes, serious or petty, were committed to jails and prisons with adult criminals (Folks 198–99; Hawes 161). To prevent this tragedy, Peattie urged parents to model moral virtues and to make their homes stimulating and happy, thus preventing their children from following the "long and treacherous road which leads at last to ruin."[9]

❧ The most valuable opinion among the many expressed at the convention of the Boys and Girls' National Home and Employment association was that given by W. S. Seavey, chief of police of the city of Omaha.

"My opinion is," said he, "that the best plan for providing against boys becoming tramps is for parents to make home more attractive and interesting for them, for parents to cultivate the acquaintance of their sons.

"Study their dispositions and desires, and in a kind, considerate, affectionate and indulgent manner, contribute to the wishes of the boys to such an

Three mischievous Nebraska boys, ca. 1900.
(Nebraska State Historical Society Photograph Collections)

extent as will win their esteem and confidence, and thus cause the attractions at Metz hall, the Coliseum, Kessler's hall, etc., to become a secondary matter.

"Parents should know where their sons are after 9 o'clock P.M. If they think the boys are at the neighbors' or at church, when in reality they are in wine rooms or houses of prostitution, the parents should know it, and knowing this, looking after them would be the best and only way to prevent many of our bright, intelligent boys becoming tramps and criminals. I believe there are about forty boys who belong in this city, whose ages range from 14 to 20 years, who are now tramps and petty criminals, and that 60 per cent of this number have Christian parents. This question of how to provide against boys becoming tramps is broad, most difficult to successfully answer, and one of the most important questions of the age. If I could be with you tomorrow, I would only attempt to deal with that part of it where boys have good homes and Christian parents, leaving the question of orphans for the other gentlemen, and my humble efforts would be to impress upon the minds of those present the apparent indifference of the parents as to the welfare of Omaha boys who are going to the bad."

Chief Seavey is quite right in thinking that the boys with fathers and mothers are even more to be pitied than the boys without them.

Benevolence finds out and cares for the boys and girls who have been robbed of their natural protectors, but it can do little for the child with home and parents.

How is benevolence going to interfere when a child is given enough to eat, drink and wear? The world is so material that we are forced to take cognizance only of these material and palpable things. It is difficult to deal with the more subtle and essential rights that belong to every child.

A child, for example, has a right to be protected. It has a right to be educated.

Yet any day you may find, in this city, truant boys and girls playing about the streets; and any night you may see them in bands, walking about together at the edges of the pavements, like little bands of conspirators. Of course, it is possible that they are not plotting at all. But a band of boys, prowling about the streets at night, bodes no good. Often, as late as 10 and 11 o'clock, I have seen children who were little more than babies, sitting about on the curb or leaning against door ways, simply waiting to see what would turn up.

If the fire engines came out, that was a happy moment! And from being listless wooden little figures, they suddenly become howling dervishes. And if the patrol wagon went by with a "drunk and disorderly" in it, that was cause for unqualified congratulation. There is nothing in this to the detriment of the little children on the curb. It's human nature at a certain period of life to like fire engines and "drunk and disorderlies." I haven't got by the fire engine stage myself.

But there is something radically wrong with the mother who does not know or care where that little fellow is who is sitting there on the curbing. For sure as the electric light dims the pale glow of the young moon, the evil that that boy learns on the curb will counteract the good that was born in him.

Night in a city is an evil book, and he who reads its pages must be armed against evil before he can do so with impunity. Oaths are the first thing the boy learns who is out at night. Blasphemy comes next. He learns to laugh at a meanness, and finally at a dishonesty. He learns first of gamblers and then of gambling; and other evils follow, until, almost before he knows it, every form of virtue seems contemptible, and his innocence is gone irremediably. At an age when he should be thinking only of his lessons, and when knowledge should be holding him with that fascination it has for the healthy youth, he is befuddled with whisky, and the lips which should have known no kiss but its mother's are befouled.

It is not a trite subject. Let no one think it is trite.

I say to you, you sleek young fellow, so sure of yourself, so comfortable in your nonchalant belief that everything is allowed to and excused in men, that this is not a woman's more sentimental objection to the "experience" about which she is supposed to know nothing. This is not preaching. It is not a theory. It is a fact.

Life cannot hold success for the fellow who insists in believing that virtue is contemptible. And success is worth thinking about. I know perfectly well how fellows of a certain age sneer at respectability and laugh at "leading citizens," and think that good manners and good books and the friendship of good girls are all very common-place, and really intended only for fools and milk sops.

Goodness knows I hate a milk sop quite as much if not a little more than anybody else. I want a fellow to have the courage to know the world. Ignorance and timidity never seem like goodness to me. But the "best fellows" are, after all, the fellows with a sense of honor, with courage, dignity, truth and courtesy. And you do not learn any of these things by sitting on the curb at night when you are 6 years old, or loafing over a poker table in a back room when you are 16.

But it is not the boys who are at fault. It is the fathers and mothers. A man and woman who have had the courage to bring a child into the world are under obligations to provide a home for that child which will make it happy.

Mind, a home is not enough. It must be a happy home. Every citizen of this country is entitled to the pursuit of happiness. That is a constitutional right, and children are entitled to it no less than grown folk.

There isn't a home in this town so poverty stricken that a corner of it cannot be set apart for the children. If you have only one room to live, cook and eat in, you can make a place for the children on one side of the stove and let them do as they please there. You grownup folks just "shinney on your own side," and don't interfere with everything the children say and do. If you fix a basilisk stare on them every time they say or do something foolish it will result in freezing up their young blood. And of all crimes in the calendar there is none so terrible as freezing young blood. It is no wonder that boys play poker in back rooms down town and that girls make appointments to meet young fellows in Jefferson square when homes are so chilly and repellant.

A flower will die if it does not have sunshine. A child will die if it does not have fun. And as the flower will make every effort in its power to get at the sunshine, and will perk its little head toward the faintest ray of light, so the boy or girl will struggle to get hold of the life and happiness which is its right.

So, if you sit around, glum, irritable, forever talking about your poverty and your nerves, and how hard you work, you foolish fathers and mothers, you can expect nothing but that your children will get out as soon as possible into some place less moldy.

You can have fun if you are poor. If you've got a fire and a mother in the house, there's material for fun. Make a noise. Noise has its moral value. It is the letting off of animal force that will be expended some way. Play together, you grown-up folks, and you folks who are not grown up. I know that after you get out of the way of it, it is hard to begin. I know when a man comes home from the smelter at night that he is pretty tired; and that his wife, who has been washing, and who has to set the bread and fold the clothes even after the supper dishes are done up, besides looking after the fretful baby, has no nervous force left to do much with. Her heart is heavy. She is starved for want of diversion, love and gladness. But let this woman make an effort to forget her cares for a moment, and make a little fun with her children, and she will be surprised to find how her own heart has been lightened.

There is nothing like making a fool of yourself now and then "to plaze the familee" – as the song has it. The children will be changed under such treatment in a way that is surprising.

There are a number of very pretty girls in this town, from 15 to 17 years of age, daughters of men and women who are, I feel sure, hard-working and honest folk. But these foolish girls, tired, perhaps, of the monotony of their homes, and filled with a natural but very dangerous desire for adventure, make a point of showing their high spirits on the street in a way which is not altogether in keeping with modesty.

For the girls one can feel only the utmost pity. For their parents, what shall be said? Why do they not know where their daughters are and what they are doing? A number of daughters of respectable citizens have been led astray through the bad influence of some women, rather more clever and respectable-seeming than most of their kind. It seems incredible that fathers and mothers do not know that. It may not always be the case, but as a general thing I feel that there is something the matter with a home from which the girls go to flirt upon the streets.

Boys and girls brought up in the intimate association of a good mother are not likely to go out from home and do things which are inconsistent with honor and decency. Men and women have a way of living too carelessly. They quarrel before their children. They talk ill of their neighbors. They get life down to a low tone. The children naturally fall into the way of thinking that coarseness and rudeness are not to be avoided. And it is so much easier to go down hill than to climb up!

Pride is a virtue. I do not think that it goes before a fall – not if it is of the right sort. Suppose, for example, that you are Wilson and that you work at the smelter. Then be proud of being Wilson and working at the smelter. Bring up your boys to say proudly that they are the sons of Jack Wilson, who works at the smelter. Make them appreciate the fact that your work requires skill, and that you take a pleasure in doing it well. Teach them that a family name has its importance; and that everyone who ever knew Jack Wilson would expect to find mechanical ability, and pride of workmanship, and honesty and temperance in his sons. We do not attach enough importance to families here in America. They make all the difference in the world. You cannot get a fine horse from low breed. And men and women ought to pay attention to these matters. It is a simple act of patriotism to do so. You want to give healthy boys and girls to your state; boys and girls who will make good citizens, who will earn their own living, who will obey good laws and understand that they have an inalienable right to reform bad ones. In a monarchy it does not matter of what stuff the citizens are composed. In a republic it matters vitally, for each person is a distinct force for good or evil there.

Vice is very democratic, and it enters the most exclusive and carefully guarded homes now and then. But the home of the workingman is particularly open to attack. There are several reasons for this. Boys and girls are given much liberty among this class. The homes are apt to be small and rather crowded, and it is not so easy to keep them as attractive, always, as they might be. The parents are too tired to make much home amusement, and they cannot afford to take their children very much to places of public amusement. The public library ought to help families of this sort to pass the evening pleasantly. There is an excellent collection of books in it. They can be found to suit all tastes. And the service at the library is perfect. I sometimes wonder if Omaha folk realize what a contrast the kindly courtesy invariably exhibited at this library is to the perfunctory and grudging service given at many of the libraries throughout the country. If you do not feel that history or biography is in your line, you can get novels enough here to keep you going for several years of your life. And novels are a great thing in a house. I sometimes think they are the most potent factor of civilization for teaching good morals and good manners to the young.

Certain it is that the parents who go selfishly along, and do not inquire why their boys and girls are out late at night, will suddenly some day be given a terrible shock. They will find some story of shame made public, and the name they have taken so little trouble to protect, will be dragged in the dirt. And their son will be "sent up" for a few months, or their daughter dismissed with a fine and a warning. All of which is apt to be but the first step in a long and treacherous road which leads at last to ruin.

It is impossible to begin too soon to protect the boys and girls. Do not make light of it when they deceive you. Do not laugh when you see them taking advantage of those who are weaker than themselves. Do not be amused at their first infantile experiments with oaths. Do not think it is funny when they are impertinent and try to "be smart." A little "tough" is no more amusing than a full-grown "tough." And you have no more occasion to laugh at these signs of incipient "toughness" in your child than you would have occasion to laugh at signs of incipient leprosy in him.

The raising of children is the most important concern in the world, for obvious reasons. No man or woman can so simply demonstrate his or her patriotism as by laboring to bring up children calculated to be self-respectful, honest, industrious and healthy. Such children become producers. It is they, who, in a very few years, will be the citizens of this town. And every child carelessly brought up represents just so much waste and expense. He is likely to be a pauper, or a convict. He is certain to be a hindrance.

The way to help the growth of a city most is to educate its future citizens.

It doesn't seem as if there were any man or woman so busy, or so thoughtless, or so ignorant that this simple truth cannot be understood or appreciated.

There is no doubt about it. The orphans will be cared for. It is the children with parents who cause the judicious to feel solicitude.

"The Women on the Farms: A Chapter of Advice for Them Which City Women Need Not Read"

24 March 1895

Even though Peattie could not comprehend the impossibility of some of her demands upon the husbands of farm wives, she did understand the reality of their everyday existence. For many women, finding the Garden of Eden in the West was more myth than reality. They learned too soon that the nineteenth-century standards of domesticity were difficult, if not impossible, to achieve on the prairie, where surviving blizzards, droughts, and frequent pregnancies became more crucial than embroidering doilies for the parlor, if they even had such a room. For most farm wives, the days were demanding, monotonous, and bleak, with no diversion and no beauty. Peattie counseled farm women to make their domiciles attractive by taking up a saw and hammer and fixing the fence around the house themselves if their husbands were disinterested or too busy. This advice was not only practical but realistic. Idealism will not mend fences.

The Charles Smith farmhouse in Lexington, Nebraska, 1904.
(Nebraska State Historical Society Photograph Collections)

This is for the women in the country, and women in town are respectfully warned that they would better not read it.

To the women on the farm the spring means a beginning of hard work. The planting and the cultivating and the harvesting of the year interest her as much as they do her husband, and, moreover, they bring almost as much added labor to her as they do to her husband. It will be difficult for her to indulge in many holidays. During the present season there will be very few women in Nebraska who will be able to go east, for a visit home. It is possible that even the prized vacation spent at the Chautauqua will be dispensed with. There is very little money. And where there is little money honest men and women do not indulge in luxuries. The thing to do, therefore, is to settle contentedly down at home, and make the best of the circumstances, and do all possible to make home attractive.

Now, if there is any one thing that is to be regretted about the country, it is the appearance of the door yards around the farm houses. It is only natural, perhaps, that it should be so. The state is young, and the men have been tillers of the soil for purposes of revenue only. They have had a hard fight with nature. Strength, energy, money and courage have been strained to their utmost in this great task of subjugating a vast territory – in reclaiming it from the wild. All things considered, the work has been prodigious – the results all that could reasonably have been hoped for.

But there is no reason, after all, why the yards should not be different than they are. In summer time a man's family lives in the yard rather than in the house. A yard may be said to be the environment of the small children, and of the mother. It is therefore obviously the duty of those who love their homes to make these yards as attractive as possible.

To begin with, the manure pile ought not to be in close proximity to the house. If it can be kept out of sight so much the better. The wagons ought not to clutter up the door ways. The men ought at least to show enough consideration for woman's natural fastidiousness to protect her from ill sights and smells and untidiness. Then the yard ought to be covered with neat sod. There is sod all over the prairies to be had for the digging, and while the grass is wild, it is nevertheless beautiful, and can be found free from weeds. There is no water to be had in the country with which to water lawns, and perhaps in many farm families there would be no one with the time to look after this duty. But the chaos of dust, rags, manure and sticks which too often makes confusion worse confounded, is inexcusable. It is healthful for the children to work in the yard, and they can make and keep it tidy. The smallest child who can toddle around may do something toward restoring order, and will enjoy the task if set about it in the right way.

There was a good deal of adroitness in the way Tom Sawyer used to farm out the painting of his fence. He began the work himself, doing it elaborately and with a look of intense enjoyment. The crowd of boys stood around and looked on. Tom delicately mentioned the pleasure he derived from his pursuit. One of the boys asked the privilege of painting for a few moments. Tom was doubtful. He explained to his listeners that the privilege was worth something. They agreed that it might be. Terms were arranged. Tom sat on a post near by while his friends painted the fence, and paid him for doing it.

Children can be induced by a strategy somewhat similar to enthusiastically undertake a task which they would have to be forced to do with ordinary treatment. When anyone has been cajoled, tricked and bewildered as I have been by the diplomacy of small boys and girls, and betrayed into doing all sorts of things I didn't want to do simply because the youngsters looked so abominably pretty, and had such alluring ways, no conscience can be expected in dealings with any of their tribe. I have been tricked into holidays, beguiled into spending more money than I had, kissed into wasting hours of time, hugged into making preposterous play houses, smiled into dealing out the last thing in the cupboard, and of going without dessert in consequence, and I am merciless. I am willing to betray the children. I intend they shall clean up my yard for me this spring and never know they did it. So I have no hesitation in advising other mothers to do the same thing.

After the yard is made tidy, the cans buried, the sticks burned, the scraps disposed of, the manure spread on the fields, or put somewhere out of sight, the next thing is to mend the fence if there is one, see that the gate swings properly, and that a nail is put in every place where a nail is required. A little gumption is needed for this almost as much as nails. There are people who never can find a board to put in the proper place. They have no board of the right sort, and never find one. It is not money, but gumption that is needed in a case like that. If you want a board to mend a hole you can get the board if you want to bad enough. Moreover if there is no man about the place who takes sufficient interest in the appearance of things to put a new hinge on the gate, or mend the shed door, or repair the fence, you can do it yourself.

Sawing is really quite interesting after one has turned one's attention to it, and the nailing of boards is really a fascinating occupation. It is nonsense to say that a woman cannot do it. She can do it just as well as a man. It requires nothing but practice. And the way to obtain practice is to practice.

The next thing needed is some flowers. Life seems like a different thing, someway, when there are flowers. It is true that on a farm there is not time to care for a large amount of flowers. For they must be faithfully watered and weeded. But there is time for a few placed near the house. At the very least a patch of pansies on the shady side of the house, a row of sweet peas on the sunny side, and some nasturtiums under the window are possibilities. By your bed room window put a few old fashioned morning glories. To wake up and see these little trumpets opening up their purple throats to you just outside your window is to get a touch of poetry and beauty at the dawning that will last the whole day. A few minutes work out in the fresh air in the morning is not a fatigue, but a rest. It seems to sweeten the day somehow, and makes the baking and ironing easier. All through the dry months you can have a bunch of blossoms on the table near you while you work. Flowers have a message brought straight from God. They are educators. They continually say:

"Beauty is as much a part of creation as use. Man does not live by meat alone. Perfume, and color, and form, and freshness are a part of the world. Put them in your own life. Enshrine them in your own heart."

It is a fact that not everyone can afford a hammock, cheap as they are. If one can be afforded, it ought to be purchased. There are few things in life that can be obtained for such a trifling price which furnish so much solid comfort as a hammock. But it is no trick to make one of ropes yourself. Swing it under the trees, or if there are not trees, put it on the porch, and seize a few minutes every day to loaf in it. If there are no trees and no porch, then put it on the side of the house where the shade is to be found in the afternoon. But have it if possible. Your husband may look at it with some disdain when you first put it up. But by the end of a week he will be glad to drop in and take a rest after supper. If it is hung out where the cool breezes can reach it, and where the eye can rest on the wonderful Nebraska sky, and watch the gloom gathering, and the stars brightening, he will not only be rested in body, but comforted in mind as well.

After the work is done there is nothing like getting out in the quiet and the cool of the summer nights and having a quiet talk with your husband. I am a very busy woman myself, and do not object to working even all the evening, or as late as midnight, in the winter time when the family can sit around the brightly lighted table, and the other people will talk to me, or read, while I work. But when the summer nights come I will work on nothing. I insist then on getting out under the stars. The work that cannot be done between sun up and sun down must go over till another day. I need the night, and the sky, and the quiet talk. It's luxury, perhaps. But it is also a necessity.

Now, no one can enjoy a talk of that sort if she is in the moist, soiled, garments she has worn while working all day. So even if you do not have time to dress freshly before supper, do it afterward. Look as well as you can. Have a fresh gown – summer gowns are so cheap that they do not mean so much expenditure of money as they do of machine stitching – put some of the flowers on your dress, comb your hair becomingly, and be as charming as you can. This delightful little diversion of looking and talking your best, with the man you like better than the whole world, under a star-lit sky, will put more energy into you, make you forget more sordidness, and bring back more of youth and joy than almost anything else of which you can think.

Youth and joy are, by the way, so very, very beautiful.

Another thing needed by the farm women is sociability. Of course they have it in a way. The picnics, the political rallies, the Grand Army gatherings, and all that sort of thing, furnish them with diversion. But, after all, these things only gratify a certain love of excitement which all human creatures have, but they do not entirely satisfy that craving for sympathy and companionship. More sociability among the women would be excellent. But it ought to be planned for. There is too much tendency among farm women to go to spend the day with their neighbors unannounced. This is sure to discommode the woman who is visited. There is a fatality about that sort of thing. Such a visit would be sure to occur on a day when a great deal of work had been planned for, and the hostess would have to drop it, and sit with folded hands and a chafing spirit, heartily wishing her guest away. The friendship between the women would thus suffer a light shock, and it might easily happen that after such an experience neither of them would feel as warmly as before. All this could be obviated by the extension of an invitation. If a day were set apart by a woman for entertaining two or three of her friends, and invitations were sent, the work arranged, the sewing laid out and the meals prepared for, a delightful day could be spent by all without any sense of hurry or fret. Nothing would remain undone that ought to be done. It is all very well to talk about informality. For a certain amount of formality is a very convenient thing with busy people. Certainly when visits are made with such difficulty that they must extend over a part or the whole of the day, prearrangement would be exceedingly sensible. Amusement that does not include one's husband is only a sorry amusement, as a general thing, and in visits of the sort mentioned there can usually be an arrangement by which the men can meet in the evening and take their wives home. A little house party would vary the monotony of existence, too. When a farm house is commodious, it is not difficult to entertain two couples over Sunday, for example. A point can be stretched – so can bed room and table accommodations. Such little gala occasions lift a life up out of the grind. They make the difference between existence and living.

There is no use in expecting much of the future. You can hope for anything you like, but be sure to "gather your rosebuds before they are withered." The present is the time. "Today is the happy dog." Let no delight of the hour pass. Do not drudge hopelessly. Work a reasonable amount, as the price you pay for living. But live and laugh between times. Do not put every cent you make on real estate. Put some on books, and some on clothes, and some on flowers. Do not rail at your neighbors. Like them. Associate with them. They are probably a little better than you are in some particulars, if a little worse in others. If you laugh together you will like each other. Do not forget to look as well as you can today. Tomorrow you may be dead. Do not neglect the cooking today. Tomorrow may find you beyond hunger. Do not forego the knowledge you might have today. Take time to read the story that attracted you. Tomorrow may find your sense past understanding. Find all the joy you can, keep all the youth you can.

Youth and joy are so very, very beautiful.

"Barriers against Women: They Are Mostly Erected by the Women Themselves through Blind Superstition"

21 August 1892

In January 1895, after reading an article about Cardinal Gibbons,[10] *one of the most outspoken churchmen against the New Woman, Peattie wrote a righteous response: "It seems then, that it is not for truth, honor, industry, sobriety, intellectual development and spiritual growth that woman is honored or exalted, but merely because she can bear children."*

Gibbons feared that education would turn women from family and religion, but Peattie disagreed: "The New Woman, as she is ridiculously called, finds in her college, her clubs, and her social intercourse, the very things that teach her how great is her responsibility to her kind. . . . Turn the light on. Let it flood the whole world – the light of learning and liberty! If this loses any woman a man's love, his love is well lost. If it keeps children from being born, they are well in their oblivion." Taking issue with Gibbons's comment that "the cardinal virtues of a woman are chastity and humility," Peattie chided, "It is unfortunate that it should seem to be the chief occupation of a large part of the men to destroy the first and to identify the second with servitude" (Peattie, "Takes Issue").[11]

Peattie reproached women, too, for restricting the growth of other women, especially by resenting each other's abilities and successes or by fearing genius. She urged them to accept the "uncommon woman" and learn to applaud.

❧ All that follows is for women. The men are not forbidden, but they are advised not to read it. A man always does anything he wants to, particularly if it is forbidden.

It is so from his earliest days.

At the age of 6 he says to himself:

"If I climbed to the top of that barn I wonder if I would see anything that I never saw before."

He climbs to the top of the barn. He sees fields, houses, woods that he did not know existed. And he perceives that the world is large – unexpectedly large. His mother comes out of the house and sees him on the barn. She does not scold him. She thinks he is splendidly adventurous. She mends his torn trousers without complaining.

But let her little daughter show any such inclination to see the world! She is called names that are a shock to her innocence. She is told that she is

Elia Peattie and her daughter, Barbara, visit the Clearys in Hubbell, Nebraska, 1891
(Photo by Michael Timothy Cleary, Cleary family scrapbooks)

a "tomboy" – terrible word! Her budding modesty is offended. She drops bitter tears into her little checked apron and admits to herself that it was very naughty indeed of her to try to find out if the world was large. She discovers that for a woman it is not large – that is to say, no larger than the door yard.

And, in a little while, she, too, has a contempt for a woman who tries to get up where she can look off and see what the world is like.

It is this placing of the limitations of women by the women themselves that always seems to me one of the most irritating of things. There are some women who always resent the success of any other woman.

After one of Mrs. Lease's peculiar and not to be forgotten addresses, I heard a woman say: "Why in the world doesn't she stay at home and take care of her children?"

There is a place where the women stay home and take care of the children. It is in India. And there the men have so little respect for them that they do not even accredit them with the possession of souls. And what is much worse, I do not think that the women suspect that this theory is wrong. They are married in infancy, their lives are doomed if their husbands die, and from birth to death they live in degrading subservience to the men. And well may these girl-mothers weep when the child they have borne is not a son! Well may they turn from the dark eyes of their little daughters, knowing what their future is to be!

There's the necessity of being mammal. Women are destined to that. But the fact is subordinated to the Woman herself. She is the Fact. Posterity is a secondary consideration.

The other night after a horribly hot day a woman was going home from Hanscom park. She had five little children. One of them seemed to be about 5 or 6 weeks old. The oldest appeared to be about 7 years. The children were all sleepy, but they didn't cry. They were good little things. They all had baskets or bundles, and had no doubt carried their luncheon to the park and eaten it there. When the mother signaled the train to stop she half arose. All the children did the same. The car stopped with a jerk. There was the usual result. Some one picked up the babies. The conductor dropped them off the car. Three of them fell getting across the street. A horse was coming and the mother had much difficulty in jerking them out of the way. The bundles seemed to be all over the block. But the tired woman gathered them up after a little and the troupe went on.

"Well," a woman on the car said, "if I had as many children as that, I'd stay home."

She hadn't as many children as that – or any at all. She is a woman who doesn't like to be inconvenienced. That is why she never had any children. Instead, she has pink luncheons.

Now, it didn't seem to me that the woman with the children was at all absurd in her little excursion. It involved fatigue, and some anxiety. But there was anticipation and enjoyment, and a lot of excitement to be counted in. There is nothing like dressing up. It gives a zest to life. And here were all these little ones in clothes that stood out with starch. They had had a day in a beautiful place. They had had their ride on the cars – a luxury not often enjoyed by them. And if they were going to bed dead tired, it was that happy fatigue which comes with a new experience.

But what is most important and significant of all is the fact that the young woman herself had not stagnated. In her soul was still the thirst for the beautiful; in her pulses still the power to leap at pleasure.

Perhaps her shuffling, overworked husband was at home waiting for her, surly at her absence, weary, wet with sweat, irritable.

What of it?

Had she not been hearing the children laugh in their play? Had she not seen the sunset through the skies, and noted the dark silhouettes against the amber west? Had she not heard the leaves whispering and watched the pallid shimmer of the fountain down through the "draw"?

She had been trying to live a little. And her effort would be sure to bring its own reward.

However, though, I think women do not always appreciate one another. I am far from thinking they are as mean to each other as they are commonly held to be in a certain class of novels. There was Mr. Trollope, who used to write interminable novels about feminine quarrels, and who seemed to work on the supposition that all any woman cared about was to get some other woman's lover away from her. That may be true in a certain class of idle and stupid society. But it isn't true here in America very much. We all seem to have all the lovers we want over here. And marriage isn't the only subject we talk about or think about. It's secondary and incidental to life itself, though it sometimes brings the chief joy of existence. I've often noticed the girls in dry goods stores. They are a good illustration of the point I wish to illustrate. There they stand, tired, dusty, harassed by senseless customers, the day stretching out before them in interminable length, yet almost always they are kind to each other, and are sisterly and courteous. There are exceptions. But the exceptions are few. On the street cars women are almost always particularly nice to each other. In the offices down town they seem to be generally kind and polite. And in society there is not half the idle gossip and ill-nature that there is commonly supposed to be. The women are sympathetic with each other. They have an admiration for each other's abilities and accomplishments.

I don't know exactly what they would do if they got a genius among them. Perhaps they would find it hard to invent excuses for her. But so long as a woman allows only well-bred mediocrity she will find affectionate friends.

Now, they want to stop the placing of limitations. They want to get over their narrowness of aspect. They want to learn to applaud. If a woman makes a success of anything from walking a tight rope to painting a picture, give her credit for it. Do not call her a crank because she has ideas. Do not cut her because she knows enough to make a living. Try to get to a point where you can admit that she is nice in spite of the fact that she has opinions. It's this fighting shy of the women who are trying to march with the marching time that I most deprecate in women.

I don't like them to be afraid of genius. Genius isn't necessarily disreputable. Make way for the uncommon woman as well as the common ones. When you hear a remarkable orator, such as Mrs. Lease, do not say that she ought to stay home and take care of the children.

The children will be taken care of all right enough. You needn't worry about that.

But give the women a chance to do something else. And it is the women themselves to whom I am talking. It is they who build the barriers.

And I want to see them all knocked down – all those moss-grown walls erected by superstition, and tradition, and prejudice. Flowers will not grow in the shadow of a stone wall. You have to let the sunshine get in at them.

"What Women Are Doing" – Protection for Working Women

2 November 1890

Redressing the inequities facing working women as early as 1890, Peattie took to task the McKinley Tariff, sponsored that year by Congressman William McKinley, chairman of the House Ways and Means Committee. McKinley supported high tariffs to protect U.S. industry from foreign competition by raising duties on many imports to the highest levels ever sanctioned. Protection for American industry did not necessary safeguard its women workers, Peattie discovered. It is no wonder that when William Jennings Bryan ran against McKinley for president in 1896, Peattie was one of the Nebraska senator's earliest and staunchest supporters.

Women workers at the Brandt Cigar Factory in Grand Island, Nebraska, 1912. (Stuhr Museum of the Prairie Pioneer)

❧ I was born with a profound admiration for "protection." I suppose it was the jugglery of the word – for really it has been a word to conjure with. And besides, I had faith in the republic. I didn't know exactly what the republic was, but I felt it represented whatever was most judicious and just in government, and confidently believed that all wretches who had the misfortune not to be born in the United States of America were spending their days in making moan over that fact. Therefore, knowing that protection was a part of the system of the republic, I concluded that it was one of those wise measures, born of necessity and preserved from a sense of right.

In course of time, having outgrown childhood and its simple and comfortable beliefs, I became a working woman in a great city, along with many thousand other women. It was only natural that I should become somewhat interested in other working women, and I took the trouble to become acquainted with a great many of them. I visited factories and shops, offices and stores. I saw them binding books, and trimming dresses, stripping tobacco and keeping books, holding confidential positions in banks and putting heads on tacks, writing on newspapers and making beds in cheap lodgings. I even became acquainted with women who got out of work, and who ended by a natural but sad sequence, in the police station, and sometimes in the penitentiary, and I came to consider the question of labor in all of its bearings, commercial, industrial, political, social and moral. Or at least, I would have considered it from a moral standpoint, if there had been any morality in it. And I ceased to believe in protection. I discovered that working women were not protected. I believed that they did not have fair and open competition, and that they were not permitted to benefit by the natural laws of supply and demand – although dozens of manufacturers have assured me to the contrary.

A memorial presented to the Senate of the United States by Charlotte Smith and Catherine Bergen, respectively president and secretary of the Woman's National Industrial League of America, contains some figures which are carefully compiled, and which it will be well for every woman to read and ponder over. The fact that she is not herself engaged in bread earning makes no difference. If she is a woman worthy of the name, she will be interested in those woman who must work. And, having no vote herself, she will attempt to influence those friends of hers who enjoy that privilege. For a woman's moral responsibility is not lessened by the fact that she cannot vote.

Immediately after the passage of the tariff bill in the house on May 21 last, when a bountiful provision of an advance of 50 per cent on the ad valorem duty was granted to the cloak manufacturers, they on the 5th day of June, notified their woman workers that their wages would be reduced by 25 per cent. Receiving themselves an advance of 50 per cent ad valorem on existing rates, they in turn decreased the wages of their workers from an insufficiency to a pittance! Any intelligent woman can decide for herself whether or not protection in this case protected the working woman of this country. This is one example of what protection can do for this country.

Protection! Great heavens, what do you women of the homes of Nebraska and the farms of Nebraska know of misery? You work hard, you think. Well, so you do. But not like the women in the shops. The women finishers in the woolen mills in Pennsylvania, according to the annual report of the secretary of internal affairs for 1888, receive only 54 cents a day. Full grown women are referred to, not girls. Women spinners get 71 cents a day; women spoolers from 42 to 64 cents a day; weavers 40 to 90 cents a day, the latter sum being paid to experts only. In the knit goods factory women receive only 55 cents a day for winding spools; women spinners 50 cents a day; yarn twisters 65 cents a day; reelers 65 cents a day. Girls at work in the shoe and boot factories receive 50 cents a day. . . . Do you know what this means? Have you ever been in the homes of these women? They are vast tenement houses, with a series of small and foul-smelling rooms. They have not clothes enough to keep the cold out; they have not food enough to sustain their moral force. They have lost the habit of chastity and the sentiment of modesty. A dozen of them will sleep together in one room, and it may be that there will be no partition between their room and the one occupied by the young men who also work in the factory. These girls no more blush for showing you the children born under these pitiable conditions than the happy wife in her safe home blushes to show you the baby which is undeniably the image of the husband that this woman respects. That is what wages like this can do.

And now that the manufacturer pays more for certain raw goods he reduces the wages of his laborers. In addition to this the girls must pay more for every article they buy – for it is the necessities of the poor which have been most affected by the McKinley bill. What comes next the optimist does not care to picture. It is sometimes a revolution which follows these things. It is sometimes a continuation of peace such as has been pictured, by the side of which the horrors of war are holy.

Protection has not protected women in America. So much is certain.

"The Woman's Club: It Will Be Distinctively Feminine and Run to Please Women"

21 May 1893

Frances M. Ford, an enterprising Omaha woman who later became very active in the General Federation of Women's Clubs, came to Peattie in early 1893 to urge her to help start a club. Peattie explained, "I thought the idea of bringing all classes of women together for social, literary and musical entertainment a most excellent idea, and wrote up our plan in the World-Herald.*"[12] The next month, Ford chaired a meeting at the* YWCA *hall to outline the purposes of such a club to interested women.*

The Omaha club held its organizational meeting on 10 May 1893 at the Lininger art gallery on the corner of Eighteenth and Davenport Streets.[13] Peattie had no difficulty interesting women in joining. In May 1894 the World-Herald *published a list of 250 women who had signed the constitution, noting that at least 50 more had applied for membership ("World Frivolous"). The club soon numbered more than 400 and by October met for the first time in its new quarters, on the third floor, elevator entrance, of the Old Boston Store owned by N. B. Falconer at 1612 Douglas Street.[14]*

❧ A young man said something peculiar the other day. He said: "I wish I were eligible to join your Woman's Club. It strikes me as being more intellectual and attractive and democratic than any movement I have ever known of here in Omaha. I saw the women coming out of the meeting the other day. And

Women of Omaha gather at the Lininger Galley in front of Bouguereau's infamous *Return of Spring*, ca. 1900. (Bostwick-Frohardt Collection, owned by KM3 TV and on permanent loan to Durham Western Heritage Museum, Omaha, Nebraska)

they looked like such nice sort of people to know that I felt it was particularly hard on me not to be able to join."

This is a nice tribute and a sincere one, and I'm sure the women of the new and astonishingly popular club cannot but be gratified. The Omaha Woman's Club certainly offers prospect of many days of deep interest. Thus far not as many working women have joined as one could desire, and it is to be sincerely hoped that they will do so in the autumn. To be sure, thus far the general meetings of the club have been held in the afternoon, and that may have made it difficult for working women to join. This was done in order that the women might attend the club without the need of escorts, for there is an idea among them that they would not like to come out in the evening without escorts. I wish that the club might, among the many reforms which it contemplates, bring about this one of educating women to go anywhere they want to go, or have need to go at night, without an escort. It would give them a fine feeling of independence, and after one or two experiments they would find that, however delightful and inspiring masculine company may be, it is not necessary as a protection.

There is one thing to be said to the working women in regard to the club, and that is that even if the regular meetings are held in the afternoon, the departments, which are the things that will offer the real opportunity for self-improvement, can meet at any hour that the majority of the members decide is best. And the women who can control the arrangement of their time will be glad, without a doubt, to make all possible concessions to women who must be at work during the working hours of the day.

In fact, I feel personally that it is the broad and kindly exchange of courtesies of all sorts that is going to give the club one of its greatest charms. It is all right for the club to be business-like and all that sort of thing, I suppose. But courtesy of the most delicate sort will be better than the finest executive ability. And there are a number of women in the club who possess just this qualification, and who can be trusted to guide this large body of women, who are, for the most part, strangers to each other, through all possible narrows and shallows in which the club might be wrecked if it had injudicious pilots.

If there is any one thing I hope for more than another concerning this club it is that it will become a point of honor among all the members not to say anything censorious of any other member, no matter what the provocation. I never was an unqualified admirer of the truth myself, and would always much rather be with agreeable people than with people who have such a mania for truth-telling that they voice it regardless of consequences. Decidedly, it is to be hoped, we will all bear with each other; that if there is anything that needs explanation we will frankly ask for an explanation, and have no sullenness or ill-natured criticism. Thus far there has been a beautiful absence of that sort of thing. But of course if serious philanthropic work is taken up it will be but a short time before some wide difference of opinion will be reached. And then the moment will have arrived for us all to remember that our differences of opinions are honest, and the majority must rule.

I heard a very clever and estimable woman complaining the other day that something that we did in the club was not as men do it. I am rather curious to know why it should be. We are not men – are not bound by their tradition – feel called to imitate them – do not want to be like them. Most of us give up the best part of our lives loving one or more of them, and that's enough. We are going to have a woman's club, fitted for woman's needs, adaptable to woman's tastes, run according to woman's fancies. The way men do wouldn't suit us at all. And any woman who imagines that by coming into the club she is going to get a sort of thin masculinity will not find there what she wants, because, on the contrary, it is going to be strongly feminine. And no one will ever be able to confound us by remarking that anything we do is "just like a woman," because we will reply: "How could it be otherwise?"

The next meeting of the club will be tomorrow, at the Lininger gallery, whither the club has been invited by the courtesy of Mrs. Haller, one of the house and home committee. The election of officers for the coming year will take place. But this work will be as hastily dispatched as possible, and the meeting will resolve itself into a social occasion. There will be a cup of tea served, by the way, and every lady is requested to bring her own cup and saucer and teaspoon. Mrs. Estabrook and Mrs. Cotton will sing, and Mme. Hesse-Fuch and Mrs. Whitmore will play the piano.

"A Word with the Women" – Stromsburg's Woman's Club

15 May 1895

In 1894 Peattie led the way in forming the Nebraska State Federation of Women's Clubs, serving as its president. Clubs from Lincoln, Crete, Fremont, Kearney, Omaha, Weeping Water, Seward, and Aurora sent representatives to a state convention. On 11–12 December the Nebraska Federation voted fourteen to seven to join the General Federation of Women's Clubs, and Nebraska became the seventh state to join the federation. Within the next six years, Nebraska boasted of more than one hundred local Woman's Clubs. Totally committed to the club movement, Peattie served on the board of directors during her entire residence in Omaha and as leader of various departments.

Peattie also traveled by train around Nebraska, assisting other towns in launching local Woman's Clubs. She visited the Stromsburg Woman's Club on its first anniversary and profiled the group as a model for other small communities throughout Nebraska. Such rural clubs, she believed, fulfilled the organization's highest purpose, offering isolated women the chance to share knowledge and beauty and uniting them in friendship and purpose in the midst of hardship and work. Praising the club for creating a strong community of women, she balanced details of their serious intellectual pursuits with a description of their lively social events.

❧ Since the formation of the State Federation of Women's Clubs there has been a constant increase in club development over Nebraska, and a number of young clubs are the result. Among them is the Stromsburg Woman's Club. Stromsburg lies in a beautiful valley, not many miles from York, on a branch of the Union Pacific.[15] The town has, perhaps, 1,500 inhabitants. It is a tiny place, in which there is an epidemic of good order. The homes are well painted, the yards bloom with plants, flowers and garden trees. In this tidy

A women's group from Central City, Nebraska, in historic costumes, ca. 1900. (Collection of Merrick County Historical Society)

town is a settlement of industrious people, most of whom are Swedes, some of whom are Germans, and a group of whom are New Englanders.

The club has twenty-three members, composed of women of all these classes, with a New England woman for its president. Miss Julia Haskell is this New England woman, and she has had the individuality to make a spot of New Hampshire life in the very heart of the Nebraska prairies. She lives amid beautiful old New England furniture, thinks New England thoughts, and has a New England manner, and is, most fittingly and naturally, the leader of the club, not only in respect to the office she holds, but in other particulars.

This club, being in existence but a few months, and wishing to have some advice concerning the laying out of the program for the next year, invited one of the officers of the federation to visit Stromsburg, review the work already done, and advise about that for the future. This officer found that the club has been exceedingly earnest. Its members had met in the evening, going about the streets to the house of meeting with lanterns, and defying all sorts of weather for the sake of their intellectual pleasures. They had made themselves conversant with a number of the most important events of the past year, had indulged in some character sketching of historical personages, had enlivened their winter's work with the consideration of some of the American poets, and had, in addition, been exceedingly sociable. Though the women had lived in the little town many years together, the club had brought a number of them into general acquaintance with their neighbors for the first time, and their acquaintance, being formed on the grounds of common intellectual ambitions, was of a sort likely to ripen into the firmest friendship. The club members all agreed that there was no time for gossiping and personal considerations when subjects of much larger interest were engaging the attention of all. They are a studious company of women, with a real earnestness for development. This is to no small degree the result of the influence exercised over them by their president and secretary, both women of unusually active brains, a vein of humor, charming addresses and much tact. Mrs. A. C. Post is the secretary as well as the wit of the club.

On the occasion of the visit of the officer of the federation the annual club banquet was given. To this the husbands and favored gentlemen friends of the members were invited. The banquet was spread in the long dining hall of the hotel, the club being entertained there by one of the members, whose husband keeps the hotel. The ladies provided the repast, which was a very delicious one. Green and white being the club colors, the ladies wore the ribbons of those colors, the table was decorated with snow balls with their plentiful green leaves, the initials of the club being made with the same flowers at the center of the table. The light was supplied by candles in brass sticks, and one mammoth candelabra – a reminiscence of the New England home previously mentioned – stood nobly in the center of the long table. Green shades covered the candles.

There were ten toasts, delivered with much wit and unction, all but one of them being by the women.

The gentlemen listened, applauded and were evidently a little surprised at the exercise of abilities of which they had not hitherto suspected the existence. After the conclusion of the toasts the tables were cleared away, and two of the members of the club showed the real club spirit by sacrificing themselves to the pleasure of the others. They seated themselves at the piano and played dance music with the best sort of spirit until an hour which will not be mentioned – for Stromsburg enjoys the reputation of being a staid hamlet and one would hesitate to destroy that reputation.

Apropos of music, the club has a number of members who have had excellent musical opportunities, and who are generous and sensible enough to endeavor to give others as much pleasure as possible by the exercise of their accomplishments. The evening's entertainment on the occasion referred to was enlivened by songs and piano playing.

The little club of women has been the means of bringing honest pleasure to this quiet town. The members are happier themselves, and have made others happier by the formation of their organization. A number of the young school teachers are in the club, and supply a deal of the verve and frolic as well as the intellect. One of the most valuable and charming members is a Swede by birth, and, having been well educated in her own country, brings to the club a different point of view from that which the Americans entertain. She writes her papers first in Swedish, to get the freedom of expression she desires, and then translates them. Another valuable member, a woman past her youth, is a German of wide experience and excellent judgment, and a habit of deep and earnest thought. Another woman is from Boston, one is from New York, several are western born. And over all is the gentle, alert, kindly spirit of the president, and from her comes an example of refined and elegant manners, an adaptability, a tolerance and a bright intellectual inspiration.

This is an example of the work being done in our Nebraska towns by the women's clubs.

"No Distinction as to Color: Chicago Woman's Club Abolishes the Prohibitory Rule at Its Last Meeting"

26 May 1895

Although Peattie voiced strong support for the Woman's Club ideal of "unity in diversity" (Wells 2) and promoted the successes of the African American community in Omaha, she remained resolute regarding the membership of African American women in the Omaha Woman's Club. When Helen Muhammitt, a well-educated African American woman, applied for membership in the Omaha Woman's Club, the sixteen women of the club's board of directors, of which Peattie was a member, voted unanimously that she fulfilled all of the conditions of membership. However, for fear of losing members, they decided not to bring the application before the club "until a stronger esprit de corps was established."[16] *Believing that racial issues could undermine the emerging unity of the nascent club movement, Peattie took an uncharacteristically conformist stance, one that she felt would safeguard her grassroots work and that of many others in the creation of local clubs as well as state and national federations.*[17]

Muhammitt may have reacted to her rejection by the all-white club with "modesty, propriety of language, and good sense," but she recognized the discrimination that existed. Her club joined the National Federation of Afro American Women, headed by the wife of Booker T. Washington, and worked toward educating and uplifting the members of their own community (Calloway and Smith 54).

❧ The color line is down in the Chicago Woman's Club.

Early last winter, Mrs. Fannie Barrier Williams, a well-known and much esteemed colored woman, applied for membership in the club, and was refused. Since then the color question has arisen again and again, till it had to be fairly faced. No palliation or compromise could keep it out of sight. The compromise was tried, however. It consisted of an amendment to the bylaws as follows:

The qualification for membership shall be character, intelligence and reciprocal advantage of membership to the club and to the individual.

It shall be the duty of those proposing candidates for membership, as well as of the committee on membership, to consider the reciprocal advantage of membership to the club and the individual.

The committee on membership shall vote upon candidates by ballot. Three negative votes shall prevent the favorable recommendation of the candidate. A two-thirds vote by ballot of the board of managers shall be required to elect to membership in the club.

It was thought by those who wished to be agreeable, and to sit comfortably on the fence, that the "reciprocal advantage" requirement would amicably settle the matter. The move to admit the colored woman could be killed painlessly. It would simply be decided in the event of the proposal of a name of any negress, that the advantage would not be reciprocal.

This weak amendment might have carried, had not Dr. Sarah Hackett Stevenson arisen to announce her principles. Many who heard her, declared that her speech was the strongest effort ever heard by them from man or woman. Dr. Stevenson is an emphatic woman, with a deep nature, positive opinions, natural and unpretentious eloquence, and absolute bravery. She told the women what she thought of the club which professed to speak for the highest achievement of womankind and yet lacked the moral courage to declare explicitly for equal opportunities for her sex. The women were swept along by her impassioned eloquence. An unconditional amendment was offered to the constitution. It reads: Membership shall be conditioned on character and intelligence without regard to race, color, creed or politics.

It went by an overwhelming majority. Dr. Stevenson had thrown her searchlight into the hearts of the women. They were ashamed of what they had seen there – ashamed of the motives that had prompted them to oppose the admission of any woman, because of the accident of race.

But the club, it must be remembered, has fought only a small part of the

Helen Muhammitt, Omaha civic leader, caterer, and businesswoman, ca. 1895.
(Great Plains Black Museum Collection)

battle. It is one of the largest and most valued clubs in the general federation of clubs, an organization numbering at present nearly 75,000 women. No club can remain in the federation which does not have a constitution conforming to that of the federation. The Chicago club will be forced to carry the federation with it, or, in course of time, in all probability, to leave the federation.

It may easily happen that this action will cause a split in the federation. Many southern clubs belong to the federation, and it was a matter of much comment at the last biennial meeting of the federation, that the southern women were among the most scholarly, influential and charming in the assembly. Some of these women have risen to an intellectual plane which leaves all race distinctions far in the background. Some of them never, at any time, would have done anything toward retarding the development of any woman, though her skin were black as tar. But these exceptional women can hardly be expected to carry with them the sentiments of their clubs, nor can they break down the sad old prejudice which shadows the south. One has not, however, any disposition to accuse the southern clubs in advance.

If the truth of the matter were known, the opposition would be strong right here in Omaha to any proposal to admit women to membership. Some time ago the matter was brought up in the board of directors of the Omaha Woman's Club. There was not a dissenting voice there, be it said to the credit of that body of sixteen representative women. But there was a decided feeling that it would be better if the question were not brought before the club for some time to come, and until a stronger esprit de corps was established. The question was proposed to the board, apropos of Mrs. Muhammitt, a young and beautiful colored woman of good education, and honest intellectual ambitions. Mrs. Muhammitt showed singular good sense. Rather than engulf the club in difficulty of any sort, she started a club among her own race, and has led that society of women along pleasant fields of study. Not long ago, as president of the Omaha Colored Woman's club she was invited to address the 500 members of the Woman's club. This she did with singular modesty, propriety of language, and good sense, and met with the warmest applause. So far, and no further have the women got on the color question in this city.

There are those in this city who feel that the club loses much by not including in its membership such women as Mrs. Muhammitt, Mrs. Pryor, Miss Lucy Gamble, and others. The strong and assertive intellect of these women, their good taste and sweetness of disposition would be an addition to the club. But there are many members of the club – and they are not all southerners – who would vote against their admission, and who, in the event of such admission, would probably leave the club.

It must be taken into account that no club is under any obligations to admit any woman, or any species of woman which it prefers to keep without its membership. A club is not a public concern. It is an organization of a private character, not chartered, composed of persons of similar tastes, organized for purposes of amusement and improvement. Such a club does not profess to be unselfish. Its first duty is to its own members. The will of its members makes its laws. If these women do not choose to assume an altruistic attitude, or a liberal attitude it is their own affair. Yet, on the other hand, insomuch as these women stand for the elevation of the sex, it seems but consistent that all persons of good character and intellectuality should be admitted to assist them.

The color question will inevitably arise sooner or later in every woman's club in the federation. Certainly it must rise in all clubs which are located in cities. The result cannot be foreseen. It is to be hoped that the women will preserve that dignity of demeanor which has thus far characterized the women's clubs, and made them impervious to the attacks of their critics. The question is one that should lead to development. It puts to the test the character of mind, heart and spirit of the women composing the enormous membership of these clubs. It will demonstrate whether these women are loftier of mind than the average, or whether they are governed by the same narrow prejudices as the unrestrained, the sectional, and the unfortunate.

CHAPTER 5

People and Places

"We are all country folk together, though some of us may not know it."

In her role as a journalist, Elia Peattie's interests extended well beyond the Omaha city limits. She loved to visit the blossoming villages on the Nebraska prairie and journeyed to all parts of the region for the Omaha World-Herald, *often coordinating these visits with her promotional work for the Nebraska Woman's Clubs. The late nineteenth century was a time of amazing transformation on the Great Plains, and Peattie especially enjoyed meeting the people who were making changes in the booming towns of Nebraska.*

In the 1880s most outsiders considered Nebraska a landscape devoid of interest or significance and without a cultural or historical past. In her interpretation of Nebraska, Peattie used her knowledge of the larger world, her understanding of human nature, and her creative imagination as a lens to observe the relationships among people, places, and events, giving her regional accounts depth and resonance, enlivening the pages of the World-Herald, *and holding up to the world a composite portrait of communities determined to be more than "merely inevitable incidents of their surroundings."*[1] *An inveterate booster of new cities, Peattie lauded the ethic of free enterprise and celebrated the myth of the American dream. To her, the citizens of these communities exemplified Walt Whitman's pioneers, marching forth to conquer and domesticate the wilderness.*[2] *The Nebraska of Peattie's writings is community-centered, forward-looking, and determined to rival the East in business as well as culture.*

In her character profiles, Peattie firmly situated her people living and striving within the Great Plains landscape. The West gave people the chance to create themselves, but it didn't make it easy. Those who rose from poverty to success, despite the physical hardships of the environment, received her highest praise. Her columns and editorials, especially those featuring women from all classes and walks of life, peopled Nebraska with extraordinary ordinary people. Like America's early nature writers, Peattie viewed the western landscape as offering haven and opportunity for women; she romanticized nature and considered it a spiritual haven.[3]

Aware that she was witnessing and recording the social history of Nebraska

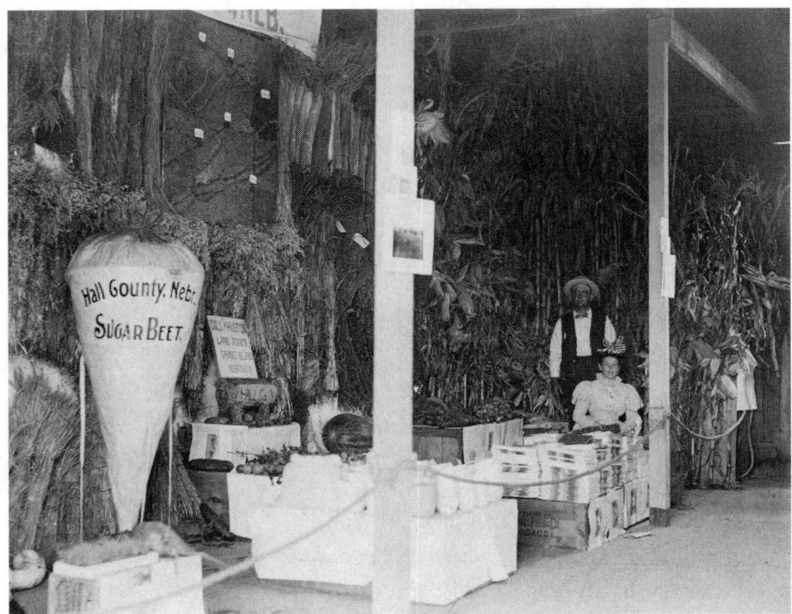

An agricultural exhibit at the Sugar Palace, situated on the 300 block of East North Front Street in Grand Island, Nebraska, from 1890 to 1894. (Stuhr Museum of the Prairie Pioneer)

as well as helping to shape public opinion and values, Peattie chose her subjects carefully, blending natural and cultural landscapes and striving always to present a balanced and honest viewpoint. Combining a journalist's attention to details and facts, a poet's sensory perception, and a fiction writer's awareness of character and plot, Peattie's interpretations of life on the Great Plains and her portraits of its inhabitants introduced her readers to the rapidly developing West and helped create a regional identity for Nebraska.

"A Bohemian in Nebraska: A Peep at a Home Which Is a Slice Out of Bohemia"

23 April 1893

Throughout her life, Peattie admired good literature, music, and art, and her columns and editorials reflected her dedication to promoting the cultural resources of the region. Peattie's most enthusiastic literary support was for her friend Kate M. Cleary, a Chicago transplant to the freshly minted town of Hubbell in south-central Nebraska. Like the Peatties, Cleary had connections

Kate and Michael Cleary entertaining guest E. A. Downey, 1891.
(Photo by Michael Timothy Cleary, Cleary family scrapbooks)

with the Chicago Tribune. *Not only did Cleary publish stories and sketches in that newspaper, but her brother Edward McPhelim was its literary and drama critic and had worked with Robert and Elia in Chicago. Peattie had much in common with Cleary, a novelist, short-story writer, poet, and humorist. Both young women shared a passion for writing, and each was devoted to her family. "A Bohemian in Nebraska" showed the respect Peattie held for Cleary, not only as a writer but as a talented and intelligent woman.*[4]

❧ It's not very often that a woman is a bohemian – a genuine bohemian. And it must be confessed that Nebraska is not the place where one would go to look for a woman of that kind, and certainly he would not journey all day along the Burlington road, over the prairie, to the tiny town of Hubbell – the quietest place, with prohibition politics – to find such a woman.

Yet, there is one there. Perhaps some night you will get in that little town, lying down among its hills, about midnight. The place will be black as Erebus. Every one of the busy, simple-living folk of the hamlet will be in bed. But up the dark, straight street one light will be shining, and it will show you inside

– for the curtain is always up – a group of people in a room which does not in the least look like a room of a quiet Nebraska farming village.

It is lined with books. It has a typewriter in it, and a writing desk, and a jolly big stove, and some chairs and sofas designed for loafing. And it has pictures not at all of the sort you would expect to find out on the prairie – little sketches of clever artists, old engravings, souvenirs of occasions, mementoes of famous folks. There never was a more informal room – never. It's a room where you say good things if it is in you to do it. There's something in the atmosphere of the place that brings the humor out of you. And when you get in one of those comfortable chairs with a glass of beer in your hand, and no particular care whether it is time to go to bed or not, and the Chicago, New York and Omaha papers at your elbow, and new books and magazines yet to be cut lying near, and the memory of a dinner that was very much more than good – that was daring and scientific in its way – then suddenly, bohemia has come to you, and the Nebraska prairie with its hard working, quiet living people seem very far away.

The big world of letters is around you. You laugh with all those who have ever, by laughing, made themselves famous. You feel as if the spirits of all those who were cleverest that ever you have known, had come out with you over the wind-racked plains, and were there, drinking beer and laughing, too.

It's the mistress of the place that brings all this about. She is a woman not unknown in this state to those who keep track of such small literature as Nebraska can turn out. Her name is Kate McPhelim Cleary, and she is an Irish woman, as her name may or may not indicate. I think she was born somewhere in Canada. But she has for a mother an elegant, most carefully reared Irishwoman of the old school, whose manners are an education in courtesy, but who has, withal, something of the reckless humor in her, which gives her daughter her individuality. Mrs. Cleary's father was a man who was a great dealer in timber, in the days when that meant ship owning, and pioneering courage, and commercial adventure, and all that sort of thing, and he had a reputation for brilliancy and wit. There was plenty of money in those days, and a very formal way of living, and Kate went to the best convent schools, and has studied French and embroidery, and never knew she was going to turn out a bohemian. Later, when her father died, her mother took her over to Ireland, to relatives there, and she lived in places where the traditions of her family would hardly let her speak to another child in the neighborhood. It is hinted, however, that about this time Kate began to slip out to the village lane to play with the baker's daughter and that, at times, she even wrote rhymes, and did other things which showed the beginning of that charming disregard for consequences which have made her what she is.

Fortunes have a sad way of dwindling, and Mrs. McPhelim had to come back from Ireland. She took her two sons out of college, and settled in Philadelphia with her three children. There were four children among them in fact, for an old country gentlewoman, brought up in the exclusion and with the protection which Mrs. McPhelim had been, was just about as well calculated to take care of herself in a bustling American city as a humming bird is to care for itself among cormorants. However, Mrs. McPhelim put her dainty heirlooms around in her little rented home, and continued to read her favorite poets, and to bring up her children in her own tender and delicate way, and she trusted to the Lord for the rest. The children, who had found that the Lord did not buy theater tickets for them, nor new novels, had begun to write verses and yarns for story papers, and as they all wrote verses with as much ease as a duck swims in water, it came about after a time that the money received began to make itself felt.

There were days of careless poverty, in which no one's heart was very heavy. With a mother who was never too tired or too proper to cook a chop at midnight, and who laughed over their funny verses and wept over their pathetic tales, and thought she had a family of poets, how could the three young folk be sad? It wasn't possible. Besides, life was interesting. At night there was the balcony of the theater to go to, if one couldn't afford anything better, and by day there was the fascinating work of story writing, and always the jolly family circle, and so time went on, and the little incomes increased, and the literary work which had been a makeshift became, for one of them, at least, a fixed occupation. For the oldest of the three, Edward McPhelim, who has been for twelve years the dramatic critic of the *Chicago Tribune*, and whose reputation is the best of that of any dramatic critic west of New York, entered newspaper work with the intention of making it a profession. And he is recognized among newspaper people as being the writer of the most limpid and well selected English to be found in the transient pages of the daily paper. Moreover he has shown a fineness of discrimination that leads him at the first to estimate the worth of an actor; and his estimates, calmly uttered in the midst of popular clamor, have all ultimately come to be accepted even by the public.

As for his sister Kate, she married. Her husband could not live in Chicago, owing to the cruel lake winds, and he came west in search of a more favorable climate, and selected Hubbell, and went in the lumber business there about ten years ago. There are four well beloved babies in the house – though two of them would probably resent being called babies. And the old bohemian life is somewhat changed.

But even the four babies, and the careful study of the household art has not put a stop to Mrs. Cleary's literary work. She writes romantic tales for the story papers; she contributes some of the brightest jokes that appear in *Puck*, she sends delightful sketches to the *Chicago Tribune*, and she occasionally writes verses. Perhaps she would do all of this work more earnestly if she did not do it so easily. What I mean to say is, that she has no definite aim in view. She does not care whether she "succeeds" or not. She wants to live as happily as possible, and she writes because she enjoys it, not because she has an ambition to write. She does without thought or care work which slower witted persons would spend sleepless nights over. And after she has done it she thinks no more about it, but sells it if she happens to want the money for anything, and if she doesn't she lets it lie in her drawer. It is, however, to persons just so careless of success that it is apt to come. Perhaps she would write more persistently if there was need for doing so from a monetary point of view. But since there is no such need, and as she has everything she wants, writing is taken up only as a form of amusement. It is valued more because it brings her into association with clever people all over the country than for any other reason. And her correspondence is of the sort that keeps her constantly in touch with eastern cities, and that gives to her days a pleasant excitement. Some charming people have been entertained in that little house up the quiet Hubbell street, and the gay little ponies that race over the hills with the family phaeton have introduced some distinguished visitors to the Nebraska hills.

To find a life so full, so interesting and – bohemian – for there is no other word for it – out on the Nebraska prairie, has never ceased to be an astonishment to me. And I hope I have not in any way betrayed the confidence imposed on me telling something of the inner life of this particular home. And I think it would not be possible to mention that home without mentioning also the genial, kindly, generous and most hospitable gentleman who is at the head of it, and whose friendship is worthy of anybody's winning.

There is one thing that distinguishes this home from most of those out on the prairies, and that is good cooking. I don't mean that the cooking in most Nebraska farming communities is not good in its simple way. But I mean when Mrs. Cleary found herself stranded, as it were, in mid-plains, and confronted by the deplorably small bill of fare of a country town, that she set about making a scientific cuisine. In all the arts of salad making, roasting, deviling, baking, preserving and mixing, she is a connoisseur – and more, she is original. It would be absurd to commend all of her methods to the busy farm woman who has neither time nor money for making fine dishes, but I am sure the isolated life out on the plains would take to itself a little more charm if other women would do as Mrs. Cleary has, and make a study of how to use cream and eggs, poultry and pork, vegetables and the native fruit. It's a great art; and it takes brains of a good sort – so no one need scorn it because of the idea that it is not intellectual.

All this may not be to the point, and may seem very vacuous and discursive; but I really think it will be a good thing for some of our serious, hard-working American women to know how humor, imagination, ability and adaptability can illuminate our lonely western life.

For say what you may, there is a little ache in the hearts of every one of us for the "place back east" which we left. In this state are hundreds of thousands of homesick people. It is inevitable. We did not grow up together here. And the new home, the new friends, however dear, cannot be quite like those we were born to. The Plymouth women used to weep when the Mayflower spread its white sails and turned toward "home," yet not one faltered, not one went with her. On them, unknown to themselves, was placed the destiny of conquering this continent. And westward still have come the pilgrims, and the subjugation of the continent is yet far from complete. And we, here in the west, a vast company of strangers from many lands, look at each other with eyes of longing, appealing for closer friendship, stronger interests, dearer compensations.

And so I think that anyone who has broken down the obstacles, who has proved that the art of living is not a thing controlled by environment and circumstances, is a fine example to us all.

And in the home in Hubbell that I have told you of such an example may be found.

Here are some of the poems that have been inspired by that life out on the prairies.[5] And they go to show that the plains are throbbing with interest for any who have the brains to perceive their charm. But then, if you have learned the art of living, what does it matter what your surroundings are? The spot does not exist on earth which is not full of interest for him who has brains enough to discover what lies hidden there. These poems are but a few of very many written there. And they do not paint the plains any better than have some of the tales written from the same place. There was one little story, for example, of a child lost in a corn field, which appeared in *St. Nicholas*,[6] which perhaps gave the atmosphere of Nebraska better than any other tale written by the story writers of this state.

"A Word with the Women" – Willa Cather

14 January 1896

Peattie earned extra money by lecturing throughout Nebraska on literary topics. At one lecture that Peattie presented on Sidney Lanier at the University of Nebraska, she met Willa Cather.[7] *In 1895, the year Cather graduated from the university, Peattie wrote a history of Nebraska women journalists for the Nebraska Press Association. Peattie complimented Cather: "Her criticisms, both literary and dramatic, are clever, original and generally just. But above all they are clever and full of 'ginger.' . . . If there is a woman in Nebraska newspaper work who is destined to win a reputation for herself, that woman is Willa Cather. . . . Indeed, without flattery, it can be said that honest workmanship already distinguishes her columns" (Brainerd 31–32). One of the first to predict Cather's future success, Peattie wrote in an 1895 column: "There is no better literary work done in this state than that on the* Lincoln Courier, *and the writing which is best in the columns of that paper is by two women, Miss Sarah Harris and Miss Willa Cather. . . . Miss Cather is exceedingly young to do such good work as she does, and her opinions, original, often dogmatic, frequently charming and piquant, are poured into those columns with all the prodigality of youth and the enthusiasm of high talent."*[8] *In 1896 Peattie devoted a column to "On the Divide," one of the first short stories written by the young Nebraska writer destined to become the first woman editor of* McClure's *magazine as well as a Pulitzer Prize–winning and internationally acclaimed author.*

Cather, in return, respected Peattie. In a letter she wrote from Pittsburgh to Kate Cleary on 25 February 1905, Cather stated that she read Peattie's stories as a young girl in Red Cloud, almost worshiping Peattie as an author, and commented that no other person had been so constant, kind, and influential in her writing career. Peattie's stimulating and charming personality and her unconscious talent for helping others, Cather wrote, always uplifted her.[9] *In her memoir, Peattie described Cather as "Always a cordial, simple friend" ("Star Wagon").*[10]

❧ Miss Willa Cather, who has done a good deal of newspaper work in Lincoln, has a story in the January number of the *Overland Monthly*. Since Miss Cather was born and raised in Nebraska, and has seen not very much of any other part of the world, she has very wisely set her characters down on the Nebraska plains. Perhaps, to speak more correctly, the tale is really one

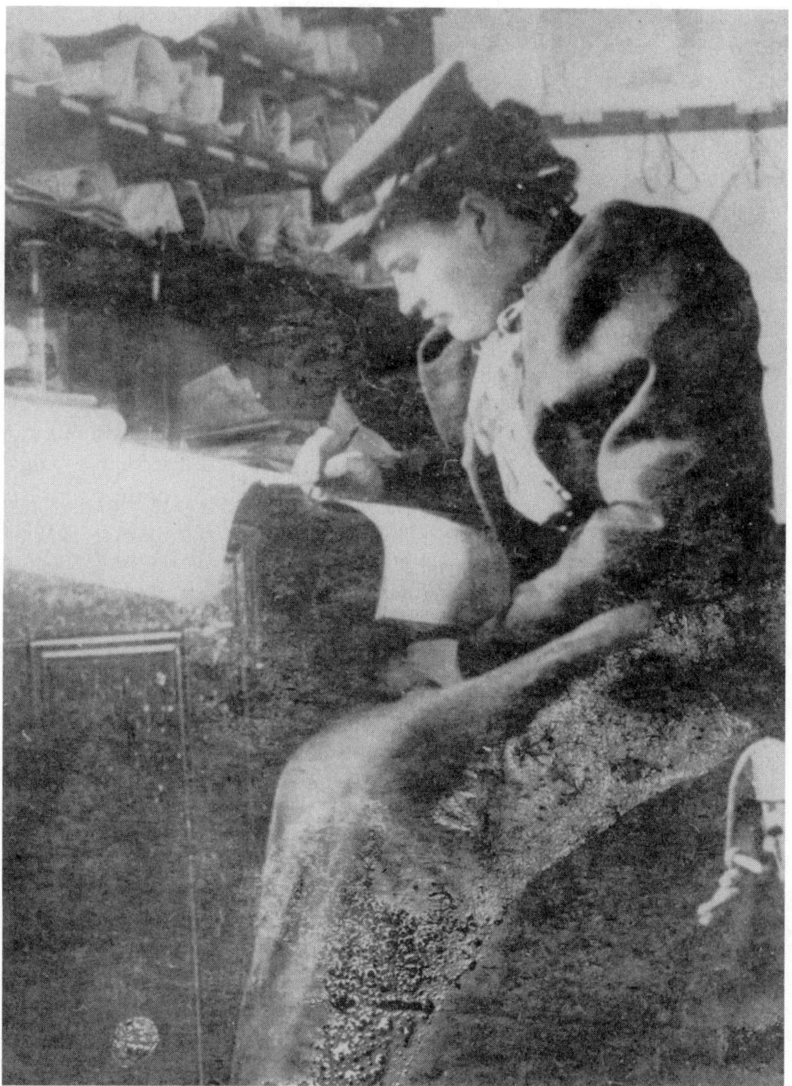

Willa Cather on the staff of the *Lincoln Journal*, ca. 1895.
(Nebraska State Historical Society Photograph Collections)

of the plains, and the characters of the people merely inevitable incidents of their surroundings. Miss Cather has long confessed herself, in her literary criticisms, an admirer of what is primitive, simple and vital in art. She likes a stirring tale, and is the young woman who said that the creative ability of women as fictionists would be demonstrated when they wrote good sea tales, or stories of battles – as if they had much opportunity of knowing about fights by sea or land! Miss Cather has not written about a fight, but she has made a mighty Norse, who, transplanted from his native hemlocks to the bare plains of Nebraska, lives in miserable and alcoholic solitude for ten long years, and who, in desperate protest against the unnatural loneliness of his situation, finally goes to a house, asks a young Swede woman to marry him, and, when she refuses, takes her in his giant arms and carries her off through a gathering blizzard to his own shack, in spite of the wails of her father and mother and her own hearty resistance. This is quite saga-like. But Miss Cather does not leave the story in this heroic simplicity. She refines it. Perhaps she was inconsistent in doing so. According to her own tenets would it not have been better to have left it there? A captured woman in a shack of logs, which was decorated with wolf skins and dried rattlesnakes, with a mighty and half-mad Norse, isn't bad as an example of the primitive. But Miss Cather makes convention send him – the Norse – for a clergyman, who performs a somewhat perfunctory marriage service in which the license required by the county clerk plays no part; and then she causes love to work a tumult in the heart of the giant, who, after having performed all the feats of which mere prowess is capable, stands baffled before the things of the spirit, and not knowing how to win a word of love from the lips of his terrified bride, lies without in the bitter storm, his head upon the doorstep, waiting for her call. The house grows cold. She calls to him. He comes in and mends the fire. Then he withdraws and sinks in the snow without. She calls again in loneliness and fright. He offers to go for her mother – to bring her in his arms as he brought his bride. She calls once more – softly, this time – "I'd rather have you, Canute." And so the Nebraska Sabine forgave her captor, as women are apt to forgive those who master them – and the story does not entirely lose its saga-like quality. As this is one of the first stories written by Miss Cather, and as it is so very original in its character, it surely should give her friends much gratification. It is written with a close attention to the verities, and is, therefore, rather dismal. It is hard to find very much that is cheerful to write about a hard-drinking Swede, who lives alone on a drouth-stricken farm in the midst of a treeless and semi-arid plain. Miss Cather says: "Canute drank alone and in solitude, not for pleasure or good cheer, but to forget the awful loneliness and level of the Divide. Milton made a sad blunder when he put mountains in hell. Mountains postulate faith and admiration. All mountain peoples are religious. It was the cities of the plains that, because of their utter lack of spirituality and the mad caprice of their vice, were cursed of god."

All of which is rather discouraging. But the stories and poems born out here on the plains all do seem to be discouraging. Are they really as bad as the fictionists paint, or have we caught a miserable melancholy from Mr. Garland, or have we not the sense to make good selections for the subjects of our fiction? Miss Cather's story, for all of its extravagancies, rings true, and seems to be sad because conditions are sad. Other writers as good have taken their mental cameras, so to speak, to the same region, and brought away equally depressing negatives. If one were rich it would be amusing to offer a prize for the best rollicking story of the plains, produced by a person who had lived on them, and await the result.

"Some Pigs and a Woman: Mrs. A. M. Edwards and Her Herd of Poland China Porkers"

9 February 1896

When Peattie, who was always delighted to showcase women with uncommon careers, learned of Mrs. Amanda Edwards, a New York native transplanted to the Nebraska plains, she traveled to Fremont to meet this successful businesswoman.[11] *Peattie headlined her as "One of the Best Known Stock Women in the Country Today" for her selective breeding of Poland China hogs. Peattie was much impressed with Mrs. Edwards, not only because of her risk taking and her business success in a man's realm but also because of her feminine side, especially the simplicity and orderliness of her home and her snug little office lined with books.*

The respect, Peattie discovered, was mutual. After a light lunch, Mrs. Edwards escorted Peattie to the stable where three hundred of her best hogs were sheltered, each registered, immaculately groomed, and fed scientific rations. "I have a surprise for you," Mrs. Edwards declared. "I have one sow here, the largest I have ever raised, that is practically perfect in all points." Taking her by the hand, Mrs. Edwards led her to a stall where Peattie saw "a vast, overwhelming mass of hog." Mrs. Edwards exclaimed, "Look at the breadth between the shoulders, look at the line of the back, look at . . ." But all Peattie was looking at was the nameplate: "Elia W. Peattie." It was the highest honor the ranch woman could bestow on the writer whom she so admired ("Star Wagon").

❧ This is a story about some pigs and a woman.

The pigs are thoroughbred – and thoroughly bred.

The woman is Mrs. A. M. Edwards, a stock breeder with a national reputation, and a very courageous and charming woman.

August Swanson's livestock near Kearney, Nebraska, 1903.
(Nebraska State Historical Society Photograph Collections)

Mrs. Edwards ought to read "Tom Grogan," which Hopkinson Smith has written for the *Century*, and which is now running there. It is, by the way, such an uncommonly good story that one marvels how it ever got in the *Century* at all. "Tom Grogan" is the story of a woman of lovely heart, who was a sort of boss stevedore, and who succeeded in all she undertook. Her nature was strong, tender, aggressive when occasion required, and loyal under all circumstances. Mrs. Edwards is like "Tom Grogan," only Mrs. Edwards is a gentlewoman. She is in the forties, as to age, with a pleasant face, rippling light brown hair, a soft voice, a vivacious manner and a tripping step.

She has not, as it happens, always raised pigs.

It came about in this way. Mrs. Edwards was born at Ames, N.Y., of such stock as the Starks, Lathrops and Binghams. She married a man with equal claim to good colonial blood, and enjoyed a brief life of married happiness with him. He died, leaving her one son, DeWayne Palmer. In course of time, she married again, her second husband being a merchant in Central New York. He had three children, two daughters and a son. It chanced one time when Mr. and Mrs. Edwards were traveling in the west that they stopped at Fremont. Driving out over the country Mrs. Edwards saw a tract of 160 acres for sale.

"I'm going to buy that," she said to her husband. "I've got the money lying idle in the bank, and I always wanted some land for DeWayne. Maybe he won't see this till he is grown, but it will be here and he can have it when he wants it."

"That garden patch!" her husband said. "Why, it isn't worth mentioning. Wait a while and we'll get a good bit of land somewhere in Colorado. A hundred and sixty isn't worth buying."

"Well, I want this," Mrs. Edwards insisted. "I feel as if I must get this, and we can have the other tract, too."

So she bought it.

Then the unexpected happened. It is always the unexpected which happens. Mr. Edwards failed in business. He lost everything he had and a good deal more beside. Mrs. Edwards sold her beautiful household furniture, took her children – for she now had two sons of her own – and her stepchildren, and fled into the wilderness. At least, she went to Fremont, and, for a person who came from Utica, N.Y., Fremont probably did seem a wilderness. There was an old house on the farm. It was built of black walnut. When the dirt was cleaned out, and such furniture as had been saved from the wreck had been put in, even the homesick children were fairly well contented. The house was built onto till it was sufficiently commodious, the children were taken into Fremont each day to school, and then Mrs. Edwards began to look about to see how she could make a living. Her husband, much broken by his losses, felt at some loss to adapt himself to conditions so different from those to which he had been used. Mrs. Edwards turned her attention to what was nearest – that is to say, farming. There were thousands of obligations to be met in the east. Frugal farming would not do. She had to go into money making. On an adjacent eighty which she purchased were a number of short-horned cattle, which were to go with the ground. These gave her the idea of raising cattle. But she had not been long in that business before she perceived that the best juice had been squeezed out of the cattle business. So she sold her stock, and began the breeding of Poland China pigs.[12]

This writes easily enough. "The breeding of Poland China pigs" is as easy to write as it can be. But it is not easy to do. Especially as Mrs. Edwards, at the outset, did not know a Poland China from any other kind of pig. But she found out. She is a magnificent example of the fact that one can do anything one sets about doing. She got the bound tabulated pedigrees of this thoroughbred stock and studied hard. She read books on the care of pigs. She examined grain, learned good grain from bad, gathered data about different feeds, and then she went to work. She had a little money, but there was need that she should make it go as far as possible. When she read of an auction of the blooded stock at an eastern farm she took the train and attended it. She would be the only woman present. It was hard, and she felt very shy. But she soon found that the auctioneers paid as much attention to her bids as to those of anyone else, and that consideration was shown her on every hand, especially when it was found that she knew how to select good stock.

"But how could you select good stock at the first?" was asked her. "How did you know a good Poland China from a poor Poland China?"

"To begin with," she replied, "I only bid on such pigs as I knew to be well bred. I took those with whose pedigree I was acquainted, carefully checking off my catalogue before I attended the sale. But even the animals with the best ancestry do not always suit. Animals sometimes degenerate, as well as human beings. I selected my stock according to an ideal of my own. I found an ideal."

"Eh! An ideal of a pig?"

"An ideal of a pig. I got fixed in my mind, the perfect pig. Top line and bottom line, flank and breadth of back, droop of ear, length of face, expression and carriage – those were all firmly fixed in my mind. Then I bid on the pig that came nearest to my ideal."

So little by little she got a fine herd. Whenever a pig was born into that herd which did not come up to her idea of approximate perfection, she weeded it out, using it for pork. She attended to the crossing herself. If she found a valuable animal with too long a nose, she saw that its progeny had shorter noses, by mating the animal with a short nosed pig. She shaped the ears, the jowl, the neck.

"I do not want an animal in my herd," she said, "that will not score ninety points."

Perhaps some of you women who read this do not know what is meant by a pig's scoring ninety points. I know. Mrs. Edwards told me. Listen then, you ignorant ones. These are the points of a pig: The head counts 5 points, the color, 3; the ears, 2; the girth around the heart, 10; the loin, 7; the back, 7; the legs – but after all, perhaps you would just as well be ignorant. Some people would. But believe me, there are those who know the points of a pig.

Mrs. Edwards knows. She knows so well that she has been able to breed on her farm such animals as Duncan, who is out in California now, and who weights 900 pounds, and is one of the best show pigs on the slope. She has bred R. U., a famous boar, and Bessie of East Grove, who sold for $500, and Lady Wilkes, Lizer's Nemo, Christmas Eve, AA 2nd, and Sensation, the last two boars with big reputations. East Grove is the name of Mrs. Edwards' place, and on it she raised every year about 200 pigs. These sell all the way from $25 to $200 apiece. In addition to the expensive animals she keeps good pigs for the farmers' trade, which she sells at prices the farmers can meet. Her farmers' trade is very large. At present there are 160 animals in stock, counting the young ones. The healthy pigs are fed corn and oats mixed, only one-third being corn. The weanlings are fed middlings. For rapid fattening the pigs are given soaked corn. But Mrs. Edwards is much opposed to force fattening. She does not think it constitutes health or normality. She gives particular attention to her young nursing pigs and the sows after they have farrowed, giving the sows little to eat, but providing them plentifully with liquids. She treats them as any nursing mother would be treated. The result is that she has no starved little pigs, no biting or devouring on the part of the sow and no fighting among the babies. Many a stockman has taken lessons at East Grove farm in these matters, and been wiser and kinder for the knowledge. When a pig is sold it is sent to its destination in a comfortable crate, and arrangements are made to have it watered and fed during its journey. Twice Mrs. Edwards has sold out. Both times she was moved to do this by personal afflictions, and both times she summoned up her courage, determined to resume her profitable and honorable business, and took up her burden again. These sales, although they were profitable and furnished her with ready money-for she derived $15,000 from the two-caused her much work, necessitating, as it did, the re-gathering of a herd. To get a perfect herd is the work of years. Mrs. Edwards has a high reputation among stockmen, and is determined to preserve it. Her farm is visited by stockmen from all over the country, and as these possible purchasers are likely to arrive at any hour of the day open house is kept at East Grove farm. There are very few meals at which the family sits down alone, and it is not unusual to have several guests who come each from a different state. The Dakotas, Colorado, Iowa, Kansas, Missouri and Nebraska furnish most of Mrs. Edwards' purchasers. Among the owners of fine herds to whom she has sold Poland Chinas are Hixson Bros. of Vermillion, S.D.; Bischel Bros. of Kearney, Neb.; H. H. Hammond of Waterloo, Ia.; Cantrall & Garrett of Waynesville, Ill.; Bert Wise of Hiawatha, Kas.; Eli Zimmerman of the same place; Levi Hayford of Seward, Neb.; D. J. Moon of Prescott, Ia.; A. C. Stowell of Cedar Rapids, Neb., and F. M. Duesler of Charter Oak, Ia.

That Mrs. Edwards is much trusted by stockmen is evidenced by the fact that Cudahy's stock man asked her to select a herd for the Cudahy farm at Albion. She was, during the World's fair, the one woman appointed to inspect cereals for the awarding of prizes. She worked on the commission with sixty men and had many a pretty triumph over the prejudice which existed against the placing of a woman in a position of such responsibility. She is the vice president for Nebraska of the Stock Breeder's association. She is always an enthusiastic worker at the Farmers' institute, is a member of the Women's Christian Temperance Union, and of the Political Equality Club of Fremont – a woman's club. Mrs. Edwards has been asked by five different counties in this state to act as a judge and appraiser of pigs at county fairs, but has refused, feeling that she must keep strictly to her particular line of work. Neither will she exhibit any more of her own pigs at fairs. It does not pay her to do so. The trouble and expense are considerable, and, after the reputation of a farm is made, the results are not appreciable.

Mrs. Edwards maintains that she keeps no stock excepting pigs, yet to a city woman a couple of hundred light brahmas, the several cows and eleven or twelve horses, seems like a good deal of livestock.

Mrs. Edwards lost her dear son DeWayne Palmer a few years ago, and since then her work has been less interesting to her in many ways. Another misfortune was the burning down of her home after she had succeeded in making it very comfortable. But her energy arose equal to the occasion. She converted her corn crib, which was a strong and well constructed building, into a home, ceiled it with Georgia pine, which was oiled and polished, and has, in consequence, a home both commodious and cozy. The warm colors of the walls, the quiet gray carpets, the books, pictures, easy chairs, hospitable table, and best of all, the gracious welcome given, make it an exceptionally interesting home.

Mrs. Edwards enjoys the friendship of the best women of Fremont. Perhaps some of these women may have hesitated before they became acquainted with "a stock woman." They probably fancied her a blustering, masculine, coarse woman with strident voice and a frowsy head. When they found instead a gentle, mild, intelligent, alert, comely and charming woman, they changed their views. Little by little the women who succeed are changing the views of the prejudiced. For it is generally found that women do not enter public life or business life from choice. They are impelled to do it by their home loving instinct. They are moved by their hearts to do clever things with their heads.

Mrs. Edwards has paid nearly all of the heavy indebtedness caused by her husband's failure, owns 200 acres not far from the 160 on which she lives, has other farms in different parts of the state, and means to keep the reputation which she has won of being one of the most reliable breeders of the Poland Chinas in the state. Thus may one conquer – even a woman, with her white brain-matter – if one tries hard enough and the gods have given her good sense.

"The Lady of the Cloister"
16 February 1896

Introducing another exemplary woman, Peattie informed her readers of a spiritual and intellectual oasis on the treeless prairie.[13] *The Academy of the Visitation originated in 1889 when Thomas Farrell, a leading Catholic businessman in Hastings, originated the idea of establishing a boarding school for girls in the sparsely populated central Nebraska region.*[14] *For most children of the plains, education stopped after the eighth grade. Parents who wanted their sons and daughters to graduate from a four-year high school would have to board them far from home at either a coeducational or Protestant institution.*

Classes commenced on 5 February 1890, offering musical instruction in voice, harp, piano, guitar, and mandolin, as well as art education in oil, watercolors, and china painting. The young women also learned French and German, taught by the "natural method," along with the more practical courses of bookkeeping, typewriting, stenography, and telegraphy – the major careers acceptable for women of the late 1800s.

From the beginning, financial difficulties plagued the academy due to the drought, crop failures, and bank closings of the 1890s. Although students from across Nebraska as well as from Hastings enrolled at the academy, the sisters had to take out two mortgages; they could not pay the interest, however, and finally had to close the doors on 1 December 1896, only eight months after Peattie's visit.[15]

❧ Deep on the convent roof the snows are sparkling to the moon.

Sister Mary Francis de Sales, at the Academy of the Visitation of the Blessed Virgin at Hastings, in this state, is one of the few literary women, worthy of the name, of whom the state can boast.

"Remember," she wrote in a letter, "that I am a cloistered nun. My personality can be nothing to the public."

One does remember. None can intrude into that cloister. Therefore may not so much of her personality be exploited as shall be of inspiration to other women? May not her fair life be set in view before us, who are weary of looking at mediocre living, at failure and "confusion worse than death"? Sister de Sales has had one great ambition: to be of use to women. She can be of no greater use than in permitting one to affectionately relate something of the story of her life. Such modest shrinking as a recluse might naturally

Faculty and students at the Academy of the Visitation in Hastings, Nebraska, 1890. (Adams County Historical Society)

feel at seeing her name in print, she may unselfishly lay aside, as she has laid aside so many other selfishnesses, for the good of others.

Before Sister de Sales entered her order and took the name that as a religious she is to bear to the day of her death, she bore the name of Chase. She is, in fact, the niece of Salmon Chase, and, as one of the family of Philander Chase, the distinguished Episcopal bishop, was quite naturally, herself of the Episcopal faith. For thirty years she "lived in the world," and was of it. She knew many distinguished persons, lived a life of some fashion, and in Springfield, Mass., one of the most intellectual towns in this country, had much social experience. She was by nature, a keen student. Books were her pleasure – her divertissement. She had also a love of teaching. To develop the human mind, whether the mind belonged to herself or to someone else, was to her a profound delight, and those whom she has instructed say she had a peculiarly luminous way of conveying knowledge.

"I never loved learning till Sister de Sales became my teacher," said a bright young nun. "She made facts stand out. She has a genius for teaching."

When she was 30 she became a Roman Catholic.

She has, in truth, a nose and mouth which suggest Savonarola. Yet her eyes are blue, soft and tender, like those of a happy, yet thoughtful child.

It was thirty years ago that she entered the cloister at Keokuk. Six years ago, when the Visitation academy was built at Hastings, that a Catholic school for girls might be held in the great central territory of the state, Sister de Sales broke her cloister to make the journey thither. For six years she has looked out upon the treeless plain, the undulating corn fields, the splendid sky, the yellow atmosphere of Nebraska. For six years she has known that peculiar silence which reigns over the vast spaces of our plains – a silence which the unceasing wind intensifies with its inarticulate voices.

But a convent life is a busy one. The women in a cloister are busier than most women in the world. The mere housekeeping of an establishment which holds twenty nuns and a varying number of pupils is no sinecure. Then the teaching of the scholars fills all the usual working hours of the day; and after those are done with, come the hours of devotion, which make up the chief part of conventual life. The Order of the Visitation of the Blessed Virgin is an educational order, its purpose being to educate women for earth and for heaven: in short, to cultivate the minds and the spirits of the young.

It is not surprising, perhaps, that in the house of an educational order there should be a noticeable degree of intelligence. But it is remarkable that in any cloister there should be a white heat of intellectuality. Yet such is the case at the Visitation academy at Hastings. All of the nuns are, of course, especially educated for teaching. But that fact alone would not create this remarkable condition. The whole place is inspired, dominated by, impregnated with the spirit of Sister Mary Francis de Sales, a woman who loves science, fine literature, knowledge of all sorts, and whose aspect of life is now so delicately spiritual, now so purely intellectual, that no one can tell where the soul ends and the mind begins. The two seem to have been soluble. Whether the soul has been made intellectual or the mind made spiritual, one would hesitate to say. There is a mental impression of something, white, vivid, luminous, something which radiates ideas and purity. To have been given such a personality is cause for reverential gratitude. Sister de Sales may feel it so – only she is too modest to think this description correct. But since it seems so, one may surely be forgiven for letting other women know. Other women, who are worried, overworked, irritated, forced into ignorance may well rejoice to read of her, serene, on her mountain top.

Sister de Sales is a writer. She contributes, under the name of F. M. Edselas, to the *Catholic World*, the *Boston Pilot*, *Donahoe's Magazine* and many lesser Catholic publications. She wrote a paper on women in religious life which was read at the [1893 Chicago] World's fair; and also a pamphlet on religious communities, which was circulated by the Catholic educational bureau at the same exposition. Many of her articles written for periodicals are of a scientific nature. In the contemplation of science, and in the making of experiments, she takes a keen delight. It is one of her amusements to weave scientific knowledge into fiction in such a way as to induce the average reader to peruse it, and gather, unconsciously to himself, some fascinating knowledge.

Her style is unaffected, her English above reproach, and her imagination very active and charming. Another pleasure of her life is to write for children. She has written numerous short stories, and also three books of the "Neptune series," known as "The Neptune Abroad," "The Neptune Afloat" and "The Neptune Homeward Bound," being stories of travel, in which the characters are hearty and natural boys and girls, who, under happy circumstances, take long journeys.

"There are subtle lessons in the geography of this wonderful world," she explained. "I do not believe the ordinary child understands the world as he learns it from physical geography. He idly says the Atlantic is east or west, and after long repetition, gets the answer right. But to make the ocean live to him, in all its beauty, to link it to the lands as God linked it, to make its palpitating history a part of his mind, is another thing, is it not? So should children be taught. I am an old teacher. I have taught nearly all my life. But I may say that I have always taught under protest. I have always been in revolt against the established regime. The day is coming when we shall have a wiser system of education. The kindergarten has the right idea in the development of the faculties. Once the mind is trained, it is easy enough to instill facts into it. If the kindergarten idea of developing the capabilities could be brought into use in the higher grades, learning would not be the difficult and repelling thing it is now."

Sister de Sales has a great love of children, and it has been part of the happiness of her life that she has been allowed to work for them, to teach them and to associate with them. A year ago, she was stricken with paralysis. Then all the sisters prayed she might be spared, to be the leader yet a little while; and prayed yet more fervently that if she lived she might retain her mind and speech. Perhaps prayer is answered. There are those who say it is. At any rate, this woman lives, and though her right hand is almost helpless and her right foot drags as she walks, and her tongue is a little heavy in speaking, still her restless, curious, alert mind is as strong as ever, and she may still make the hours of recreation brilliant with her conversation. She is excused now from her teaching, and no compulsory labor of any sort is put upon her. Yet she is always busy in little deeds of charity, in the offices of her life, or in her writing – for she writes now, with her left hand, on the typewriter. Her cell is strewn with books, pamphlets, papers and clippings.

"We may own nothing," she explained, "not even our rosary. That will next year be given to another. It is not for us to become attached to anything in this world. Yet we are permitted to use whatever is necessary for our work, and this litter of stuff is necessary for my work. I have time to read, and can thus keep myself and those around me in touch with the world, with literature and discovery."

The library is the room in which she sits on such rare occasions as she visits with the secular, and this is an interesting room. Its two great windows look off over the western plain. A piano, a harp and some mandolins form a part of its furniture. Great bunches of peacock feathers decorate the wall. One side of the room is covered with book cases, in which are such standard works of philosophy, belles lettres or fiction as would be found in any well selected private library. There are also souvenirs from many parts of the world, sent to the sisters in general, and to Sister de Sales in particular. A tiny bronze statue of Bartholdi's Liberty, a basket of white woven cedar roots from the Thinglets of Alaska, a crystal from the mammoth cave, a stone from the pyramids, a bunch of edelweiss from Alpine snows, a sea bean from the blue bay of Tampa, coral from Naples, a jug from Mexico, a scrap from the petrified forests, fossils of moss, fish and grass.

"These are the fragments of a world," said Sister de Sales, smiling. "You see I am a great traveler, in mind. And indeed, there is no country which I cannot penetrate, no mountain which I cannot climb without fatigue, no river which I cannot penetrate without expense. I have but to shut my eyes, choose my path, and go wherever I will, while you, who are in the world, must needs be hampered in your journeyings by so many things."

Is not this contentment? Is not this a triumph of mind over walls of brick, over vows of poverty, over the limitations of the body? Yet such joys as these all may know.

The Order of the Visitation of the Blessed Virgin was founded in 1610 by Jane Francis de Chantal, a pious widow, and Frances de Sales, Bishop of Geneva. It was intended particularly for those who were feeble, blind, lame, or incapacitated for work, poor and afflicted. The sisters of the order were first known as visitandines. In time, however, the order became a closed one, and its function was that of prayer. Later, it began to take in "sisters of the little habit," young girls, who were instructed in letters and religion. In course of time it came to be known as one of the active educational orders. Its first house in America was at Georgetown, Md., a house founded by Leonard Neale, bishop of Baltimore, in 1793. That house stands today and bears a wide reputation. Many of the prominent women of the country have been educated here. The order was founded, the legend goes, as the result of visions which appeared to its two founders, who, at that time, were strangers to one another. The whole course of its history has been marked by episodes of the supernatural sort, a history of which may be found in an interesting book by George Parsons Lathrop and Rose Hawthorne Lathrop, called "A Story of Courage."

The customs of the sisters have not materially changed since the Baroness Jane de Chantal of France learned of St. Frances de Sales, the rule of conventual living, and the art of suffering. To eat at a bare board in silence, the coarse and simple food, to listen in the midst of this abstemious eating to the reading from some life of the saints by a sister who sits as the reading desk above the table; to dress in gown and veil of black, and coif of snowy linen, to have for a jewel only the cross of silver marked with the letters I. H. S.; to spend the time in the services of God, not allowing even so much egotism as that involved in scourging the body for the good of the soul; to bear life in patience, cheerfulness, piety and peace, is the duty of the sisters of the Order of the Visitation.

The great building at Hastings, Neb., stands about two miles from town, its bare red walls rising up from the dull yellow plain. The building appears to be 200 feet long, or perhaps, more. But half of it is finished. The chapel is not yet completed, and a modest room is used for that purpose – a room made interesting with the altar and its statues, with its kneeling life-sized figure of a Sister of the Visitation, and with some excellent pictures. These were brought from Mexico by an Omaha gentleman, who learned that at the time of the Mexican war with this country, they were taken from a church in Mexico. Three of these hang above the altar, and represent different stages of the tragedy of the crucifixion. They are beautiful, and of great workmanship. Much could be written about them-but that another time.

The convent school is modern in its teachings, and its method. Such accessories as telegraphy, stenography, typewriting, bookkeeping, etc., are taught. But all this information is not interesting. One only means to say that the school aims to be in keeping with the times, and that the institution is good and ambitious. But the nuns are more attractive than their retreat, as jewels are than their setting.

There is the energetic "out-sister," by whose energies the convent is partly maintained, the school not being self-supporting in these pinched times; there is the mother superior, who is a fine and much esteemed woman, and one of executive ability; there many sisters, young and middle aged, whose own strong personalities have been enriched and deepened by living in an atmosphere of great books, interesting reminiscence, and liberal thought, such as Sister de Sales has thrown around them. For she has played with Harriet Hosmer in her youth, corresponded with Longfellow, known Emerson, been a friend to Father Doyle, the leader of the Catholic temperance movement; been intimate with Miss Conway, the poet; had letters from Prof. Agassiz and a correspondence with the Rev. Martin S. Brennan, priest and astronomer, who, laboring among the stars, while he preached at this little church of St. Thomas of Aquin of St. Louis, became the author of great books, the fellow of exclusive scientific societies.

Sister de Sales is in favor of the development of woman's abilities. She sympathizes with growth, development, new powers. She is not so foolish as to set herself against the laws of evolution. She writes, in one of her articles, "let woman fill up her measure of capacity, whether large or small." She writes of whatever is most stirring and vital. She is of the present age, and even cloister walls cannot rob her of her interest in what is going on without those walls. In fact, to her the cloister is as a lofty height from which she may review the procession of the world-contemplate the kaleidoscopic time.

Sometimes with sadness,
Sometimes with confidence,
Always with superb intelligence.

"A Woman Doctor"

15 March 1891

Dr. Freda Lankton, a well-known Omaha physician and surgeon for more than twenty years, was a graduate of Iowa State University at Iowa City. In May 1888 she joined her former mentor, Dr. Amelia Burroughs, the first recorded woman practitioner in Omaha. Dr. Burroughs, a homeopath, had moved to Omaha in February 1883 from Council Bluffs.[16] *Within the next six years, more than half a dozen women followed Burroughs's example, most of them also homeopaths, and by 1892, when all practitioners were required by law to register, fifty-six women were licensed to practice in Nebraska, thirteen of them in Omaha. By 1894, Dr. Lankton's reputation was well established among her peers, and she was elected president of the Nebraska State Homeopathic Society (Tyler and Auerbach 179–81, 186–87, 364–66).*

Peattie became acquainted with Dr. Lankton through the Omaha Woman's Club, of which Lankton was a member, as well as through her own work in support of the Open Door. Considered one of Omaha's most charitable women, Dr. Lankton also contributed her services, and sometimes material assistance, to the Old People's Home and the Visiting Nurses' Association. In addition, she generously supported the education of several youths of Omaha. Among these, one young man became a prominent Omaha physician and two young women became teachers ("Dr. Freda M. Lankton Dead"). Asserting that women could

Male and female students at the Omaha Medical College, ca. 1890. (Nebraska State Historical Society Photograph Collections)

be both successful and feminine, both learned and humane, Freda Lankton personified for Peattie the professional woman.[17]

❧ . . . In Omaha there are at present eight women physicians. One of these is Freda Lankton, a woman who may be said to be a physician in spite of herself.

"When I was young," she said the other day, "my dolls were always sick and I was doctoring. I killed my cats by administering to them the most extraordinary compounds. After I got old enough to think about what my course of life was to be, I determined to become a doctor. So I redoubled my energies at school and after hours nursed all the old ladies who would do me the favor to imagine themselves ill. I determined, of course, that I would never marry. At the age of 18 I changed my mind suddenly, impelled by circumstances over which I had – and have – no control. That is to say Mr. Lankton. But I apologized to myself for this act of frivolity by reminding myself that my eyes and health had failed me, and that I could not possibly follow my studies.

I thought then that my life would be like that of other married women, and I tried to content myself with home making, expecting always that by and by I would have little patients of my own to raise up in ways of health. But the babies did not come, and the old appetite for study and for work came back stronger than ever. It seemed more than an inclination to me. It was the voice of duty. We thought it best, my husband and I, that I should go to New York and study. I did so for two years. Then again my health and eyes failed me. I came home, rested, and went to the Iowa medical school, intending to ultimately to return to New York. But I found the instruction where I was so excellent that I staid until I received my graduation."

Dr. Lankton did not mention that she carried off the honors of her class, though such was the case. She then came to Omaha and practiced under Dr. Amelia Burroughs for several years. At length, gaining confidence, she hung her sign before her door and started out on the profession alone.

That was three years ago. Since then Dr. Lankton has made a somewhat remarkable record in her profession. The reason of it is that she is never perfunctory in her work. She has love for her occupation which rises above all monetary consideration. In personal appearance she is as slight as a girl, with a self-contained, scrutinizing sort of face; the expressing of intellectuality being increased by the glasses which she always wears. Her manners are gentle but decisive; her speech quiet, firm, but not in the least dogmatic. Dr. Lankton has, in fact, a sense of humor, and a humorous person is not apt to be dogmatic. Her dress is stylish, but not so notably stylish as fastidious. Something in the particularity with which the bodice of her dress fits, in the whiteness of the bits of linen at throat and wrist, and in the neatness of the gloves and boots, betrays the personal daintiness of this professional woman.

There is nothing about Dr. Lankton that is not absolutely feminine. Even her pitifulness is of a feminine character.

For example, she will stay up all day and all night with some suffering creature at the Open Door and never relax her enthusiasm or her best efforts. A man might pity these poor girls. He might be generous in his judgment. But would he stay up all day and night nursing a shame-stricken, unknown woman as tenderly as if she were the wife of a millionaire? Would he spend a part of every day – such valuable days – among these poor girls – knowing that no monetary reward would ever be his?

That is what Dr. Lankton does in common with the other women physicians of the city. They take turns, do these women, in performing this labor for the wonderful home of mercy over which Mrs. Clark presides. The willingness of Dr. Lankton to sacrifice herself in this noble work can be estimated by the fact that out of the 100 births at the Open Door, thirty-seven have been attended by her. But all the physicians are most kind, and a great debt of gratitude is due them from the suffering women who have been cared for by them.

It is not impossible that a few persons adversely criticize Dr. Lankton for this. Perhaps there are some who would employ her if she were not so unselfishly associated with this institution. There are people like that. I am glad to say I do not know any of them. If I did, I should cut their acquaintance. The mental processes of such persons would be too complicated for me.

I was at the Open Door the other day when Dr. Lankton came. She wore a tidy little brown walking suit, with a sealskin cap on her dark hair, and in her hand she carried the neat medicine case – for she is a homeopathist.

"Dear me," she said, looking in the door brightly, "is this a committee meeting?"

It wasn't, and the doctor came in and chatted for a moment. But she did not stay long, for there was a girl next door who was coming down with pneumonia – or so Mrs. Clark said.

"So glad you diagnosed the case for me," the doctor said jocularly.

The faint smell of disinfectants meets the nostrils as one enters the Open Door. The white, bare floors remind one of a hospital, but before the beds are squares of bright carpet, and on the walls hang a few pictures and scrolls of comforting scriptural selections.

"How's the coal, dear?" the doctor asks Mrs. Clark.

"All out," says Mrs. Clark. "We're burning soft coal now. Don't see how we're going to get any more."

"Soft coal's bad for the furnace," sighed Dr. Lankton, unbuttoning her gloves.

"It isn't as bad for the furnace as freezing to death would be for my poor girls," said Mrs. Clark.

The doctor went in the quiet first room. There lay two girls. One was the girl sent out from a home in this city a few weeks ago in convulsions. She contracted pneumonia in that journey through the bitter cold. For hours frightful convulsions tormented her. Her little child died. And days of delirium followed, in which the endurance of the nurse and doctor were taxed to the utmost. In the other bed lay a deserted wife, with her 4-day-old baby beside her. The doctor looked about her cheerfully.

"Hope you had a good night," she said. They had. Both of them had good nights. She sounded the lungs of one.

"We are better," she announced, as if the pneumonia had been a sort of co-operative affair. "The air is getting into our lungs in great shape. A little patience and we shall be well."

Then she went to the other bed. Pulse, temperature, were as they should be. Appetite good. Patient comparatively happy – as happy as a deserted wife with a 4-days-old baby could be expected to be.

"No medicine needed here," said the doctor, smiling. "Let's see the baby."

The baby was looked over.

"Sound as a nut," said the doctor, rolling it up and snuggling it in bed again.

Upstairs was the poor, feverish creature, who had been turned from a hotel in this city where she had become useless. She could not work, being sick. She could not pay her board, having no money.

Of what use is such a creature to a practical hotel keeper? Obviously, none. So he lets her go out where she pleases, keeping her pitiful trunk full of clothes as security. A poor woman's scanty garments are of so much use to a hotel proprietor! And besides, the law gives him a right to keep them – no one denies that.

It is under such circumstances that women commit suicide – in cities where there is not an Open Door.

"It's not pneumonia," said the doctor, after ten minutes of careful examination. The girl still turned mute, appealing eyes on her. Behind those hot glances was a torrent of unshed tears. Apprehension and loneliness drew down the lines of the young face. The doctor laid a hand on the throbbing head.

"You will be better by night," she said, gently. "It is only a bad cold that you have. The medicine will take down your fever. Do not fret. Remember you are among friends. There is no need to fret."

She prepared the medicine, looked to the temperature of the room, smiled reassuringly and went out.

In the next room were the babies. Some of them were playing and cooing as if all the good things of life were theirs and an honorable heritage among them. One was ailing and weeping.

"Colic," said the doctor. "Don't feed it so much. Its stomach isn't strong. You over tax it."

Another baby lay on the bed snapping like some vicious little animal. It was beyond the reach of human surgery or physic. Like Richard III, it had been sent into the world but half made up. Such an unfortunate is a great exception at the Open Door. Most of the infants born there are vigorous and healthy in body and mind.

The doctor turned this little compound of nerves and twitching muscles over on its side, and looked at it a long time. Then she laid it back as it was and went away, saying nothing, and the child snapped at her viciously.

But another flung out its hands and sent a ripple of laughter after her.

The doctor's visit for the day was over. She put on her things and started for the door.

"Wish you had some coal, dear," said she to Mrs. Clark.

Mrs. Clark smiled. So did that most adroit and patient of nurses, Mrs. Ecles.

"The Lord will provide," said Mrs. Clark. The doctor nodded in acquiescence and farewell. Then she caught the south bound train.

"It has been a light day for her," said Mrs. Clark, "and I am glad to have her rest on her laurels for a while, for she has had some terrible cases here lately."

That is a glimpse of Dr. Freda Lankton's forenoon. The afternoon is spent among her regular patients. The evenings, so far as may be, are at home reading with her husband.

Pretty good sort of a life that, take it for all in all. . . .

"A Singular Institution: The Christian Home of Council Bluffs and Its Founder"

1 March 1891

The Christian Home of Council Bluffs, Iowa, was founded by Rev. Joseph Goff Lemen, who studied law at Harvard University and moved to Lebanon, Missouri, where he practiced law, published newspapers, and at age twenty-eight was ordained in the Baptist Church. In 1880, when Rev. Lemen accepted the pastorate at the First Baptist Church, he moved with his wife and four children to Council Bluffs.

Two weeks after their arrival, Rev. Lemen began his special mission to assist the needy when a poor widow refused aid because there were others as desperate as she. That winter, Rev. Lemen organized a charity that provided for every poor family in the city. Soon, people began bringing homeless children to him, so in 1883 he incorporated the Council Bluffs Home of the Friendless, using personal funds he had saved during his years of legal practice. Rev. Lemen received homeless children and helpless aged, who served as grandparent figures for the orphans, and also provided adoption services. He insisted that families of young children never be separated, and many of the children grew to adulthood under his and his wife's loving care.[18] *The home's "Newsboys' Department" intrigued Peattie, too, for it provided a shelter for vagrant and misbehaving boys, a much better consequence than the jails where young Omaha miscreants were housed (Peattie, "Papa Lem[e]n").*

When Rev. Lemen died in 1904 at age fifty-six, the institution covered two and

Homeless children and elderly residents of Rev. Joseph Lemen's Christian Home of Council Bluffs, 1898. (Christian Home Association–Children's Square U.S.A.)

one-half blocks and included three parks, twenty cottages, a public chapel, and a printing office. The home had cared for more than fifteen hundred children.[19]

❧ There is one town in these United States where, if a child is homeless or forsaken, or miserable or wicked, he will be received with affectionate cordiality and cared for with tender consideration.

In fact, not a motherless or hungry child is permitted to wander the streets of this city. This is very extraordinary. It has almost no parallel.

The city referred to is Council Bluffs.

The home where they find shelter is the "Christian Home," conducted by the Rev. J. G. Lemen and his wife. At present there are in it over sixty children, all of whom might be homeless – and worse – but for this protection. The peculiarity of this home is, however, that the little ones are taken in that they may have shelter from the street. It is not that the pangs of hunger may be spared. No child is turned from the door. There is no attempt to foster them upon other institutions.

"What we want is to reach the immortal souls of the children," says Mr. Lemen. "We do not try to find homes for them because we do not want to let them go. We would as soon take a deformed child as a strong and comely one, for our only thought is to save their souls from the wickedness of the world. Of course we incidentally give them physical comforts, and the manner in which the Lord provides for them through His people is a continual marvel."

But though there is no desire to put a single child adrift, or put the expense and worry of its raising on anyone else, yet homes have been found for 200 of them since the beginning of the institution eight years ago. These homes are most exceptional. They have been selected with the greatest care. Mr. Lemen will not permit one of his children to leave the home unless the one to which it is going is presided over by Christian people. They must also be well enough provided with the world's goods to give the child such comforts that it will not need to drudge through those years when it should be acquiring an education. And the persons taking the child must legally adopt it, and must promise that the child shall attend divine worship. When these conditions have been fulfilled with many parting expressions of affection it is permitted to leave the home. Perhaps to be correct the home should be spelled with a capital H. Homes where children of various parentage are cared for usually are spelled that way. But a home spelled with a capital H is such a desolate thing! It is so often a place where there is tyrannical order; where every impulse of individuality is crushed; where no child ever learns the word "mamma"; where a kiss is unknown; where tears must be hidden and dropped at night, with stifled sobs.

In this home all the children say "mamma." There are two persons who answer to this name – the matron and Mrs. Lemen. These two women are the recipients of every confidence. They even have time to kiss the children, and kissing is considered quite as necessary a part of the day's duties as the washing of faces.

He who does not believe that every occurrence of earth is a part of a vast design may well be excused for considering this remarkable place an accident.

Mr. Lemen has so quaintly told in his little journal of the Christian Home just how it all began that perhaps the best estimate of the man's character can be conveyed by printing his own words. They are as follows:

In the spring of 1882, a mechanic, who some months before had taken the temperance pledge and violated it, in a fit of despondency, committed suicide. We were called to preach the funeral. The poor wife, with babe in arms, and five little children, standing around the coffin, was a sight never to be forgotten. The poor woman was left penniless and had to go out and wash for families in order to support her little ones, made fatherless. Her oldest child was only 11. The babe had to be left in the care of this little one during the day. The little sister probably did the best she could, but was too young to properly care for the babe. The result was that the little one took cold, and in just two weeks from the time of the funeral of the father we were called to preach the funeral of the babe.

The next day we ordered supplies for the family for the winter, and, moved of the Lord, visited a large number of other poor families who were as destitute as the one in question. Late in the evening, returning home, happy in spirit, but very tired in body, the reporter of the *Council Bluffs Daily Nonpareil* met us and asked for a report. After he had received it, he said:

"Why not let me announce in the morning that you will be in your study from 10 a.m. to 12 p.m. to receive any additional donations that citizens desire to bring in?"

"Why, we can't do that," we replied. "Those are our hours for study, and we can't do it. We must look after the interests of the church."

"But look here," he said, "if you are the means of feeding and clothing these people, what better work can you do?"

The Lord blessed the words of that worldly man to our good. He meant them to be ironical, but we let that pass, and said, "Well, do as you like. Shrink from it, but if you see fit to announce it, I will do my part."

He did announce it. The citizens of this city responded most liberally. He came around daily, and each morning wrote up the work, because he took special pride in it, having suggested it. His name was Clark. He was a man of the world, did not claim to be anything else, but he had a tender heart. We do not know where he is now, but wherever he is, may God bless him and eventually lead him unto Himself. The work rapidly grew into large proportions, until we had the chapel of the church open from 7 a.m. to 10 p.m., had a man to attend to it, had committees, sometimes had a half dozen express wagons engaged in the service of the committees, fed and clothed scores of families, made extensive repairs on dilapidated houses, where the sick were, furnished stoves, beds and bedding, sent nurses to the sick, and, in short, by the co-operation of all the churches and charitable organizations of the city, did a work for the poor that winter that will ever be remembered to the credit of the good people of Council Bluffs.

While this work was at its height, about the middle of December, 1882, a drunken man staggered into the chapel one day. Approaching us he said, "I want you to take my three girls." We explained to him that we had no place for his girls, that we were simply dispensing food and clothing, and that if he and family were in need and in the opinion of the committee, worthy, we would assist.

"I don't want that," he exclaimed. "My wife died a few days ago. I am a wreck! There is no hope for me, and if you won't take my children they will have to go to the poor house, and then God only knows what will become of them!"

This language touched our heart, as God intended it should. We took the girls and hired their board, praise the Lord! As soon as it was noised abroad that we had so done, other homeless, forsaken little ones, were brought to us. Having commenced, our heart was softened, and we simply followed on, as the Lord led. Soon we had more than we could afford to board out, and so we rented a little house and hired a matron. In the spring of 1883, March 16, we called some earnest brethren together and organized a legal association for the holding of property. We may not here go on with the long struggle we then had before the Lord saw fit to lead us out into a comparatively large place. He tried us. We are well aware that it was for our best good, and devoutly praise Him for the dark days of the work, as well as the bright ones.

The mercies of the Lord certainly have been very substantial – or, at least, the sacrifices made by men and women – for the unfortunate little ones have been very numerous, if one is to judge by the many comfortable cottages that stand close grouped in a shady cul-de-sac in the shadow of the Bluffs. This being no thoroughfare, the children are left uninterrupted in their play in the long summer afternoons, and the petunias and geraniums grow unmolested in their great, square garden patch. Mr. Lemen, his wife and their four children have a house of their own, and preserve a family life in spite of all their labors. Back of their very comfortable and homelike dwelling stands the little chapel – "a gift of the Lord." Within, the worn carpet testifies to the tramping of many small feet. About the walls hang cards and small mottoes. At one end of the platform is a snug cabinet organ; at the other, a generous stove. Here all the family meet after breakfast for a song and a word of prayer and praise. Then at night, after school hours, the older children tidy it up. The tidying up is as much a part of the day's devotions as is the prayer. Everything done in the home is done to the glory of God.

"Even the help in the kitchen," says Mr. Lemen, "are Christian ladies. We have no servants here. We all give our services to the Lord." If cleanliness is an indication of godliness the kitchen is certainly the dwelling of God-fearing women. Its long, bare benches, its worn floors, its cupboards and ranges are scrupulously clean. The dining room has a series of pine tables, some of them lower and some higher – to match the children. Red cloths cover the table, and bowls and spoons stand ready for soup or porridge, whatever the fare may be. No state institution is run on so little as this, yet the children all look well fed as anyone may see who watches them scampering home – a group of hearty, noisy boys and girls from the public schools.

"We like them to seem as much like other children as possible," said Mr.

Lemen, "so we send them to the public school. And at any rate we could not give them such good instruction as they receive there. We feel sure that they are very kindly treated." There are other children in the institution who do not go to school, and who do not look hearty and who never will. Some of them have had for their only heritage some noxious disease, and their innocent souls wait in those unclean bodies for a happy translation. Some are deformed, some maimed. There is one intelligent little girl whose legs and feet are shriveled so as to be quite useless. Mr. Lemen wants to get her a typewriter. Everyone who visits the home gives her a few pennies toward this, and already she has nearly enough to make the purchase. Meantime she studies away patiently at her English speller. Her abilities are really very good, and in spite of her terrible misfortune she looks to an independent living.

"You have some new shoes, my child," said a lady who entered the room and who wanted to say something agreeable.

"My shoes are always new," the little girl said looking up without smiling. Then she went back to her spelling book.

The home has one little soul who is such a monument of suffering and patience as well as of precocious sanctity that he is usually mentioned before any other child in the institution. His name is Willie McCourt. His body is wrenched and twisted with pain. His back has sores which never heal. He has undergone operations that the veteran of many battles might well have shrunk from. It is impossible for him to lie on his back, but he lies day and night face downward on a pile of pillows. His head is disproportionately large, his face most piteous with suffering, but his eyes are alight with ecstasy such as must have been in the eyes of the little ones who left the Rhineland six centuries ago to follow their sires to the crusades. Whatever is best in the home is brought to this bedside. If there is a picture book, it is placed on this counter-pane. If there is a canary bird it hangs above this bed. If there is a flower, it blooms in a window near. This extraordinary little sufferer looks forward to heaven as most children do to the next Christmas, and his fame has gone broadcast. His unchildlike speeches of devotion are quoted by Sunday school superintendents to their awed and youthful listeners. One could hardly expect a little boy who did not have the hip disease, or to say the least, ulcers on the back, to keep up to this pitch of somewhat hysterical devotion, and not a mother who sees him but could wish that the sad and angelic little child were rid of his spirituality and possessed of a whole body, a red sled and some desirable, boyish naughtinesses. (The writer, like the reporter, whose haphazard words caused the starting of this institution, is also a "worldly man.")

One of the sources of regular income for the home is that which comes from the paper, the *Christian Home*, which has a circulation of 8,000 a week. There is also a monthly paper called the *Word and the Way*. The circulation of this is about 8,000 also. The *Word and the Way* and also the Marion tract depository were established by Dr. B. J. Kendall and wife at Saratoga Springs, N.Y., in memory of their little daughter, Marion Kendall. In March, 1890, they gave the *Word and the Way* and the Marion tract depository to the Christian Home orphanage. They also erected a neat building, which contains a composing room, a press room and most agreeable editorial apartments. The press runs ingeniously by water power, the water being furnished without cost by the company which supplies the water to Council Bluffs. Mr. Lemen does most of the writing for these papers. His son has learned practical printing and, with the assistance of two of the boys of the home, sets up and prints two papers which commend themselves to any practical printer so far as typography is concerned. The subscriptions from the publications, together with cash donations, form the income of the home. As showing the figures involved as receipts, those for April of the last year were $1,056.51; May, 922.66; June, 634.34.

But the money received is far from representing the entire receipts of the home. For example, the floors everywhere are covered with neat rag carpeting, the work of an army of dear old women from New Hampshire to Texas. In the cosy, clean dormitories there is the most wonderful array of bed quilts pieced in patterns of competing intricacy, the work also of women who had a thought for the children who are motherless. The children are kept well clothed and fortunately with no attempt at uniformity. As soon as the girls are old enough they are taught to sew, but most of them are taken from the home before they have arrived at an age when they can be of much use. One little girl makes the proud boast that she has lived there seven years, and she looks on herself as quite an aristocrat in consequence. There is one bit of a house in this group of cottages, the original purpose of which is not known by the writer, but which is used at present as the room of two of the larger boys. A bed with a bright, pieced cover, a gay rag carpet, a stove and a box of wood, a shelf of books and a pine writing table, with some common chairs, make up the contents. It is just such a room as boys can enjoy themselves in.

It would be possible to write indefinitely of the beautiful institution and of the remarkable man who presides over it and who shelters and gives love to so many shelterless and loveless little ones, but it is only possible to hint at the life of the place. One object, however, must not go unmentioned. It is a large album in which are kept many of the photograph portraits of the children who have been sent into other homes. It is a book full of histories – more, it is a book full of melodies. One turns a page, for example, to look at the faces of a middle-aged, well-to-do, hearty, lovable couple. In the midst of the pleasant lines on their faces there is the hint of a little hardness or disappointment. It is the ungratified child-hunger – the longing for that close love which never came. But between them in the freshly purchased clothes, garnished out with clean muslins and laces, stands the little one they have just taken to appease this yearning.

Expectancy, pride and trust are there on the face, under the stiffly-plaited braids. Out of incompleteness completeness has been brought. The brook searching for a channel has found its way into the arid land which ached for it.

"Grand Island and Its Beets: The County Seat of Hall and What Beet Cultivation Has Done"

5 February 1893

Always on the lookout for a chance to promote Nebraska communities, Peattie investigated the sugar beet industry in 1893, traveling first to Grand Island, Nebraska, and then to Norfolk to feature the Oxnard brothers' operations.[20]

Sugar beets were late immigrants to Nebraska. In 1863, Henry A. Koenig, formerly of Prussia, who had served with the First Nebraska in the Civil War, settled in Hall County and began planting experimental fields with seeds imported from France and Germany. The crops proved successful, and soon more farmers began planting sugar beets. Meanwhile, the four Oxnard brothers, after studying the soil and climate requirements of raising the crop, both in Europe and the United States, began considering Grand Island, Nebraska, as the site for their factory. Citizens raised $60,000 of the needed $100,000 to commit the Oxnard Company to the Grand Island location.[21]

Numerous difficulties arose for the producers and manufacturers alike.[22] *However, the sugar beet economy persevered, thanks to the indefatigable German farmers and to the state of Nebraska, which offered a "bounty" of one cent per pound on sugar produced in Nebraska. During the next few years, beet farmers continued to suffer. The plains states endured a drought, slowing beet production; the state repealed the bounty, obliging factories to reduce the price for beets; and the election of 1892 forecast the repeal of the McKinley tariff, which lowered crop prices even more. It was not until 1896, however, that the weather, the government, and experience pulled together to produce more sugar beets than the factories could handle (E. S. Anderson 17–20). Impressively, Peattie captured all sides and issues of the sugar beet industry in her two articles.*

❧ "I've been here thirty-five years," he said, "and I've raised about every kind

Young Grand Island boys thinning sugar beets behind the cultivators, 1891. (Stuhr Museum of the Prairie Pioneer)

of crop that comes up on this part of th' country. And I think beets pay best on th' whole. Yes, I do. I didn't think so at first. And I said I didn't think so. But I've tried it. And I know."

He was a weather-hardened little man, just as sound as a nut; and as he spread out his strong, short legs, in their felt boots, before the fire in his "front room," and nodded his head briskly to give emphasis to what he was saying, he impressed one as being just the sort of man who would say what he thought regardless of consequences.

"Yes," he went on, "been here thirty years. Came from way east-Iowa. I thought it was fun. Boys like starting off, they don't know where. I didn't know where I was going. Hadn't an idea. Had a schooner and four yoke of cattle, and I just drove west. Sometimes," and he dropped his voice as if he wouldn't like anyone on the outside to hear his next remark, "sometimes I think I ought to have gone farther west. I believe California is a better place than Nebraska." He said this last as if he had made a statement that would lay him open to suspicion of high treason. "The climate," he went on, "I believe the climate is better."

Seeing that the thermometer without stood at 10 above zero, and that the wind was drifting the pulverized dust around this lonely dwelling, and that each particle of dust was somehow as cold and sharp as ice, it was easily imagined that he was right.

"But Nebraska's a great state," he continued. "I've had thirty-five years of it. Built this house thirty-five years ago and lived here ever since."

The house, by the way, was built of logs, the walls were two feet thick if they were an inch, and the whole place was cozy and warm and cheerful.

"Corn don't pay," he said, with some sadness. His wife, who did not look as if she had stood the vicissitudes of thirty winters and summers as well as he, shook her head to acquiesce in his statement. "Lately corn don't pay. It ain't necessary to tell th' reasons. One thing there's too much of it. It's a cheap crop. So you might as well set about raising a crop there's a demand for. And there is a demand for beets. At first, when Mr. Oxnard came in here, he paid $3.50 a ton for beets that ran 12 1/2 per cent of sugar to th' pound. That wa'nt enough. It got t' be generally agreed all 'round that that wa'nt enough. Now he pays $4 a ton for beets running 12 1/2 per cent. He pays $4.50 per ton for those running 15 per cent, and fifty cents more for every addition of 1 per cent sugar above that.

"A man can get as much as $7 a ton for beets. I know a man that got $7 a ton for some of his beets. I got $5 for a part of mine. But, on the whole, mine didn't run as well last year as they did the year before. We had a long dry spell that hurt them; and then I planted them in ground that had been plowed the fall before. The ground got too hard."

"Couldn't get up the weeds," broke in his wife in a tone of interest that showed she knew what she was talking about.

"No," went on the man, "I made a mistake. What I ought to have done was to have plowed in the spring. A good crop of beets is a thing you've got to take care of if you want it to turn out well.

"It doesn't take work alone. It takes brains. That's why some of the farmers have been slow about going in it. They have been used to planting hundreds of acres of stuff, and then having it take care of itself almost. Now that would be well enough if it paid. But I don't think it does. It didn't pay me. With beets it is possible to make as much as $70 an acre. Now that gives a chance to a farmer."

"But you can't hire help," said his wife. "It don't pay to hire help."

"No," acknowledged her husband, "not if you have to pay $1.50 a day, and your men will work only eight hours a day. Men don't really work at weeding beets as well as boys and you can get a boy for 75 cents a day and he will do more work and better work than a man. He ain't so long about getting up and down, and his fingers are more limber. I've got children, and they help me out. And last summer I hired two boys."

"Yes, but you have to watch boys," said his wife with conviction. This seemed to be such an obvious proposition that no one attempted to deny. It would probably be admitted on the Cannibal islands that you have to watch boys.

"The state hasn't been fair," the farmer went on after a bit. "Mr. Oxnard built his factory here when the state paid a bounty on his sugar – a bounty of 2 cents a pound. He put in his money here expecting that he was going to have that bounty for several years. But no sooner had he got down to work than the bounty was taken away. It wasn't fair.

"It wasn't according to contract, so to speak. I think myself that the bounty was not placed where it would do the most good. If beet sugar is a success in this part of the country, it will be because the farmers get over their nonsense and take to raising beets. They need encouraging. Very well, then. Where ought the bounty to go? Why, to the agriculturalist. When the legislature took up the question of the bounty on sugar what it should have done was to have passed a law making it payable to the farmer. I'm not saying this because I'm a farmer and want to get the money. I'm saying it because I want to see the beet industry succeed. And I believe that is the way to make it do so. It seems to me as if this state has just set itself out to discourage one of the best industries ever started in this state. And it doesn't look to me like good sense."

"No," interrupted his wife, as she crocheted on some white cotton edging for the pillow cases, "it ain't good sense to hit a child on the head the minute it's born-not if you want it to live."

I asked the farmer what he considered the most profitable crop he had raised during the last two years. His reply was unhesitating and emphatic.

"Beets," he said. "If you manage 'em right, there's more money in beets than any crop you can raise in these parts. But you have to realize the fact that the raising of beets ain't so much farming as gardening. You have to get right down and go at them. And some men are too big to do that. They think an American citizen ought to ride around over 200 or 300 acres. As soon as they get out their naturalization papers they are too proud to get down and garden. They need encouraging. That's right. They ought to have the bounty." And he rubbed his legs where the felt boot tops had got to smoking from the close proximity to the fire.

Now that is the farmers' point of view faithfully recorded. It shows, in fact, the whole situation; even the undeniable reluctance of the Nebraska farmer to take up with this new crop.

M. Emile Brysselbout, the chemist and superintendent of the Grand Island sugar factory, said concerning this:

"It does not seem at all peculiar to anyone who is acquainted with the introduction of the beet industry in France and Germany. Farmers are conservative the world over, and they are particularly slow to take up with the raising of a new crop. But it seems to me as if, by this time, the farmers ought to be convinced that there is more money for them in beets than in any other crop. Of course, every farmer cannot raise sugar beets. It is scientific farming. It appeals to the very best class of farmers. In fact, it gives an opportunity to farmers capable of doing scientific work, to show what they are made of."

There is a general feeling, not only among the people at the factory, but generally in and around Grand Island, that the prejudice against sugar beet raising is gradually giving way. It has been due in no small extent to the constant opposition and misrepresentation of some of the local papers.

I pride myself on being able to see the point of view of almost everybody, but I am obliged to confess that after much honest endeavor the only argument against sugar beet raising that I can find is that it involves manual labor and the exercise of the brains. I do not know which of these things it was that aroused the local papers to opposition.

But that this conservatism is disappearing is evidenced by the rapidly increasing number of contracts that are being made with the company this year. Mr. Ferrar, the superintendent of the agricultural department of the factory, said:

"Some of those who have been most opposed to us are coming in this year and making large contracts. I think such reluctance as has existed has been largely due to the natural timidity of the farmers in taking up with a crop with which they were unacquainted. You see, the beet has to be treated with great tenderness. The sweetness has to be worked into it so to speak. First, you must be careful in the selection of your ground. It must be deep soil, with a soft sub-soil that will allow the water to pass through. Unworked land will not do, as the weeds are apt to be too rank; sandy soil will not do, because it will flow; freshly-manured ground makes too course a beet; wet ground will not do at all, because, while the beets need a good deal of moisture, they must not be allowed to stand in the water.

"Deep plowing is most essential. You see, the ground must be soft and yielding. It's not safe to plant before the first week in April, and the last planting ought not to be later than the middle of May. If a man has a large field, there is some advantage in sowing different blocks of it at different times because that allows the farmer more time to attend to them. When the plant has formed good leaves, which under the right conditions is about five or six weeks, then is the time for thinning out. And much depends upon having this well done. Up to this time the beet has not been touched, except in the way of light but frequent cultivation. In the thinning out, the bunches are so separated that each beet left remaining in the ground stands quite by itself. If two beets are left together they twist around one another and neither amounts to anything. They should be left from six to eight inches apart in the row, the rows being, you understand, far enough apart to allow a horse to pass between them.

"In order to do it so as not to loosen the beet that is left in the ground, and at the same time to get up the entire root of the one you are uprooting requires a peculiar twist of the wrist. But when it is once learned one does it instinctively. After this thinning has been thoroughly done the crop is practically assured. The sun, the rain and the wind does the rest. It takes about five months for the beet to mature. Then it is brought here and put in our sheds."

Mr. Ferrar spoke again of the great satisfaction he felt at the manner in which the farmers who raised beets last year were renewing their crops and the manner in which those who had not hitherto essayed beet-raising were now making arrangements to do so this coming summer.[23]

Concerning the factory at Grand Island, it stands a mile or more from town, and wears at present, it is unnecessary to say, a look very different from that which it has during the "campaign." The long, neat building of red brick, the channels for floating the beets, the kiln, with its half melted bricks, the great pallid "dumps" of refuse from the limestone, the still smouldering heaps of the burned slack, are there. But the place is silent. The pump house, through which there passes 2,100,000 gallons of water daily drawn from eighty great wells, is bolted now; and the pipes and sluices are empty. Within the machinery, much of it is apart, and a few men spend their time cleaning it and getting it ready for the coming year. Up in the laboratory there is always something to do.

One of the reasons that the expense of running the factory is greater than usual is, that while, thus far the factory has run only 100 days in a year, the company has to hire its chemists and managers by the year. If the supply of beets was such that the factory could run fifty days longer, it stands to reason that there would be much better results all around.

When once the fires are started and the mill is in operation, there is no let up either day or night. The men work in shifts. Last year about 250 were employed continuously in the factory. And during the growing season nearly 400 persons were employed in the beet fields, for the Oxnard company raised 1,000 acres of beets themselves last year.

Last year the Grand Island factory turned out 21,101 bags of sugar, which is equal to 2,110,100 pounds of the same delicious material. And still they have stored in forty great iron tanks 1,773,200 gallons of syrup, which will be made into sugar next year. Some idea of the labor and material that all this represents can be guessed at from the fact that sixty tons of coal and thirty tons of limestone are used daily during the campaign. The limestone, after its trial by fire in two kilns, is used as a clarifier.

In one way the Oxnard company is a typical western company. That is to say, every one concerned with it is young. Mr. Oxnard himself is young and a bachelor, and he came into his present business by heredity, so to speak. His father was a sugar refiner somewhere in New York state. Mr. E. C. Howe, the manager of the Grand Island factory, is not yet 30; the superintendent, M. Emile Brysselbout, is barely that age, though he has already had much experience in the business in various parts of France. Mr. H. S. Ferrar, the superintendent of the agricultural department, is a gentleman with an Irish name, an American tongue, and what may be termed the "country eye" – that is, the eye made for close observation of things rural. All of these men have an amount of enthusiasm for their work, and a belief in it, that would be surprising anywhere else than in America. But here some sort of microbe appears to diffuse itself through the mental system, causing an intense and indefatigable earnestness. It is this which has conquered the "Great American Desert," and made it one of the rich places of the world.

Grand Island itself seems to have not a little of this same intensity. Everyone is working with a single eye to success. And this unity of motive, and diversity of action has produced the usual results.

Where a few years ago there stood an untamed prairie, is now a characteristic western town. Its enthusiastic citizens say that it has 10,000 inhabitants. Its more accurate and conscientious citizens claim 8,000. It has many really fine and beautiful homes, though, as usual in a western town, the criticism might be made that they are too far apart. An effort to direct future building so as to make the town more compact would not be amiss.

The more recent architecture shows the influence of the aesthetic movement which began in the east fifteen years ago, and has steadily kept its way toward the west.

The public schools are, of course, a prominent feature, as they may well be, supporting as they do about 1,300 pupils and forty teachers. The attendance has spilled over out of the school buildings into church rooms and stores, just as is the case at Omaha; and the board of education is said to have a large task on its hands in providing school facilities to keep up with the rapidly growing population.

The town is conspicuous for nothing more than the number of church spires which arise from it. There cannot be less than ten churches in the town, and some of them are beautiful. There are five banks, four papers, two of them being daily papers and two weekly; a fine new Baptist college, which is a co-educational institution and which has started with a fine number of pupils; and a business college which is said to be very thorough in its methods, and to be much thought of.

The city, like Omaha, has not yet provided itself with a hospital, but hires beds in the excellent institutions conducted by the Sisters of Mercy, and stands conspicuously out on the plains, with its gold cross announcing its message of pity and protection.

At present ice cutting appears to be one of the most flourishing industries of the place. The ice is cut from private ponds or lakes, Mr. Koehler having some carp and trout ponds, clear as crystal, and Mr. Wasmer two small lakes.

I must say that the ice looked like glass, not a weed marring its beautiful transparency. The output of ice from these sources and the river is said to be large.

In the way of manufactories Grand Island has not much to offer. There is a cigar factory – not in the union – which employs fifty women and turns out a cigar that has found its way over a very wide territory. And there is a successful, but not very large broom factory. It does seem as if the place was a fine one in which to locate factories that turn out articles of common use.

The Union Pacific repair shops are, of course, a great factor in the industrial life of the place. One hundred and seventy-five men are constantly employed here. The buildings are of unhewn stone, very picturesque in their way. And more are to be put up next year. Something of the amount of work that goes on there can be guessed at from the fact that $18,000 worth of material is always kept in the store house.

Something of the character of the workingmen employed there may be gathered from the statement of Mr. B. C. Howard, the foreman of the works, who says he does not know what it is to have to watch a man to keep him from whisky. The place seems indeed to be pervaded by an atmosphere of cordiality. Many of the men have been with the company for years. Mr. Howard himself has been in the employment of the Union Pacific for twenty-five years, and at these shops ever since they were erected.

He is a man very much respected in the community, as is borne evidence to by the fact that one of the finest school houses is named after him. Which is an honest tribute to an honest man – an old-fashioned artisan, in love with his work, thoroughly informed concerning it; and as much elated at the sight of a fine locomotive as an artist with a master-piece on canvas.

Grand Island is divided in its attitude toward the Union Pacific, between dissatisfaction at its discrimination in rates, and appreciation of its expenditure of $60,000 in improvements during the last year.

The Burlington & Missouri also runs into the town and plays its part in commercial and civic affairs.

The mayor of the town is Henry D. Boyden, a republican, and the leading druggist of the place. His home is one of the most attractive among the substantial homes of Grand Island.

One of the places of attraction is the Soldiers' home, which stands northwest of the town, making with its turreted main structure, its hospitals and homes for soldiers and their wives, an impressive and prosperous little colony.

Not far from this is the suburb of West Lawn, which has some of the best houses in Grand Island, and which is reached by a semi-occasional horse car. The place has been made very attractive, but it does seem to the casual observer as if a suburb is a sort of superfluity in a place like Grand Island.

A new wholesale grocery house has just been started in Grand Island, which will make a total of two in operation and will serve to keep the greater part of the wholesale trade of the surrounding country within near limits.

Grand Island rejoices in the possession of electric lights and excellent gas, water and sewerage systems which have made it famous among the towns of the state. It likewise has several good hotels, and is altogether one of the most progressive of Nebraska's cities.

The importance played by the Oxnard Beet Sugar company will be readily perceived. The benefit of the ready money it represents will be appreciated. And it is generally admitted alike by farmers and business men that the policy of the company is one of great liberality. From the outset this has been the case. The farmers who have had dealings with the company admit that in every way they have been treated with something more than justice.

Nebraska stands today as a state of good average achievements and of extraordinary capabilities and promise. The industry of sugar beet raising is conspicuous among her opportunities. It seems impossible that it should be allowed to fall into desuetude.

"The State Fish Hatchery: Where the Rivers of Nebraska Get Their Stock of Gamey Fish"

3 July 1892

In July 1892 Peattie traveled by train to South Bend, southwest of Omaha, to research the fish hatchery, allowing her to escape the summer heat and bustle of Omaha as well as the dull reporting of facts. Her editorial became a refreshing blend of poetry, personality, and reality.

The Nebraska legislature created the Board of Fish Commissioners in 1879, the forerunner of today's Game and Parks Commission, to oversee the stocking of the state's rapidly depleting rivers and streams. At first the board contracted

Succession of fish-holding pools at the Gretna fish hatchery, ca. 1900. (Nebraska State Historical Society Photograph Collections)

for fish from the private Santee Hatchery between Gretna and Louisville on the Platte River. The location was a perfect hatchery site, with its natural springs filling the canyon ponds with fresh water. Three years later the board purchased the hatchery and fifty-four acres of land for four thousand dollars.[24]

The area, now considered the state's oldest recreation grounds, became popular with the public, which enjoyed hiking, picnicking, and viewing the abundant wildlife on the scenic Platte River. At the turn of the century, with the leisure class no longer limited to the "idle rich," men, women, and children from all walks of life were searching for places to spend their newly acquired free time. Meeting the need for public lands where nature could be rediscovered, the soul rejuvenated, and families reconnected was becoming a national priority (Doell and Twardzik 7).

❧ Omaha in summer is a sort of occidental Arabia.

A sky of burning sapphire hangs above it, aching for a cloud. The wind is laden with sand, and even while it promises to cool the flesh of man, it wounds it. The air is a white glare – the stone pavements, hot as glass, flash reflected light into the eyes almost with the intensity of mirrors. The clay cuttings blanch in the sun until they, too, are white, and from their dry surfaces the incessant wind drifts the powdered dirt.

But the last few days I have not particularly minded all this because I have been looking with the mind's eye – always so much stronger than the eye of the body – at a scene very different.

I have been seeing a "draw" cutting down between quiet hills where the white oak and the elm grows, and down the draw, from pool to pool, trickles a stream of water. Neither rain nor drought affects this, for it bubbles tirelessly from the black rock at the head of the little ravine. In winter the pools never freeze, although just beyond, the Platte may be solid. In summer, cool and alluring, the water flows among the cresses and the mosses, and holds up its mirror to the butterflies and the birds.

The Platte is a good quarter of a mile wide at this point, and its yellow waters lie off at the west, and go swirling around the shallow sand-bars at the rate of five miles an hour. Over this river the sun sets in scarlet and gold, and you can sit on the hillside and watch these "ineffectual fires" burn themselves out, till they leave only that purple dimness which is the ashes of a sunset, and all the while the water in the draw will sing and slug, and the whip-poor-will call to you from the solemn groves, and the firefly prick the darkness with his point of vivid flame.

Now, with such a scene in my mind, what does it matter to me that the blast of heat which rises from the pavement seems to draw my eyeballs out?

Not a bit! It does not matter in the least.

I can hear katydids while I am looking at paving blocks. I can smell wild roses and white cloverfields, while the bell of the electric car jangles in my ear, and above the noise of the street rises the silence of the fields.

This spot, which so haunts me, can be reached in a very short time. It is in Sarpy County, and it is at the state fish hatchery. If you journey thither by the Rock Island road, South Bend is the station at which to get off. On the Burlington & Missouri the station is Ashland.

The river lies between the slovenly little town of South Bend and the hatchery, and the person who drives there over Mr. Clark's bridge pays the enormous toll of 25 cents a person, or if he is a stranger he pays at the rate of $1 for horse and driver. Even a foot passenger pays 25 cents for the privilege of walking over the uneven boards. It would really seem as if nothing but the grimmest necessity would take the farmers of the neighborhood over the bridge at such rates.

However, once over, you drive along an uneven road beside the river, with the bluffs rising on your right, and the sumac and elderberry giving promise of autumnal glory, and so presently find yourself going beneath an arched gateway, which announces to you that the state fish-hatchery has been reached.

It is fourteen years since the state fish commission became a fact. The rivers of Nebraska were not any too well stocked with fish, and the depletion was greater than the increase. For three years the state fish commission contented itself with being a name. It did, however, make a discovery. It found fifty-one acres of wooded land upon the Platte for sale at a very reasonable sum. Upon this land were a number of remarkable springs which bubbled out a rock at the head of a ravine, and ran, with a fall of twenty feet in its pleasant descent, down to the rushy bottom lands of the river. An old raiser of fish had settled upon this place as a desirable locality for a private hatchery, but he sold out cheap to the state – for a sum, if my memory serves me, of not more than $1,400.

Ten years ago Martin O'Brien was put in charge, and he has placed in the rivers of this state, no less than 100,000,000 fish.

Mr. O'Brien had begun his professional association with piscatorial matters when he assumed superintendency of one of the public hatcheries of Canada. Afterward he had charge of the Michigan state hatchery, and later of one of the Wisconsin state hatcheries. When he came to Sarpy County to take charge of the Nebraska state fishery, he found a wilderness – but a wilderness which contained great possibilities.

Now, a succession of pools greets the eye, a fine, large hatchery house, a pleasant residence on the cap of a wooded hill, and all the other evidences of thrift, system and industry.

Carp, rainbow and speckled trout, bass, croppies and pike are raised. Certain fish are, of course, adapted for certain streams, and Mr. O'Brien is acquainted with the nature of every stream and lake in the state and knows what kind of fish it should be stocked with. When applications are made for fish he therefore sometimes refuses to send the sort of fish applied for, and sends instead those fish which he has learned, by experience, are calculated to live in those particular waters. A bass, for example, has no objection whatever to a mesh of weeds and a miry river bed. But a trout is an aristocrat, and insists upon pellucid waters.

The hatching house preserves 95 per cent of the fish eggs, brings them to safe maturity, whereas, of the eggs which are laid in a river not more than 1 per cent ever reach maturity. In the river the eggs of one fish frequently furnish the food of another, but in the hatching house the spawn is permitted to ripen in troughs, over which the clear spring water flows, and the little fishes – when the little fishes have become evolved out of the mysterious egg – are fed and cared for in a manner which insures health and finny happiness to their young days.

Then, in the autumn and spring, the young fish are carried from their native troughs, so to speak, put in a car adapted for the purpose, and conveyed to some distant stream or lake, where they grow up into respectable black bass, or wall-eyed pike, or mountain trout, and disport themselves with as much independence as if they had never had their early hours watched over by a mere man, without fins or gills, or any of the other accessories – from the point of view of a fish – necessary to the pursuit of happiness.

There is a good deal of work connected with the place – enough to keep three men busy – but the life there must be a pleasant one. Mr. O'Brien has lived in the neat house on the hill for ten years now, and has seen his labor bring its excellent results, and looks forward to greater accomplishments.

He knows all there is to know about the raising of fish, but I hesitate to repeat anything he told me on the subject lest I should misinterpret him. He is a hospitable, unpretentious, straightforward sort of a man – still young and remarkably vigorous. He has a very interesting family, which, it can easily be understood, offers him compensations for his isolated life. Five thoroughbred dogs, four of which are good bird dogs, are the companions of his hunting expeditions. Then there are the other animals that are to be found in country homes, and one which is not usually found in such places. This is a large gallinaceous bird, with beautiful plumage, capable of eating seventy-five fish in fifteen minutes. This gluttonous but graceful creature was winged by Mr. O'Brien's rifle shot beside a Nebraska river, but it certainly belongs in warmer climes.

It would never have self-control enough to sit beside trout pools in the twilight, as Mr. O'Brien does, to watch the fish leap from their crystal element, a foot in the air after the incautious fly. If that bird were privileged to look on such a scene as that, he would go mad in excess of rapture. But he is safely caged – fortunately for the fish.

At Fountainbleau and Versailles it is an amusement to fish for carp, which bear in their noses rings, which have engraved upon them a date more than 100 years past. In France the carp appears to live forever. Whether it does so in Nebraska or not has not yet been determined.

There is a circular tank on the lawn in front of Mr. O'Brien's house, where hundreds of variegated Japanese gold-fish glide and flash and dart; and down in the hatching house are many curious water animals – newts and frogs, turtles and eels, catfish and water spiders. Some of the catfish in the ponds weigh seventy pounds; but, then, that isn't of half so much importance as that some of the black bass weight five pounds.

It would be easy to chat for another half hour about the hatchery, but probably not very much would be said.

Mr. May and Mr. Kenneny of Omaha and Mr. Burlingham of Seward are the present fish commissioners.

"A Word with the Women" – The Hunting Mania

29 April 1895

In the newly developing West, hunting became a sport available to everyone. Not only was hunting a symbol of masculine strength, but it attested to man's superiority in the natural world and the dominance of white culture in civilizing the frontier. The West had long been considered a Garden of Eden, and the plentitude of wild game supported this myth. New settlers on the plains believed that they had a right to hunt to sustain their families; market hunters, encouraged by the high demand from urban centers for meat, pelts, and plumage, considered hunting a business; and wealthy business and professional men as well as the European elite were accustomed to enjoying adventure at any price. States, too, joined in the mania, often competing with their neighbors to see whose hunters could kill the greatest number of waterfowl before the flocks migrated to the next range (Trefethen 162–64).

Behind the humor of the hunting obsession, however, hid the very serious problem of declining game populations and the struggle among local, state, and national groups for control of wildlife regulations. The lack of defined hunting seasons allowed spring shooting, which prevented successful breeding and nesting. With the development of the repeating shotgun, entire flocks could be decimated. However, it was not until 1913, nearly two decades after Peattie's sketch, that the federal Migratory Bird Act passed, setting limits on hunting and banning spring hunting and night shooting.[25]

❧ "It was the most absurd thing," said my hostess, drawing her chair nearer the fire, which the chill spring evening had made necessary, "at least it would have been absurd if it had not resulted in a tragedy. They loved each other, and were married, though they were poor, and young. Moreover, their prospects were such, that, while it seemed more than likely that they would outgrow their youth, there was no reasonable possibility that they would ever outgrow their poverty. They came out here to Nebraska, and went onto a small claim. She was a lady born, and used to fine living in every sort of way. But she loved him – and so nothing else mattered. He set out a garden, and worked it industriously. She did the housework. They had a good crop of saleable

Canada geese shot on the North Platte River between Sutherland and Paxton, 1908. (NEBRASKAland Magazine/Nebraska Game and Parks Commission)

things, and lived very economically. It was really surprising, all things considered, that they should be so sensible. All went well until one day, as the two were standing at the back of their little cottage watching the sunset, a wild cry disturbed them, and looking overhead, they saw a gander leading his flock up from the south. She was interested in the sight, of course. But he was more than interested. He had lived in a city all his life, and so had never known or suspected it, but the truth is, that he was a modern Nimrod.[26] No sooner did he see these great birds than he was seized with a mania to kill them. I do not use the word mania lightly. All that evening he spent his time cleaning his gun, and looking up the proper ammunition. The next morning instead of attending to his usual duties, he sat watching the sky. He had not long to watch before the cry of a gander came down to him. He was up and away on the moment, and it was two days before his wife saw him again.

"From that time on he followed the wild geese. The garden was neglected, the animals were fed by his wife, it was she who drove to town for such provisions as they could afford to buy, it was she who finally took in sewing and ground gunpowder to supply their living. She was ashamed to write home and confess the truth to her friends. And, moreover, what she had to write was too ridiculous. How could she say that her husband was away on a wild goose chase? How could anyone possibly imagine that a flock of wild geese would destroy a woman's happiness?

"The next season it was the same. He had become a victim of the hunting mania. He no longer took any interest in any occupation except that of hunting. He was no longer married to her, but to his shotgun. At home he was restless, impatient, and querulous. He complained if she did not provide the things to satisfy his ever growing appetite. He ceased, in a sense, to be a civilized or domesticated man. His habits, to a degree, became those of the savage. There were, in fact, no pleasures for him, save those of the chase. So it was not surprising that when the first flock of geese appeared on the third season that she should pack her trunk, leave a batch of bread, a ham, and a note for him, and tell him that she had left him to his gun, and gone back to the haunts of civilized men.

"No, I don't know what happened next. I only know that they never met again. He was a Nimrod, and should have been married to a wild woman of the jungle who could skin his beasts for him when he brought them in. I don't say that I particularly blame him. He ought to have been born under different conditions. He should have lived in the age of the cave dwellers. His most inexcusable mistake lay in selecting this century for his incarnation."

CONCLUSION

A Writing Life

1896–1935

"Make room for the uncommon woman as well as the common ones."

In October 1896, Peattie left the *Omaha World-Herald*, and she and her children, her mother-in-law, and her sister Bertha joined Robert in Chicago, where he was serving in several successive capacities for the *New York Tribune*. He functioned as exchange editor and editorial writer, managed the Voice of the People and the Friend of the People features, and oversaw what Robert termed "general housework" ("Bob Peattie Retires"). The family moved into an apartment on Eerie Street across from the McCormick mansion. To help support the family, Elia wrote anything that would bring in income: histories, short stories, even a romantic opera.

Two years later, in 1898, the Peatties' fourth child, Donald Culross, was born to the sound of a clattering typewriter; writing was the family business, and the machine hardly rested. Elia did all of her writing from home, stealing minutes here and there between her household chores and caring for the four children, often writing late into the night. *The Shape of Fear*, a collection of Peattie's ghost stories, came out that year. Because short stories sold well and the family needed the income, she sent out fiction to every periodical imaginable, from serials in the *Youth's Companion* to short stories for *Atlantic Monthly*, *Harper's*, and *Cosmopolitan*. Sometimes she would dictate to her husband at night so that she could finish her sewing or mending (Bremer, "Introduction" xiii). The next year, 1899, Peattie boasted of writing one hundred stories and sketches in one hundred days. These were printed successively on the front page of the *Chicago Tribune* to pay for the renovation of the family home ("Mrs. Elia Peattie Retires").

Peattie gained further recognition as literary critic for the *Chicago Tribune*, a post she held from 1901 to 1917. During this time, her husband estimated, she typically read and reviewed ten books a week, writing more than five thousand columns.[1] Robert carried these books home to her like a "pack-horse." However, she realized how much else she owed to her husband: "It was he who guarded me against mistakes, who edited my writing, who stayed late one night a week to see the book page to press; he who conducted the

Elia Peattie at home in Chicago. From *The Pilgrim*, 1903.

correspondence regarding the books, who got specialists to review scientific and highly philosophic volumes, and saw that the most interesting and stimulating books came to me and who let me have all the credit."

Peattie also initiated a daily column she titled "Poems You Ought to Know," featuring verses by various poets. Later she collected them into two editions, *Poems You Ought to Know* (1902) and *To Comfort You: Poems of Comfort Selected by Elia W. Peattie* (1903). After the publication of her novel *The Edge of Things* (1903), about sheep ranchers in southern California, her creative writing almost came to a standstill. She complained in her memoir that reviewing books "destroyed my originality and ate up my vitality . . . but the bills were paid, the children educated." In the Chicago of Peattie's day, the newspaper was the only institution where a writer could earn a living by writing (Duncan 153).

To refill Elia's creative well, the Peatties attended Eagle Nest camp in 1907, a writer's retreat in Oregon, Illinois, frequented by prominent scholars, politicians, and writers such as Hobart and Rose Chatfield-Taylor, Ernest Thompson Seton, Fanny Bloomfield-Zeisler, Lorado Taft, Anna Morgan, and Harry Pratt Judson, president of the University of Chicago. Although the companionship was stimulating and the evenings with their tableaux, musicals, and dramatic productions were entertaining, Peattie's manuscript rejections,

Elia Peattie with her son Donald, ca. 1904. (Cleary family scrapbooks)

which were delivered to her at camp, disappointed her. She commented, "I wrote and wrote and wrote and my manuscripts came back like hungry cats." Once thought of as too radical for a woman writer, she now had become too conservative. "My writing was regarded as nauseatingly virtuous, amiable and reminiscent."

To help fill the family coffers, Peattie increased the number of literary presentations and readings of her own works she gave in drawing rooms or clubs around the Midwest – Michigan, Indiana, Nebraska, Iowa, Ohio, and Minnesota. In some instances her audience only came to socialize. "Their elaborate hats hid their faces; their costumes were charming," she complained, "but seldom were they able to pay me more than $10 or $15." She usually received from sixteen to one hundred dollars for each of these presentations, but she donated her readings at Hull House, the Northwestern Settlement House, and other community centers as charity.

Reinvigorating Her Writing

The next spring, April 1908, several of Peattie's friends, patrons of the arts, collected money to send her on a tour of Europe. They had decided she needed a change, and as they were of the class used to conferring scholarships and supporting artists, they generously funded her travel. Peattie arrived in Naples and traveled across Italy, where she witnessed volcanic eruptions from Aetna. She visited Paris, and while in London she lunched with the daughter-in-law of Charles Dickens. Although the sights and experiences invigorated her, she was sorry that Robert, who always gave his family opportunities for travel, was unable to visit "the rich, dark old world."

During her writing career, Peattie occasionally collaborated with her children. Once, when Roderick needed money for graduate work, the two collaborated on a girl's book – Peattie wrote the narrative, and her son outlined the plot and copied the finished draft for a ten-installment serial for the *Youth's Companion*. They split in half the twelve-hundred-dollar payment for "Sarah Brewster's Relatives," which ran from July through September 1913, and Roderick used his share to help pay his expenses at Harvard.

Peattie began channeling her creativity into other venues. She and Robert became celebrated for their Sunday-morning brunches at the Peattie home, which they called the "old house home." An invitation to one of these gatherings marked an author's acceptance into the Chicago literary establishment (Bremer and Falcone 679). Eugene Field, Lorado Taft, Hamlin Garland, Willa Cather, Edgar Lee Masters, Zona Gale, and Ellen Glascow were frequent guests. A member of several exclusive clubs – the Fortnightly, the Little Room, Colonial Dames of America, the Chicago Woman's Club, and the Cordon Club for professional women (which Peattie helped found and presided over when women were not admitted into the prestigious Cliff-Dwellers Club organized by Hamlin Garland) – she influenced the taste of a wide public. Peattie's membership in the Little Room was especially significant, for although people in all of the arts were welcome, most of Chicago's literary women belonged to it (Bremer, "Willa Cather's Lost Sisters" 221). Comprising representatives of Chicago's "genteel protest," men and women alike, it was the strongest cultural force in Chicago and served to bridge the community of artists and local society, especially the wealthy patrons of the arts (Duffey 55, 57).

Peattie's list of admirers is long and includes Hamlin Garland, Wallace Rice, Henry Blake Fuller, Willa Cather, and John Stahl.[2] Her literary contributions were so respected that Northwestern University presented Peattie, who only completed sixth grade, with an honorary Phi Beta Kappa key, validating her lifelong dedication to learning and intellectual self-fulfillment.

In 1914, when Peattie was fifty-two, she published *The Precipice*, a suffrage novel about a turn-of-the-century social work pioneer who tried to balance her career with the traditional roles and values of her day. Partly based on the life of Katherine Ostrander, a social worker who lived with the Peatties, the heroine, Kate Barrington, interacts with a spectrum of women, both professionals and residents of the settlement house, as they try to find their place in society. Promoting a wider urban family, the novel echoes the themes of Peattie's earlier columns concerned with municipal housekeeping and the social interdependence of classes. The book received laudatory reviews from the *New York Times Book Review*,[3] and the *Omaha Daily News* praised the novel of its former resident, saying, "*The Precipice* pictures the modern, purposeful woman who has retained her charm and womanliness throughout the changing civic and economic standing" and ranked Peattie as "one of the foremost critics of the day, her work being marked by a depth of analysis and knowledge of human nature which gets well under the written word."[4]

After the publication of *The Precipice*, Peattie continued writing for young people. Earlier she had collected fifteen short stories in *Ickery Ann and Other Boys and Girls* (1899). Her works now included *Edda and the Oak* (1911); a series of three novels based on Azalea, a girl from the Blue Ridge Mountains; and many stories first serialized in the *Youth's Companion* and later published as books. Her stories departed from the gloomy didacticism of the past and offered children adventure and fantasy, vital factors, most progressive parents

Elia Peattie in New York City at age fifty-six, 1918.
(Chicago Historical Society)

believed, in developing children's imaginations. Meanwhile, she remained as literary editor for the *Chicago Tribune*, churning out daily book reviews.

New York City and Retirement

In 1915, tragedy struck the Peatties. Their daughter, Barbara, a poet and the mother of three boys, died at age thirty of a streptococcus infection. The family was devastated, and in 1917 they moved to New York City to be closer to their three motherless grandsons. While there, both Elia and Robert worked part-time for the *New York Tribune*, he as a correspondent and she as a literary reviewer. Although World War I was on with its shortages and high prices, the Peatties made good money and enjoyed life in New York City. Their little apartment was near Fifth Avenue, and they attended the theater often. However, both suffered serious illnesses – Robert was hospitalized after a bout with pleurisy, and Elia underwent gallbladder surgery. Because of their health problems, coupled with their unremitting grief over the loss of Barbara and their concern about their oldest son, Rod, who was serving in the war, they decided to take advantage of the *Chicago Tribune*'s pension system. Robert retired on 1 January 1921, after twenty years' service on the editorial staff. At his surprise retirement party, his colleagues joked that when the newspaper transferred "Old Bob" to New York they had to hire two or three men to take over his roles ("Bob Peattie Retires"). Elia officially retired from the *Tribune* in the fall of 1922.

Accompanied by Elia's mother, the Peatties moved to "Dunwandrin," their retirement home on Broadway Street in the mountain town of Tryon, North Carolina. However, in six months, the New York news branch of the *Tribune* begged Robert for a seven-hundred-word daily editorial, and he agreed to provide it until a new writer could be found. That December he retired again, because, he joked, he was afraid he might have to give back his engraved watch.

In Tryon the Peatties became involved in local dramatic groups, and Elia turned her attention to writing plays and poetry. Earlier she had written short dramas for the *Omaha World-Herald*, published *The Love of a Caliban: A Romantic Opera in One Act* in 1898, and composed *Time and Manners: A Pageant* for the Chicago Woman's Club, so this was not a new genre for the multifaceted writer. The new twist was that she could now write for herself, her family, and her friends – not for economic survival. She published *The Wanderweed, and Seven Other Little Theater Plays* in 1923 and *Massimilliano: The Court Jester* in 1925.

In 1928 the Peatties' son Donald and his wife moved to southern France for

Robert Burns Peattie nearing retirement, ca. 1920. (Cleary family scrapbooks)

their health, and Robert and Elia visited them early the next year. For Robert it was "a pleasure which I had given up hoping would come to me," and it provided them with rich experiences and happy memories (Robert Burns Peattie 78). While there, both began their memoirs: Robert's was matter-of-factly called *The Story of Robert Burns Peattie*, and Elia's, characteristically poetic, was titled *Star Wagon*.

Two years later, Robert died at age seventy-three after many years spent battling illness. His son Donald wrote: "No one who heard him whistling bits from *The Pirates of Penzance* and *The Bohemian Girl* had any idea that he clung to life with a grip terrifyingly light. That, indeed, he did not open his hands and let it go, only for the sake of his children." Robert had spent his life quietly sacrificing for his family. "For almost fifty years he worked for newspapers," explained Donald, "turning out editorials of a rare charm and delicate fancy while the stuttering telegraph battered on his eardrums. His life long, he never signed a word he wrote." Elia had kept Robert alive until he was seventy-three, her son wrote, "by her own passionate vitality. It burned like two tiny candles in her sea-colored eyes. Or perhaps she did it by laughter; their marriage rang with it." On her husband's tombstone Peattie had engraved the following words: "Journalist, Wit, and Gentleman Unafraid" (Donald Peattie 54–56).

After her husband's death, Peattie published only two more works: a collection of poems, *Songs from a Southern Garden* (1930), and another play, *The Great Delusion: A Drama in One Act* (1932). Most of her writing now was to her two sons and her eight grandchildren, and she remained an active member of the Tryon Garden Club and Tryon's Woman's Club and helped with the Lanier Library ("Her Life Is a Busy One").

On 12 July 1935, while visiting her grandchildren in Wallingford, Vermont, Peattie died from heart disease at age seventy-three. Knowing her aversion to traditional funerals, her family planned her last rites to imitate her life.[5] They placed a simple casket in the streaming sunlight in front of a window through which her beloved mountains could be viewed. Upon the casket, the family placed flowers that Peattie had picked from the garden the day before. They played her favorite records and read excepts from Omar Khayyam and a poem of Thomas Hardy's. Then the casket was carried out to a carriage so that she could be buried in Tryon City Cemetery beside her husband, side by side in death as they had been in life (Roderick Peattie 235–36).

"There was mirth around her like a scent; there were always people around her, or stories of people," Donald wrote about his mother. "Interesting conversation was as much a necessity to her as bread; she fed multitudes with her magical loaves. She could create not only feast but festival from nothing, pinning on a rose for her children, pouring the sparkling wine of her daily adventure. She could fight like an Indian; she could make anyone her friend." On her stone the family etched the words, "She ate of life as if 'twere fruit" (Donald Peattie 55).

Elia Peattie shortly before her death, ca. 1930s. (Courtesy of Peattie family)

Peattie's Legacy

Peattie was a consummate professional in her writing career. Because of her understanding of the complexities and demands of the literary marketplace, she was able to publish writings that ranged from romanticized and pastoral children's stories, realistic local color tales, and naturalistic depictions of lower-class society's struggles to logically argued political and social essays. Peattie's editorials crossed borders, and she borrowed ideas, techniques, and subjects from literature and journalism, shaping her style to fit readers' tastes. Moving comfortably within several genres, her editorials conveyed information with authority, yet she transcended the simply factual with style and grace, interpreting ideas, presenting her opinions, and employing metaphor, images, irony, and wit. Although her editorials can be viewed as social and cultural documents meant to inform, educate, and entertain the public, it is the literary aspect of her writing that makes them stand up over time.

Lacking a descriptor for her own literary approach to journalism, Peattie labeled her writings "editorials." Writers of the late nineteenth century were equally at odds in naming their genre, referring to their own work as "stories," "sketches," "studies," "scenes," or "travels." In a 1907 literary review, an anonymous writer in the *Bookman* termed writing stories as opposed to news "literary journalism," a term still debated heatedly today.[6] Peattie's "editorials" featured narrative techniques such as dialogue, characterization, scene, concrete detail, contrast, imagery, and irony and emphasized a reporter's interpretation as well as impressions and emotions of a person, place, or event. Peattie embraced the freedom and leisurely style that this form allowed, declaring in her 1890 novel, *The Judge*, that "a newspaper man should see the world with the eye of a novelist, and not an amanuensis" (119). Arguing for literary license, Peattie's protagonist states: "I hope you are not one of those dull persons who require that a story be true. . . . You might as well refuse to buy a beautiful picture because you do not know where it is painted" (62).

Peattie's editorials and columns are also significant for their human interest and the dramatization of the lives of ordinary people, a type of writing that dominated late-nineteenth-century newspapers and periodicals. By portraying specific individuals, journalists, much like novelists and short-story writers, were able to interpret universal human experiences and report on the "texture of our human life."[7] This new emphasis on human interest in journalism paralleled William Dean Howells's promotion of realism in his column as editor for *Harper's*, in which he encouraged a distinctly American literature based on fidelity to individual human traits and commonplace experiences.

Although Peattie needed to publish for her family's economic survival, writing was more than a vocation for her – it was her ambition. Nothing could have kept her from a career as a writer, but a companionate husband who supported her aspirations and who also was able to help her with revision and editing was crucial to her professional success (Willard 562). Her family also figured significantly in her life. Devoted to her husband and children, she never resented the time spent with and for them and considered her domestic responsibilities a joyful and rewarding aspect of her life. As a result, from the very beginning of her marriage, her life became an endeavor to balance both of her passions: her family and her career. "It was a simple life for all of its diverse activities," Peattie summarized in her memoir. "I was never ashamed of the fact that I tried to improve my condition, socially as well as any other way. I couldn't see what America was for, if not for expansion, and I certainly didn't mean to let my family stop where I left off."

In her 1890 editorial "Barriers against Women," Peattie railed against the placing of limitations on women, especially by other women. "Do not call her a crank because she has ideas. Do not cut her because she knows enough to make a living," she wrote. "Genius isn't necessarily disreputable. Make way for the uncommon woman as well as the common ones." Peattie's life and writings are a challenge to each individual to demolish restricting barriers for all people and, like her, to have the courage to be uncommon.

NOTES

PREFACE

1. Historians vary on the dates of these periods, but the Gilded Age would extend approximately from 1876 to 1898, while the Progressive Era is often dated from 1890 to 1917.

2. In a 1 August 1892 letter to Hamlin Garland she commented about a clipping she sent him: "It's much harmed by the proof reader, but the poor man has six children and a run of boils on the back of his neck and I am not scolding him as much as usual" (Doheny Memorial Library, University of Southern California–Los Angeles).

INTRODUCTION

1. In 1936 Ishbel Ross of the *New York Tribune* wrote that women reporters were never "thoroughly welcome in the city room and they are not quite welcome there now. . . . [W]hat every city editor thinks in his black but honest heart is: 'Girls, we like you well enough but we don't altogether trust you' " (13).

2. Biographical material and quotations from Peattie, unless otherwise noted, have been taken from her unpublished memoir, "Star Wagon."

3. Eugene Field (1850–95), a nineteenth-century American humorist and children's poet, is best known for his poems "Little Boy Blue," "Wynken, Blynken, and Nod," and "Jest 'Fore Christmas." His volumes of poetry include *A Little Book of Western Verse* (1889) and *Love Songs of Childhood* (1894).

4. Set in 1835, "A Tale of Early Chicago" recounted in three chapters a romantic intrigue set during a Christmas snowstorm.

5. Peattie's claims cannot by verified; however, Ishbel Ross in *Ladies of the Press* credits Minnie Roswell Langstadter as being the earliest female reporter in Chicago. Langstadter began working for the *Chicago Record* in 1878 at age fifteen. Ross also mentions Peattie as working "side by side with the men reporters in the late eighties." The only other women Ross mentions are Nora Marx, Mary Abbott, Margaret Sullivan, and Mrs. Amber Holden, who appear to have been reporters in the late 1890s and at the turn of the century (551). Peattie mentions Sullivan in a 17 September 1896 "Word with the Women" column: "She was a true friend, and once, long ago, when she was a great woman, a little girl took a manuscript to her to read. She might have refused, or consenting, been rude, or careless, or amused. She was courteous, patient and explanatory. It brought the first gleam of hope for literary excellence to that timid child, who now writes with regret the words that Margaret Sullivan is dying."

6. A personal and financial battle raged between Rosewater and Hitchcock for years, and it wasn't until 1898, when the *World-Herald* acquired the wire services of Hearst's *New York Journal* as well as the *New York Herald* during the Spanish-

American War, that Hitchcock's paper edged into the number one spot in circulation (Limprecht 12–13).

7. An offshoot of the Grand Tour of Europe enjoyed by the elite, travel in the United States became an affordable option to the rising middle class in America, 90 percent of whom were receiving annual paid vacations and now had more money for leisure. Indeed, travel by rail had become cheaper, faster, more convenient, and even comfortable, and tourism began emerging as big business (Webb).

8. In her 1 August 1892 letter to Hamlin Garland, Peattie commented on the work, saying that F. J. Schulte and Company of Chicago "wouldn't have my 'American Peasant.' I don't know just why. Perhaps he and Mr. Tibbles couldn't agree as to terms. I don't know where the manuscript is now. I wish for poor old Tibbles' sake that some one would bring it out. Personally, I am rather indifferent." An agreement must have been made, because it came out that fall.

9. The subjects of these literary papers are unknown, but one was probably on Sidney Lanier (1842–81), a favorite topic for Peattie. Lanier was a poet, critic, and musician from Georgia. He wrote an antiwar novel called *Tiger-Lilies* (1867), but his most famous works were published posthumously: *Poems of Sidney Lanier* (1884), *The English Novel and the Principle of Its Development* (1883), *Music and Poetry* (1898), *Retrospects and Prospects* (1899), and *Shakespeare and His Forerunners* (1902).

10. Agnes Hooper Gottlieb, in *Women Journalists and the Municipal Housekeeping Movement, 1868–1914* (Lewiston NY: Edwin Mellen Press, 2001), discusses the joint efforts of women journalists and clubwomen in furthering their reforms in social housekeeping.

11. Goldberg states that "organizations offered emotional support to their members in a new, unstable, and often threatening environment" (42).

12. Other women who edited small Nebraska newspapers include Mrs. E. M. Correll of the *Hebron Journal*; Harriet S. MacMurphy, who assisted her husband on the *Blair Times* and the *Beatrice Times*; Edith M. Pray of the *Geneva Gazette*; Lena Pear of the *Central City Democrat*; and Annie Vio Gates of the *Blair Tribune* (Peattie, "Newspaper Women of Nebraska" 23–37).

13. Such women journalists, although often negatively labeled "sob sisters" for their sentimental accounts, continually struggled against cultural and political barriers that persisted in the newspaper world. Although Peattie was not as well known as Bly and Tarbell, she was groundbreaking in that, unlike Bly, who quit journalism when she married, and Tarbell, who never married, she was able to successfully combine her marriage, her career, and her causes.

14. Between 1880 and 1900 the population of the United States increased by 50 percent, the national wealth more than doubled, and people began crowding into cities, especially the new urban centers of the Midwest and the West (Marzolf 7).

1. EARLY OMAHA

1. "A Word with the Women," *Omaha World-Herald* 4 Mar. 1896: 8.

2. After St. Paul's Church burned in 1895, the incident Peattie described, the Poles worshiped again at St. Joseph until they could build another church, this time the Immaculate Conception on Twenty-fourth and Bancroft. As the Omaha Polish community grew, other churches were erected: St. Francis of Assisi in 1899 and St. Stanislaus in 1919 (Otis 248).

3. For news stories about the cholera outbreak see the *Omaha World-Herald* articles from 12 September 1892: 1, 2; 15 September 1892: 2.

4. The fall of 1892, in its end-of-year report, the Creche noted that its total cash receipts for 1892 were $2,080.20; its expenditures of $1,748.63 left the benevolent society with a net balance in their treasury of $331.57 (Peattie, "Work of the Day Nursery"). Certainly Peattie's repeated pleas for support in her editorials and columns helped the Creche succeed.

5. Baker coined the term "municipal housekeeping" in "The Domestication of Politics." Perry argues that this is a simplification of women's role in the Gilded Age and Progressive Era, for women were tireless in moral and political reform as well (35). Elshtain supports this idea, offering Jane Addams as an example of a municipal housekeeper who understood the importance of politics (163). Peattie, too, went well beyond civic housekeeping in her social activism.

6. The movement, begun in England in 1855, entered the United States in 1858. Throughout its history, the caring women of the YWCA took up the task of responding to the needs of other women, especially those emigrating from supportive, rural areas who had come to cities for work.

7. In addition to chairing several committees and serving as temporary chair of the legislature (the only black man to serve in that capacity), Ricketts introduced a bill to legalize interracial marriages, which passed the legislature only to be vetoed by the governor, and to strengthen Nebraska's 1885 civil rights laws by prohibiting the denial of public services on account of race (Polk 41; Calloway and Smith 53–54).

8. The brothers bought out the Armour interest in 1890, making Michael Cudahy one of several local multimillionaires ("Michael Cudahy").

9. Here the article included a lengthy description of a steer's trip to market (13).

10. Here the article included a listing of the largest receipts of stock in one day, in one week, in one month, and in one year (13).

11. Here the article included Cudahy's statistics for 1991, including total distributive sales, payroll, number of employees, number of acres of buildings, floor area, and cold storage as well as various numbers of animals killed and processed (13).

2. FACT AND FICTION

1. Although it was unusual for a young journalist (Peattie was twenty-eight at this time) to be allowed a byline, it was even more rare for a woman to be allowed into an "old boys" establishment on a major western newspaper (Halper 148).

2. Alarmed by the sensationalism and superficiality of this new "penny press," the more expensive, traditional newspapers, which sold for five cents a copy and main-

tained strong political alliances, attacked the commercialism of the more aggressive newspapers, calling their reporting "yellow journalism," a color they associated with decadence and the decay of urban society. The term "yellow journalism" originated from a popular comic strip in the *New York World* that featured a street-smart slum urchin who wore a yellow nightshirt – a new experiment with color ink – and he became known as the "Yellow Kid." Two other New York editors, Ervin Wardman of the *New York Press* and C. A. Dana of the *New York Sun*, used the term to describe what they believed were the "extremes of decadence" of Hearst's *New York Journal* and Pulitzer's *World* (Marzolf 23).

3. Having a byline was one of the most sought-after rewards on a newspaper, and many journalists become local or even national celebrities. According to Maria Braden, "Columnists enjoy fame, independence, and a special relationship with readers. . . . Unfettered by the need to be objective or fair, columnists can be scathing in their criticism, unabashed in their praise, funny or poignant, arrogant or intensely personal" (ix).

4. The Burnt District included the area from Douglas Street six blocks north to Cass and from the Missouri River west to Sixteenth Street.

5. In 1890 Omaha reported forty-three houses of "questionable character." From time to time, citizen committees would be formed, letters would be written, and wholesale arrests would be carried out, but soon life would resume its nightly routine as the city treasury and the city officials' pockets overflowed. The male customers or the landlords who charged exorbitant rates were never arrested (Bristow 202–20). Josie Washburn, an Omaha prostitute at the turn of the century, provided the best description of this life in her book *The Underworld Sewer*. She explains that the cribs were little shacks crammed in the alleys of Capitol Avenue between Ninth and Tenth Streets. "Each crib consists of two small rooms, about six feet high; a door and a window forms the whole front" (qtd. in Bristow 202). The two-block-long alley was paved, with iron gates at either end, and one of the alleys had a fancy roof painted with red designs and hung with electric lights. "At night these cribs are brilliantly lighted, the shades are never drawn, and through the glass front or large windows therein," Washburn continues, "that which transpires on the inside may be observed from the street. High school boys and boys of tender age are allowed to visit the district and here take their first step into vice" (qtd. in Bristow 203).

6. It was no secret that while the legislature was in session the profits from prostitution were enormous. One news story reported: "There is one house in this city the proprietress of which has grown rich from the earnings during the legislative sessions. It was in this house that the scheme to abduct State Senator Taylor was concocted in 1891, and in 1892 the railroad lobby chartered this establishment, paying for it and its inmates a stated sum per day." Kitty Paxton, madam of two of the principal houses in Lincoln, and Nellie Roberts, at Seventh and L Streets, told

reporters that they and their girls would be leaving the business and reforming. However, most of the others, such as Cora Hoffman at 736 L Street, and Georgie Wade, 800 N Street, scoffed at the order, predicting that the storm would blow over and that the situation would be worse than before. May Brown was unavailable for comment, but she had hung a "Restaurant" sign in front of her building, and it was common knowledge that her girls would be waitresses in the "so-called restaurant" ("Fast Women Depart").

7. Washburn admired these young mothers. "It is said that 'Greater love hath no man than this, that a man lay down his life for his friends,'" she wrote. "But it is not the hardest act to DIE for those we love, BUT TO LIVE IN DISGRACE, SELL BODY AND SOUL and to devote a life to a condition where men expect us to take part in all kinds of degradation for their entertainment, IN ORDER TO SUPPORT OUR CHILDREN, is a far GREATER SACRIFICE THAN DEATH" (Bristow 205).

8. One example of negative stereotyping appeared on 14 July 1895 in the *World-Herald*. It was written by Viola Pratt, who had lived for a year among the Poncas (the headline calls them "Sioux" as if tribal differences didn't exist) with her father (first name unknown, but not Richard Henry), who was appointed Indian trader and whom the Indians called "Long Beard." Although the body of her firsthand report contained interesting facts about the tribe, Pratt's introductory comments upheld their status of "other," one she vehemently maintained throughout. "There is a current saying to the effect that 'a good Indian is a dead Indian,'" Pratt asserted, "and I believe, all things considered, that the originator of that remark knew whereof he spake when he made that observation." When six thousand Native Americans turned out to greet Pratt's family upon their arrival, she exclaimed, "The first look inspired me with a dread of them that our year's residence among them never quite dispelled." Another woman, Elsie Robertson, romanticized the Omahas and Winnebagos as "noble savages." Her 28 August 1892 *World-Herald* article described Omaha Indian Agent R. H. Ashley as "a well-read gentleman and an excellent conversationalist" who had "the interests of his Indian charges thoroughly at heart." Mrs. Smith, the matron, announced that the children were "Not much trouble, not bright enough to get into mischief." The two women reporters then traveled to the Blackbird Mission, superintended by Mr. Morris, declaring the region right out of "Hiawatha" and "Evangeline." Mingling with the Indians who gave them gifts of beadwork and descriptive Indian names, the women declared them to be "poetic children of the forest." The article closed with the description of a "blood-red" sunset and an allusion to the myth of the vanishing American Indian: "The day's death is beautiful as its birth. It is gone as all things beautiful must go."

9. In 1890 the *World-Herald* sent Tibbles and his second wife, Susette LaFlesche (Bright Eyes) of the Omaha tribe, to the Pine Ridge area of northwestern Nebraska and southwestern South Dakota to cover the Messiah craze and the troubles developing there. While other correspondents were sensationalizing war rumors, Tibbles

and his wife saw the reality of the situation – that the Sioux were going about their everyday activities while Seventh Cavalry troops began surrounding the Sioux camp in order to begin collecting the weapons of the Native Americans (Tibbles).

10. When Schlatter reached Hot Springs, Arkansas, barefoot, bareheaded, and claiming to be guided by "the Father," local authorities arrested him for lunacy, tried him in a kangaroo court, sentenced him to fifty lashes on his bare back, and confined him to jail for more than five months because he had no money to pay the fine. After purportedly healing many of his fellow prisoners, he escaped and headed west, where he was again jailed for three days, this time as a vagrant, in Throckmorton, Texas. The sheriff released him and told him to leave town, so he headed to El Paso, and then through the Yuma desert to San Diego. From there he traveled by boat to San Francisco, then walked barefoot down the central valley of California to the Mojave Desert, following the railroad lines and subsisting on flour and water (Mayfield 2). For a detailed history of Schlatter and his legend, see Norman Cleaveland's *The Healer: The Story of Francis Schlatter.*

11. A delegation from Omaha was even sent to induce Schlatter to come to Omaha: J. A. Connor, a grain merchant; C. K. Spearman, a Gretna banker, and W. S. Raker, editor of the *Gretna Reporter* (Magill 115–16).

12. Among those reportedly cured were J. L. Brandeis, senior owner of the Boston Store, who had suffered from stomach trouble for many years, and Louis Metz, son of the Omaha brewer, who had been in ill health many years.

13. Neal climbed the fourteen-foot gallows and addressed the crowd: "I want to ask pardon of the people of this city, and especially of the Jones family, because I am sorry for what I have done." A black hood was placed over his head, the noose secured around his neck, and Sheriff Boyd pulled the trap door lever at 12:06 p.m. ("Douglas County Hangings"; "Justice at Last" 8).

14. Coe/Smith, a waiter, was married, the father of one child, and supporting his mother and brother. Lizzie's grandmother had briefly talked to a garbage collector and could give no accurate description of the rapist; all she could remember was that he was black. Lizzie could not be induced to look at the assailant in order to identify him. As the community awaited Neal's hanging, stories spread that Smith had been let off on an earlier rape charge because of a jurisdiction technicality and that Lizzie was supposedly his fifth victim. One hour after Neal's hanging, an emotional mob of reportedly ten thousand people gathered, fueled by what Peattie was convinced was bloodlust from the execution. Sheriff Boyd was abducted by masked men and held prisoner. Neither Captain Cormack nor Governor Boyd could dissuade the mob. The next morning more than six thousand people went to Heafey and Heafey Undertakers to view Smith's body, which had been put on display with the rope still around his neck (Bristow 227–67; "Followed Ed Neal").

15. In a 15 January editorial, "Let the Law Be Amended: Give Juries the Option of Pronouncing the Death Penalty or Life Imprisonment," she took a more analytic

approach in her appeal, citing facts, giving supporting examples from other states as well as Nebraska, and systematically refuting opponents' arguments.

3. COMMUNITY CONCERNS

1. Large-scale industrial development after the Civil War had transformed America from an agricultural state into the world's leading industrial power. Controlled by a few giant corporations, headed by business barons such as J. P. Morgan, Cornelius Vanderbilt, John D. Rockefeller, Andrew Carnegie, and Jay Gould, industry wrought many economic changes upon Americans. By 1896, one-eighth of the nation's people owned seven-eighths of its wealth (Hart 180).

2. The wealthier Omaha residents included people such as Grenville Dodge, surveyor and railroad promoter; Edward Creighton, telegraph executive; Charles Turner, civil engineer; Andrew J. Poppleton, real estate agent; Christian Hartman, founder of the Omaha Lead Works and city treasurer; William Paxton, Gustavus F. Swift, and Michael and Edward Cudahy, meatpackers; Edward Rosewater, editor of the *Omaha Bee*; and Anna Wilson, queen of the underworld. Unfortunately, the Gilded Age was also the beginning of the polarization between rich and poor. In 1890, eleven million of America's twelve million families earned less than twelve hundred dollars a year, with half of them below the poverty level ("Gilded Age"). Between the Civil War and 1900, the urban population increased at twice the rate of the population as a whole (Goldfield et al. 594). Between 1880 and 1890, Nebraska's population increased from 452,402 to 1,058,910 (Larsen and Cottrell 71). In 1880 Omaha's population was 30,518, and by 1885 it had reached nearly 60,000 (Limprecht 4; Chudacoff 14).

3. Peattie, "Word with the Women," 4 June 1895.

4. In response to Peattie's stinging 1893 editorial "Stand Up, Ye Social Lions," Mr. Chase of the *Excelsior*, "the editor of the journal of society in this town," accused Peattie of jealousy because she could not "get in Omaha society." Peattie scoffed: "He might as well say that my criticisms upon train robbers were inspired by my inability to join the ranks of the train robbing gentry. I dare say I would not be invited to join any sort of society. I certainly never claimed to have had any such opportunity. I have a few friends, it is true, some of whom I know, and some of whom I do not, but they are my friends all the same, and give comfort to me, as I hope I do to them. Some of these friends of mine live in houses with frescoing on the walls, and some of them in houses where the walls are covered with patches of old newspapers. I move in human society, I believe. But not by invitation. No one asked me to. Further than that I can lay no claim to social distinction. But I have become so accustomed to this state of things, it having existed from my birth, that I really cannot plead guilty to pique. And it must really be admitted that in this controversy society has had the best of me, because I had to arraign it generally, and as a body, whereas it could put me straight up in a public pillory and hurl arrows at me. But they were not poisoned arrows, and I am none the worse, thank

you, and have been quite exhilarated at the commotion. And I feel almost proud of myself when I think of the things I might have said – and haven't" ("Word with the Women," 21 January 1894).

5. Taylor goes more specifically into mourning jewelry, especially the jet industry (224–47). A widow could wear no lace or jewelry for this period, and her social life had to be restricted. She could not leave the house for the first month, except to attend church, and during the first year she could accept no invitations. After one year and one day, a widow could begin to reenter society and receive callers, but no men. The second stage normally lasted eighteen months and was itself divided into three stages. During the first half of second mourning, the widow could wear a shorter "weeping veil" of black net, trim her collar and cuffs with white, and add jewels such as pearls, amethysts, black cut-glass, or jet. Jewelry made from the hair of the deceased or curls enshrined in lockets or brooches were especially appropriate (Morley 66). If a woman wore the wrong kind of jewelry, however, it could be socially disastrous. The following three months were called "ordinary mourning," and this period allowed black fabrics of silks or velvets with lace or ribbon trims and jewelry. During the last stage of mourning, called "half-mourning," women could wear gray, purple, mauve, lavender, lilac, and white, and prints in these shades were allowed. After completing her two and a half years of mourning, the widow could return to her normal life and even receive gentleman callers.

6. For Sullivan's 1889 fight with Jake Kilrain, originally scheduled for New Orleans, approximately three thousand spectators had to board special trains that transported them to a secret location. Most major fights occurred in semi-secrecy, often on riverboats or near state lines, so that the participants as well as the spectators could escape across borders to avoid arrest. When the bout concluded after seventy-five rounds, Sullivan was declared the winner and became a national celebrity. This was the last bare-knuckle championship prize fight in America (Isenberg 269–75).

7. When Sullivan recovered his senses, he went to the ropes and spoke to the audience: "All I have to say is that I came into the ring once too often – and if I had to get licked I'm glad I was licked by an American." His humble speech brought more response from the crowd than Corbett's winning blow ("King Corbett" 1).

8. More interested in his theatrical career and his ghostwritten autobiography than in conditioning for the championship title, Sullivan weighed 246 pounds only two months before the fight and trained sporadically. Years of drinking and carousing also took their toll, and after the Corbett bout his alcoholism contributed to his financial failure, his public brawls and arrests, and his broken friendships. Although he detested his image as a drunkard, he could not stop drinking, and, like so many celebrities today, could not live up to his gloried past (Isenberg 327–28).

9. Davis's story has been omitted.

10. Revivals were emotionally cathartic, and participants did not simply believe but intensely experienced an altered sense of self. See Donald Scott's *Evangelism as*

a Social Movement and *Evangelicalism, Revivalism, and the Second Great Awakening* for a more thorough discussion.

11. Since most new cities did not have an auditorium large enough to seat the crowds that routinely attended his revivals, Mills's method was to divide cities into sections, scattering his meetings through the different neighborhoods and holding a culminating session in the largest hall he could find. This system, which he termed the Mills District Combination Plan, left little to chance. After a period of singing by a trained choir of 100 to 150 people, Mills would preach his evangelical message, concentrating on the need for personal repentance and conversion, attacking the sins of pride, vanity, dissatisfaction, and impatience (McLoughlin 335–37). After each rousing sermon, Mills would distribute "decision cards" to the audience, who were to sign their name, address, and preferred church under the statement, "I have an honest desire henceforth to lead a Christian life," thus securing them as converts while the proverbial iron was still scorching. Afterward, the cards were counted and the success of the revival was assessed by dividing the number of converts into the cost of the campaign (Schaff 16; Weisberger 237–40). Although putting a bottom line to spiritual matters seems overtly materialistic, during the economic depression of the 1890s churches needed to spend their money wisely.

12. Believing that it was the duty of the churches to do more than rehabilitate the drunkard and prohibit card-playing, theatergoing, and dancing, Mills preached that it was "the business of the Church . . . to see that there is better care of the poor . . . to be concerned about the physical welfare of all cities and citizens, better pavement, cheaper heat and light and transportation and communication, pure water and more of it." Unfortunately, his progressive social vision did not play well with conservative evangelists, so in 1899 he retired from the revival circuit and became pastor of the First Unitarian Church in Oakland, California (McLoughlin 339–44).

13. In 1893 Peattie wrote an editorial titled "Salvation Lassies at Home," which explained the continuing success of the organization, described its school, and honored its members for their spiritual heroism in hedonistic Omaha. "Without doubt, here in Omaha today," she began, "in the midst of the greed, that disguises itself as shrewdness, in the midst of materialism that masks as industry, in the midst of the selfishness that governs almost all of us, the Salvation Army remains an honest protest against our display, our selfism, and our pride of purchasable things" (11 December 1893).

4. A WORD WITH THE WOMEN

1. Welter employs the phrase "the cult of true womanhood," while Cott prefers "the cult of domesticity." The phrase "Angel in the House," often used to describe the True Woman, originated in Coventry Patmore's 1854 poem about his wife titled "The Angel in the House."

2. Sarah Grand coined the term "New Woman" in her essay "The New Aspect of the Woman Question," published in *North American Review* in 1894. Ouida

popularized it in her response "The New Woman" published in *North American Review* that same year (Ledger 8).

3. Also known as the American Girl, the New Woman demanded to enter a career outside of her home, to remain unmarried by choice, and to vote, smoke, and ride a bicycle in bloomers (Fowler xvii–xviii). The New Woman had multiple and contradictory identities, for she was known as "a feminist activist, a social reformer, a popular novelist, a suffragette playwright, [and] a woman poet" (Ammons 7) as well as a part of the "new socialism, the new imperialism, the new fiction and the new journalism" (Ledger 1). See also Lerner, Thomas, Cunningham, Cogan, Honey, Woloch, and Schneider and Schneider for complementary definitions of the New Woman.

4. Journalism encouraged this subversion of women's roles, for only in newsprint and in the theater could they "fashion themselves so persuasively as men" (Roberts 153.)

5. In a 16 November 1890 discussion of Tolstoy's novel *The Romance of Marriage* (in an early "What Women Are Doing" column), Peattie elaborated on her views of marriage. When Tolstoy's characters Marie and Serguei Mikhailovitch wed, they enjoyed a marriage filled with joy, tenderness, and beauty. However, after a time Serguei changed, becoming arrogant and severe with his young wife. Marie, too, felt the need of something more in life, but neither understood the other's fears and longings. Then one day,they discovered a new relationship centered around the children – different from the old passion but happy and satisfying.

6. As in the earlier part of the century, women's private sphere served as a source of strength and identity, providing women with a positive role in society and a supportive sisterhood (Cott 197).

7. Elliott West agrees: "Children were often described in romantic and idealized terms and were contrasted favorably with adults corrupted by a sinful world" (148). In 1911, after Peattie moved back to Chicago, she wrote *Edda and the Oak*, which is about a lonely girl who lives with her mother and father on the top floor of a six-story building in a crowded city. One summer, Edda's parents send her to the country to visit her grandmother. There, Edda meets elves, fairies, and the dryad of the oak tree; converses (literally) with all of nature; and, for one glorious night, becomes a fairy herself. The story closes with Edda's parents rejecting urban materialism and moving back to the country to farm the grandmother's sixty-five acres, a place "where daddies were not too tired, and where mammas who liked yards could have them." *Edda and the Oak* exemplifies Peattie's pastoral ideal, a united, extended family living in harmony with nature, and with the physical, emotional, and imaginative development of the child at its center.

8. Lomax comments that at the end of the nineteenth century, medical texts on infant care considered children's needs as precise, measurable, and applicable to all, with little consideration for individual difference. She cites L. Emmett Holt's

1894 *The Care and Feeding of Children* as typical of such scientific guides. Lomax explains: "Everything possible was regulated, including the time and numbers of feeding; the quantity of food given; the temperature of the nursery; the precise time of bathing, and the order in which its face, body, and limbs were washed; and the amount of sleep it required" (14). A patriarchy of doctors and scholars, rather than networks of mothers, took over the guidance of women, whose private sphere suddenly became public. Young girls learned about child care in Little Mothers' Leagues in their schools and brought the latest advice home to their parents (Weiss 284–85). In 1914 the newly established Children's Bureau published Mrs. Max West's *Infant Care*, which continued to support these guidelines: "The rule that parents should not play with the baby may seem hard, but it is without doubt a safe one. A young, delicate, or nervous baby especially needs rest and quiet" (59).

9. In *The Spirit of Youth and the City Streets* (1909), Jane Addams would echo Peattie's warnings, explaining that youth demands excitement: "May we not assume that this love of excitement, this desire for adventure, is basic and will be evinced by each generation of city boys as a challenge to their elders." Particularly concerned about the children of lower-class workers and immigrants, Addams continued, "These are the children who hear a thousand calls to vice where they listen to the merest whisperings of virtue" (67–68).

10. In 1868, James Gibbons, who wrote *Faith of Our Fathers*, became the first Vicar Apostolic of the North Carolina mission territory. Later he served as archbishop of Baltimore, and in 1886 Pope Leo XIII named him the second American cardinal. Peattie erroneously placed him in Philadelphia ("Cardinal James Gibbons").

11. Although Peattie did not like the designation "New Woman," she soon aligned herself with the movement, defining the term and herself in her 21 March 1895 "Word with the Women" column: "I think the best definition would be, 'the woman who denies the definite limitation of feminine life as set down for her by tradition, and strives for the best development of which she may be capable.'" All women, whether professionals or homemakers, according to Peattie, could exalt in being categorized a New Woman. The following December, she wrote "In Defense of Her Own Sex": "As 'Yankee' was a term to contempt, yet came to be born with honest pride by those to whom it was applied, so 'the new woman,' which was meant for a slur, has come to be a shibboleth, and the women who work in science, in art, in the professions, in the trades, in the home, the church and the school have come to accept with dignity that appellation and to fraternize under it."

12. On 26 March 1893 the *Omaha World-Herald*, presumably under Peattie's direction, collected essays written by prominent Omahans, such as Anna L. P. Duryea, Jennie E. Keysor, Harriet C. Towne, Grace B. Sudborough, M. Garard Andrews, and Dr. Metha Helpritz Jonas, that expressed the intellectual, cultural, and educational advantages of such a club for women ("Uses of a Woman's Club").

13. George W. Lininger, an Omaha pioneer who made his fortune in the im-

plement business, built an addition onto his home for his private art collection. Many of these works, including William-Adolphe Bouguereau's *Return of Spring*, are currently exhibited at Josyln Art Museum in Omaha.

14. The rooms, "Furnished with Refined Taste through the Exertions of the House and Home Committee," were carpeted in blue and olive with draperies of brocade and olive lace. The committee secured a buffet "to be filled with cups, saucers, and teaspoons donated by members," covered the tables with embroidered linen, and decorated the platform with palms ("Enjoys a House Warming" 8).

15. Stromsburg, approximately one hundred miles east of Omaha, was established by Lewis Headstrom, a Swedish real estate agent. For a history of Stromsburg, see Rystrom.

16. According to White, "Virtually all nineteenth-century white Americans were racially prejudiced – that is, they thought that nonwhites were inferior to whites." He explains that racists considered nonwhites permanently inferior, destined to servitude or extinction. Assimilationists also believed in the inferiority of nonwhites but thought they could "redeem themselves by imitating white Americans" (321).

17. One month after Peattie wrote "No Distinction as to Color," Lena Wilson of the *Progress*, an Omaha newspaper published by the African American community, accused her of being "on the fence." Peattie responded: "I am surprised that one of Miss Wilson's race should do me that injustice. I do not wish to see the clubs injured, divided or destroyed by any question – they could certainly be of little use to any one in such events. I recommend patience, and Miss Wilson will learn in time that patience is best. I am not on the fence in regard to the color question." After alluding to her abolitionist parents, she added, "But because of all this, I am not therefore indifferent to the ideas and prejudices of other women in the club, who may not agree with me, and who have as much right to hold their views." Peattie concluded, "I stand, always have stood, and always will stand for the breaking down of all race distinctions (Peattie, "Word with the Women," 18 June 1895). Ironically, after Peattie moved to Chicago and became a leader in the Chicago Woman's Club, she publicly approved of maintaining the "color line" for membership at the annual meeting of the Illinois Federation of Women's Clubs in 1900. Peattie compared the situation to men's clubs that did not admit women, calling the separation a natural partition recognized by everyone, completely reversing her 1893 stance of sexual unity. Destroying this boundary would benefit no one, she argued, maintaining her belief that it would be too divisive for the local clubs as well as the state and national federations ("Talks Plainly").

5. PEOPLE AND PLACES

1. Peattie uses this phrase in her review of Cather's "On the Divide," included in this chapter.

2. According to Gene M. Gressley in *West by East: The American West in the Gilded Age*, Peattie's boosterism was typical: "Middle class in perspective, optimisti-

cally hopeful for material progress, the Westerner was imbued with a strong booster psychology, a trait which many an Eastern entrepreneur and Western promoter capitalized on again and again, often to the disastrous embarrassment of all concerned" (6).

3. Such narratives, explains Glenda Riley in *Women and Nature*, make the West appealing to women, presenting it as a place where they "could survive, endure, and even triumph on their own." Riley focuses on women nature writers, especially nineteenth-century ecological romanticists, who played a role as early conservationists. However, Peattie should probably not be counted as a conservationist. In "The State Fish Hatchery," for example, she lauds the progressive superintendent for having "found a wilderness which contained great possibilities" and for domesticating the springs, building a large hatchery house, and scientifically improving upon nature.

4. When Cleary's short stories and sketches began appearing regularly in the *Chicago Tribune* and popular periodicals across the United States, Peattie continued to support her friend, reprinting her poems and even one of her short stories, "A Racehorse to the Plow," in her 3 May 1895 column. Perhaps encouraged by Peattie's support, in 1897 Cleary published a novel about Nebraska, *Like a Gallant Lady*, with Way and Williams, who had published Peattie's collection of western stories, *A Mountain Woman*, the year before. When both women moved back to Chicago in the late 1890s their friendship deepened, especially after Cleary's release from the Illinois Northern Hospital for the Insane at Elgin. Cleary had undergone treatment for morphine addiction, caused by her country doctor's treatment of her bout with childbirth fever in 1894, and stayed with the Peatties for several months after her release from Elgin. For a full biography and bibliography as well as selected writings of this Nebraska/Illinois author, see *Kate M. Cleary: A Literary Life with Selected Works* by Susanne K. George [Bloomfield].

5. The poems have been omitted.

6. "Lost in a Cornfield," *St. Nicholas* Sept. 1891: 812–17.

7. While attending a dinner given by University of Nebraska chancellor James Canfield and his wife, artist Flavia Camp Canfield, who was active in the Nebraska State Federation of Women's Clubs, Peattie met the Canfield's daughter, Dorothy, already a writer with promise, and Cather, then an undergraduate.

8. Peattie, "Word with the Women," *Omaha World-Herald* 28 Nov. 1895: 8.

9. Cather also stated that she continued to follow Peattie's work, especially her literary criticism, and was hoping to spend an afternoon with both women when she passed through Chicago during the first part of July on her annual visit to Nebraska (the Peatties and Clearys had returned to Chicago by this time). Cleary died that July, but the Peatties remained in touch with Cather. Cather was their guest during their short stay in New York City, and they dined with her in her house on Bank Street.

10. In her memoir, Peattie reflected on the famous Nebraska author: "Miss Cather has become the foremost woman fictionalist of our country. She had then as now, simple and downright manners. She has written about the things that interested her and done it without any manner of affectation. Owing to the vitality of her intellect and the depths of her human sympathy and to her instinctive literary taste, which has kept her from all forms of sentimentality, she has achieved an excellence which wins the respect even of the professional scoffers" ("Star Wagon").

11. The 1890–91 *Nebraska State Gazetteer–Dodge County Business List* registers A. M. Edwards, who lived a quarter mile east of Fremont on Military Road, as breeder of Poland China hogs. In 1897, one year after Peattie's visit, Edwards moved to Milford, where she was superintendent of the Omaha Child Saving Institute, and from 1902 to 1907 she served as assistant superintendent of the institute ("Mrs. Amanda Edwards" 3).

12. The Poland China hog was a cross of several breeds developed in southwestern Ohio in the 1830s and 1840s. Although its color was originally white, the solid black pig with white feet, legs, and tail, became more popular, especially in the show ring. The Poland China, the leading breed at the turn of the century in America, was well suited for grazing, making it common in the Midwest and Great Plains. A middle-weight, early maturing breed, it was a compact animal with much meat-producing capacity whose chief characteristics included its straight nose, droopy ears, broad, curved back, superior hams, and short legs (Plumb 485–96).

13. How Peattie became acquainted with Sister Mary Francis de Sales, a nun and teacher at the Academy of the Visitation of the Blessed Virgin at Hastings, Nebraska, is unknown. They might have met in 1893 at the Chicago World's Fair. Peattie mentioned that Sister de Sales's paper on women in religion was read at the exposition and that the Catholic Educational Bureau distributed there a pamphlet she had written. Whether the sister herself attended the fair is unknown, but Peattie was present and read three papers in the company of James Whitcomb Riley and Eugene Field, American poets and the Peatties' former Chicago newspaper associates. Peattie also mentioned in her memoir that her columns and editorials solicited responses from people across Nebraska, including "women in convents." Perhaps a letter from the Hastings nun prompted Peattie's visit to central Nebraska, for the trip would have occasioned a new friendship with an intellectual woman writer like herself and a chance to expand her own knowledge of religion, education, and geography. Although Peattie mentioned a letter from the nun in the article, it may not have been their first interaction or correspondence.

14. Farrell sold a plot of ten acres at Pine and Fourteenth Streets to the Sisters of Visitation for $6,500 so that the region's young women could receive instruction "free from temptation and evil influences." Work began immediately on the three-story, 184-by-80-foot academy, which in 1889 would cost nearly $100,000. Constructed of Colorado red sandstone from Farrell's quarries, the building had

two wings; the east wing housed the convent for the sisters in charge of the school, while the west wing accommodated the students and reception hall. The chapel occupied the central portion of the building. Surrounding the structure, a ten-foot-high wooden fence safeguarded the girls and women (Adams County Historical Society, "Academy of Visitation" 4).

15. Interestingly, in the six years of the academy's existence, the chapel, as Peattie noted, had never been completed, an ominous foreshadowing for a religious institution. Farrell, it seems, reaped the most profit from the enterprise. Two sisters, Margaret and Anastasia, remained in Hastings as nurses, but Mary Francis de Sales presumably returned to Chicago with the rest of her order. For the next twelve years the academy stood vacant except for the years when a family occupied it as caretakers, stabling domestic animals in the basement and ignoring the rats infesting the hallowed halls. Finally, in 1908, the town raised funds to bring the Sisters of Saint Dominic of Saint Catherine, Kentucky, to Hastings to reopen the school. Renamed the Immaculate Conception Academy, it offered a traditional curriculum for young women through twelfth grade as well as a bachelor of education degree. Immaculate Conception weathered a 1930 tornado, but another economic depression forced the school's closure in 1932. The Crosiers bought the building and grounds to house a college and monastery for men that endured through 2000. The building is currently an office park (Adams County Historical Society, "Academy of the Visitation" and "Academy Building").

16. As a homeopath, her treatment methods were based on the belief that "like cures like" and that treatments as well as prescribed drugs, usually in minute quantities, should mimic the symptoms in healthy people of the disease being treated. To many, especially women, homeopathy was a welcome relief from the bleeding, purging, large doses of drugs, and other heavy-handed medical techniques of the day ("Homeopathy").

17. Dr. Lankton died in 1907, a widow, at age fifty-five, of septic poisoning. According to the newspaper account, her illness had not been considered dangerous until the last two days of her life. She was buried in Prospect Hill cemetery ("Dr. Freda M. Lankton Dead").

18. Information about the Christian Home is taken from "The Christian Home"; "The Christian Home: Wonderful Work of Charity"; Wood, "History and Heritage"; and Children's Square U.S.A., "History of the Christian Home Association."

19. Serving the Christian Home was a generational endeavor for the Lemens. Rev. J. G. Lemen served from 1883 to 1904 as the home's first director. His son H. R. Lemen assumed the position from 1905 to 1947; his daughter Ethel Lemen Smith was director from 1947 to 1957; and great-grandson David A. Lemen served from 1957 to 1972 ("History").

20. In "Grand Island and Its Beets," the first of two companion articles, printed one week apart, Peattie focused on a general overview of the factory and sugar

beet processing as well as the farmer's side of the story. One week later, in "Norfolk and Its Sugar," she described in detail the actual process of manufacturing sugar from sugar beets. As orderly as the beets moving on the conveyor belts, Peattie continued a meticulous description of the process in the Norfolk article – adding facts, records, quotes, and human interest. Making sure to include all aspects of Norfolk in her account, she reported stories about inmates at the asylum for the insane and complimentary descriptions of the town, its inhabitants, and the natural surroundings. Norfolk, she summarized, had a "grace and charm all its own." She explained, "The transformation of a dirt-covered beet into many thousand white and glistening granules of sugar is an interesting and remarkable process – it is a thing of such fine ingenuity, such nice adjustments and such accurate tests. The sugar turned out by the Nebraska sugar beet factories ranks with the best granulated sugar made" (Peattie, "Norfolk" 5).

21. In December 1890, Henry T. Oxnard, president of the Beet Sugar Company, began erecting the four-story building, 292 feet long and 85 feet wide. The factory, requiring two hundred operators and using fifty tons of coal and about two million gallons of water daily, could refine over 350 tons of sugar beets every twenty-four hours. On 16 April 1890 a steam engine, pulling part of a shipload of machinery imported from France, puffed across the prairie while people thronged along the tracks to see the spectacle. Signs adorned the railroad cars, proclaiming "Sugar Is King, Grand Island Is Its Throne," "Grand Island Beets the World for Sugar," and "Machinery for the Million Dollar Factory Will Employ 8,000 Men." The mammoth steam engine bore a huge wooden sugar beet with green tin leaves on its front ("Beet Sugar Factory"; T. Anderson).

22. As Hall County farmers were the first to experiment with the crop, they had no examples or experiments from which to learn. First, most Nebraska farmers were unacquainted with raising beets and made many mistakes: they prepared the ground incorrectly, chose the wrong types of ground, or failed to realize the amount of hand labor necessary for cultivation. Then the Nebraska weather did not cooperate. The dry season of 1890 produced a low yield and was followed by extremely wet conditions the next year, discouraging supporters and encouraging detractors. To add to the injury, animal pests and plant diseases for which there were as yet no known remedies further decreased yields. Lewis Hoche, a French expert, was hired to supervise sugar beet production in the Grand Island area. He implemented the use of day laborers, men who would travel from the city to the fields to hoe beets. The daily wage for fourteen to fifteen hours of work was $1.50 (E. S. Anderson 18–20).

23. A table listing area farmers, their number of acres, and their averages has been omitted from the original.

24. This location is now the Schramm Park State Recreation Area (*Schramm Park* 1).

25. The strongest voice at the turn of the century came from John C. Lacey, Iowa congressman and the father of American conservation. "For more than three hundred years destruction was called 'improvement,' " he stated, "and it has only in recent years come to the attention of the people generally that the American people were like spendthrift heirs wasting their inheritance." Deeply concerned about the misuse of the environment, he helped create the Forest Reserve Program in 1891 and the Lacey Bird Act of 1891 (Beisker and Olson).

26. Noah's great-grandson, a great hunter and king.

CONCLUSION

1. Duffey states that Peattie's book reviews were considered "openly and incisively conservative" (257) with a preference for the "wholesome" (137).

2. In his autobiography, *Growing with the West*, Stahl called Peattie "one of the most discriminating, acute, and liberal literary critics of the country. Because of her generosity, helpfulness, and sympathy, no other Chicago author has had more warm friends" (368).

3. *New York Times Book Review* 22 Feb. 1914.

4. Untitled clipping, *Omaha Daily News* 15 Nov. 1915. For more about *The Precipice*, see Sidney Bremer's excellent introduction to the republished edition as well as her critical articles and book: "Willa Cather's Lost Sisters," "Lost Continuities: Alternative Visions in Chicago Novels, 1890–1915," and *Urban Intersections*. Joan Falcone's "The Bonds of Sisterhood in Chicago Women Writers: The Voice of Elia Wilkinson Peattie" also analyzes Peattie's Chicago writings.

5. See Peattie's editorial "Evil of Expensive Funerals: It Is Vanity as Often as Affection Which Dictates Ornate Burials," *Omaha World-Herald* 7 May 1893: 7.

6. Hartsock's introduction to his book *A History of American Literary Journalism* contains an excellent dialogue about this debate. The term he prefers is "narrative literary journalism" (9). Connery's articles, especially "Discovering a Literary Form," also discuss the "Defining and Naming" of this genre (8). Connery in "A Third Way to Tell the Story" further explains that "literary journalism often reconciled fact and fiction, reality and language, by being a mode of expression more imaginative than conventional journalism but less imaginative than fiction" (6). Rather than reporting the traditional who, what, when, and where, literary journalists explored the how and why (Connery, "Discovering" 5).

7. Frank Luther Mott in *The News in America* continues, "Human life everywhere came to be used as newspaper material. People on the streets, in their homes, in the shops and factories, in the theaters, at fairs and at sports events – all of them were subject matters for the writers of these stories" (58).

WORKS CITED

Adams County Historical Society. "Academy Building Reaches Century Mark." *Historical News* 22.4 (1989): 1–5.

———. "The Academy of the Visitation." *Historical News* 6.4 (1973): 1, 5–6.

Addams, Jane. *The Spirit of Youth and the City Streets.* New York: Macmillan, 1909.

Ambrose, Stephen E. *Nothing Like It in the World: The Men Who Built the Transcontinental Railroad, 1863–1869.* New York: Simon and Schuster, 2000.

Ammons, Elizabeth. *Conflicting Stories: American Women Writers at the Turn into the Twentieth Century.* New York: Oxford UP, 1991.

Anderson, Esther S. *The Sugar Beet Industry of Nebraska.* Bulletin 9, 2nd ed. Conservation Department of the Conservation and Survey Division, University of Nebraska. Lincoln: State of Nebraska, Apr. 1937.

Anderson, Tom. "Arrival of Trainload of 'Strange and Ponderous' Machinery Marked Beginning of New Agricultural Era in the Great Plains." *Prairie Pioneer Press* 24.4 (1990): 1, 3.

Baker, Paula. "The Domestication of Politics: Women and American Political Society, 1780–1920." *American Historical Review* 89 (1984): 620–47.

Beasley, Maurine H., and Sheila J. Gibbons. *Taking Their Place: A Documentary History of Women and Journalism.* Washington DC: American UP, 1993.

"The Beet Sugar Factory and Refinery at Grand Island." *Beet Sugar Enterprise* 1.1 (1890): 1.

Beisker, Greg, and Jay Olson. "John F. Lacey: Champion for Birds and Wildlife." Iowa Natural Heritage Foundation. 12 Oct. 2001 <http://www.inhf.org/lacey/laceyhome2.htm>.

Blair, Karen. *The Clubwoman as Feminist: True Womanhood Redefined, 1868–1914.* New York: Holmes and Meier, 1980.

"Bob Peattie Retires after Strenuous Career." *The Trib* Jan. 1921: 6.

Braden, Maria. *She Said What? Interviews with Women Newspaper Columnists.* Lexington: U of Kentucky P, 1993.

Brainerd, Henry Allen. *History of the Nebraska Press Association.* Book 2. Lincoln: Wood Printing, 1923.

Bremer, Sidney H. "Elia Wilkinson Peattie." *American Women Writers: A Critical Reference Guide from Colonial Times to the Present.* Ed. Lina Mainiero. New York: Frederick Ungar, 1979. 1: 360–62.

———. "Introduction." *The Precipice: A Novel.* Elia W. Peattie. Urbana: U of Illinois P, 1989. ix–xxxvi.

———. "Lost Continuities: Alternative Visions in Chicago Novels, 1890–1915." *Soundings: An Interdisciplinary Journal* 64 (1981): 29–51.

———. *Urban Intersections: Meetings of Life and Literature in United States Cities.* Chicago: U of Illinois P, 1992.

———. "Willa Cather's Lost Sisters." *Women Writers and the City: Essays in Feminist Literary Criticism.* Ed. Susan Merrill Squier. Knoxville: U of Tennessee P, 1984. 210–29.

Bremer, Sidney H., and Joan Falcone. "Peattie, Elia Amanda Wilkinson." *Women Building Chicago, 1790–1990: A Biographical Dictionary.* Ed. Rima Lunin Schultz and Adele Hast. Bloomington: Indiana UP, 2001. 678–80.

Bristow, David. *"A Dirty, Wicked Town": Tales of Nineteenth-Century Omaha.* Caldwell ID: Caxton P, 2000.

Calloway, Bertha W., and Alonzo N. Smith. *An Illustrated History of African Americans in Nebraska.* Virginia Beach VA: Donning, 1998.

"Cardinal James Gibbons." *Today in History.* Library of Congress. 5 Oct. 2002 <http://memory.loc.gov/ammem/today/jul23.html>.

"Caring for the Children at the Creche." *Omaha World-Herald* 31 Jan. 1909: 3M.

Casper, Henry W. *The Catholic Church in Nebraska: Catholic Chapters in Nebraska Immigration, 1870–1900.* Milwaukee: Bruce Publishing, 1966.

Cather, Willa. Letter to Kate Cleary. 25 Feb. 1905. Private collection of Connie Koepke.

Children's Square U.S.A. "History of the Christian Home Association—Children's Square U.S.A." Ca. 1986.

"The Christian Home." *Trans Mississippi* Feb. 1891: 36.

"The Christian Home: Wonderful Work of Charity Being Done Here." *Nonpareil* 31 Dec. 1902.

Chudacoff, Howard P. *Mobile Americans: Residential and Social Mobility in Omaha, 1880–1920.* New York: Oxford UP, 1972.

Cleaveland, Norman. *The Healer: The Story of Francis Schlatter.* Santa Fe NM: Sunstone Press, 1989.

Cogan, Frances B. *The All-American Girl: The Ideal of Real Womanhood in Mid-Nineteenth-Century America.* Athens: U of Georgia P, 1989.

Connery, Thomas B. "Discovering a Literary Form." *A Sourcebook of American Literary Journalism: Representative Writers in an Emerging Genre.* Ed. Thomas B. Connery. New York: Greenwood Press, 1992. 2–37.

———. "A Third Way to Tell the Story: American Literary Journalism at the Turn of the Century." *Literary Journalism in the Twentieth Century.* Ed. Norman Sims. New York: Oxford UP, 1990. 3–20.

Cott, Nancy F. *The Bonds of Womanhood: "Woman's Sphere" in New England, 1780–1835.* New Haven: Yale UP, 1977.

"Count John R. Creighton." *Omaha World-Herald* 3 Jan. 1895: 6.

Cunningham, Gail. *The New Woman and the Victorian Novel.* London: Macmillan, 1978.

"Denver the Mecca." *Omaha World-Herald* 10 Nov. 1895: 1.

"Detroit Free Press: The Storey Era." *Detroit Free Press.* 1997. 12 Nov. 2003 <http://www.freep.com/jobspage/club/fphiststorey.htm>.

Doell, Charles E., and Louis F. Twardzik. *Elements of Park and Recreation Administration.* Minneapolis: Burgess, 1973.

Douglas, Anne. "Victorian Mourning Customs." Pagewise. 2001. 29 July 2002 <http://ky.essortment.com/victorianmourni_rlse.htm>.

"Douglas County Hangings." *Omaha Daily Bee* 3 Aug. 1896.

"Dr. Freda M. Lankton Dead: Prominent Physician and Friend of the Needy Ends Her Work." *Omaha Bee* 6 Dec. 1907.

Duffey, Bernard. *The Chicago Renaissance in American Letters: A Critical History.* East Lansing: Michigan State UP, 1956.

Duncan, Hugh Dalziel. *The Rise of Chicago as a Literary Center from 1885 to 1920: A Sociological Essay in American Culture.* Totowa NJ: Bedminster Press, 1964.

Elshtain, Jean Bethke. *Jane Addams and the Dream of American Democracy: A Life.* New York: Basic Books, 2002.

"Enjoys a House Warming." *Omaha World-Herald* 16 Oct. 1894: 8.

Falcone, Joan. "The Bonds of Sisterhood in Chicago Women Writers: The Voice of Elia Wilkinson Peattie." Diss. Illinois State U, Normal, 1992.

"Farewell to Mrs. Peattie." *Omaha World-Herald* 13 Oct. 1896: 2.

"Fast Women Depart." *Omaha World-Herald* 1 Mar. 1894: 1.

Finnicum, Barbara. "The First Army Nurses." 3 Jan. 2001. *Indian Country Today* 26 Aug. 2002 <http://www. IndianCountry.com/?2414>.

Folks, Homer. *The Care of Destitute, Neglected, and Deliquent Children.* London: Macmillan, 1907.

"Followed Ed Neal." *Omaha Daily Bee* 10 Oct. 1891: 1.

Fowler, Marian. *In a Gilded Cage: From Heiress to Duchess.* Toronto: Random House, 1993.

"General Booth in Omaha." *Omaha World-Herald* 2 Dec. 1894: 13.

"'Gentleman' Jim Corbett." Cyber Boxing Zone. 1999. 28 June 2001 <http://cyberboxingzone.com/boxing/corbett.htm>.

George [Bloomfield], Susanne K. *Kate M. Cleary: A Literary Life with Selected Works.* Lincoln: U of Nebraska P, 1997.

"Gilded Age." The American Experience. PBS Online. 26 July 2002 <http://www.pbs.org/wgbh/amex/carnegie/ gildedage.html>.

Goldberg, Michael L. *An Army of Women: Gender and Politics in Gilded Age Kansas.* Baltimore: Johns Hopkins UP, 1997.

Goldfield, David, et al. *The American Journey: A History of the United States.* Vol. 2. Upper Saddle River NJ: Prentice Hall, 1998.

Green, Harvey. *The Light of the Home: An Intimate View of the Lives of Women in Victorian America.* New York: Pantheon Books, 1983.

Gressley, Gene M. *West by East: The American West in the Gilded Age.* Provo UT: Brigham Young UP, 1972.

Halper, Donna L. *Invisible Stars: A Social History of Women in American Broadcasting.* Armonk NY: M. E. Sharpe, 2001.

Hart, James D. *The Popular Book: A History of America's Literary Taste.* New York: Oxford UP, 1950.

Hartsock, John C. *A History of American Literary Journalism: The Emergence of a Modern Narrative Form.* Amherst: U of Massachusetts P, 2000.

Hawes, Joseph M. *Children in Urban Society: Juvenile Delinquency in Nineteenth-Century America.* New York: Oxford UP, 1971.

"Head of Christian Home Goes to His Reward." *Nonpareil* 27 Oct. 1904.

"Her Life Is a Busy One." *The Trib* Jan. 1934: 5.

"A History of Omaha." Accessomaha. 18 Mar. 2000 <http://acccessomaha.com/living/history.html>.

"Homeopathy." *Encyclopaedia Britannica Online.* 24 Sept. 2001 <http://search.eb.com/bol/topic?eu=41775&sctn=1>.

Honey, Maureen. *Breaking the Ties That Bind: Popular Stories of the New Woman, 1915–1930.* Norman: U of Oklahoma P, 1992.

Isenberg, Michael T. *John L. Sullivan and His America.* Urbana: U of Illinois P, 1988.

"Is Opposed to Hanging." *Omaha World-Herald* 3 Mar. 1895: 8.

Jensen, Richard, R. Eli Paul, and John E. Carter. *Eyewitness at Wounded Knee.* Lincoln: U of Nebraska P, 1991.

"Justice at Last." *Omaha Daily Bee* 10 Oct. 1891: 1, 8.

Kennedy, Joseph. *The Cudahys: An Irish-American Success Story.* Callan, Co. Kilkenny: Michael J. Cudahy, 1995.

"King Corbett." *Omaha World-Herald* 8 Sept. 1892: 1.

"Large Audience Welcomes Mrs. Peattie 'Back Home.'" *Omaha World-Herald* 17 Feb. 1923.

Larsen, Lawrence H., and Barbara J. Cottrell. *The Gate City: A History of Omaha.* 1982. Lincoln: U of Nebraska P, 1997.

Ledger, Sally. *The New Woman: Fiction and Feminism in the Fin de Siecle.* Manchester: Manchester UP, 1997.

Leighton, George R. *Five Cities: The Story of Their Youth and Old Age.* New York: Harper, 1939.

Lerner, Gerda. "Introduction." *An Improved Woman.* Janice C. Steinschneider. New York: Facts On File, 1993. ix–xvii.

Limprecht, Hollis J. *A Century of Service, 1885–1985: The World-Herald Story.* Omaha: Omaha World-Herald Company, 1985.

Lomax, Elizabeth M. R. *Science and Patterns of Child Care.* San Francisco: W. H. Freeman, 1978.

Lomicky, Carol S. "Frontier Feminism and the *Woman's Tribune*: The Journalism of Clara Bewick Colby." *Journalism History* 28.3 (2002): 102–11.

MacLeod, Anne Scott. *American Childhood: Essays on Children's Literature of the Nineteenth and Twentieth Centuries*. Athens: U of Georgia P, 1994.

Macleod, David I. *The Age of the Child: Children in America, 1890–1920*. New York: Twayne, 1998.

Magill, Harry B. *Biography of Francis Schlatter, The Healer, with His Life, Works and Wanderings*. Denver: Schlatter, 1896. Reprint, Pomeroy WA: Health Research, 1968.

Marzolf, Marion Tuttle. *Civilizing Voices: American Press Criticism, 1880–1950*. New York: Longman, 1991.

Mayfield, Eugene O. "'Christ Man' of the West." *Omaha World-Herald* 18 Nov. 1895: 1–2.

McLoughlin, William G., Jr. *Modern Revivalism: Charles Grandison Finney to Billy Graham*. New York: Ronald Press, 1959.

Mescher, Virginia. "Mourning in the Nineteenth Century: An Overview." *The Campbell Crier* (Mar. 1998) <http://users.erols.com/va42nd/mourning.html>.

"Michael Cudahy Science Hall." Loyola University Archives. 22 June 2001 <http://www.luc.edu/depts/archives/cudsci.html>.

Morley, John. *Death, Heaven, and the Victorians*. Pittsburgh: U of Pittsburgh P, 1971.

Mott, Frank Luther. *The News in America*. Cambridge: Harvard UP, 1962.

"Mrs. Amanda Edwards." *Fremont Herald* 12 Aug. 1910: 3.

"Mrs. Elia Peattie Retires from Trib." *The Trib* 4.4 (1922): 3.

"Mrs. Elia Wilkinson Peattie." *A Woman of the Century*. Ed. Frances E. Willard and Mary A. Livermore. Buffalo: Charles Wells Moulton, 1892. 562–63.

Omaha Board of Trade. *Nebraska's Progress: The Advantages and Resources of Omaha and Douglas County, Neb. as Set Forth by the Omaha Board of Trade*. Omaha: Herald Printing, 1880.

———. *Omaha: The Western Metropolis*. Omaha: H. N. Blood, 1891.

Otis, Harry B. *E Pluribus Omaha*. Omaha: Lamplighter Press, 2000.

Peattie, Donald Culross. *The Road of a Naturalist*. Boston: Houghton Mifflin, 1941.

Peattie, Elia W. "Barriers against Woman: They Are Mostly Erected by the Women Themselves through Blind Superstition." *Omaha World-Herald* 21 Aug. 1892: 16.

———. "Brother Lemen's Work." *Omaha World-Herald* 15 Nov. 1891: 5.

———. *Edda and the Oak*. Chicago: Rand McNally, 1911.

———. "In Defense of Her Own Sex." *Omaha World-Herald* 1 Dec. 1895: 24.

———. *The Judge*. Chicago: Rand McNally, 1890.

———. "Let the Law Be Amended." *Omaha World-Herald* 15 Jan. 1893: 16.

———. "Newspaper Women of Nebraska." *History of the Nebraska Press Association: Book Two*. Ed. Henry Allen Brainerd. Lincoln: Wood Printing, 1923. Rpt.

"Nebraska Women Journalists." *The Story of the Nebraska Press Association, 1873–1973*. Ed. Arthur J. Riedesel. Lincoln: Nebraska Press Association, 1973.

———. "Norfolk and Its Sugar." *Omaha World-Herald* 12 Feb.: 1893: 5.

———. "Papa Lem[e]n and His Home." *Omaha World-Herald* 30 July 1893: 9.

———. "Salvation Lassie at Home." *Omaha World-Herald* 11 Dec. 1893: 5.

———. "Star Wagon." Ed. Joan Falcone. Unpublished manuscript.

———. "Successful Public School." *Omaha World-Herald* 16 Apr. 1893: 16.

———. "Takes Issue with Gibbons." *Omaha World-Herald* 27 Jan. 1895: 10.

———. "Was Not a Partisan Fight: Mrs. Peattie Explains Wherein Women Voters Were Misled." *Omaha World-Herald* 11 Nov. 1894: 10.

———. "What Makes Home Home: Some People Mistake an Aggregation of Rooms for One." *Omaha World-Herald* 22 May 1892: 13.

———. "What Women Are Doing." *Omaha World-Herald* 19 Nov. 1890: 3.

———. "A Word with the Women." *Omaha World-Herald* 21 Jan. 1894: 9; 10 Mar. 1895: 8; 18 Mar. 1895: 8; 21 Mar. 1895: 8; 18 June 1895: 8; 24 June 1895: 8; 3 July 1895: 8; 28 Nov. 1895: 8; 4 Mar. 1896: 8; 17 Sept. 1896: 8; 10 Oct. 1896: 8; 11 Oct. 1896: 8.

———. "Work of the Day Nursery: The Creche and What It Does for Women Who Must Work." *Omaha World-Herald* 7 Feb. 1892: 13.

Peattie, Robert Burns. *The Story of Robert Burns Peattie*. Ed. Mark Robert Peattie, Noel Roderick Peattie, and Alice Richmond Peattie. N.p.: n.p., 1992.

Peattie, Roderick. *The Incurable Romantic*. New York: Macmillan, 1941.

Perry, Elizabeth Israels. "Men Are from the Gilded Age, Women Are from the Progressive Era." *Journal of the Gilded Age and Progressive Era* 1.1 (2002): 25–48.

Plumb, Charles S. *Types and Breeds of Farm Animals*. Boston: Ginn, 1906.

Polk, Donna Mays. *Black Men and Women of Nebraska*. Lincoln: Nebraska Black History Preservation Society, 1981.

Pratt, Viola. "One Year among the Sioux." *Omaha World-Herald* 14 July 1895: 12.

Raftery, Judith. "Chicago Settlement Women in Fact and Fiction: Hobart Chatfield-Taylor, Clara Elizabeth Laughlin, and Elia Wilkinson Peattie." *Illinois Historical Journal* 88 (Spring 1995): 37–58.

Riedesel, Arthur J. *The Story of the Nebraska Press Association, 1873–1973*. Lincoln: Nebraska Press Association, 1973.

Riley, Glenda. *Women and Nature: Saving the "Wild" West*. Lincoln: U of Nebraska P, 1999.

Roberts, Mary Louise. "True Womanhood Revisited." *Journal of Women's History* 14.1 (2002): 150–55.

Robertson, Elsie. "On the Omaha Reservation." *Omaha World-Herald* 28 Aug. 1892: 11.

Ross, Ishbel. *Ladies of the Press: The Story of Women in Journalism by an Insider*. New York: Harper, 1936.

Rystrom, Geraldine, ed. *History of Stromsburg, 1872–1972: Centennial Book of the*

Swede Capitol of Nebraska. Stromsburg NE: Woman's Civic Improvement Club, 1972.

Saltzman, Joe. "Sob Sisters: The Image of the Female Journalist in Popular Culture." *The Image of the Journalist in Popular Culture*. 2003. 5 Mar. 2004 <http://www.ijpc.org/sobessay.pdf>.

Schaff, Philip. "Revivals of Religion." *New Schaff-Herzog Encyclopedia of Religious Knowledge*. Vol. 9. Grand Rapids MI: Baker Book House, 1953. 9–19.

"Schlatter Blessed Them." *Omaha World-Herald* 19 Nov. 1895: 8.

Schneider, Dorothy, and Carl J. Schneider. *American Women in the Progressive Era, 1900–1920*. New York: Facts on File, 1993.

Schramm Park State Recreation Area: A Park for All Seasons. Lincoln: Nebraska Game and Parks Commission, 2001.

Scott, Donald. *Evangelicalism, Revivalism, and the Second Great Awakening*. National Humanities Center. 25 July 2001 <http://nhc.nc.us:8080/tserve/nineteen/nkeyinfo/nevanrev.htm>.

———. *Evangelism as a Social Movement*. National Humanities Center. 25 July 2001 <http://www.nhc.nc.us:8080/tserve/nineteen/nkeyinfo/nevansoc.htm>.

Stahl, John M. *Growing with the West: The Story of a Busy Life*. London: Longmans, Green, 1930.

"Steady Stream to Denver." *Omaha World-Herald* 12 Nov. 1895: 8.

Stephenson, John S. *Death, Grief, and Mourning: Individual and Social Realities*. New York: Free Press, 1985.

"Talks Plainly to Club Women." *Chicago Tribune* 19 Oct. 1900: 7.

Taylor, Lou. *Mourning Dress: A Costume and Social History*. London: George Allen and Unwin, 1983.

Thomas, Mary Martha. *The New Woman in Alabama: Social Reform and Suffrage, 1890–1920*. Tuscaloosa: U of Alabama P, 1992.

Tibbles, Thomas Henry. "Red Blood Flows." *Omaha World-Herald* 30 Dec. 1890: 1.

Trefethen, James B. *Crusade for Wildlife: Highlights in Conservation Progress*. Harrisburg PA: Stackpole, 1961.

Tyler, Albert F., ed., and Ella F. Auerbach, comp. *History of Medicine in Nebraska*. Omaha: Magic City Printing, 1928.

Untitled clipping. *Omaha Daily News* 15 Nov. 1914.

"Uses of a Woman's Club." *Omaha World-Herald* 26 Mar. 1893: 16.

Walakafra-Wills, Delpaneaux. *A Short Historical Analysis of the Urbanization of the African-American in Nebraska*. N.p.: n.p., Jan. 1976.

Washburn, Josie. *The Underworld Sewer: A Prostitute Reflects on Life in the Trade, 1871–1909*. 1909. Lincoln: U of Nebraska P, 1997.

Webb, Dottie. "Nineteenth Century Regional Writing in the United States." Diss. University of Michigan. 28 Feb. 2000. 22 July 2001 <http://www.traverse.com/people/dot/default.html>.

Weisberger, Bernard A. *They Gathered at the River*. Boston: Little, Brown, 1958.

Weiss, Nancy Pottishman. "Mother, the Invention of Necessity: Dr. Benjamin Spock's *Baby and Child Care*." *Growing up in America: Children in Historical Perspective*. Ed. N. Ray Hiner and Joseph M. Hawes. Urbana: University of Chicago Press, 1985. 283–303.

Wells, Mildred White. *Unity in Diversity: The History of the General Federation of Women's Clubs*. Washington DC: General Federation of Women's Clubs, 1953.

Welter, Barbara. *Dimity Convictions: The American Woman in the Nineteenth Century*. Athens: Ohio UP, 1976.

West, Elliott. *Growing Up with the Country: Childhood on the Far Western Frontier*. Albuquerque: U of New Mexico P, 1989.

West, Mrs. Max. *Infant Care*. Washington DC: Government Printing Office, 1914.

White, Richard. *"It's Your Misfortune and None of My Own": A New History of the American West*. Norman: U of Oklahoma P, 1991.

"Who Is This Strange Man?" *Omaha World-Herald* 17 Nov. 1895: 2.

Woloch, Nancy. *Women and the American Experience*. 2nd ed. New York: McGraw Hill, 1994.

"Women in Journalism." *Hebron Journal* 20 Dec. 1895: 4.

Wood, Carol. "The History and Heritage of Children's Square U.S.A." *Around the Square*. Jan. n.d.: 5–6.

"A Word from the Women." *Omaha World-Herald* 14 Oct. 1896: 8.

"The World Frivolous." *Omaha World-Herald* 14 May 1894: 6.

"Writer Who Comes Here to Lecture Says Babies Her Greatest Happiness." *Omaha World-Herald* 11 Feb. 1923.

A BIBLIOGRAPHY OF THE WORKS OF ELIA WILKINSON PEATTIE

To say that Elia Peattie wrote voluminously would be an understatement. Because she published in diverse newspapers and periodicals for approximately fifty years (1882–1932), a definitive bibliography would be nearly impossible to collect. This bibliography includes her major works and stories from leading periodicals as well as her writings from the Omaha World-Herald, *but it does not include the many reviews of her books and the hundreds of stories, poems, and book reviews she published in the* Chicago Tribune *and other newspapers or in less well-known periodicals.*

Books

America in War and Peace. Chicago: W. B. Conkey, 1898.

The American Peasant: A Timely Allegory. With Thomas Henry Tibbles. Chicago: F. J. Schulle, 1892, 1900; Indianapolis: Vincent Bros., 1892.

The Angel with a Broom. Chicago: R. F. Seymour, 1915.

Annie Laurie and Azalea. Chicago: Reilly and Britton, 1913.

Azalea at Sunset Gap. Chicago: Reilly and Britton, 1912, 1914.

Azalea's Silver Web. Chicago: Reilly and Britton, 1915.

Azalea: The Story of a Girl in the Blue Ridge Mountains. Chicago: Reilly, 1912.

The Beleagured Forest. New York: Appleton, 1901.

The Book of the Fine Arts Building. Chicago: Fine Arts Building, [1911?].

Edda and the Oak. Chicago: Rand McNally, 1911.

The Edge of Things. Chicago: F. H. Revell, 1903.

The History of Gibson County. Owensboro KY: Cook and McDowell 1980. Reprint of "Gibson County" from *The History of the United States, Indiana, and Gibson County*, 1897.

How Jacques Came into the Forest of Arden: An Impertinence. Chicago: The Blue Sky P, 1901. (Of this book there have been printed seven hundred copies on Van Gelder handmade paper, twenty-five copies on Japan Vellum, and three copies on parchment. Cover and illustrations were drawn by Walter J. Enright. The initial letters designed by Harry Everett Townsend and illuminated by Barbara Peattie.)

A Journey through Wonderland: Or, The Pacific Northwest and Alaska, with a Description of the Country Traversed by the Northern Pacific Railroad. Chicago: Rand McNally, 1890.

The Judge. Chicago: Rand McNally, 1890, 1891.

Lotta Embury's Career. Boston: Houghton Mifflin, 1915.

The Newcomers. Boston: Houghton Mifflin, 1917.

*Our Chosen Land: A Romantic Story of America from the Time of Its Discovery and

Conquest to the Present Day. An Interesting Account of the Progress and Development of Our Country, Written Especially for Young Folks. Chicago: Wabash, 1896. (An abridgment of the author's *Story of America*)

Our Land of Liberty, or The Wonderful Story of America, Containing the Romantic Incidents of History, from the Discovery of America to the Present Time. Chicago: International Publishing Company, 1895.

The Pictorial Story of America Containing the Romantic Incidents of History from the Discovery of America to the Present Time. Chicago: Amer. Pub. and Engraving, 1895; Union Pub., 1896; National Pub., 1896; Tombaugh Publications, 1982.

Pictorial Story of America: Part 3, Fulton County, Indiana. Chicago: National Pub., 1896.

The Precipice: A Novel. Boston: Houghton Mifflin, 1914; Urbana: U of Illinois P, 1989.

Sarah Brewster's Relatives. Boston: Houghton Mifflin, 1916.

The Story of America: Containing the Romantic Incidents of History, from the Discovery of America to the Present Time. San Francisco: R. S. King, 1889; Chicago: Midcontinent Pub., 1891, 1892; Cleveland: Neff, 1893; Chicago: W. B. Conkey, 1898.

With Scrip and Staf: A Tale of the Children's Crusade. New York: A. D. F. Randolph, 1891.

Collections of Poems, Short Stories, and Essays

Ghost, Window, Mountain. Holicong PA: Wildside Press, 2003. Includes short stories from *The Shape of Fear*, *A Mountain Woman*, and *Painted Windows*.

Ickery Ann and Other Girls and Boys. Chicago: H. S. Stone, 1899. Includes short stories "Ickery Ann," "The Genius," "Grizel Cochrane's Ride." "Bertha's Debut," "The Shut-ins," "The Message of the Lilies," "The McCulloughs of the Bluff," "Tarts," "Jock, the Chipmunk," "How Christmas Came to the Santa Maria Flats," "Christmas at Goldberg," "The Dead Letter," "The Wooing of Fan Tod," "The Breeziest Reunion," and "Tommy, the Beach Cat."

A Mountain Woman. Chicago: Way and Williams, 1896; Freeport NY: Books for Libraries, 1969; Blue Unicorn Editions, 2000; IndyPublish.com, 2002. Includes short stories "A Mountain Woman," "Jim Lancy's Waterloo," "The Three Johns," "A Resuscitation," "The Two Pioneers," "Up the Gulch," "A Michigan Man," and "A Lady of Yesterday."

Painted Windows. New York: George H. Doran, 1918. Includes essays "Night," "Solitude," "Friendship," "Fame," "Remorse," and "Travel."

Pippins and Cheese: Being the Relation of How a Number of Persons Ate a Number of Dinners at Various Times and Places. Chicago: Way and Williams, 1897. Includes short stories "Dinner for Two," "The Price of a Dinner," "At Luncheon," "The Princess Dines," "The Stop Gap," "Covers for Twelve," "A Diminuendo," "The Blood Apple," and "A Mess of Pottage."

Poems You Ought to Know. Selected by Elia W. Peattie. Chicago: Jamieson-Higgins, 1902; Chicago: Fleming H. Revell, 1903; Freeport NY: Books for Libraries, 1969; Columbia, NY: Granger Index Reprint Series, 1978.

The Shape of Fear and Other Ghostly Tales. New York: Macmillan, 1898, 1899; Freeport NY: Books for Libraries, 1969. Includes short stories "The Shape of Fear," "On the Northern Ice," "Their Dear Little Ghost," "A Spectral Collie," "The House That Was Not," "The Story of an Obstinate Corpse," "A Child of the Rain," "The Room of the Evil Thought," "The Story of the Vanishing Patient," "The Piano Next Door," "An Astral Onion," "From the Loom of the Dead," and "A Grammatical Ghost."

Songs from a Southern Garden. Tryon NC: Pacolet, 1930. Includes poems "Lanier in the Valley," "Easter Greetings," "These Be the Mountains That Comfort Me," "The Two Griefs," "In the Cool of the Day," "The Garden Pool," "To Barbara," "January Jasmine," "Query," "Wood Smoke," "Little Brides of Tryon," "The Hester Bank," "Christmas Candles," "To You, Unforgotten," "Betty in the Fig Tree," "Autumn Twilight," "Contentment," and "Ole Jacob's Turkey."

To Comfort You: Poems of Comfort Selected by Elia W. Peattie. Chicago: Fleming H. Revell, 1903.

Plays

Castle, Knight, and Troubadour: In an Apology and Three Tableaux. Chicago: Blue Sky Press, 1903.

The Great Delusion: A Drama in One Act. Chicago: Dramatic Publishing, 1932.

The Love of a Caliban: A Romantic Opera in One Act. Wausau WI: Van Vechten and Ellis, 1898, 1980, 1986.

Massimilliano, the Court Jester. N.p.: n.p., 1925, 1926.

Time and Manners: A Pageant. Chicago: Ralph Fletcher Seymour for the Chicago's Woman's Club, 1918.

The Wander Weed, and Seven Other Little Theater Plays. Chicago: C. H. Sergel, 1923.

Short Stories

"After the Storm." *Atlantic* Sept. 1897: 393–405.

"Anne St. Cross: Parts I, II, and III." *Women's World* May–July 1913.

"As Far as Angels Ken." *Chicago Tribune* 17 Aug. 1886: 9.

"The Brothers." *Smart Set* Aug. 1903: 121–32.

"Bundle of Life." *Collier's* 7 May 1910: 20–21, 26, 28–31.

"The Call of the City." *Ainslee's* Apr. 1903: 112.

"Cap'n Patti." *Lippincott* 53: 523.

"A Childless Madonna. *(Omaha) Woman's Weekly* 7 Apr. 1894; rpt. in *Prairie Schooner* 41.2 (1967): 143–51.
"The Christmas Lady." *Woman's Home Companion* Dec. 1900.
"Confessions of a Cheerful Person." *Ainslee's* June 1903: 122.
"The Counterfeiter." *Chicago Tribune* 3 June 1900: 34.
"Crime of Micah Rood." *Cosmopolitan* 4: 383.
"Cupid and the Hurdy-Gurdy." *Harper's Bazaar* July 1907: 636–42.
"A Deadwood Incident." *Chicago Tribune* 3 Oct. 1885: 16.
"Dinner for Two." *American Magazine* 7: 173.
"The Door." *Reader* Jan. 1906: 168–76.
"Esmeralda Herders." *Atlantic* Jan. 1901: 111–16.
"The Executioner of the Revolution." Historical fiction. No publication data available.
"The Functions of Society." *Frank Leslie's Popular Monthly* 8.5: 44.
"Ged." *Scribner's Monthly* Nov. 1903: 580–94.
"Greater Love Than This." *Harper's Bazaar* (serial) 26 May 1900: 212–19; 2 June 1900: 268–77.
"His Christmas Eve." *Chicago Tribune* 24 Dec. 1887: 12.
"House of the Golden Song." *Harper's Bazaar* 9 Dec. 1899: 1056–57.
"Ill-regulated Courtship." *Harper's Bazaar* Mar. 1904: 252–61.
"In Husking Time." *Harper's Weekly* 8 Aug. 1891: 993–94+.
"Instructress of Men." *Smart Set* Feb. 1903: 109–18.
"The Invisible House." *Frank Leslie's Popular Monthly* May 1901: 66–76.
"Jim Lancy's Waterloo." *Cosmopolitan* June 1894: 211.
"Man at the Edge of Things." *Chicago Daily News* 1 Sept. 1899: 8; *Atlantic* Sept. 1899: 321–42.
"Madonna of the Desert." *Harper's* Sept. 1905: 507–18. Rpt. in *The Argosy* (UK) Nov. 1932.
"Maloney's Masterpiece." *Harper's Weekly* 8 Aug. 1891: 593–95.
"Michigan Man." *Lippincott* 47: 394.
"A Month of Her Life." *Woman's World* Jan. 1911.
"Mountain Woman." *Harper's Weekly* 14 Nov. 1891: 889–91.
"Mozart: A Fantasy." *Atlantic* Nov. 1902: 634–36.
"Off His Beat." *Chicago Tribune* 31 Oct. 1885: 16.
"Outlaw." *Collier's* 5 Mar. 1910: 28–29.
"Painted Windows." *McCalls* May 1913.
"The Parish House Wraith." *Chicago Tribune* 6 Apr. 1901: 16.
"The Place of Dragons." (serial) *Everybody's* Mar. 1903: 226–358; Apr. 1903: 358–66.
"Resuscitation." *Harper's Weekly* 13 June 1891: 441–42.
"Rubiayat and the Liner." *Harper's Bazaar* 29 Sept. 1900: 1360–66; rpt. in *Quaint*

Courtships: Harper's Novelettes, ed. W. D. Howells. New York: Harper and Brothers, 1906.
"The Sandwich Man." *American Magazine* 8: 700.
"Seaweed." *The Red Book* Sept. 1903.
"Shenens' Houn' Dogs." *Reader* June 1907: 73–84.
"Stage Coach." *Atlantic* June 1904: 787–96.
"The Story behind a Personal Advertisement." *Chicago Tribune* 31 Aug. 1902: 43.
"A Story of Block Island." Historical fiction. No publication data available.
"A Tale of Early Chicago." *Chicago Tribune* 26 Dec. 1885: 3.
"Their Dear Little Ghost." *Outlook* 29 Oct. 1898: 530–32.
"Thorold Viborg." *Atlantic* Feb. 1903: 228–35.
"The Three Johns." *Harper's Weekly* 26 Dec. 1891: 1037–39.
"Tobias Vesey's Opera Box." *Chicago Tribune* 8 June 1901: 16.
"The Voyager." Historical fiction. No publication data available.
"Wilderness Station." *Munsey* May 1903: 272–75.
"Wild Fruit." *The Teepee Book* July 1915: 4–18.

Young Adult Fiction

"At Aunt Frank's Service." *Youth's Companion* 1 Feb. 1900: 49.
"At Dr. Merriwether's Service." *Youth's Companion* 11 Aug. 1904: 374.
"Barbara's Valentine." *St. Nicholas* Feb. 1902: 76.
"Bertha's Debut." *Youth's Companion* 17 Jan. 1890: 217–21.
"The Color Bearers." *Youth's Companion* 17 Sept. 1914: 477.
"A Declaration of Independence." *Youth's Companion* 10 Dec. 1903: 619.
"The Disgrace of Grandfather." *Youth's Companion* 7 Sept. 1916: 492.
"Dressmaking." *Youth's Companion* 5 July 1917: 377.
"The Family He Found." *Youth's Companion* 25 Jan. 1900: 37.
"The Fourth Chaperone." *Youth's Companion* 28 Sept. 1905: 448.
"Grandmother's Fete." *Youth's Companion* 2 Oct. 1902: 470.
"Grizel Cochrane's Ride: Founded on an Incident of the Monmouth Rebellion." *St. Nicholas* Feb. 1887: 271–78.
"The Home Road." *Youth's Companion* 26 Aug. 1915: 429–30.
"In Memoriam." *Youth's Companion* 30 May 1912: 281.
"Kenyon's Bride." *Youth's Companion* 7 Jan. 1904: 1.
"The Last Sedan-Chair." *Youth's Companion* 22 Feb. 1906: 85.
"The Lion Light." *Youth's Companion* 1 Nov. 1917: 621–22.
"Lotta Embury's Career." (serial) *Youth's Companion* 10 Dec. 1914–11 Jan. 1915.
"The McCulloughs of the Bluff." *Youth's Companion* 16 June 1898: 285–86.
"The Mean Little Town." (serial) *Youth's Companion* 5 Oct. 1916–7 Dec. 1916.
"Message of the Lillies." *Youth's Companion* 7 Apr. 1898: 161–62.

"Old Kaskaskia." *Youth's Companion* 21 Apr. 1904: 196.

"The Pageant." *Youth's Companion* 2 Aug. 1917: 430.

"Sarah Brewster's Relatives." (serial) *Youth's Companion* 24 July 1913–25 Sept. 1913.

"A Singing Bird." *Youth's Companion* 20 June 1912: 331.

"Some Odd Figurines." *Youth's Companion* 10 Oct. 1901: 491.

"Tapestry." *Youth's Companion* 18 June 1903: 293.

"Tarts." *Youth's Companion* 21 Apr. 1898: 191.

"True Hospitality." *Youth's Companion* 19 Apr. 1900: 215.

"The Utilization of Uncle Reginald." *Youth's Companion* 25 May 1899:262.

"Wan Tsze-King." *Youth's Companion* 2 June 1901: 229–30.

Essays

"Artistic Side of Chicago." *Atlantic* Dec. 1899: 828–34.

"The Breeziest Reunion: How and Where It Was Held and What Happened." *Chicago Tribune* 24 Nov. 1887: 9.

"Child Studies by Chicago Sculptors." *Good Housekeeping* Oct. 1910: 415–20.

"Churches of Old London." *Harper's Bazaar* Jan. 1910: 16–17.

"Defense of Fine Writing." *Critic* June 1903: 546–47.

"Friends of the Family: The Teacher." *Good Housekeeping* Feb. 1910: 179–87.

"Fun at Narragansett." *Chicago Tribune* 27 Aug. 1886: 9.

"Groves, Worms, Epitaphs: The Thoughts Inspired by a Ramble around Narragansett." *Chicago Tribune* 27 Aug. 1886: 10.

"Life at Long Branch." *Chicago Tribune* 17 Aug. 1886: 9.

"Love and Death." *Harper's Bazaar* Sept. 1911: 408–9.

"Newspaper Women of Nebraska." *Nebraska Editor* 1895, rpt. in *Nebraska Press Association: Book II*, ed. Henry Allen Brainerd. Lincoln: n.p., 1923. 23–33.

"Not So Exclusive Now." *Chicago Tribune* 19 Aug. 1886: 9.

"One's Self: A Dissertation for the Middle-Aged Woman." *Harper's Bazaar* 5 Mar. 1910: 437–39.

"Outskirts of Thought." *Open Court* 25 (Dec. 1911): 708–19.

"Woman's Note-book of Events." *Delineator* 76 (Dec. 1910): 510.

"Women of the Hour." *Harper's Bazaar* Oct. 1904: 1003–8.

"A Word on 'The New Woman.'" (unidentified clipping, 1899).

"Wren's Little Steeples." *Harper's Bazaar* Jan. 1911: 18–20.

"Your Wife's Pocketbook." *Delineator* 66 (June 1911): 466.

Poems

"The Babes at Danbury Cross." *Omaha World-Herald* 22 May 1892: 4.

"Compensations." *Harper's Bazaar* Sept. 1910: 538.

"The Growing of the Grain." *Omaha World-Herald* 12 July 1891: 4.

"Interruption." *Harper's Monthly* Nov. 1896: 924.

"A Knight in the Nineteenth Century." In "Is the Goat a Reality?" *Omaha World-Herald* 26 Nov. 1893: 16.

"Lanier in the Valley." *Scribner's* Nov. 1922: 625.

"The Little Brides of Tryon." *Youth's Companion* 28 July 1921: 412.

"Little Flowers from a Milliner's Box." By Sade Iverson (pseudonym). *The Little Review* Jan. 1915: 7–8.

"Love's Delay." *Atlantic* Feb. 1897: 257.

"On a Blank Leaf in the Marble Faun." *Century* Oct. 1891: 847.

"The Pine Forest Speaks." *Lorado Taft's Indian Statue "Black Hawk": An Account of the Unveiling Ceremonies at Eagles' nest Bluff, Oregon, Illinois, July the First Nineteen Hundred and Eleven, Frank O. Lowden Presiding.* Chicago: University of Chicago Press, 1912. 25–29.

"Star i' the Darkest Night." *Munsey* Nov. 1900: 285.

"Trinity." *Harper's Bazaar* 43 (July 1909): 690; *Current Literature* 47 (Aug. 1909): 217–18; reprinted in *Dreams and Voices: Songs of Mother, Father, and Child from the Writings of American and English Poets of To-day.* Comp. Grace Hyde Trine. New York: The Woman's Press, 1920. 102.

Short Stories Collected in Anthologies

"A Bohemian in Nebraska." *The Nebraska of Kate McPhelim Cleary.* Ed. James Mansfield Cleary. Lake Bluff IL: United Educators, 1958. 5–10.

"From the Loom of the Dead." *Famous Psychic and Ghost Stories.* Ed. J. Walker McSpadden. Freeport NY: Books for Libraries Press, 1976.

"A Grammatical Ghost." *A Treasury of Victorian Ghost Stories.* Ed. Everett F. Bleiler. New York: Simon and Schuster, 1981.

"A Grammatical Ghost." *Bodies of the Dead and Other Great American Ghost Stories.* Ed. David G. Hartwell. New York: Tor Books, 1995. 77–84.

"Grizel Cochrane's Ride." *Heroines of History and Legend.* Ed. Elva S. Smith. Lothrop, Lee, and Shepard, 1921.

"How Christmas Came to the Santa Maria Flats." *Children's Book of Christmas Stories.* Ed. Asa Don Dickinson. Garden City NY: Children's Crimson Series, 1913.

"Madonna of the Desert." *Under the Sunset.* Ed. William Dean Howells and Henry Mills Alden. New York: Harper, 1906.

"A Michigan Man." *Short Story Classics (American).* Vol. 3. Ed. William Patten. New York: Collier, 1905. 827–37.

"Rubyiat and the Liner." *Quaint Courtships.* Ed. William Dean Howells and Henry Mills Alden. New York: Harper, 1906.

"Their Dear Little Ghost." *Ghosts for Christmas.* Ed. Richard Dalby. Secaucus NJ: Castle Books, 1988. 103–8.

From the *Omaha Daily Herald*

1888

FICTION

"A Diminuendo." 16 Dec. 1888: 9.

1889

EDITORIAL

"The Wabash Corner." 20 Jan. 1889: 4 [6].

FICTION

"Dr. de Launy of Omaha." 6 Jan. 1889: 6.

"Lisette." 21 Apr. 1889: 16.

COLUMN: "THE WOMEN OF THE WORLD"

6 Jan. 1889: 4 [Lace caps; tea gowns; Jessie Bartlett Davis, opera singer; Frances Willard's maid; writer Mary Hartwell Catherwood].

13 Jan. 1889: 4 [Queen Victoria's lack of accomplishments; women in science; Omaha's new "Training School of Expression"; apathy of women in Omaha boardinghouses].

20 Jan. 1889: 4 [Cleaning gloves; women and higher education; flannel jackets; practical church weddings].

10 Feb. 1889: 4 [Miss Mae Wentworth, actress; Edna Carey, actress and connoisseur of tea gowns; the Woman's Exchange to assist needy women].

From the *Omaha World-Herald*

1889

FICTION

"Tragedy of Ward 3." 6 Nov. 1889: 6.

"Born: Two Souls." 24 Nov. 1889: 5.

"Christmas at Goldberg." 22 Dec. 1889: 13.

1890 [January 1890–March 1890 not available]

EDITORIALS

"How Not to Treat Babies." 20 Apr. 1890: 12.

"All the Men Were Angry." 8 June 1890: 18.

"Very Fast Men." 3 Aug. 1890: 9.

"How to Loaf Gracefully." 10 Aug. 1890: 11.

"They Were from Missouri." 17 Aug. 1890: 9.

"Vale, the Departing Man." 24 Aug. 1890: 9.

"Carleton's Lady Singers." 31 Aug. 1890: 13.
"What Four Women Did." 7 Sept. 1890: 12.
"Rev. Duryea and His Flock." 21 Sept. 1890: 4.
"And Still They Do Not See It." 26 Sept. 1890: 4.
"Dr. Miller's Stone Castle." 28 Sept. 1890: 12.
"A Needed Reform: Farmers' Wives Should Have More Amusement." *Weekly World Herald* 1 Oct. 1890: 1.
"What Women Have Done." 12 Nov. 1890: 5.
"What Is Shown in Oil." 13 Nov. 1890: 5.
"Don't Want Separation: The Women Don't Want a Separate Exhibit at the Fair." 23 Nov. 1890: 11.

FICTION

[Philomon]. 6 Apr. 1890: 10.
"The Orphans of Omaha." 12 Nov. 1890: 4.

COLUMN: "WHAT WOMEN ARE DOING"

5 Oct. 1890: 12 [Salvation of the farmers' wives].
12 Oct. 1890: 12 [Home decorating].
19 Oct. 1890: 12 [Pressures of women on farms].
26 Oct. 1890: 12 [Sealskin cloaks].
2 Nov. 1890: 11 [Economic protection for working women].
9 Nov. 1890: 12 [Farm women and barns].
16 Nov. 1890: 12 [Tolstoi's "Romance of Marriage" and marriage].
23 Nov. 1890: 18 [Caroline Dodge, tobacco shop owner and piano teacher].
30 Nov. 1890: 12 [Asks for help for unfortunate in Nebraska].
7 Dec. 1890: 16 [Christmas, children, and charity].
14 Dec. 1890: 12 [Ill-natured comments about women; defends women and shopping].
21 Dec. 1890: 15 [On poverty and superfluous wealth].
28 Dec. 1890: 16 [Response to *Omaha Excelsior* and Mora Balcombe concerning women on sleeping cars).

1891

EDITORIALS

"Lovely Woman and Indians." 4 Jan. 1891: 10.
"Home Life and Home Duty." 11 Jan. 1891: 12.
"Who Will Help the Women." 25 Jan. 1891: 8.
"A Singular Institution: The Christian Home of Council Bluffs and Its Founder." 1 Mar. 1891: 11.
"The Owner of Dox Box." 8 Mar. 1891: 10.
"A Woman Doctor." 15 Mar. 1891: 4.
"A Salvation Army Funeral." 18 Mar. 1891: 4.

"Two Pioneers: The Easter Story of Council Bluffs." 29 Mar. 1891: 10.
"An Omaha Poet (Alonzo Hilton Davis)." 5 Apr. 1891: 17.
"Grapes and Nebraska Soil." 12 Apr. 1891: 7.
"A People's Church Which Failed." 19 Apr. 1891: 13.
"Stirred the Whole Nation." 26 Apr. 1891: 17.
"Shakes a Stick at Them." 10 May 1891: 11.
"She Fires Her Own China." 17 May 1891: 5.
"They Improve Their Minds: The Cleofan Society of Omaha and Its Bright Members." 24 May 1891: 6.
"Of a Family of Musicians." 31 May 1891: 16.
"Your Graduation Dress." 14 June 1891: 16.
"Five Young Graduates." 21 June 1891: 5.
"They Wear a Little Cross." 28 June 1891: 12.
"Allen Root the Pioneer." 5 July 1891: 7.
"A Hoche-Pot of Gossip: Chatter about Souvenir Spoons as an Incentive to Travel." 12 July 1891: 10.
"Seen with One's Eyes Open: What Is to Be Seen from an Open Motor Car in Omaha." 19 July 1891: 16.
"Methodist Episcopal Smith." 26 July 1891: 10.
"The Law and the Lynchers." 18 Oct. 1891: 13.
"Lanier's Place in Letters." 25 Oct. 1891: 7.
"With Works of Charity: St. Joseph's Hospital and the Good Sisters Who Do Its Work." 1 Nov. 1891: 13.
"Brains in the School Room: Some Pertinent Remarks Regarding the Needs of the Public Schools." 8 Nov. 1891: 13.
"The Judge Objects." 14 Nov. 1891: 4.
"Brother Lemen's Work: The Christian Home of Council Bluffs and What It Does for Children." 15 Nov. 1891: 5.
"The Sentimental Meredith: The Late Lord Lytton and His Place in the Literature of His Age." 6 Dec. 1891: 6.
"Within Learning's Circle: Something about the Chatauqua Circles in This City." 13 Dec. 1891: 14.
"Sir Edwin Arnold's Poetry." 20 Dec. 1891: 18.
"Rooms of Noted Heroines." 27 Dec. 1891: 5.

FICTION

"The Triumph of Starved Crow." 4 Jan. 1891: 4.
"Leda." 1 Feb. 1891: 12.
"A Diminuendo." 7 June 1891: 16.
"Polly Merrick's Rise: A Story for Young People." 16 Aug. 1891: 11.
"The Postmistress of Weeping Willow." (serial) 27 Sept. 1891; 4 Oct. 1891: 11; 11 Oct. 1891: 11.

COLUMN: "WHAT WOMEN ARE DOING"

8 Feb. 1891: 12 [Omaha women should shop in Omaha].

1892

EDITORIALS

"Camden's Good Gray Poet: Walt Whitman and His Bizarre Democracy." 10 Jan. 1892: 13.

"The Servant Girl Problem: The Large Proportion of Vicious Incompetents in That Class of Workers." 17 Jan. 1892: 12.

"The Plague of the Decade." 24 Jan. 1892: 9.

"Killing, Yet No Murder: A Day at the Stock Yards in South Omaha." 7 Feb. 1892: 13.

"Work of the Day Nursery: The Creche and What It Does for Women Who Must Work." 7 Feb. 1892: 13.

"A Rational Christian: A Vigorous Thinker and a Christian Gentleman in the Best Sense [Gilbert C. Monell]." 14 Feb. 1892: 16.

"Nebraska Women's Exhibit: Something about the Opportunity Nebraska Women Will Have at the Fair [Chicago World's Fair]." 21 Feb. 1892: 7.

"Bernhardt's Intense Art: The Great French Actress Appears in Sardou's Drama of 'La Tosca.'" 23 Feb. 1892: 2.

"The True Poet of Nature: James Whitcomb Riley and His Familiar Works." 28 Feb. 1892: 13.

"The Cooperative Charities: A Work Lately Commenced in Omaha." 6 Mar. 1892: 7.

"The Faults of the Drama: Shakespeare's Inconsistencies and Incongruities as a Playwright." 13 Mar. 1892: 9.

"Where Are the Children? A Lay Sermon Suggested by Chief Seavey to Colonel Hogeland." 20 Mar. 1892: 10.

"David, the Magnetic Man: 'The Sweet Psalmist of Israel' and His Great Personal Magnetism." 27 Mar. 1892: 7.

"For an Educational Park: What Colonel Daniels Is Here Moving For." 10 Apr. 1892: 17.

"Rights of the Immigrant: A Plea for the Poor Foreigner Who Seeks an Asylum with Us." 17 Apr. 1892: 10.

"An American Realist: Hamlin Garland, a Western Writer, Whom Gosse Would Term a 'Sensitivist.'" 24 Apr. 1892: 9.

"What Makes Home Home? Some People Mistake an Aggregation of Rooms for One." 22 May 1892: 13.

"The Working Girls' Home: A Description of the Place on Seventeenth Street, between Douglas and Dodge." 5 June 1892: 18.

"The St. James Orphanage: Happy Days Spent by the Inmates of a Worthy Charitable Institution." 12 June 1892: 18.

"Nature's Sweet Restorer: Delicate Sleep and the Unavailing Chase Her Devotees Sometimes Pursue." 19 June 1892: 7.

"The Creighton Hospital: The Opening of a Noble Monument to a Philanthropist's Charity." 26 June 1892: 4.

"Omaha's Manual Training: The Excellent Workshop in the High School Building and Its Teacher." 26 June 1892: 6.

"The State Fish Hatchery: Where the Rivers of Nebraska Get Their Stock of Gamey Fish." 3 July 1892: 11.

"Hot Weather Thoughts: The Delight of Being Absolutely without Ideas—Block Island's Happy Idiot." 24 July 1892: 16.

"Woman, Modern and Feudal: A Distinction between Women of the North and of the South." 31 July 1892: 12.

"Fascination of the Circus: It Is Like Striped Candy and Endures Only during Your Callow Days." 7 Aug. 1892: 4.

"The Midsummer Magazines: A Comprehensive Review of the Aug. Periodicals with Comments." 14 Aug. 1892: 9.

"Barriers against Woman: They Are Mostly Erected by the Women Themselves through Blind Superstition." 21 Aug. 1892: 16.

"Want to See a Knock-Out: Americans Seem to Feel That Way in Spite of Their Civilization." 4 Sept. 1892: 13.

"Omaha's Season of Opera: Something about Nov. Operatic Season This Year in Omaha." 11 Sept. 1892: 6.

"Women and the Cholera: Upon Them Much of the Work of Preventing the Cholera Depends." 18 Sept. 1892: 7.

"Omaha's Black Population: The Negroes of This City—Who They Are and Where They Live." 25 Sept. 1892: 13.

"The Fair Dedication Ode: Miss Harriet Monroe's Noble Composition for the World's Fair." 2 Oct. 1892: 7.

"Consistency in the Opera: Do Operatic Performances Satisfy the Demand for the Natural and Consistent?" 9 Oct. 1892: 5.

"The Democracy of Nature: That Is What Henry D. Thoreau Represented—A Review of His 'Autumn.'" 9 Oct. 1892: 10.

"Kindergartens in Omaha: The Introduction of This Excellent Instruction into Our Public Schools." 16 Oct. 1892: 14.

"Songs from Out a Silence: Angie Fuller Fischer's Beautiful Spirit Triumphs over Terrible Physical Defects." 30 Oct. 1892: 10.

"The Nebraska University: A Splendid Educational Institution of Which the Whole State Is Proud." 6 Nov. 1892: 19.

"The Women and Politics: They Are Too Prone to Worship a Name, Most Are Republicans." 20 Nov. 1892: 13.

"Governors as Litterateurs: Samples of Their Literary Products in Thanksgiving Proclamations." 27 Nov. 1892: 5.

"Omaha's Inadequate Jail: This Miserable Quarters in Which It Is at Present Housed." 4 Dec. 1892: 10.

"For the Younger Readers: The Adventures in a Squashed-Out Land and His Final Descent to Earth Again." 11 Dec. 1892: 19.

"The Work of the Worker: Qualities in Evangelist Mills That Give Him Success in Soul Winning." 15 Dec. 1892: 5.

"A Talk with Annie Besant: The Remarkable Woman Discusses Weirdly Her Strange Faith and Philosophy." 25 Dec. 1892: 7.

FICTION

"Candy Kitchen Romance." 3 Jan. 1892: 9.

"A Case of Love." 3 Apr. 1892: 14.

"Who Will Finish It?" 17 Apr. 1892: 10.

"Who Would Fardels Bear?" 8 May 1892: 12.

"The Proof of the Pudding" [On centenary of the guillotine]. 29 May 1892: 11.

"The Suicide of a Hero." 10 July 1892: 13.

"How Jacques Came to the Forest of Arden." 17 July 1892: 10.

1893

EDITORIALS

"Homes for the Homeless: The Aims and Work of the American Educational Association." 1 Jan. 1893: 5.

"Gold Cure and the Curse: A Peculiar Change Noticed in the Mental Make-Up of the Graduates." 8 Jan. 1893: 5.

"Let the Law Be Amended: Give Juries the Option of Pronouncing the Death Penalty or Life Imprisonment." 15 Jan. 1893: 6.

"Grand Island and Its Beets: The County Seat of Hall and What Beet Cultivation Has Done." 5 Feb. 1893: 13.

"Norfolk and Its Sugar: The Second Town in Nebraska Which Has a Sugar Beet Factory." 12 Feb. 1893: 5.

"A Contrast of Extremes: A Comparison of Nebraska and Florida by One Who Knows Them Both." 19 Feb. 1893: 5.

"Cuba and Its Annexation: The Queen of the Antilles Is Anxious to Come Into the Union." 26 Mar. 1893: 9.

"Our Women as Workers: A Discussion of the Emancipation of Women through Work." 9 Apr. 1893: 10.

"A Successful Public School: A Sketch of the Park School's Wonderful Growth and Achievement." 16 Apr. 1893: 16.

"A Bohemian in Nebraska: A Peep at a Home Which Is a Slice Out of Bohemia." 23 Apr. 1893: 7.

"The Mockery of Mourning: Thoughts upon Outward Signs of Inward Grief Prescribed by Convention." 30 Apr. 1893: 5.

"Evil of Expensive Funerals: It Is Vanity as Often as Affection Which Dictates Ornate Burials." 7 May 1893: 7.
"A Sociological Soliloquy: Some Thoughts Suggested by the Proposed Exodus from the Bottoms." 14 May 1893: 9.
"The Woman's Club: It Will Be Distinctively Feminine and Run to Please Women." 21 May 1893: 6.
"Bourget's 'Cosmopolitan': The French Analyst's Great Novel of Composite Human Types." 21 May 1893: 6.
"About Chicago's White City: The Great Fair Is Approaching Completion." 4 June 1893: 9.
"A Move for a Half Holiday: The Pros and Cons of the Agitation for a Half Day's Rest." 18 June 1893: 14.
"Through a Woman's Eyes: Text of an Address on the Fair Delivered at Y.M.C.A. Hall." 25 June 1893: 7.
"About Children's Books: How Children's Literature Has Progressed from 'Gulliver' to 'Lord Fauntleroy.'" 16 July 1893: 16.
"Work of the Woman's Club: It Has Been Systematized and Sections Are Organized." 30 July 1893: 9.
"Papa Lem[e]n and His Home: How the Christian Home at Council Bluffs Flourishes." 30 July 1893: 9.
"Things Remembered." 13 Aug. 1893: 5.
"With the Free Methodists: An Afternoon at the Free Methodist Camp Meeting in Syndicate Park." 20 Aug. 1893: 5.
"The Judges Are Named: Parties Who Will Pass on Exhibits at the Douglas County Fair." 27 Aug. 1893: 6.
"A Few Ill-Natured Remarks." 3 Sept. 1893: 6.
"Do You Want Children? Three Places Where They May Be Had for the Asking." 10 Sept. 1893: 4.
"Some Legal Notes." 17 Sept. 1893: 13.
"That Vital Thing, Debt: Mrs. Peattie Discourses on It in Connection with Mortgage Statistics." 25 Sept. 1893: 3.
"Some Casual Remarks." 16 Oct. 1893: 18.
"The Men of the Mountains: Mrs. Peattie Writes of Them and of the Capital of the Rockies." 22 Oct. 1893: 10.
"All for Humanity's Sake: A Story Told to Show the Good Which Comes of Good Action." 29 Oct. 1893: 16.
"It Is of Everyday Service: Mrs. Peattie Speaks of the Use of Beauty in Ordinary Life." 5 Nov. 1893: 4.
"Literature of France: Not the France Today, but That of Years Ago." 12 Nov. 1893: 12.

"The Fall of the Kitchen: Mrs. Peattie Writes of the Mournful Decay of That Housekeeping Feature." 19 Nov. 1893: 4.

"Odd Corners of the Earth: Mrs. Peattie's Address at Rescue Hall on Places of Living Interest." 27 Nov. 1893: 5.

"Sunday Sermons." 3 Dec. 1893: 4.

"Will Sing in the Spring: How the Omaha Operatic Festival Is Progressing toward a Smooth Finish." 3 Dec. 1893: 7.

"Salvation Lasses at Home: Mrs. Peattie Writes of the Blue Frocked Sisterhood of the Lord." 11 Dec. 1893: 5.

"Character in Furniture: Mrs. Peattie Tells How Human Nature Crops Out in House Arrangements." 17 Dec. 1893: 22.

"A Hodge-Podge for Sunday: About Men, Women, Books, Crimes, Christmas, Clubs, Religions, Ideas, and Things." 24 Dec. 1893: 11.

FICTION

"Gospel Chariot Romance." 11 June 1893: 5.

"A Mess of Pottage." 9 July 1893: 16.

"A Letter Carrier's Story: How He Came to Fall in Love with the Minier Family." 23 July 1893: 9.

"Mary and John on the Situation." 6 Aug. 1893: 5.

"Ned." 8 Oct. 1893: 16.

"The Story of a Cut." 10 Dec. 1893: 10.

1894

EDITORIALS

[Headline missing]: "Love Scenes in Well-Known Books: An Anglo-Saxon Literary Characteristic." 1 Jan. 1894: 7.

"Stand Up, Ye Social Lions: Mrs. Peattie Arraigns the Sickly Forms That Sin from Nature's Rule." 7 Jan. 1894: 12.

"A Little Bit about Art: It Is Not Languishing, So Far as the City of Omaha Is Concerned." 28 Jan. 1894: 11.

"Mrs. Peattie in Rebuttal: Just a Word or Two in Passing Concerning the Society Question." 21 Jan. 1894: 9.

"Garland's Prairie Songs: The Western Writer Produces a Small Volume of Verses." 4 Feb. 1894: 11.

[Headline missing]: The Problems of "Scientific Charity." 11 Feb. 1894: 11.

"Home for the Girl Clerk: There Is No Reason Why It Should Not Be Made Cheerful." 25 Feb. 1894: 19.

"On Whitman, the Gray Bard: Mrs. Peattie Lectures on the Good Poet before the Unity Club." 27 Feb. 1894: 2.

"No Need for Prostitution: Mrs. Peattie Refuses to Accept the Claim That the Wanton Is Necessary." 4 Mar. 1894: 11.

"Writers Who Live Here: Several People Whose Works in a Literary Way Are Quite Well Known." 11 Mar. 1894: 20.

"The Bride of a Soldier: Something Concerning the Life of the Woman Who Weds a Private." 18 Mar. 1893: 19.

"Identifying One's Self: The American Aversion of Uniforms Is Unwittingly Disregarded in Many Cases." 25 Mar. 1894: 11.

"Ties Which Do Not Bind: The Matrimonial Knot and the Ease with Which It Is Broken." 1 Apr. 1894: 11.

"A Talk about Cheap Dress: Mrs. Peattie Tells the Girls How to Garb Themselves Tastily and Economically." 8 Apr. 1894: 11.

"Scholars and Christians: They Are Made at Doane College Out on the Prairies." 15 Apr. 1894: 10.

"The Woman's Suffrage Fad: Equal Rights Getting to Be a Fashionable Thing Nowadays." 29 Apr. 1894: 13.

"Are They Anarchists? Nineteenth Century Crusade, Its Expectations, and Its Devoted leader." 22 Apr. 1894: 11.

"Roads in Douglas County: Ways in Which They Might Be Improved." 6 May 1894: 12.

"Brain and Heart Broken: The Story of a Girl Whose Folly Has Ended in Madness—A Nameless History." 6 May 1894: 17.

"Clubs Made Up of Women: Mrs. Peattie Writes of Some Things She Learned at Philadelphia." 3 June 1894: 11.

"The Brave Missionaries: Examples of Privation and Danger Encountered by Congregational Ministers." 10 June 1894: 4.

"Florence Pumping Works: A Glance over the Pulsating Heart and Arteries of the Water System." 17 June 1894: 10.

"A Summertime Medley: A Young Violin Maker of Omaha and His Work; Nebraska School for the Deaf; the Negro Question and a Word for the Indians." 1 July 1894: 16.

[Headline missing]: "Mrs. Peattie Writes of the Recent Academy Exhibition in This City." 8 July 1894: 12.

"Mrs. Peattie on Lynching: The Blot on the Name of Civilization and Why It Is There." 24 June 1894: 11.

"Built around an Idea: That Is How Tabor, Va. Was Founded Many Years Ago." 30 July 1894: 5.

"Boys in a Natural State: How They Are Transformed during a Vacation in Camp." 12 Aug. 1894: 12.

"Of Emerson, the Giant: Mrs. Peattie Defends the Literary Memory of the Philosopher of Concord." 2 Sept. 1894: 11.

"The Delight of Trilbyism: Du Maurier's Novel Has Given a New Word to the Literary World." 16 Sept. 1894: 11.

“Where the Sun Goes Down: At Last a Dignified Literary Production from Omaha.” 25 Sept. 1894: 16.

“Through French Optics: A Critical View of the American People by Paul Bourget.” 7 Oct. 1894: 11.

“Great Harm Is Inflicted: Christian Science as Practiced Results in Very Serious Things.” 14 Oct. 1894: 11.

“How a Woman Viewed It All: Mrs. Peattie Writes of the Impressions Given a Feminine Mind.” 21 Oct. 1894: 11.

“Was Not a Partisan Fight: Mrs. Peattie Explains Wherein Women Voters Were Misled.” 11 Nov. 1894: 10.

FICTION

“Covers for Twelve.” 14 Jan. 1894: 8.

“Nance Oldfield: A Comedy in One Act.” 18 Feb. 1894: 13.

“A Waking Dream.” 3 June 1894: 17.

“A Reconciliation: A Comedy in One Act.” 5 Aug. 1894: 12.

“Tom Wallace’s Bewitchment.” 27 Aug. 1894: 4.

“A Forgotten Woman: The Aftermath of the ‘Hot Thursday.’ ” 30 Sept. 1894: 11.

“The Fountain of Youth: A Romance of the Supernatural.” (serial) 28 Oct. 1894: 18; 4 Nov. 1894: 10; 11 Nov. 1894: 18; 18 Nov. 1894: 18; 25 Nov. 1894: 18; 2 Dec. 1895: 18; 9 Dec. 1894: 18; 16 Dec. 1894: 22; 23 Dec. 1894: 18; 30 Dec. 1894: 10; 6 Jan. 1895: 10; 13 Jan. 1895: 10.

“A WORD WITH THE WOMEN”

30 Mar. 1894: 5 [Hired girls; local meetings; spirited Omaha newspaper woman].

10 Apr. 1894: 5 [Revivals for children; tea and coffee].

28 Apr. 1894: 9 [Omaha suburbs].

2 June 1894: 5 [The *Women’s Signal* of WCTU; physical culture; pathetic coaching parties].

8 June 1894: 3 [Rpt. letter about smart women and marriage; Woman’s Christian Association lodging house and employment agency for women; Calhoun].

10 June 1894: 11 [Woman’s Club and philanthropy; a woman shopper; Elsie Robinson, Omaha writer].

12 June 1894: 8 [Omaha Humane Society; women as railroad passengers].

15 June 1894: 3 [Women and sewing; simple room décor].

16 June 1894: 8 [Repeats June 15].

1 July 1894: 16 [Conkey’s “The Congress of Women”; Kathleen Blake Watkins, newspaper woman; rebukes Lily Langtry].

15 July 1894: 5 [Women swimmers; working women and the Woman’s Club].

18 July 1894: 5 [Sentimental sketch of old woman and sewing scraps].

19 July 1894: 2 [Little girl and her horse, Popcorn; Frances Willard and her bicycle].

29 July 1894: 8 [Omaha Theosophical Society and Annie Besant].

31 July 1894: 8 [Visit of Nana, English animal trainer].
4 Aug. 1894: 5 [Rpt. from *Mission of Our Merciful Savior* about fallen women].
5 Aug. 1894: 16 [Omaha Order of the Good Shepherd for wayward women].
11 Aug. 1894: 3 [Protests morbidity and lack of morals in fiction].
12 Aug. 1894: 12 [Omaha and Havana merry-go-rounds].
22 Aug. 1894: 5 [Women and housekeeping].
25 Aug. 1894: 8 [Comment on Lincoln train wreck and shameful conduct of women].
26 Aug. 1894: 12 [Clinic at Omaha Medical College].
28 Aug. 1894: 5 [Two Omaha girls retreat to forest for summer; unpleasant Mondays].
29 Aug. 1894: 5 [Sketch of separated husband and wife reunited].
30 Aug. 1894: 5 [Various philanthropies; Bryant's mother and rpt. of "Thanatopsis"].
4 Sept. 1894: 8 [Omaha cyclists; YWCA].
5 Sept. 1894: 8 [Omaha traveling saleswoman and men].
7 Sept. 1894: 8 [Bits of literary news].
12 Sept. 1894: 5 [Protests opposition of women on Municipal League].
18 Sept. 1894: 3 [Comment on Colonel Breckinridge's morality].
20 Sept. 1894: 5 [Derides New York newspaper *Womankind*].
23 Sept. 1894: 8 [Plea to give jobs to poor to help through winter].
25 Sept. 1894: 8 (Need for household science classes in Omaha].
3 Oct. 1894: 7 [Woman's Club; remarkable Omaha girls].
9 Oct. 1894: 5 [YWCA classes; WCTU coffeehouse].
14 Oct. 1894: 11 [Omaha laundrywoman; Woman's Club program; notable Englishwomen].
17 Oct. 1894: 5 [Rpt. of article about "Women in Finance"].
18 Oct. 1894: 8 [Beauty of fall in Omaha; poem by Peattie].
22 Oct. 1894: 2 [Poet Thomas Chatterton].
23 Oct. 1894: 5 [Denver women].
26 Oct. 1894: 3 [Women and politics; Omaha interest].
27 Oct. 1894: 7 [Western Art Association exhibit of china painters].
28 Oct. 1894: 11 [Stories of romance, drama, realism, and idealism in the newspaper].
31 Oct. 1894: 7 [Urges women to vote; matrimonial ads].
10 Nov. 1894: 8 [Twelfth-century writer and martyr Marguerite Porete].
21 Nov. 1894: 5 [Report of speech on women's responsibilities at Iowa College].
15 Nov. 1894: 5 [New York women watchers at polls; reclamation of homeless women].
18 Nov. 1894: 5 [Conference schedule of National Council of Women].
2 Dec. 1894: 7 [Delegates for formation of State Federation of Woman's Clubs].
5 Dec. 1894: 2 [Women's need for a special corner; women's wages and work].
13 Dec. 1894: 8 [Various topics; women of the "Bottoms"].
18 Dec. 1894: 7 [Afternoon socials; old exposition building; single tax].
22 Dec. 1894: 7 [British political etiquette; woman mistakenly summoned as a juror].

23 Dec. 1894: 15 [Response to comments about society columns].
28 Dec. 1894: 5 [Duties of and need for matron of city jail].

1895

EDITORIALS

"The Year in Music: Most of It Connected with Churches—Advance Steady but Marked." 1 Jan. 1895: 7.

"Takes Issue with Gibbons: Mrs. Peattie Discusses the Cardinal's Position Regarding the 'New Woman.'" 27 Jan. 1895: 8.

"The Latest Play of Ibsen: 'Little Eyolf,' in Which He Lays Bare the Human Heart." 10 Feb. 1895: 10.

"An American Aristocracy." 10 Feb. 1895: 15.

"Differences of Worship: How People Worship God in Various Lands—Havana and Philadelphia." 24 Feb. 1895: 18.

"Bunn's Obituary Bunncombe: The North Carolina Congressman Runs Amuck in Rhetoric." 3 Mar. 1895: 13.

"Arraigns the Missionaries: Thomas G. Sherman Blames Them for the Troubles in Hawaii [Queen Liliuokalani]." 10 Mar. 1895: 13.

"Merely Domestic Column: A Rambling Talk on Domestic Subjects Written for Women Only." 17 Mar. 1895: 18.

"The Women on the Farms: A Chapter of Advice for Them Which City Women Need Not Read." 24 Mar. 1895:18.

"How They Live at Sheeley: Pen Picture of a Strange Settlement and Its Queer Set of Inhabitants." 31 Mar. 1895: 18.

"Mrs. Mumaugh's Pictures: And Something about Local Artists and What They Are Doing." 7 Apr. 1895: 18.

"100 Books for Girls." 14 Apr. 1895: 18.

"All Fuss and Feathers: Wedding Ceremonies Which Are Almost Grotesque Because of Their Flummery." 21 Apr. 1895: 20.

"What She Saw in Japan: Mrs. Scipio Dundy and the Funny Little Dragons She Brought from Abroad." 5 May 1895: 18.

"Association of Teachers: Protective Organization for the Mutual Benefit of Pedagogues." 12 May 1895: 11.

"Stanton Bible for Women: It Is to Be the Work of the Sex for Whom It Is Prepared." 19 May 1895: 18.

"No Distinction as to Color: Chicago Woman's Club Abolishes the Prohibitory Rule at Its Last Meeting." 26 May 1895: 13.

"A Forgotten Book." 8 Sept. 1895: 18.

"For Cuba: An Episode of '95." 27 Oct. 1895: 13.

"In Defense of Her Own Sex: Mrs. Peattie Writes a Reply to the Communication of A.M.M." 1 Dec. 1895: 24.

FICTION

"Jan Paulsen: The Bookman." (serialized novel) 16 June 1895: 20; 23 June 1895: 10; 30 June 1895; 7 July 1895: 16; 14 July 1895: 11; 21 July 1895: 11; 28 July 1895: 11; 4 Aug. 1895: 11; 11 Aug. 1895: 11; 18 Aug 1895: 11.

"Coronado of Salamanca: Dedicated to the Knights of Ak-Sar-Ben." 15 Sept. 1895: 6.

"A Ghost Story." 29 Sept. 1895: 17.

"Witch's Gold: A Story in Three Parts." 3 Nov. 1895: 21; 10 Nov. 1895: 11; 17 Nov. 1895: 18.

"A Little Story of Sentiment." 15 Dec. 1895: 19.

"His Christmas Dinner." 22 Dec. 1895: 18.

COLUMN: "A WORD WITH THE WOMEN"

2 Jan. 1895: 8 [The New Year for women].

4 Jan. 1895: 8 [Harriet Monroe].

12 Jan. 1895: 8 [Girls and military drills].

14 Jan. 1895: 8 [North and South prejudice].

15 Jan. 1895: 8 [When the twentieth century begins].

17 Jan. 1895: 8 [Distress in Keith County].

18 Jan. 1895: 8 [Various topics].

19 Jan. 1895: 2 [Woman's Club].

20 Jan. 1895: 8 [Prominent women].

21 Jan. 1895: 8 [Women's organizations].

22 Jan. 1895: 8 [Du Maurier's "Trilby"].

24 Jan. 1895: 8 [Against wearing fur].

25 Jan. 1895: 8 [Young women skating].

26 Jan. 1895: 8 [Strikes; women's hats].

27 Jan. 1895: 8 [Colored posters].

29 Jan. 1895: 8 [Women's rights].

30 Jan. 1895: 8 [Woman's Club].

31 Jan. 1895: 8 [Symbolism in literature and English playwright William Sharp].

1 Feb. 1895: 8 [Women's study group; Rescue Home].

2 Feb. 1895: 8 [Women's suffrage; teachers' salaries].

5 Feb. 1895: 8 [Cardinal Gibbons; drought aid; Cleary poem].

6 Feb. 1895: 8 [Queen Victoria; Working Girls' Home].

7 Feb. 1895: 8 [Sketch on warmer climates].

8 Feb. 1895: 8 [Belle Bilton, British dancer].

9 Feb. 1895: 8 [Nurseries; public schools].

10 Feb. 1895: 16 [View of back streets of Omaha].

11 Feb. 1895: 8 [Woman's duty; dancing teas].

12 Feb. 1895: 8 [Omaha women in business].

13 Feb. 1895: 8 [Omaha's Dr. Duryea].

14 Feb. 1895: 8 [Story of Maria and temperance].

15 Feb. 1895: 8 [Mothers-in-law].

17 Feb. 1895: 13 [Methodist deaconesses].

18 Feb. 1895: 8 [Hygienic luncheons].

19 Feb. 1895: 8 [YWCA].

20 Feb. 1895: 8 [Women clergy].

21 Feb. 1895: 8 [University of Chicago's Alice Freeman, Harriet Monroe; New Woman].

22 Feb. 1895: 8 [Christina Rossetti].

23 Feb. 1895: 6 [Patriotic sketch of George Washington]

25 Feb. 1895: 8 [Need for women undertakers].

26 Feb. 1895: 8 [Trial of Queen Liliuokalani of Hawaii].

27 Feb. 1895: 8 [Indian education].

28 Feb. 1895: 8 [Rpt. of sketch by Thomas Wentworth Higginson about Lady Kew of Newport].

1 Mar. 1895: 8 [Women undertakers; Red Cross women in Japan; James Whitcomb Riley; need for women jail matrons].

2 Mar. 1895: 8 [Omaha woman Baptist evangelist].

3 Mar. 1895: 8 [Omaha men's attire].

4 Mar. 1895: 8 [Nebraska poet Isabel Richey of Plattsmouth; women undertakers].

5 Mar. 1895: 8 [Mary Lowe Dickinson of New York; artificial violets].

6 Mar. 1895: 8 [Jails and matrons for women; Ninth Street prostitute district].

7 Mar. 1895: 8 [Anna Gould's international marriage].

8 Mar. 1895: 8 [The SPCA; Rex, neighborhood dog].

9 Mar. 1895: 8 [Response to criticism of her column on Ninth Street "Burnt District" problems].

10 Mar. 1895: 8 [News stories about women].

12 Mar. 1895: 8 [Women's age of consent].

13 Mar. 1895: 8 [Women legislators; international marriages].

14 Mar. 1895: 8 [Women's fashion].

15 Mar. 1895: 8 [Chase County farmers and women's work].

16 Mar. 1895: 8 [Autobiography of Michigan childhood].

17 Mar. 1895: 8 [Mississippi steamboat couple].

18 Mar. 1895: 8 [Frances Willard; children anecdote; Omaha woman "handyman"].

19 Mar. 1895: 8 [Chapel of the Carpenter; "fallen woman" desires a friend].

20 Mar. 1895: 8 [Omaha Chautauqua College; a stupid husband].

21 Mar. 1895: 8 [Definition of New Woman; appeal from Hayes County for warm clothing].

22 Mar. 1895: 8 [Success story of Omaha girl].

24 Mar. 1895: 8 [Hayes County follow-up; Age of Consent bill; cigarette bill; keeping Sabbath].

25 Mar. 1895: 8 [Miscellaneous news about women].

26 Mar. 1895: 8 [Professional women and their health].
27 Mar. 1895: 8 [Foreign-born nurses in Chicago and Omaha].
28 Mar. 1895: 8 [Capital punishment; women deans and college presidents].
29 Mar. 1895: 8 [New Woman; authors; Omaha woman Miss Kountze].
31 Mar. 1895: 8 [WCTU; spring clothing; flowers and lawns].
1 Apr. 1895: 8 [Supporting goldenrod as state flower].
2 Apr. 1895: 8 [Formal and personal names].
3 Apr. 1895: 8 [School lunch; Omaha water troughs].
4 Apr. 1895: 8 [Woman who owns boardinghouse and loves music].
5 Apr. 1895: 8 [Truancy; raising boys; a male chauvinist].
6 Apr. 1895: 8 [New woman; mortuary eulogies; Mozart Club].
7 Apr. 1895: 6 [Rpt. of 1792 letters from a colonel to his wife].
8 Apr. 1895: 8 [Response to criticism of Sheely article; *American Jewess* magazine].
9 Apr. 1895: 8 [Various topics; women in law and politics; bloomers].
10 Apr. 1895: 8 [Cuban women].
11 Apr. 1895: 8 [City politics; women market gardeners; Woman's Club; women street sweepers].
12 Apr. 1895: 8 [Men's and women's clubs; Max Nordau's *Degeneration*; standards of justice for women].
13 Apr. 1895: 8 [Suffrage meeting; women unable to vote in churches; response to *Globe-Democrat* article on women].
14 Apr. 1895: 8 [Poem by Omahan Prudence Spencer Lamb; Autobiographical poem of Michigan forests].
15 Apr. 1895: 8 [Protests long gowns for little girls; notable women].
16 Apr. 1895: 8 [Strike of girl waiters; notable women; Mrs. Canfield; women physicians].
17 Apr. 1895: 8 [Cripple Creek bootblacks].
18 Apr. 1895: 8 [Parisian men and American women].
19 Apr. 1895: 8 [Women's shoes; *Pall Mall Budget*].
21 Apr. 1895: 8 [Poems by Howells; curfews].
22 Apr. 1895: 8 [Chadron curfew; married women teachers; women's trousers].
23 Apr. 1895: 8 [Gardens and Alaska].
24 Apr. 1895: 8 [WCTU; Omaha and drinking; women lawyers].
25 Apr. 1895: 8 [Fashion of silk waists and dark skirts].
26 Apr. 1895: 8 [Summer housekeeping and clothing].
28 Apr. 1895: 8 [Lauds Kate Field's paper *Washington*].
29 Apr. 1895: 8 [Hunting mania].
30 Apr. 1895: 8 [Capital punishment; beauty and hope of spring; Omaha newspaper *Excelsior*].
1 May 1895: 8 [Various topics; Brooklyn schoolchildren; Kate Cleary, Nebraska author].

2 May 1895: 8 [French Marquis's criticisms of America; Jane Addams as garbage collector].

3 May 1895: 8 [Kate Cleary's story "Racehorse to the Plow"].

4 May 1895: 8 [Women's edition of the *Omaha Bee*; Woman's Club; children onstage].

5 May 1895: 8 [Controversy over Chicago monument to Confederate dead].

6 May 1895: 8 [*Omaha Bee*; women architects; women's property rights].

7 May 1895: 8 [Allegory about a new goat in neighborhood].

8 May 1895: 8 [Ellis Meredith; New York woman who planted trees; curse of apprehensive people].

9 May 1895: 8 [Rpt. of letter from a working girl and Peattie response].

10 May 1895: 8 [*Omaha Bee*; woman bacteriologist].

11 May 1895: 8 [Sculptor Clio Hinton Huneker, creator of General Frémont statue].

12 May 1895: 8 [Beauty of Oriental rugs].

13 May 1895: 8 [New York woman choir director of workingmen].

15 May 1895: 8 [Stromsburg Woman's Club].

17 May 1895: 8 [Response from another Working Girl; women's fencing club; WCTU].

19 May 1895: 8 [Eulogy of Mrs. George Leavitt of Omaha, whose son was afflicted with paralysis].

20 May 1895: 8 [Stupid lectures].

21 May 1895: 8 [Derides *Ladies Home Journal*; Omaha Mission of Our Merciful Savior].

22 May 1895: 8 [YWCA; child-stealing].

23 May 1895: 8 [Home for Working Girls; Open Door].

24 May 1895: 8 [Mary Abigail Dodge near death].

25 May 1895: 8 [Comment on news of Mrs. Notson, who killed self and children; cloak maker's union; Madam Modjeska; an objectionable woman].

26 May 1895: 8 [Woman's Club nomination process].

27 May 1895: 8 [Eulogy of Dr. Mary Thompson, Chicago surgeon].

28 May 1895: 8 [Literary criticism of Gertrude Atherton].

29 May 1895: 8 [Open Door; Camilla Collet, Scandinavian feminist].

30 May 1895: 8 [Polish villa and women's interest in houses].

31 May 1895: 8 [Children beggars in Omaha; Park School exercises].

2 June 1895: 8 [Birth announcements and father's names; Chicago art].

3 June 1895: 8 [Bloomers].

4 June 1895: 8 [Public school, physical culture, kindergarten].

5 June 1895: 8 [Chinese and interracial marriage].

6 June 1895: 8 [Women and athletics].

7 June 1895: 8 [Women's voices].

8 June 1895: 8 [Against kindergarten on Indian reservations].

9 June 1895: 8 [Easter story about a child and a cross].

10 June 1895: 8 [Support for woman teacher fired for being married].

11 June 1895: 8 [Deaf girl graduate].
12 June 1895: 8 [Protests bishop against women's vocations].
13 June 1895: 8 [Comments on Mary E. Krout and women's settlement houses].
14 June 1895: 8 [Eulogy of two writers: Miss Emily Faithfull and Frederick Locker Lampson].
15 June 1895: 8 [Commentary on Omaha murder, Ish-Chapple case].
16 June 1895: 8 [Mothers and scarlet fever].
17 June 1895: 8 [Women and the census report].
18 June 1895: 8 [Response to critics about Woman's Clubs and the color question; cycling race; Chapple murder case].
19 June 1895: 8 [Supports Indians eating dogs].
20 June 1895: 8 [Asks charity for specific people; eulogy of Sister Xaveria of St. Joseph's].
21 June 1895: 8 ["The Jewish Woman"; school for women in Iceland].
23 June 1895: 8 [Women, bicycling, and bloomers].
24 June 1895: 8 [Frances Willard and Negro lynchings].
25 June 1895: 8 [Establishment of Omaha's Tabor College settlement for girls].
26 June 1895: 8 [New York society love match].
27 June 1895: 8 [Daughter Barbara's vacation].
28 June 1895: 8 [*New York World*'s woman's edition].
29 June 1895: 8 [Raising children].
30 June 1895: 8 [Vanderbilts and summer seclusion].
2 July 1895: 8 [Men's fashion; divorce; Ida B. Wells].
3 July 1895: 8 [Omaha man climbs Alps; unhappy housewives].
4 July 1895: 8 [Patriotism].
6 July 1895: 8 [Vignettes about children].
7 July 1895: 8 [American/British politicians].
9 July 1895: 8 [Love vignette; woman hero].
10 July 1895: 8 [Letter from reader about raising children].
11 July 1895: 8 [Curfew; children's literature].
12 July 1895: 8 [Men's/women's tastes].
13 July 1895: 8 [Clevelands' baby].
14 July 1895: 8 [Maria Deraismes, French feminist].
15 July 1895: 8 [Women and railroad travel].
16 July 1895: 8 [Response to critics; women cyclists].
17 July 1895: 8 [Omaha Opera Festival].
18 July 1895: 8 [Women's rights and business].
20 July 1895: 8 [Women and fads].
21 July 1895: 8 [Women shoppers].
22 July 1895: 8 [Benefit play for WCTU].
23 July 1895: 8 [Women and bloomers].

24 July 1895: 8 [The New Man].
25 July 1895: 8 [Reform schools].
26 July 1895: 8 [Interracial adoption].
27 July 1895: 8 [Omaha Nurses' Training School].
29 July 1895: 8 [Saint Joseph's Hospital].
30 July 1895: 8 [Women's movement].
31 July 1895: 8 [Doane College].
1 Aug. 1895: 8 [Meetings; lightning].
2 Aug. 1895: 8 [Book agents; Valley Women's Club; fashion].
5 Aug. 1895: 8 [Women and Atlanta Exposition].
6 Aug. 1895: 8 [State Federations of Women's Clubs].
7 Aug. 1895: 8 [New Woman; Sunday closings of saloons].
8 Aug. 1895: 8 [Forests in California, Maine, Colorado, Michigan].
9 Aug. 1895: 8 [Wood fires versus coal fires].
10 Aug. 1895: 8 [Pastoral country life].
11 Aug. 1895: 8 [Simple life in log cabin].
12 Aug. 1895: 8 [Beauty of oceans].
14 Aug. 1895: 8 [Pleasure of being without books].
15 Aug. 1895: 8 [Studying people on city streets].
16 Aug. 1895: 8 [New cafeterias].
17 Aug. 1895: 8 [Dramatization of "Trilby"].
18 Aug. 1895: 8 [Chewing grass and confidentiality].
19 Aug. 1895: 8 [*Chicago Daily News* and Women's Sanitarium in Lincoln Park].
20 Aug. 1895: 8 [Flaw in American art].
21 Aug. 1895: 8 [New Woman].
22 Aug. 1895: 8 [State institutions and private lives].
23 Aug. 1895: 8 [Noonday Rest institution for working women].
24 Aug. 1895: 8 [Women and journalism].
25 Aug. 1895: 8 [Chicago Greek letter club for working women].
26 Aug. 1895: 8 [House decoration].
28 Aug. 1895: 8 [Autobiographical sketch about Peattie's son].
29 Aug. 1895: 8 [Cuban bullfights; women working in rolling mills].
30 Aug. 1895: 8 [Rainy night fantasy].
1 Sept. 1895: 8 [Colored teacher; school beginning].
2 Sept. 1895: 8 [American flag laws].
3 Sept. 1895: 8 [Women's gymnastics; WCTU; Omaha artist].
4 Sept. 1895: 8 [Mrs. Holyoke's private school].
5 Sept. 1895: 8 [Water cure of Father Sebastian Kneipp].
6 Sept. 1895: 8 [Letter from Omaha principal; comments about *Women's Tribune* and suffrage].
7 Sept. 1895: 8 [Walter Besant's theory on teaching writing].

8 Sept. 1895: 8 [Legal status of women in the District of Columbia].
9 Sept. 1895: 8 [Grand Army of the Republic women protest age limit in employment of old soldiers].
10 Sept. 1895: 8 [Rpt. of old love letter found in trunk].
11 Sept. 1895: 8 [Girls walking to school; healthy schools].
12 Sept. 1895: 8 [Postage glue; modern inventions].
13 Sept. 1895: 8 [Eulogy of librarian Miss Jessie Allan].
14 Sept. 1895: 8 [Woman's Club; woman farmer].
16 Sept. 1895: 8 [Raising boys].
17 Sept. 1895: 8 [State Fair].
20 Sept. 1895: 8 [Preparing for State Fair ball].
21 Sept. 1895: 8 [Improvements for State Fair].
22 Sept. 1895: 8 [Hot weather; State Fair race horse].
23 Sept. 1895: 8 [State Fair agricultural exhibits].
24 Sept. 1895: 8 [McPhelim poem; Lily Langtry].
25 Sept. 1895: 8 [Methodist organist; Woman's Club annual meeting].
26 Sept. 1895: 8 [Tennyson manuscript; suffrage].
27 Sept. 1895: 8 [Artificial beauty devices].
28 Sept. 1895: 8 [New Woman].
30 Sept. 1895: 8 [House of the Good Shepherd for Women; elocution].
1 Oct. 1895: 8 [Christmas and toys].
2 Oct. 1895: 8 [Streetcar vignette].
3 Oct. 1895: 8 [School discipline].
4 Oct. 1895: 8 [Music teacher and children; streetcar tickets].
6 Oct. 1895: 6 [State Women's Club meeting].
7 Oct. 1895: 8 [Hamlin Garland poem].
8 Oct. 1895: 8 [Funerals].
9 Oct. 1895: 8 [Teacher response to column on school discipline].
10 Oct. 1895: 8 [Response to *Omaha Bee* about Woman's Clubs; women cyclists].
11 Oct. 1895: 8 [Slaughter at butchers' picnic].
12 Oct. 1895: 8 [Response to *Lincoln Journal*; women and politics].
13 Oct. 1895: 8 [Omaha soprano to study in Berlin].
15 Oct. 1895: 8 [Eulogy of children's writer Clara Doty Bates].
18 Oct. 1895: 8 [Public school teaching].
19 Oct. 1895: 8 [Women journalists; Falconer's bankruptcy].
20 Oct. 1895: 8 [Various topics; attacks *Ladies Home Journal*].
21 Oct. 1895: 8 [Women in sweatshops; New Woman].
22 Oct. 1895: 8 [Miss Vanderbilt and journalists].
23 Oct. 1895: 8 [Spain's moral degeneracy and bullfighting].
25 Oct. 1895: 8 [Purpose of Woman's Clubs].
26 Oct. 1895: 8 [Vignette of a fake healer].

27 Oct. 1895: 8 [Mother's kindergarten classes].
28 Oct. 1895: 8 [WCTU].
29 Oct. 1895: 8 [Nebraska Suffrage Association meeting; Nebraska City Woman's Club; autumn].
30 Oct. 1895: 8 [Frances Willard].
31 Oct. 1895: 8 [New York women's headquarters; American girls in Paris].
5 Nov. 1895: 8 [Nebraska City's library].
17 Nov. 1895: 8 [Large sleeve fashions].
18 Nov. 1895: 8 [Schlatter, religious healer].
20 Nov. 1895: 8 [Waitresses and bloomers; professional Women's League; child labor].
21 Nov. 1895: 8 ["Teed's Heaven" commune; women's suffrage].
26 Nov. 1895: 8 [Eugene Field; flower hints].
28 Nov. 1895: 8 [Field monument; *Lincoln Courier* and Willa Cather].
29 Nov. 1895: 8 [A Thanksgiving sermon].
5 Nov. 1895: 8 [*Nebraska literary Magazine*; actress Clara Morris].
3 Dec. 1895: 8 [Literary criticism in *Woman's Weekly*].
5 Dec. 1895: 8 [Omaha lecturer Elizabeth Poppleton; violets].
6 Dec. 1895: 8 [Field monument; Stanton's *Woman's Bible*].
7 Dec. 1895: 8 [Author Isaac Zangwell; W. D. Howells; Garland and humor; H. C. Barnabee].
8 Dec. 1895: 8 [Dr. Duryea; Daughters of the American Revolution; Cuban revolutionists; bloomers].
9 Dec. 1895: 8 [China missionaries; Kipling].
10 Dec. 1895: 8 [Woman's Club; adoption].
11 Dec. 1895: 3 [Mme Mojedka's home, the "Forest of Arden"].
13 Dec. 1895: 8 [Woman's Club; new Holdrege library].
14 Dec. 1895: 8 [Lombroso].
15 Dec. 1895: 8 [Boys in Cook County jail].
16 Dec. 1895: 8 [Field; poverty at Christmas].
17 Dec. 1895: 8 [Peattie poem "Suicide Weather"].
18 Dec. 1895: 8 [Trained nurses].
20 Dec. 1895: 8 [Field monument; Christmas presents for needy children].
21 Dec. 1895: 8 [Fashionable women thieves].
24 Dec. 1895: 8 [Women's news; swearing in print].
25 Dec. 1895: 8 [Woman's Club room; WCTU "punch"; Christmas charity].
27 Dec. 1895: 8 [Omaha woman artist; Field monument; charity; Dickens's "Christmas Carol"].
28 Dec. 1895: 8 [Omaha's opera].
29 Dec. 1895: 8 [Poem by Omaha's Mr. Gale].
31 Dec. 1895: 8 [Omaha and London Woman's Clubs].

1896

EDITORIALS

"About the 'Crazy Store': An Emporium of Wonderful Merchandise Which Delights the Children." 12 Jan. 1896: 17.

"Students of Calvinism: Something about the Presbyterian Theological Seminary of Omaha." 2 Feb. 1896: 9.

"Some Pigs and a Woman: Mrs. A. M. Edwards and Her Herd of Poland China Porkers." 9 Feb. 1896: 16.

"The Lady of the Cloister." 16 Feb. 1896: 11.

"The Bible in the Public Schools." 3 May 1896: 18.

"Grandmother's Stories." 24 May 1896: 18.

"Her Dearest Foe." 28 June 1896: 18.

"Three Children of Galilee." 20 Sept. 1896: 18.

"Victoria of England." 27 Sept. 1896: 18.

"Lesson from the Past: Open Door." 4 Oct. 1896: 18.

COLUMN: "A WORD WITH THE WOMEN

1 Jan. 1896: 8 [Miscellaneous Christmas women's news].

2 Jan. 1896: 8 [National Woman Suffrage convention; Woman's National Progressive Political League].

3 Jan. 1896: 8 [London woman mountain climber].

4 Jan. 1896: 8 [Women-only revival; Nebraska State Humane Society].

5 Jan. 1896: 8 [Benevolent Omaha women].

6 Jan. 1896: 8 [Clara Barton; journal about newborns].

7 Jan. 1896: 8 [Lake poem; *Ladies' Home Lournal*; Colorado woman miner).

8 Jan. 1896: 8 [Austin's British laureateship].

9 Jan. 1896: 8 [*Harper's* cartoon; Dambrosch's lecture; enfranchisement; Bernhardt].

10 Jan. 1896: 8 [Vitality of sexes; "The Little Room"].

11 Jan. 1896: 8 [Starving horses; YWCA].

12 Jan. 1896: 8 [Suicide of Lieutenant Swift of Ninth Calvary; women as burdens].

13 Jan. 1896: 8 [Union station; courtesy; Paul Verlaine's death].

14 Jan. 1896: 8 [Willa Cather].

15 Jan. 1896: 8 [Longfellow and Stoddard].

16 Jan. 1896: 8 [Southerners; Miss Lucy Andrews; Ruth Kimball Gardner, journalist].

17 Jan. 1896: 8 [Rapist released; Cuban insurgents].

18 Jan. 1896: 8 [Ethics of marriage].

20 Jan. 1896: 8 [Woman's Club *New Cycle* has new name; lecturers; damp weather].

21 Jan. 1896: 8 [Elegies of Beatrice Pope of Omaha, and Martha Holden of Chicago].

22 Jan. 1896: 8 [Roosevelt and child spies; child labor; melancholy businessman].

23 Jan. 1896: 8 [South African woman novelist].

24 Jan. 1896: 8 [Older women and younger men].

25 Jan. 1896: 8 [Young men and suicide].

26 Jan. 1896: 8 [People with friendly dispositions; colored women in Chicago Woman's Club; Cuba].

27 Jan. 1896: 8 [Woman's Bible; Zangwill's poor tales].

28 Jan. 1896: 8 [Associated Charities; a woman and a union].

29 Jan. 1896: 8 [Anatole France; Woman's Clubs and separatism].

30 Jan. 1896: 8 [W. D. Howells's pessimism].

31 Jan. 1896: 8 [Custody rights; Russian typewriter; Beatrice cooking class; Cuba].

1 Feb. 1896: 8 [Art education in Omaha public schools].

3 Feb. 1896: 8 [Nebraska Press Club Auxiliary misunderstanding].

4 Feb. 1896: 8 [*Woman's Weekly*; public school examinations].

5 Feb. 1896: 8 [Woman's Club letter and peace movement].

6 Feb. 1896: 8 [Survey: "If I Were Queen Victoria?"].

7 Feb. 1896: 8 [Shoes for schoolchildren; streetcar patrons].

8 Feb. 1896: 8 [Oscar Wilde's mother].

10 Feb. 1896: 8 [Theosophist wedding].

11 Feb. 1896: 8 [Mexican women postal workers; South Dakota rescue home; congressman's strong wife].

12 Feb. 1896: 8 [Universities and the sexes].

13 Feb. 1896: 8 [Mrs. Wynne's "Little Room"; talented people].

14 Feb. 1896: 8 [Women and mortgages].

15 Feb. 1896: 8 [Women art students in Paris].

17 Feb. 1896: 8 [Mary Lease, populist lecturer].

18 Feb. 1896: 8 [Souvenirs and remembrances].

19 Feb. 1896: 8 [Poems by women poets].

20 Feb. 1896: 8 [State Press Association rebuttal; Mrs. Mason, revivalist at African Methodist Church].

21 Feb. 1896: 8 [Mrs. Pugh's lectures on cooking; supporting woman for school board].

22 Feb. 1896: 8 [Mrs. Pugh misunderstanding; Amelia Barr and "Discontented Women."]

23 Feb. 1896: 8 [Mrs. Ormiston-Chant's free lecture on "The New Heaven and the New Earth"].

24 Feb. 1896: 8 [Capital punishment].

25 Feb. 1896: 8 [Animals and personality types; Bill Nye, philosophers and jesters].

26 Feb. 1896: 8 [Musical events; Mrs. Ormiston-Chant and obstinate children].

27 Feb. 1896: 8 [Sir Henry Irving; *Trilby*; the occult; women's friendship].

28 Feb. 1896: 8 [Wisconsin's New Woman's Club; inhumanity of dissection in schools].

29 Feb. 1896: 8 [Local lectures; criticizes petition against loitering in front of church].

2 Mar. 1896: 6 [South Omaha YMCA and Women's Auxiliary; Mrs. Geary for school board].

3 Mar. 1896: 8 [Statue of Jesuit Father Marquette].

4 Mar. 1896: 8 ["Anecdotes of Omaha" and Omaha history].

5 Mar. 1896: 8 [News tidbits].

6 Mar. 1896: 8 [Discussion of *Lyrics of the Ideal and Real*].

7 Mar. 1896: 8 [Nebraska Woman's Clubs; murderer poet].

8 Mar. 1896: 8 [Men and children].

9 Mar. 1896: 8 [Art department of Woman's Club; poem by Coates Kinney].

10 Mar. 1896: 8 [Various topics; Kearney attorney; Mrs. Fisk of Chicago].

12 Mar. 1896: 8 [British woman who murdered her husband; domestic tyrants; *Nebraska Literary Magazine*].

13 Mar. 1896: 8 [Women as principals].

14 Mar. 1896: 8 [Various topics; Lady Somerset; raising children].

16 Mar. 1896: 8 [Woman physician and food supplements for poor children].

17 Mar. 1896: 8 [Laurel NE children's "Telling Club"].

18 Mar. 1896: 8 [Various topics; Woman's Club news].

19 Mar. 1896: 8 [Memorial Hospital on Dodge Street].

20 Mar. 1896: 8 [Raising chicory in Nebraska and women farmers; Kate Cleary].

21 Mar. 1896: 8 [Woman's Club; physiognomy, insanity, and criminality].

23 Mar. 1896: 8 [Discrimination against prostitutes].

24 Mar. 1896: 8 [Plattsmouth Woman's Club; Omaha Woman's Club].

25 Mar. 1896: 8 [Strange dreams; protests Omaha curfew law].

26 Mar. 1896: 8 [Woman's Auxiliary of Armenian Relief].

27 Mar. 1896: 8 [Journalism and literature; prostitutes].

28 Mar. 1896: 8 [Woman lawyer not disbarred; killer elephant; typhoid in Denver].

30 Mar. 1896: 8 [Dr. Mary E. Green's Woman's Club lecture on hygienic food products].

31 Mar. 1896: 8 [Local readings, lectures, contests].

1 Apr. 1896: 8 [Children eating dirt].

3 Apr. 1896: 8 [Paris theater; women's tennis; Omaha woman].

4 Apr. 1896: 8 [Woman's Club; WCTU Home for Working Girls].

6 Apr. 1896: 8 [Omaha library refuses to order *Woman's Journal*; X-rays; Chicago businesswoman].

7 Apr. 1896: 8 [Chides woman's edition of *Enterprise*; Chapel of the Carpenter in "Bottoms"; gardening].

9 Apr. 1896: 8 [Woman's Club; woman mine superintendent and woman monk; women's clothes].

10 Apr. 1896: 8 [Women and politics; protests school superintendent Corbett's sexism].

11 Apr. 1896: 8 [Omaha women physicians].

13 Apr. 1896: 8 [Chewing and spitting tobacco].

14 Apr. 1896: 8 [Various topics; popular literature; women out of work].

15 Apr. 1896: 8 [Various topics; women and insurance discrimination].
16 Apr. 1896: 8 [Plays by James A. Herne].
17 Apr. 1896: 8 [Woman's Club; Omaha minister refuses burial of girl from Open Door].
18 Apr. 1896: 8 [Water for horses; school for household economics; new biography of Amelia Bloomer].
21 Apr. 1896: 8 [Slates and poetry in public schools].
22 Apr. 1896: 8 [Monday-morning Omaha scene].
23 Apr. 1896: 8 [Homer NE girl's poem and poetry].
24 Apr. 1896: 8 [Gardening].
25 Apr. 1896: 8 [Autobiographical memory of Michigan woman].
28 Apr. 1896: 8 [Recipes for cooking mushrooms].
29 Apr. 1896: 8 [Woman's Club; boys and music; nurses].
30 Apr. 1896: 8 [Women's independence].
2 May 1896: 8 [Christian Civic League; incorrigible boy].
3 May 1896: 8 [Woman's charity to "vagrant"].
4 May 1896: 8 [Portraits; Omahans distrust of "outsiders"].
5 May 1896: 8 [Union depot; Omaha woman leaves; Anderson historical boarding-house on Thirteenth and Capitol].
6 May 1896: 8 [Rebuttal to *Bee* about women organists].
7 May 1896: 8 [Beauty of plains in May].
8 May 1896: 8 [Corbett; Dunroy poem; Nebraska farmhand who translates poems].
9 May 1896: 8 [Women and courage].
10 May 1896: 8 [Cooking class craze; ambitious women of leisure].
13 May 1896: 8 [Beauty of Council Bluffs]
14 May 1896: 8 [Woman's Club building; discrimination against married women teachers].
15 May 1896: 8 [Ghost child on Omaha streetcar].
17 May 1896: 8 [Endorses woman for state superintendent of schools and discharge of Professor Norton from Peru].
18 May 1896: 8 [Opposes forced retirement of two Methodist bishops].
19 May 1896: 8 [Sketch of woman in Colorado mining camp].
20 May 1896: 8 [Women organists; decline of pie-making].
21 May 1896: 8 [Woman's Club and music program].
22 May 1896: 8 [Sarah A. King, Christian Scientist in Michigan Woman's Club].
23 May 1896: 8 [Cycling popularity in Omaha; French versus American girls].
24 May 1896: 8 [General Federation of Women's Clubs; Chadron artist Mary Bartow].
27 May 1896: 8 [Nebraska china painter; Nebraska Ceramic Club].
28 May 1896: 8 [Imaginations of girls and boys].
30 May 1896: 8 [Sketch of man and perfumed handkerchief].

31 May 1896: 8 [Oratorio ballad singer Antoinette Sterling].

1 June 1896: 8 [Illustrating poems; daily bathing; Nebraska Federation of Women's Clubs and *Lotus*].

2 June 1896: 8 [Omaha Colored Women's Club; Afro-American *Enterprise*; family rose jar].

3 June 1896: 8 [Chicago Woman's Club; juvenile offenders in Omaha; need for women to be political in Omaha].

5 June 1896: 8 [Educating all parts of the body].

7 June 1896: 8 [Sketch of spendthrift wife and result to husband].

8 June 1896: 8 [St. Louis tornado devastation; Helen Gould charity].

9 June 1896: 8 [Harriet Monroe's book about John Root and Chicago Fair; Field Museum].

10 June 1896: 8 [Besant and Chicago as new literary center].

11 June 1896: 8 [Henry Estabrook; Garland's *Rose of Dutcher's Cooly* and women].

12 June 1896: 8 [Harriet Monroe, cycling, bloomers; Winnifred Black; visiting Russian on prairie mushrooms].

13 June 1896: 8 [Omaha people; Hamlin Garland as farmer].

16 June 1896: 8 [Bessie Potter, Chicago sculptor].

17 June 1896: 8 [Chicago and Omaha Women's Clubs; Armenian relief Association].

18 June 1896: 8 [Various topics; women physicians; Robert Louis Stevenson and Harriet Monroe].

19 June 1896: 8 [Advocates Thursday half-day holidays; Hilliard poem about plains; love for sea].

20 June 1896: 8 [English reform for uniform divorce laws].

22 June 1896: 8 [Colored women in Woman's Club; pure and impure women].

23 June 1896: 8 [Reform at Omaha State Boys' School].

25 June 1896: 8 [Michigan Woman's Club; tidbits about Lansing].

26 June 1896: 8 [Oscar Wilde in prison; novels and sermonizing].

29 June 1896: 8 [Loveliest women; actress Adelaide Neilson].

2 July 1896: 8 [Sketch of little girl and fairies].

5 July 1896: 8 [The Creche day care].

6 July 1896: 8 [Woman's Club].

7 July 1896: 8 [Chicago's fresh-air fund].

8 July 1896: 8 [Assorted stories about women; UNL caps and gowns].

9 July 1896: 8 [Party at Lenox castle; NY Associated Charities].

10 July 1896: 8 [Woman's Club; men/women and time].

11 July 1896: 8 [Lemons; bathing and Omaha water].

12 July 1896: 8. [Responses to William Jennings Bryan's Chicago convention speech].

14 July 1896: 8 [Pleasure of birds].

15 July 1896: 8 [Germs and streetcars, humorous].

16 July 1896: 8 [Library buildings; heroic women].

17 July 1896: 8 [Extreme wealth].
18 July 1896: 8 [Death of Logan train victim].
19 July 1896: 8 [Symmetry and Japanese art].
20 July 1896: 8 [Women's suffrage; women wage earners].
21 July 1896: 8 [Birds].
22 July 1896: 8 [*Lady Cyclist* and *Woman's Club Magazine*; bloomers].
23 July 1896: 8 [Various topics; NY woman dentist; professional singers].
24 July 1896: 8 [Two charity cases; stands up for Omaha].
25 July 1896: 8 [Overheard conversation at Crete Chautauqua].
26 July 1896: 8 [Responses to charity call; children needing adoption].
27 July 1896: 8 [Women and cycling].
28 July 1896: 8 [Women's life insurance].
29 July 1896: 8 [Response to charity call; babies and hot weather].
30 July 1896: 8 [Omaha YWCA].
31 July 1896: 8 [Adapting to seasons; garden hoses].
2 Aug. 1896: 8 [Nebraska Children's Home; Eugene Field poem].
3 Aug. 1896: 8 [Armenian atrocities].
4 Aug. 1896: 8 [Tabor College settlement; Alaska].
6 Aug. 1896: 8 [Ghost story].
7 Aug. 1896: 8 [Neglected children; Tabor suburb].
9 Aug. 1896: 8 [Omaha man to study music in Germany].
10 Aug. 1896: 8 [Response to Peattie's column on garden hoses].
11 Aug. 1896: 8 [Eulogy of Omaha's Rev. Charles Gardner; "Our Day Out" and Salvation Army].
12 Aug. 1896: 8 [Francis Hodgson Burnett].
13 Aug. 1896: 8 ["Our Day Out" picnic contributions; French nun; Omaha language teacher].
14 Aug. 1896: 8 [Alaska].
16 Aug. 1896: 8 [Max O'Rell and the New Woman].
17 Aug. 1896: 8 [Girls' hayrack ride; bon mots].
18 Aug. 1896: 8 [Boys who need homes; bicycling family].
19 Aug. 1896: 8 [Women's work and philosophy].
20 Aug. 1896: 8 [Against Corbett; death of writer Gail Hamilton].
21 Aug. 1896: 8 [Ride on Thirteenth Street car].
26 Aug. 1896: 8 [Poem by Elsie Robertson of La Platte NE].
27 Aug. 1896: 8 [Woman's Club; Omaha whist and other social clubs].
30 Aug. 1896: 8 [Women on Farnam Street car].
10 Sept. 1896: 8 [Woman's Club].
11 Sept. 1896: 8 [Boswell and Dr. Johnson].
13 Sept. 1896: 8 [Woman's Club and benevolence].
14 Sept. 1896: 8 [Interesting women; YWCA].

15 Sept. 1896: 8 [Charity; marriage and secrets; Woman's Club].
16 Sept. 1896: 8 [Actresses and dancers].
17 Sept. 1896: 8 [Tribute to Chicago journalist Margaret Sullivan].
18 Sept. 1896: 8 [Omaha writers Ida Edson and Mary Fairbrother; Mrs. Notson].
19 Sept. 1896: 8 [Opening of first Woman's Club; Omaha acting teaching; call for aid].
20 Sept. 1896: 8 [Chicago Independent Church and woman leader from Woman's Club].
21 Sept. 1896: 8 [Art of reading; good/bad housewives].
22 Sept. 1896: 8 [May Sewall and International Congress of Women].
23 Sept. 1896: 8 [Ellen Burns Sherman; Women and Trans-Mississippi Congress].
24 Sept. 1896: 8 [Woman's Club; Nebraska women's exhibit at Tennessee; responses to request for aid].
25 Sept. 1896: 8 [State fair; women and bicycles; fashionable sleeve].
27 Sept. 1896: 8 [Salvation Army; Charles Dudley Warner; children].
30 Sept. 1896: 8 [Chinese and American women physicians].
1 Oct. 1896: 8 [Woman's Club; waist sizes; fashion].
2 Oct. 1896: 8 [Omaha women musicians; Woman's Club].
5 Oct. 1896: 8 [Neglectful husbands].
6 Oct. 1896: 8 [Richard Harding Davis].
7 Oct. 1896: 8 [An amiable woman].
8 Oct. 1896: 8 [Need for private kindergartens in Omaha; elopements and materialism of weddings].
10 Oct. 1896: 8 [Salvation Army Rescue Home].
11 Oct. 1896: 8 [Farewell column and women reporters].
13 Oct. 1896: 8 [News story about Peattie's farewell reception].
14 Oct. 1896: 8 [Tribute to Peattie: "A Word *From* the Women"].

Autobiography

"Night—A Reminiscence." *Youth's Companion* 18 July 1912: 371.
Painted Windows. New York: George H. Doran, 1918. Reprinted from *McCalls* 1913.
"Solitude—Another Reminiscence." *Youth's Companion* 15 Aug. 1912: 419.
"The Star Wagon." Unpublished manuscript. ca. 1930–31.
"Western Hospitality." *Youth's Companion* 8 Sept. 1910: 467.

Biographical Backgrounds

Brown, Edith A. "Chicago Literary Women." *The Pilgrim* 6.2 (1903): 13–14. *Chicago Tribune* 10 Oct. 1897: 13.

"Chicago Women's Club: Elia Talks of French Troubadours." *Chicago Tribune* 7 Oct. 1900: 43.

"Chicago Women Who Have Gained Recognition in Arts And Letters." *Chicago Tribune* 29 Aug. 1897: 45.

"Elia Peattie, Obituary." *Omaha World-Herald* 13 July 1935: 1.

"Elia Wilkinson Peattie." *Eminent Sons and Daughters of Columbia: The Lives and Photographs of Prominent People of the Time.* Stanley Waterloo and John Wesley Hanson Jr. Chicago: International Publishing Company, 1896.

"Elia Wilkinson Peattie." *Famous American Men and Women: A Complete Portrait Gallery of Celebrated People, Whose Names Are Prominent in the Annals of the Times.* Ed. Stanley Waterloo and John Wesley Hanson Jr. Chicago: Robert O. Law, 1895. 365.

"Elia W. Peattie." *Blue Book of Nebraska Women.* Winona Evans Reeves. Missouri Printing and Publishing, 1916: 114.

"Farewell to Mrs. Peattie." *Omaha World-Herald* 13 Oct. 1896: 2.

"Her Life Is a Busy One." *The Trib* Jan. 1934: 5.

"Large Audience Welcomes Mrs. Peattie 'Back Home.'" *Omaha World-Herald* 17 Feb. 1923.

"Meeting of ILL State Federation of Women's Clubs." *Chicago Tribune* 13 Oct. 1901: 44.

"Mrs. Elia Peattie Retires from Trib." *The Trib* Oct. 1922: 3.

"Mrs. Elia Wilkinson Peattie." *A Woman of the Century.* Ed. Frances E. Willard and Mary A. Livermore. Buffalo: Charles Wells Moulton, 1892. 562–63.

"News of Women's Clubs." *Chicago Tribune* 31 Mar. 1901: 38.

Peattie, Donald Culcross. *The Road of a Naturalist.* Boston: Houghton Mifflin, 1941.

Peattie, Robert Burns. "Story of Robert Burns Peattie." Second edition edited and annotated by Mark Robert Peattie, Noel Roderick Peattie, and Alice Richmond Peattie, 1992. Family papers.

Peattie, Roderick. *The Incurable Romantic.* New York: Macmillan, 1941.

Rascoe, Burton. *Before I Forget.* Garden City NY: Doubleday, Doran, 1937.

Reeves, Winona Evans, ed. *The Blue Book of Nebraska Women: A History of Contemporary Women.* Mexico MO: Missouri Printing and Publishing Company, 1916.

"Sketch." *Book Buyer* 22 (July 1901): 446.

"Sketch." *Critic* 43 (Nov. 1903): 396–98.

Stahl, John M. *Growing with the West: The Story of a Busy, Quiet Life.* London: Longmans, Green, 1930.

"Talks Plainly to Clubwomen." *Chicago Tribune* 19 Oct. 1900: 7.

"Writers and Readers." *The Reader* 4 (June–Nov. 1904): 455.

"Writer Who Comes Here to Lecture Says Babies Her Greatest Happiness." *Omaha World-Herald* 11 Feb. 1923.

Critical Analysis

Bremer, Sidney H. "Elia Wilkinson Peattie." *American Women Writers: A Critical Reference Guide from Colonial Times to the Present.* Vol. 1. Ed. Lina Mainiero. New York: Frederick Ungar, 1979. 360–62.

———. "Introduction." *The Precipice.* 1889. Urbana: U of Illinois P, 1989.

———. "Lost Continuities: Alternative Visions in Chicago Novels, 1890–1915." *Soundings: An Interdisciplinary Journal* 64 (1981): 29–51.

———. *Urban Intersections: Meetings of Life and Literature in United States Cities.* Chicago: U of Illinois P, 1992.

———. "Willa Cather's Lost Sisters." *Women Writers and the City: Essays in Feminist Literary Criticism.* Ed. Susan Merrill Squier. Knoxville: U of Tennessee P, 1984. 210–29.

Bremer, Sidney H., and Joan Falcone. "Peattie, Elia Amanda Wilkinson." *Women Building Chicago, 1790–1990: A Biographical Dictionary.* Ed. Rima Lunin Schultz and Adele Hast. Bloomington: Indiana UP, 2001. 678–80.

Butcher, Fanny. "Books and Writers in an Earlier Day." *Chicago Tribune* 15 Mar. 1964.

Duffey, Bernard. *The Chicago Renaissance in American Letters: A Critical History.* East Lansing: Michigan State UP, 1956.

Falcone, Joan. "The Bonds of Sisterhood in Chicago Women Writers: The Voice of Elia Wilkinson Peattie." Diss. Illinois State U, Normal, 1992.

Inglehart, Babette. "Illinois Women and Their Fiction." *A Reader's Guide to Illinois Literature.* Ed. Robert Bray. Springfield: Illinois Humanities Council and Illinois State Library, 1985. 83–106.

Raftery, Judith. "Chicago Settlement Women in Fact and Fiction: Hobart Chatfield-Taylor, Clara Elizabeth Laughlin, and Elia Wilkinson Peattie Portray the New Woman." *Illinois Historical Journal* 88 (Spring 1995): 37–59.

Szuberla, Guy. "Peattie's *Precipice* and the 'Settlement House' Novel." *Midamerica: Society for the Study of Midwestern Literature* 20 (1974): 59–75.

Woolley, Lisa. *American Voices of the Chicago Renaissance.* Dekalb: Northern Illinois UP, 2000.

INDEX

Page numbers in *italics* refer to illustrations.

Academy of the Visitation, 223–29, *224*, 282–83nn13–15
Adams, A. O., 62
African Americans, 58–65, 151, 280nn16–17
Alexander, W. H., 16
Allen, Luella, 50
American Peasant, The, xix, 11, 270n8
Anthony, Susan B., xix, 14, 17
Armour, Philip D., 65
Armour-Cudahy Company, 65–72, 271nn9–11
Associated Charities, 38

Balcomb, Nora, 17
Barnett, F. L., 61
Barnett, Laura, 62
Bellamy, Edward, 33–34, 37
Bly, Nellie, 18, 270n13
Board of Fish Commissioners, 249–50
Booth, General William, 148
boxing, 134–41
Boyden, Henry D., 249
Brooks, Mrs. Datus, 17
Bryan, James S., 61
Bryan, William Jennings, xix, 11, 12, 192
Brysselbout, M. Emile, 244–45, 247
Burroughs, Dr. Amelia, 229, 231
Butler, Bert, 50
Butler, Dr. S. Wright, 99

Cable, George W., 81
Cahill, Edward, 2
Cahill, Frank, 2
Cameron, Ray, 78
Campbell, Thomas, 62
capital punishment, 103–05, 110–11, 274n15
Cather, Willa, 17, 214–17, *215*, 260, 261, 280n1, 281n4, 281n7, 281n9, 282n10
Chase, Lizzie, 4
Chicago Daily News, 4, 5, 261
Chicago Mail, 6
Chicago Morning News, 4
Chicago Times, 2, 4, 6
Chicago Tribune, xvii, xix–xx, 5, 209, 212, 257, 263
Chicago Woman's Club, xix–xx, 47, 202, 204, 261, 263, 280n17
Chicago World's Fair (1893), xix, 12, 15, 282n13
child care, 42–46
children: delinquent, 176–82, 234, 272n5, 279n9; education of, 152, 155–60; infant, 169–76, 278n7, 278n8; older, 44, 117–19; in poverty, 32, 33, 36–37, 43–46, 67, 234–41
cholera, 33, 34, 271n3
Christian Home of Council Bluffs, 234–41, *235*, 283nn18–19
City Mission, 38, 141, 146
Clark, Mrs. A. W., 231, 232, 234
Cleary, Kate McPhelim, 208–14, *209*, 281nn4–6, 281n9
Coe, Joe (alias George Smith), 103, 106, 109–10, 111, 274n14
Colby, Clara Bewick, 17–18
Corbett, Jim, 134–35, *136*, 137, 141, 276n7
Council Bluffs (IA), 15, 20, 45, 151, 229, 234, 235
Craft, Father Francis M. J., 92, 94–95, 96
Crèche Day Nursery, 38, 42–46, 271n4
Creighton, Edward, 19, 53, 275n2
Creighton, John A., 53, 55, 56, 65, 67
Croly, Jane Cunningham, 18
Cudahy, Edward A., 65, 67, 275n2
Cudahy, Michael, 65, 72, 271n8, 275n2

Dahlman, Jim, *31*
Darcy, J. M., 61
Dargaczewski, Nick, *31*
Dargaczewski, Xavier, 29
Davis, Richard Harding, 136, 276n15
De Sales, Sister Mary Francis, 223–29, 282n13, 283n15
Detroit Free Press, 10
divorce, 164, 166, 167, 168, 169
Dodge, Grenville, 19, 275n2
Donnelly, John H., 65
Dupont School, 33

Eagle Nest, 258, 260
Edda and the Oak, 261, 262, 278n7
Edge of Things, The, 258
education: in boarding schools, 223–29, 283n15; in Grand Island, 247; in orphanages, 43, 238–39; from parents, 179–82, 188; and school boards, 114–15, 152–55, 156, 159–60; and school buildings, 155–56, 158; from the streets, 178, 272n5; and teachers, 152, 156–60
Edward, Amanda M., 217–22, 282n11
Erskine, Barbara Peattie (daughter), xix, 5, *189*, 263
Evans, Miss, 47, 49

Fairbrother, Mary, 17
faith healing, 97–102
farmers, 64, 183, 186, 241–46, *242*, 284nn22–23
feminism: and labor rights, 192–95; and sexism, 128, 188, 190–92, 196, 197, 268, 278n4; and suffrage, 114–15, 152–55
Ferrar, Henry S., 245–46
Field, Eugene, 4, 12, 260, 269n3, 282n13
fish hatchery, 249–54, *250*, 281n3
Florence Crittendon Mission, 79, 80
Ford, Frances, 12, *13*, 195
Fortnightly Club, xix, 261
Franklin, Rabbi Leo M., 99
Fremont (NE), 22, 217, 218–19, 222
funerals, 133–34, 148, 150–52, 285n5

Gapen, Dr. Clarke, 57
Garland, Hamlin, vii, xix, 15, 40, 126, 217, 260–61, 269n2, 270n8
George, Henry, 34, 35, 37, 39
Gibbons, Cardinal James, 188, 279n10
Gilded Age, xv, 18, 113, 169, 269n1, 271n5, 275n2
Glassman, Stena Christensen, 148–52
Grand Island (NE), *193*, *208*, 241, 245, 246, 247–49, 284nn21–22
Great Delusion, The, 265
Gretna (NE), 250
"Grizel Cochrane's Ride," 6

Hall, Fred, 5
Hanscom, Andrew J., 23
Hanscom Park, 23, 29
Hanscom Park Methodist Church, 32
Hanscom Park School, 152
Hartman, Christian, *114*, 275n2
Haskell, Julia, 199
Hastings (NE), 78, 223, 224, 228, 282–83nn13–14
Hearst, William Randolph, 73, 269n6, 271–72n2
Hedwig, Sister Superior, 55
Higgins (Sullivan), Elizabeth, 81–82
Hitchcock, Gilbert, 8, 73, 269n6
homeopathy, 229, 232, 283n16
Howard, Blake C., 248
Howells, William Dean, 267
Hubbell (NE), 208, 209–10
hunting, *255*, 255–56

Ickery Ann, xix, 261
Iler Distillery, 20
immigrants: Bohemian, 68; Czech, 23; English, 30, 151; and ethnic neighborhoods, 23, 27, 33–39; German, 20, 23, 27, 30, 199, 241; Irish, 30, 134, 151, 173; Italian, 30; as laborers, 19, 70, 113, 115; Norwegian, 216; Polish, 29–33, *31*, 271n2; and poverty, 29–42, 176; and religion, 29–31, 141, 271n2; Swedish, 23, 27, 30, 146, 151, 199, 201; Welsh, 151
Independent, 11

Jackimowicz, Father T., 29
Jackson, Helen Hunt, 90
Jardine, Mrs. J. B., 36
"Jim Lancy's Waterloo," *11*, 11–12
Johnson, Virgie, 61
Journey Through Wonderland, A, xix, 8, *9*
Judge, The, xix, 10, 267

Kaminski, Stephen, 29
Kimball, Mrs. T. L., 42
King, Lizzie, 62
Koenig, Henry A., 241
Kountz, Augustus, 19
Kraycki, Frank, 29

Laflin, John, 138–39
Lanier, Sidney, 214, 270n9
Lankton, Dr. Freda, 229–34, 283nn16–17
Lease, Mary Elizabeth, 190, 192
Lemen, Rev. Joseph Golf, 234–39, 240, 283n19

Lewis, John, 62
Lincoln (NE), 19–20, 22, 75–76, 78, 83, 272n6
Lininger Gallery, 195, *196*, 198, 279n13
Littlefield, Lillian, 152
Little Room, xix, 261
Love of a Caliban, The, xix, 263
lynching, 60, 103–11

marriage, 79–80, 123, 125–27, 130–31, 164–69, 278n5
materialism, 15, 113, 115, 119, 125–28, 130–34, 169, 275nn1–2, 280–81n2
McCafferty, Nora, 49
McKinley, William, 192
McKinley Tariff, 192, 194, 195, 241
McPhelim, Edward, 209, 211
McPhelim, Margaret, 210, 211
McShane, John A., 65, 67
meatpacking plants, 19, 65–72, 113
Megeath, James G., 23
Millard, Anna, 36
Miller, George L., 7
Mills, Benjamin Fay, 141–48, *143*, 277nn11–12
Mission of Our Merciful Savior, 81
Missouri River, 20, 21, 105
Mobley, Maggie, 17
Mountain Woman, A, xvi, xix, 12, 14, 15
mourning, xvi, 128–34, 150, 151, 276n5, 285n5
Muhammitt, Helen, 201, *203*, 204
Murphy, Frank, 65

National Federation of Afro American Women, 201–02
Native Americans, 73, 88, 89–96, 273–74n9, 280n16
Neal, Ed, 103, 104, 105, 111, 274nn13–14
Nebraska State Federation of Women's Clubs, 198
Nelson, Morris, 65
Nelson, Nell, 170–76
New Journalism, 73–75, 267, 285nn6–7
Newman, Wright, 62
New Woman, xv, 14, 161, 163, 188, 277n2, 278n3, 279n11
New York Tribune, 15, 257, 263, 269n1
Noonday Rest, 46
Norfolk (NE), 241, 283–84n20
Northside Colored Citizens' Protective Association, 63

O'Brien, Martin, 252–53
Omaha (NE): Bottoms, 33–42; Burnt District, 75, 272nn4–5; climate of, 21–22, 250–51; corruption in, 20–21, 22, 78, 271n5; economy of, 15, 19–21, 65, 113, 119–23; history of, 19–21, 23–72, 75, 103–11, 113, 114–15, 119, 141, 146–48, 152, 195, 229–30, 271nn2–4, 271nn7–8, 272nn4–6, 274nn11–14, 275n2, 279–80nn13–14, 280n17; neighborhoods in, 20, 22, 23–36, *41*, 44; schools in, 152, 155–60; Sheelytown neighborhood of, 29–33; society in, 36, 39–42, 115, 117–19, 123, 125–28, 275n4; South, 65–72
Omaha Bee, 8
Omaha Colored Woman's Club, 201, 204
Omaha Daily Herald, xv–xvii, *7*, 8
Omaha Daily World, 8
Omaha Medical College, *230*
Omaha Woman's Club, xix, 12, 13, 14, 16, 103, 195–98, 201, 204–05, 229, 279n12, 280n14
Omaha Woman's Press Club, 16
Omaha World-Herald, 1, 2, 8, 16–17, 73, 88, 103, 114, 135, 269n6, 273nn8–9, 279n12
Open Door, 38, 75, 79, 83, 87–88, 229, 231–34
orphanages, 38, 83, 234–41
Our Chosen Land, xix, 15
Overall, E. R., 58, 62
Oxnard Brothers Beet Sugar Company, 241, 244–47, 249, 283n20, 284nn21–23
Oxnard, Henry T., 284n21

Palmer, De Wayne, 218–19, 222
Parker, A. W., 61
Parkvale Congregational Church, 32
Parkman, Francis, 91
Patterson, Robert Wilson, 5
Paxton, William A., 65, 67, 275n2
Peattie, Barbara. *See* Erskine, Barbara Peattie
Peattie, Donald Culross (son), xix, 257, *259*, 263–65
Peattie, Edward Cahill (son), xix, 5
Peattie, Elia: birth of, xix, 1; on censorship, 21; in Chicago, xix, 1–6, *6*, 15,

Peattie, Elia (*continued*)
209, 257, *258*, 258–63; and the *Chicago-Tribune*, xix–xx, 5, 257–58, 263; childhood of, xix, 1–4; and children, xv, 169–76, *189*, *259*, 261, 263; and clubs, 12–14, 16, *74*, 163, 195–202, 204–05, 261, 265; death of, xx, 265, *266*; and education, 1–2, 12, 114–15, 152–60, 167, 178, 188, 223, 226, 228, 247, 283n15; in Europe, 260, 264; and family, xv, 161, 176, 179–82, 190–91, 267–68, 278n7; and health, 4, 263; marriage of, xv, xix, 4–5, 14–15, 161–63, *162*, 164, 257–58, 267–68; and nature, 21–22, 23–24, 56, 63–64, 207–08, 250–52, 281n3; in New York, *262*, 263, 281n9; in Omaha, xix, 7–19; and *Omaha World-Herald*, xv–xix, 1, 7–8, 10–12, 14–18, 114, 195, 207, 257, 263, 279n12; and Populist Party, xix, 11–12, 33, 37, 114; racial attitudes of, 58–60, 63–65, 152, 201–05, 280n17; retirement of, xx, 263, 266; social activism of, 14, 16, 18, 33–42, 46, 78–83, 169, 271n5; in Tryon (NC), xix, 263, 265; writing career of, xv, xix–xx, 1, 4–12, 14–18, 21, 73–75, 88, 113–15, 163, 207–08, 214, 257–58, 260, 261, 263–64, 265, 266–68, 270nn8–9, 270n13, 271n1, 275n2, 275n4, 278n7, 281n4, 285n1
Peattie, Elizabeth Culross (mother-in-law), 2, 5, 7, 8, 257
Peattie, John (father-in-law), 2
Peattie, Robert Burns (husband): birth of, xix, 2; in Chicago, xix, 2–6, *3*, 15, 209, 257, 262; death of, xx, 265; in Europe, 264; health of, xix, 10, 14–15, 263; journalism career of , xix–xx, 2–7, 10, 163, 257–58, 263, *264*, 265; marriage of, xix, 4–5, 14–15; in New York, 15, 263, 281n9; in Omaha, xix, 7–16, 19; retirement of, xx, 263; in Tryon (NC), xx, 263, 265
Peattie, Roderick (son), xix, 10, 19, 21, 260
Phillips, Rev. J. B., 150–51
Pictorial Story of America, The, xix, 14
Platte River, 250, 251, 252, 255
politics: and capital punishment, 103–07, 110–11; and leaders, 113–14; and McKinley Tariff, 192–95; and Native Americans, 88–90, 92; of populists, 11–12; and prostitution, 75–76, 78–79, 83; and school board, 114–15, 152–56, 159–60, 241; and sugar beet bounty, 241, 244
Post, Mrs. A. C., 200
poverty: and charity, 53–58, 79–81; and children, 32, 33, 36–37, 43–46, 67, 176, 179–81, 234–41, 279n9; and farmers, 11; and immigrants, 26–42, 176; and Native Americans, 89–90, 93, 94–95; and women, 52, 79–81, 83, 193–95, 231–41, 272n5, 273n7
Pratt, Viola, 17, 273n8
Precipice, The, xvi, xx, 261, 285n2
Progress, 61, 280n17
Progressive Era, xv, 18, 169, 269n1, 271n5
prostitution, 20–21, 73, 75–76, 78–83, 86–87, 89, 272nn4–6, 273n7
Pulitzer, Joseph, 73

realism, 74–75, 267
Reed, Byron, 19
religion: Catholic, 29–30, 141, 271n2; and Christianity, 79, 81, 146–48; and City Mission, 38, 141, 146; and death, 128, 132–34; and evangelism, 141–48, 276n10, 277nn11–12; and faith healing, 97–102; and Grand Island churches, 247; and marriage, 164, 166, 167–69; and Omaha churches, 29–30, 32, 141; and Salvation Army, 148–52, 277n13
Ricketts, Dr. Matthew Oliver, 58, *59*, 61, 271n7
Riley, James Whitcomb, 12, 282n13
Robbins, Silas, 61
Robertson, Elsie, 273n8
Rosewater, Edward, 8, 269n6, 275n2
Ross, Ishbel, 269n1, 269n3
rural women, 64, *170*, 182, *183*, 184–87, 217–22, 243–44, 254–56, 282n11

Salvation Army, 148–52, 277n13
Sanderson, Rev. F. H., 99
Schlatter, Francis, xvi, 97, *98*, 99, *100*, 100–101, 274nn10–12
Seavey, Chief W. S., 176–77
Shape of Fear, The, 257
Singleton, Millard F., 61
Sisterhood of St. Francis, 53–55, 57–58
Smith, A. J., 35
Smith, George. *See* Coe, Joe
Songs from a Southern Garden, 265

Stanton, Elizabeth Cady, 17
"Star-Wagon," xvi–xvii, 11, 214, 264, 269n2
Stephenson, Dr. W. H. C., 61
Stevenson, Dr. Sarah Hackett, 202
St. Joseph Hospital, 53–58, *54*
stockyards, xv, 58, *66*
Stone, Melville E., 4, 5
Storey, Wilbur F., 3
Story of America, The, xix, 9
Story of Robert Burns Peattie, 264
St. Paul's Catholic Church, 29, 30, 31, 271n2
streetcars, 23, *25*
Stromsburg (NE), 198–201, 280n15
Stromsburg Woman's Club, 198–201
Students' Home, 26
Sullivan, John L., 134–41, *136*, 276nn6–8
Sullivan, Margaret, 269n5
Sundown Club, 16
Swan, Alexander, 65
Swift, Gustavus, 65, 275n2

Tennyson, Lord Alfred, 141
Tibbles, Thomas Henry, 11, 88, 270n8, 273n9
True Woman, xv, 17, 161, 163, 164, 277n1, 278n6

Union Pacific Railroad, 19, 20, 58, 65, 99, 113, 198, 248
Union Stock Yards Company, xvi, 29, 58, 65, *66*

Voss, Henry, 56

Wallace, J. Laurie, 51
Washburn, Josie, 83, 272n5, 273n7
Weir, Mayor Austin H., 75–76, 78, 83
Wells, Ida B., 18
Whitman, Walt, 40, 207
Wilkinson, Amanda (mother), xix, 1, 2, 4
Wilkinson, Bertha (sister), 2, 8, 218, 257
Wilkinson, Frederick (father), xix, 1–4
Wilkinson, Hazel (sister), 4
Willard, Francis, 18, 113–14
Williams, Minnie, 17
Williams, Rev. John A., 60
Wilson, Lena, 280n17
Windsor Park (IL), xvi, 3–4, 21
With Scrip and Staf, xix, 10
Woman of the Century, A, 6, 163
Woman's Christian Temperance Union, 38, 52, 80, 113, 195, 271n6
women's occupations: in business, 203, 282n13, 283n15; in childcare, 43–44, 173; as clerks, 49, 83, 85–86; as doctors, 229–34, *230*, 283nn16–17; as journalists, 5, 15, 16–18, 170–76, 269n1, 269n5, 270n10, 270nn12–13, 271n1, 273n8; as laborers, 68, 69–70, 72, 192–95, *193*, 197; as nurses, 53–54, 57–58; as prostitutes, 75, *76*, *77*, 78–83, 86–88, 272nn5–6, 273n7; in religion, 148–52, 223–28; as social workers, 36, 42–49, 231–34, 235–36, 238, 261, 271nn5–6; as teachers, 28, 113, 152, 157–58, 201, 223–28, 282n13, 283n15; as telephone operators, *48*, 49; as writers, 17, 81–82, 208–17, *209*, *215*, 260, 261, 272n5, 273nn7–8, 279n9, 280n1, 281nn4–9
women's clubs, xix, 12–14, 16, 103, 114, 163, 195, 198–205, 207, 261, 270nn10–11, 279n12, 280nn14–15, 280n17
working girls' home, 46–52
Wounded Knee, 88, *89*, 90, 92, *93*, 95–96, 273–74n9

Xavier, Sister Superior, 55

Young Women's Christian Association (YWCA), 38, 46–78, 95, 195, 271n6
Youth's Companion, 261